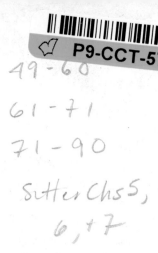

US-China Relations

Perilous Past, Uncertain Present

Third Edition

Robert G. Sutter
George Washington University

ROWMAN & LITTLEFIELD
Lanham • Boulder • New York • London

Executive Editor: Susan McEachern
Assistant Editor: Rebeccah Shumaker
Senior Marketing Manager: Kim Lyons

Published by Rowman & Littlefield
A wholly owned subsidiary of
The Rowman & Littlefield Publishing Group, Inc.
4501 Forbes Boulevard, Suite 200, Lanham, Maryland 20706
https://rowman.com

Unit A, Whitacre Mews, 26-34 Stannary Street, London SE11 4AB,
United Kingdom

British Library Cataloguing in Publication Information Available

Library of Congress Cataloging-in-Publication Data
Names: Sutter, Robert G., author.
Title: U.S.-China relations : perilous past, uncertain present / Robert G. Sutter, George
    Washington University.
Description: Third edition. | Lanham, Maryland : Rowman & Littlefield, 2018. | Includes
    bibliographical references and index.
Identifiers: LCCN 2017039755 (print) | LCCN 2017043456 (ebook) | ISBN
    9781538105351 (electronic) | ISBN 9781538105337 (cloth : alk. paper) | ISBN
    9781538105344 (pbk. : alk. paper)
Subjects: LCSH: United States—Foreign relations—China. | China—Foreign relations—
    United States.
Classification: LCC E183.8.C5 (ebook) | LCC E183.8.C5 S884 2018 (print) | DDC
    327.73051—dc23
LC record available at https://lccn.loc.gov/2017039755

Printed in the United States of America

Contents

Chapter One

Introduction

Relations between the United States and China constitute the most important bilateral relationship in world affairs in the twenty-first century. China's global economic importance and rising political and military power came about in a world order where the United States faced many challenges but still exerted broad leadership reflecting its superpower status. Whether the two powers will support international peace and development and pursue more cooperative ties, will become antagonistic as their interests compete, or will pursue some other path in world affairs remains the subject of ongoing debate among specialists and policy makers in both countries.[1]

BALANCING CONVERGING AND CONFLICTING INTERESTS

The first edition of this book was written in 2010 following the latter years of the administration of President George W. Bush (2001–9) and the first year of the administration of President Barack Obama (2009–17). Officials in China and the United States emphasized positive aspects of their relationship. As explained in detail in chapters 6 and 7, these included ever closer trade and investment ties leading to deepening economic interdependence of the United States and China. Converging security interests involved dealing with international terrorism, North Korea's nuclear weapons program, UN peacekeeping, and other issues involving sensitive situations in Asia and the world. China had come far in the post–Mao Zedong (d. 1976) period in adopting norms of free-market economic behavior supported by the United States and essential to China's success in dealing with the conditions of economic globalization of the current era. China also substantially changed policies on proliferation of weapons of mass destruction to conform more to US-backed international rules. US-China collaboration on climate change and environmental issues was prominently featured, and bilateral discussion on human rights continued amid mixed reviews on progress in China toward accepting US-backed international norms. US-China differences over Taiwan subsided with the coming to power of Taiwan President Ma Ying-jeou (2008–16), who sharply shifted Taiwan toward a more cooperative stance in relations with China. In broad terms and with some reservations, the US government accepted and supported the Chinese Communist government as a leading actor in world affairs; the Chinese government seemed to tacitly accept, at least for a time, the existing international order in which the United States exerted leading power in Asian and world affairs.[2]

The Chinese and American governments had strong reasons to emphasize the positive aspects of their relationship and to minimize public discussion of negative aspects. Sino-American differences were dealt with through private conversations among senior leaders and channels of diplomacy called dialogues. The number of these dialogues grew to more than ninety by the end of the Obama administration. The most important was the US-China strategic and economic dialogue, which held its first meeting in July 2009.

During this seemingly positive period, students, media commentators, and other readers inexperienced with the complicated background and context of the Sino-American relationship had a tendency to be misled by the benign image of US-China relations that had flowed from the public discourse of US and Chinese officials in the previous decade. Adding to the mix was the point of view of some commentators, particularly in the United States, that emphasized the convergence of interests between the United States and China. At the outset of the Obama administration, some argued for an international order determined chiefly by cooperation between the two governments, what is called a G-2 world order, for the twenty-first century.[3] The first edition of this book took issue with what it saw as an overly benign image of Sino-American cooperation; it concurred more with scholarly and other assessments in the United States, China, and elsewhere that viewed Sino-American relations as more complicated and conflicted than official discourse and arguments by commentators who favored a Sino-American international condominium led many to expect.

The second edition came in 2013 amid the increasing competition and public acrimony evident in Sino-American relations since 2010. It depicted a fragile balance between converging and diverging interests in the relationship, notably with China's newly appointed party leader and president Xi Jinping (2012–) pursuing assertive and often bold initiatives at home and abroad that seriously challenged key American security, economic, and political interests. Though registering sometimes strong public opposition to China's advances at the expense of its neighbors and the United States and taking some military, economic, and diplomatic moves in response, the Obama government on the whole continued to rely on private summit talks and other dialogues to manage tensions. The Xi Jinping government also avowed support for such diplomatic managing of key differences, but China's actions on sensitive territorial disputes, trade and investment matters, international governance issues, and restrictive treatment in China of Chinese citizens and of US and other foreign businesses and nongovernment organizations undermined the previous benign image of cooperation with the United States.[4]

The Obama government remained positive about the status of US-China relations to the end of its tenure in January 2017. However, sharply critical treatment of China in the 2016 US election campaign came from the leading Democratic Party candidate, Hillary Clinton, the secretary of state in the first term of the Obama government (2009–13). Clinton's negative assessment of Chinese policies and practices complemented criticisms by Republican frontrunner and later President Donald Trump.[5] Together, the two candidates reinforced a broad trend seen among American experts, specialists, members of Congress, and the media that the previous moderate and forthcoming US engagement of China was failing; a new, tougher approach would be required to deal with the rising challenges posed by Xi Jinping's government.[6] For their part, Chinese specialists and media were on guard in the face of these negative trends. They claimed that China would seek to work constructively with the president-elect. Hillary Clinton was viewed negatively as an official who was familiar with Sino-American differences and determined to push Beijing on these matters. Trump was depicted as a newcomer and much less committed to key differences with China; a prevailing view in China saw him as a pragmatic businessman turned political leader who could be "shaped" to accord to Chinese interests through bargaining and negotiations.[7]

The third edition was written against this background after five months of the Trump presidency in 2017. US-China relations were tense at first, as President-elect Trump in December 2016 took a controversial step in accepting a congratulatory phone call from Taiwan's president. When China complained, President-elect Trump replied by criticizing Chinese economic policies and military advances in disputed islands in the South China Sea, and he later went on to repeatedly question why the United States needed to support a position calling for one China and avoiding improved contacts with Taiwan.[8]

These rapid-fire actions upended Chinese forecasts of smoother sailing with Trump than with Hillary Clinton. In a few gestures and blunt messages to the media and on Twitter, the president-elect showed President Xi and his lieutenants that the new US leader would be capable of a wide range of actions that could be done easily and would surprise Chinese counterparts with serious negative consequences. During the long US election campaign, President Trump made clear that he preferred unpredictability and did not place the high value President Obama did on policy transparency, carefully measured responses, and avoidance of dramatic actions. He has been much less constrained than the previous US administration by a perceived need to sustain and advance US-China relations. Like President Xi and unlike President Obama, President Trump has been characterized as (1) not averse to conflict, (2) presumably willing to seek advantage in tensions between the two countries, and (3) prepared to seek leverage through linking his policy preference in one area of the relationship with policies in other areas of the relationship.[9]

In June 2017 the outlook for US-China relations seemed heavily influenced by one bold leader interacting with another bold leader. President Trump eventually was persuaded to publicly reaffirm support for the American one-China policy during his first phone conversation with President Xi on February 9. Xi reportedly refused to speak with President Trump until he did so.

The informal summit meeting with President Xi at the Trump resort Mar-a-Lago in early April 2017 went well, though it sandwiched President Trump's surprise announcement of fifty-nine US cruise missiles striking a Syrian airfield that was being used to carry out a widely condemned chemical weapons attack. After the summit, the Trump government kept strong political pressure on China to use its economic leverage to halt North Korea's nuclear weapons development. While stoking widespread fears of conflict on the peninsula, President Trump stressed his personal respect for President Xi. He promised Beijing easier treatment in negotiations on the two countries' massive trade imbalance and other economic issues.

The crisis over North Korea put a premium on US interaction with China. Planned arms sales to Taiwan, freedom-of-navigation exercises in the South China Sea, and other US initiatives that might complicate America's search for leverage to stop North Korea's nuclear weapons development were put on hold.[10]

Overall, the US leader put his Chinese counterpart on the defensive, compelling Beijing to prepare for a wide range of contingencies from the American president. Gone was the Obama government's commitment to positive ties with China. It became clear that Beijing could no longer rely on the policy transparency, measured responses, and avoidance of dramatic action or spillovers among competing interests that characterized the previous administration. As discussed in chapter 7, in the view of American critics, "no-drama" Obama enabled Xi to expand in the South China Sea and carry out other bold moves at American expense without the danger that the resulting tensions would lead to serious US retaliation.

China's new uncertainty over the American president added to reasons for Beijing to avoid—at least temporarily—controversial moves at US expense, such as expansionist actions in the disputed South China Sea and especially sensitive Chinese interchange with North Korea. How long this discretion would last would be a guessing game.

Meanwhile, the respective interests of the two countries in pragmatic cooperation over common concerns amid serious differences remained important determinants; they are assessed in the following chapters. The incentives to avoid serious US-China confrontation or even war have been enormous[11] and seemed obvious to all; but the differences have been growing in importance. The evolution and influence of incentives to cooperation versus differences are treated in the following chapters.

ENDURING DIFFERENCES:
DIVERGING INTERESTS AND VALUES

The lessons of history over US relations with China and especially relations with the People's Republic of China (PRC) provide the basis for findings of lasting importance in determining the course of Sino-American relations. The following chapters show that on balance the historical trajectory has not been positive, with tensions reaching a high point of conflict and confrontation during the first two decades of the Cold War. A major breakthrough took place under the leadership of President Richard Nixon (1969–74) and Chairman Mao Zedong. After that historic thaw, major turning points over the next forty years showed that without powerful, practical reasons for pragmatic accommodation and cooperation, strong and often deeply rooted and enduring differences between the two governments and their broader societies were likely to emerge. Even in the best of times, those differences tended to obstruct improvement in Sino-American relations.

The differences between the United States and China in the early twenty-first century are summarized in the sections that follow.

China

China's many disagreements with the United States can be grouped into four general categories of disputes that have complicated US-China relations for years. Based on Chinese statements and commentary in official Chinese media, the four categories are (1) opposition to US support for Taiwan and to US diplomatic and other involvement with other sensitive sovereignty issues, including Tibet, Xinjiang, and Chinese territorial disputes with neighbors along China's eastern and southern maritime borders; (2) opposition to actual or perceived US efforts to change China's political system; (3) opposition to the United States playing the dominant strategic role along China's periphery in Asia, including US military involvement in Taiwan and military activities in disputed and other territory along China's rim; and (4) opposition to many aspects of US leadership in world affairs. Some specific issues in the latter two categories include US policy in Iraq, Iran, Syria, and the broader Middle East; aspects of the US-backed security presence in the Asia-Pacific, seen notably in the Obama government's so-called pivot or rebalance policy in the region; US and allied ballistic missile defenses; periodic US pressure on such governments as Myanmar (Burma), North Korea, Sudan, Zimbabwe, Cuba, and Venezuela; US pressure tactics in the United Nations and other international forums, and at times the US position on global climate change. [12]

United States

US differences with China continue to involve clusters of often contentious economic, security, political, sovereignty, and foreign policy issues. Economic issues center on inequities in the US economic relationship with China that include a massive trade deficit, Chinese currency policies and practices, US dependence on Chinese financing American budget deficits, and China's lax enforcement of intellectual property rights and wide use of industrial espionage targeting US firms. Security issues focus on the buildup of Chinese military forces and the threat they pose to US interests in Taiwan and the broader Asia-Pacific. Political issues include China's controversial record on human rights, democracy, religious freedom, and family planning practices. Sovereignty questions involve disputes over the status of Taiwan, Tibet, Xinjiang, and Hong Kong, and the often intense disputes in contested territory along China's eastern and southern rim that involve maritime transit and security issues of importance to the United States. Foreign policy disputes focus on China's support for states deviating from US-backed norms, notably including at various times North Korea, Sudan, Myanmar (Burma), Iran, Syria, Cuba, Zimbabwe, and Venezuela; and Chinese trade, investment, and aid involving resource-rich and poorly governed states in Africa and other parts of the developing world, which undermines Western sanctions and other measures designed to pressure these governments to reform. [13]

The following chapters show that these differences reflect conflicting interests and values that often bedeviled US-China relations before the establishment of the PRC in 1949 as well as since that time.

On the US side:

- US policy and practice demonstrates the strong rationale to seek change in China in directions favored by the United States. This values-based American approach often clashes with the realities in US-China relations, arguing for greater US policy pragmatism.
- US government and nongovernment opinion shows wariness and is disinclined to accept China until and unless it accommodates satisfactorily to US values and norms.

- US exceptionalism prompts US policy makers backed by broader American opinion to often see their actions in morally correct terms, so they have a tendency to play down or ignore the negative implications of their actions for China and Chinese interests.
- Nongovernment actors play a strong role in influencing policy, reinforcing the need for US government policy to deal with domestic US determinants in relations with China as well as the international aspects of those relations. These nongovernment actors tend to reinforce the three above-noted elements of a US values-based approach to China seen as less accommodating to Chinese policies and practices at odds with US norms.
- The long-standing US strategic interest in China saw a prolonged reluctance to undertake the risks, costs, and commitments of leadership in relations with China until forced to do so by the Japanese attack on Pearl Harbor at the start of World War II. This period disappointed those in China seeking help from the United States. Since then, US leadership and resolve generally has continued amid often great sacrifice and trauma, caused in particular by repeated, sometimes very costly, and often unpredicted shifts in China. The resulting distrust in Sino-American relations seems strong.

On the China side:

- China's "victim mentality," a long-standing dark view of foreign affairs strongly propagated by the Chinese government, compels China to sustain and advance national power and independence in order to protect its interests in the face of perceived acquisitive and often duplicitous world powers, notably the United States.
- Chinese exceptionalism places the PRC clearly in the lead in the small group of countries that view their foreign behavior in more self-righteous ways than the United States does. Concurrent with the state-fostered "victim mentality," Beijing fosters a view that effectively sways opinion among the Chinese elite and populace that China is always morally correct in its foreign decisions. Information on China's many episodes of aggression and coercive practices for self-interest is suppressed or controlled. In this view, disputes between China and other countries are not China's fault; they arise because of erroneous policies of other countries or sinister manipulation by larger powers, notably the United States. Since China is never at fault, the PRC has never recognized making a mistake in foreign affairs.
- China shows particular worry about the leading world power (usually the United States) and how it will use its presence and influence along China's periphery, broader international influence, and involvement in Chi-

nese internal affairs to enhance its own power and influence at the expense of Chinese interests and influence.

- As China rises in international power and influence, the leading power (the United States) is seen to be inclined to constrain and thwart the rise in order to preserve its dominant position.
- Chinese suspicions and wariness toward the United States and toward foreign affairs in general are reinforced by strong currents of nationalism and Chinese domestic politics sensitive to perceived foreign pressures or impositions.

Adding to these determinants and values is the fact that the United States and China are big countries—the world's most powerful. Their approaches to each other will not be easily changed by smaller powers or other outside forces.

Meanwhile, the checkered record of the United States and China in managing their differences in the interest of pragmatic cooperation since the Nixon-Mao breakthrough more than forty years ago has given rise to experiences on each side that add to bilateral wariness and friction. They include:

- Taiwan: Private and until recently secret Nixon administration interaction with China shows US leaders at the outset giving assurances to China about Taiwan that appeared to open the way to unification on terms agreeable to China. Subsequently, Chinese leaders were repeatedly confronted with US actions that were at odds with earlier US promises and impeded Chinese ambitions regarding Taiwan. Chinese distrust of US policy, especially regarding Taiwan, became deep and long lasting, and continues today.
- Secrecy: Beginning with Nixon, various US administrations determined to hide US concessions on Taiwan and other sensitive issues through secret diplomacy with China in order to keep Congress as well as US media and other interested Americans in the dark on these sensitive questions. One result was repeated backlash from these forces against US administration China policy. Such backlash was seen in congressional action drafting the Taiwan Relations Act of 1979 and congressional and media reaction to the George H. W. Bush handling of China policy after the Tiananmen incident of 1989. The perceived duplicity of the US administration on sensitive issues of China policy has led to continued suspicion among congressional officials, the media, and other US opinion leaders regarding the purpose and implications of sensitive US policies toward China. The US domestic backlash and suspicion poses a significant drag on US administration efforts to move forward on sensitive issues in US-China relations.
- Respective costs and benefits: Debate in the United States and China repeatedly centers on whether one side or the other is gaining dispropor-

tionately in the relationship while the other side defers and makes concessions. The Chinese government, given its authoritarian system, has done a better job than the United States in keeping such debate from spilling over publicly to affect policy in negative ways. Nonetheless, the tendency of both sides to be wary of being taken advantage of by the other remains strong.

• Nongovernment actors: Elites in the Chinese and US governments have been the key decision makers in Sino-American relations. However, foreign policy in the United States, and particularly US policy toward China, has a long history of American nongovernment forces influencing policy. These groups and individuals have been especially important when broader international and domestic circumstances do not support a particular elite-led policy toward China. Thus, they were very important in the years after the Tiananmen incident and the end of the Cold War. Chinese leaders for their part say they are constrained by patriotic public opinion in China, which they aver runs counter to Chinese compromises on Taiwan or other sensitive issues in the interests of fostering better US-China relations.

PURPOSE AND SCOPE OF THIS BOOK

The review offered here synthesizes and analyzes the views of various assessments regarding the background, issues, and trends in Sino-American relations. It shows enormous changes over time, with patterns of confrontation, conflict, and suspicion much more prevalent than patterns of accommodation and cooperation. The past four decades have featured sometimes remarkable improvements in relations as leaders on both sides have pursued practical benefits through pragmatic means. That the base of cooperation is often incomplete, thin, and dependent on changeable circumstances at home and abroad is evident as the societies and governments more often than not show salient differences over a variety of critical issues involving security, values, and economics. Even during periods of public cooperation, probing below the surface shows officials, elites, and public opinion on both sides demonstrating persisting suspicion and wariness of the other country and its possible negative intentions or implications affecting Sino-American relations.

The purpose of the book is not to argue against continuing efforts in both the United States and China to promote a positive trajectory in Sino-American relations. Such efforts are viewed as reasonable and based on common interests of both countries in seeking greater cooperation. Nor does it argue against US and Chinese public disagreements and competition in peaceful pursuit of their respective interests. Instead, this volume conveys the perspective of experienced policy makers and specialists on both sides who understand that perceived advances or setbacks in Sino-American relations involve only part of a complicated relationship. It seeks to assess more fully the complexity of the relationship, so improvements and frictions in official relations between the two nations are placed in balanced context.

Partly because of the salience of US-China relations for international politics, political scientists and other experts devote impressive effort to understanding the relationship and charting its future trajectory, notably using international relations (IR) theories. Nevertheless, experience with many past failed predictions and often unexpected twists and turns in the relationship argues against adherence only to one IR theory in addressing Sino-American relations. Prominent IR scholar Aaron Friedberg early in this century usefully showed how different American and other IR specialists viewed China's rising power and influence through the lens of realism, liberalism, or constructivism—the leading theories in the IR field.

Indeed, the complex American relationship with China has many features that may best be assessed using different perspectives from IR theory. Deepening strategic competition and a massive security dilemma between China and the United States in the Asia-Pacific region underline forces and phenomena that seem best understood through a realist lens. At the same time, American stress on open trade and investment, related social and political liberalism, and deepening Chinese engagement with the existing world order seem best assessed through a liberal perspective in IR theory. In addition, a fundamental reason US efforts to engage and change China's policies and practices have occurred on the US side and have been resisted on the Chinese side has to do with a profound gap between the national identity in China and that in the United States, a topic well explained by constructivist IR theory.

While written by a specialist who sees US-China dynamics best viewed through a realist lens, this study sees the wisdom of using an eclectic approach in applying IR theory to explain varied developments in US-China relations. Meanwhile, the complexities and perceived shortcomings in assessing Sino-American dynamics discussed above lead this author to employ throughout the book the type of contextual analysis used by US government and other policy and intelligence analysts. The author's intention is to offer a comprehensive assessment of the various determinants seen in the context of Chinese and US decision making in order to provide (1) a realistic view of why and how government officials and others influential in decisions relevant to the United States-China relationship have made their choices and (2) a realistic view of the implications of those decisions. Those determinants take into account the changing interplay of power, interests, development, identity, norms, and values present in different countries and regions.

OUTLINE

This book assesses determinants—historical and contemporary—that explain the uncertain situation prevailing today between areas of convergence and areas of divergence in contemporary US-China relations. It also thoroughly examines those issues (i.e., areas of convergence and divergence) and offers a likely forecast for US-China relations.

Proceeding from this introductory chapter, which provides a summary of some findings and explains the purpose and scope of the book, chapters 2 through 7 treat the historical development and status of US-China relations with an eye toward discerning historical determinants relevant to contemporary US-China relations. Chapters 8 through 11 examine four major issue-areas in contemporary US-China relations, endeavoring to discern determinants relevant to the status and outlook of the relationship. Chapter 12 concludes the study by articulating an outlook for Sino-American relations.

Chapter Two

Patterns of US-China Relations Prior to World War II

Throughout much of the nineteenth century, the United States played a limited role in Chinese affairs. Initial American traders and missionaries had no choice but to accommodate the restrictive and sometimes capricious practices of Chinese regulation of trade and other foreign interaction at Canton in southeastern China, part of the Chinese government's broad Tribute System restricting and regulating Chinese interaction with foreigners.[1]

The US government followed the lead of Great Britain, France, and other powers that used wars to compel the declining Qing dynasty (1644–1912) to meet foreign demands and grant privileges to foreigners, including Americans who did not take part in the fighting. Americans in China supported and benefited from the resulting Treaty System. The emerging new order gave foreigners extraterritoriality, the right to reside in China under foreign laws and jurisdiction. The series of foreign treaties imposed on China in the nineteenth and early twentieth centuries opened Chinese ports to foreign commerce and residence; established equal diplomatic relations between the foreign powers and China, with foreign diplomats stationed in the Chinese capital, Peking; allowed foreign missionaries and others to live and work throughout China; provided for concessions of land and development rights that made parts of China, like Shanghai, into foreign-ruled enclaves; and allowed foreign military forces to patrol Chinese coastal and inland waterways and eventually to deploy ground forces in China to secure their interests. The treaties also marked the loss of substantial pieces of Chinese territory to foreign ownership.[2]

A few American companies made significant profits in China trade, but the scope of US trade and investment there remained very small. Christian missionaries comprised the largest and most influential group of Americans in China until the start of World War II, but for much of the period they numbered only in the hundreds.[3]

American diplomats, merchants, and missionaries reacted with concern as European powers and later Japan began at the end of the nineteenth century to carve up Chinese territory into exclusive spheres of influence. However, US government actions in response were mainly symbolic, using nonbinding measures such as diplomatic notes and agreements to support the principles of free access to China and Chinese territorial integrity. US importance in China also grew by default as previously active European powers withdrew forces and resources during World War I. Imperial Japan used military and other coercion to solidify Japanese control in parts of China, notably Manchuria.[4]

Though there often was strenuous US debate, the prevailing US official position was that limited US capabilities and interests in China argued against the United States confronting increasingly dominant Japanese power in East Asia. US officials endeavored to use international agreements and political measures to persuade Japanese officials to preserve Chinese integrity and free international access to China. The US efforts were seriously complicated by political disorder in China and by US leaders' later preoccupation with the consequences of the Great Depression. In the 1930s, Japan created a puppet state in Manchuria and continued encroachments in northern China. The United States did little apart from symbolic political posturing in response to the Japanese aggression and expansion.[5]

US-China relations in this more than century-long period saw the emergence of patterns of behavior that influenced US and Chinese attitudes and policies toward one another. American officials and elite and popular opinion tended to emphasize what they saw as a uniquely positive role the United States played as a supporter of Chinese national interests and the well-being of the Chinese people, with some commentators seeing the emergence of a US special relationship with China. Chinese officials and elites, including a rising group of Chinese patriots in the late nineteenth and early twentieth centuries, tended to see American policies and practices as less aggressive than other powers but of little substantive help in China's struggle for national preservation and development. Chinese officials often endeavored to manipulate American diplomacy to serve Chinese interests, but they usually were disappointed with the results. American government policies and practices were seen at bottom to serve narrow US interests, with little meaningful concern for China. Gross American discrimination against and persecution of Chinese residents and Chinese immigrants in the United States underlined a perceived hypocrisy in American declarations of special concern for China.[6]

US INTERESTS, ACTIONS, AND PERCEPTIONS

Beginning in the late eighteenth century, new American freedom from British rule brought American loss of access to previous British-controlled trade partners. This prompted an American search for new trading opportunities in China. Though actual US trade with China remained relatively small, the China market often loomed large in the American political and business imagination. Meanwhile, US officials sometimes sought to channel US investment in ways that would preserve American commercial opportunities in China in the face of foreign powers seeking exclusive privileges and spheres of influence. [7]

Americans also were in the vanguard of Protestant missionaries sent to China in the nineteenth century. US missionaries came in groups and as individuals to work in the treaty ports and eventually grew to many hundreds working throughout China to spread the gospel and to carry out relief, education, medical, and other activities of benefit to Chinese people. Part of a well-organized network of church groups that reached deep into the United States for prayers and material support, American missionaries explained Chinese conditions to interested Americans, fostering a sense of special bond between the United States and China. They also served as advisers to US officials dealing with China, and sometimes became official US representatives in China. Their core interest remained unobstructed access to Chinese people for purposes of evangelization and good works carried out by the American missionaries and their foreign and Chinese colleagues. [8]

Though commercial and missionary interests remained at the center of US priorities in China well into the twentieth century, a related strategic interest also had deep roots. In 1835, several years before the first US treaty with China in 1844, the United States organized the Asiatic Squadron. This US Navy group began in 1842 to maintain a regular presence along the China coast. It later was called the Asiatic Fleet. Initially two or three vessels, it grew to thirty-one vessels by 1860 before forces were recalled on account of the American Civil War. It varied in size after the Civil War, but was sufficiently strong to easily destroy the Spanish forces in Manila harbor during the Spanish-American War in 1898. It protected American lives and commerce in China and throughout maritime East and South Asia and reinforced American diplomacy in the region. [9]

Strong American interest in commercial, missionary, and strategic access to China seemed to contrast with only episodic American diplomatic interest in China. The US government occasionally gave high-level attention to the appointment of envoys or the reception of Chinese delegations. Caleb Cushing, Anson Burlingame, and some other nineteenth-century US envoys to China were well connected politically. Some US envoys endeavored to use their actions in China to influence broader US policy or to advance their own political or other ambitions. US envoys sometimes came from the missionary community in China. On the other hand, the post of US minister in China often was vacant, with an interim official placed in charge in an acting capacity. Generally speaking, whenever nineteenth-century US envoys pushed for more assertive US policies that involved the chance of significant expenditure of US resources or political risk, Washington decision makers reflected the realities of limited US government interests in the situation in China and responded unenthusiastically. This broad pattern continued into the twentieth century, though US officials from time to time took the lead in low-risk political and diplomatic efforts in support of US interests in unimpeded commercial and other access to China. [10]

Not surprisingly, the Americans with an interest in China tended to emphasize the positive features of US policy and behavior. Thus, the United States was seen to have behaved benignly toward China, especially when compared with Japan and the European powers that repeatedly coerced and attacked China militarily. The US government repeatedly voiced support of China's territorial and national integrity. Through missionary and other activities, including education activities that brought tens of thousands of Chinese students for higher education in the United States by the 1940s, Americans also showed strong sympathy and support for the broader welfare of the Chinese people. [11]

US officials, opinion leaders, and commentators tended to ignore or soft-pedal negative features of US relations with China. Most notable was the so-called exclusion movement that grossly discriminated against and often violently persecuted Chinese immigrants to the United States. The movement took hold in US politics beginning in the 1870s and lasted for almost a hundred years. At first centered in western states with some significant concentrations of Chinese workers, the exclusion movement reflected widespread American prejudice and fear of Chinese workers amid sometimes difficult economic times in the United States. American elites and common people took legal and illegal actions, including riots and the murder of hundreds of Chinese in the United States, to stop Chinese immigration to the United States and drive away those Chinese already in the United States. Various state governments and the national government passed an array of laws and the US courts made a variety of decisions that singled out Chinese immigrants for negative treatment and curbed the legal rights of Chinese residents and Chinese citizens of the United States. The movement eventually broadened to include all Asians. The National Origins Act of 1924 barred all new Asian immigration. US mistreatment of Chinese people in the United States became a major issue for the Chinese government, which complained repeatedly against unjust US actions, but with little effect. It was the target of a Chinese anti-American boycott in 1905. [12]

CHINESE INTERESTS, ACTIONS, AND PERCEPTIONS

The Chinese side of the US-China relationship during the more than century-long experience prior to World War II saw Chinese officials and elite opinion in the nineteenth and early twentieth centuries remain preoccupied with massive internal rebellions and disruptions. In this context, the United States figured secondarily in Chinese government and elite concerns. The opinion of the Chinese populace was less important in China-US relations until the occurrence of anti-Christian and anti-missionary riots later in the nineteenth century and grassroots nationalistic actions like the 1905 anti-American boycott reacting to the US mistreatment of Chinese immigrants.[13]

Qing dynasty officials often were too weak to confront foreign aggression and military pressure in the nineteenth and early twentieth centuries. Their diplomacy frequently amounted to versions of appeasement. Forced to give ground to foreign demands, the Qing officials gave special emphasis to capitalizing on real or perceived differences among the foreign powers, hoping to use some foreign powers to fend off others. Chinese officials repeatedly tried to elicit US actions that would assist Chinese interests against other generally more aggressive and demanding powers. Although US envoys in China often would be caught up in these Chinese schemes and argue for US positions at odds with other powers in China, Washington decision makers tended to adhere to a low-risk approach that offered little of substance to support the Chinese efforts.[14]

Qing dynasty initiatives endeavoring to use possible US support against other foreign powers did not blind Chinese government officials to US interests in China that worked against Chinese government concerns. The spread of foreign missionaries throughout China as a result of treaties reached in 1860 meant that these foreign elites soon ran up against strong resistance from local Chinese elites. The local Chinese leaders, the so-called gentry class, often fomented popular outbursts and riots against the foreigners and their Chinese Christian adherents. The American missionaries sought the support of their official representatives in China who backed their demands to the Chinese government for protection, punishment of Chinese malefactors, and compensation with strong diplomacy and frequent use of gunboats. This posed a very difficult dilemma for Qing officials, who needed to deal with the threats from the Americans and other foreign officials pressing for protection of missionaries and punishment of offending Chinese elites, while sustaining the support of local Chinese elites who provided key elements of Chinese governance at the local levels.[15]

Meanwhile, American government officials were seen by Chinese officials and other elites as transparently hypocritical in demanding protection of special rights for American missionaries and other US citizens in China, while US officials and people were carrying out repeated and often violent infringements on the rights and basic safety of Chinese workers in the United States. In this context, Chinese officials tended to be sympathetic with the merchant-led and student-encouraged anti-American boycott that took hold in Chinese coastal cities in 1905 and that focused on Chinese anger over US discrimination against Chinese immigration to the United States and poor treatment of Chinese in the United States.[16]

With the withdrawal of the European powers to fight World War I, the United States loomed larger in the strategies of the weak Chinese governments following the end of the Qing dynasty in 1912. However, the United States remained unwilling to take significant risks of confrontation with the now-dominant power in China: imperial Japan. The US reaction to the gross Japanese infringements on Chinese sovereignty in the so-called Twenty-One Demands of 1915 elicited statements on nonrecognition and not much else from the United States. President Woodrow Wilson gravely disappointed Chinese patriots by accepting Japan's continued control of the former German leasehold in China's Shantung province at the Versailles Peace Treaty ending World War I.[17]

The Nine Power Treaty at the US-convened Washington Conference of 1921–22 pledged to respect Chinese territorial integrity, but when Japan took over Manchuria, creating a puppet state in the early 1930s, the US government offered little more than words of disapproval. Given this experience, Chinese patriots were not persuaded by the protestations of some American commentators that the United States had developed a special relationship with China based on concern for the well-being of the Chinese people and preservation of China's sovereignty and integrity. When Japan, after occupying Manchuria, moved in 1937 to launch an all-out war against China and the United States did little in response, Chinese patriots became even more cynical about American intentions and policies.[18]

NINETEENTH-CENTURY ENCOUNTERS

American traders and seamen were the first from the United States to interact with China. When American traders went to China prior to the Opium War of 1839–42, Chinese regulations under the Tribute System in foreign affairs confined them, along with most other foreign maritime traders, to Canton, in southeastern China. There, local officials supervised and taxed foreign trade, foreigners were required to live and work in a designated area of Canton during the trading season, and foreign interaction with Chinese was kept to a minimum; certain Chinese merchants were designated to deal with foreign merchants.[19]

Chinese foreign relations under the Tribute System were unequal; they emphasized the superiority of China, its system of governance, and the emperor. The foreigners were expected to abide by Chinese laws and regulations and to accord with Chinese instructions. As a result, although American and other foreign merchants and their foreign employees benefited from the trading opportunities at Canton, they were subject to interventions from Chinese authority that appeared unjust from a Western perspective and dangerous to those concerned.

A graphic illustration of the vulnerability of foreigners in China was the case of Francesco Terranova. A Sicilian-born sailor on an American ship trading at Canton in 1821, Terranova was accused of the murder of a boatwoman selling fruit to the ship. He and his shipmates denied the charge. A standoff resulted, with Chinese authorities cutting off American trade until Terranova was handed over. The American merchants and shipowners gave in; Terranova was handed over, tried in secret under Chinese procedures with no American present, convicted, and executed. Trade between the United States and China resumed.[20]

Like their British colleagues, American merchants brought opium into China, balancing their purchases of tea and other Chinese commodities. The burgeoning trade in illegal opium entering China in the period before the Opium War was carried out mainly by British merchants, though American merchants carried Turkish opium to China and held about 10 percent of the Chinese opium market. American opium along with British opium was confiscated and destroyed by Chinese authorities in Canton in 1839, leading to Great Britain going to war. The US government took no part in the fighting.[21]

After the British in 1842 negotiated the Treaty of Nanjing ending the Opium War and opening five Chinese treaty ports for foreign residency and trade, the United States appointed Caleb Cushing as commissioner to China to negotiate a US treaty with China. He negotiated the Treaty of Wang-hsia in 1844, obtaining the rights and privileges Britain had gained by force of arms. Chinese negotiator Ch'i-ying followed a general policy of trying to appease foreign demands, and the US treaty included language to the effect that Chinese concessions made to other foreign nations would apply to the United States as well. American merchants, missionaries, and others were free to settle in the five treaty ports; and Americans, like other foreigners in China, had the right of extraterritoriality. This legal system meant that foreigners and their activities in China remained governed by their own law and not Chinese law.[22]

Emblematic of the wide-ranging influence some American missionaries exerted over the course of US policy toward China during that period was the role of Peter Parker (1804–88). Parker was a medical missionary in Canton in the 1830s. He assisted Caleb Cushing in negotiating the Treaty of Wang-hsia. He was an interpreter and also helped facilitate the talks by being on good terms with the chief Chinese government negotiator and his aides.

Parker eventually became US commissioner in China in 1856. Faced with a harder Chinese line at that time toward foreign demands for broader commercial and missionary privileges, Parker favored Britain's approach emphasizing firmness and appropriate use of force to advance foreign interests. When Chinese forts in Canton in 1856 fired on US warships under the command of Commodore James Armstrong, Parker backed Armstrong's destruction of the forts. Parker later had ambitions for the United States to gain a foothold in Taiwan and to have a more active naval presence in China, but these initiatives were not supported by the US government. [23]

The upsurge of the massive Taiping Rebellion beginning in 1850 caught Chinese authorities and American and foreign observers by surprise as the rebel movement came to dominate southeastern China and most of the Yangtze River valley. Some Americans at first were attracted by Taiping leader Hung Hsiu-ch'uan's avowed Christian beliefs. Hung came to his own unique views of Christianity, though he had three months of study in 1837 with an American missionary in Canton, Issachar Roberts. As the Taiping leader's warped views of Christianity became clearer to Americans, they added to reasons Americans and other foreigners shied away from the radical rebel leader and his destructive activities. [24]

Though seeing US interests resting with continued Qing dynasty rule, American officials nonetheless were ready to join with Great Britain, France, and others in pressing for treaty revisions that would open more treaty ports, allow for missionary activities outside the treaty ports, and establish foreign legations in the Chinese capital. Britain and France used military force to back up their demands, and in 1858 the Chinese government signed treaties with them as well as with the Americans, who did no fighting. When British and French envoys returned in 1859 to exchange ratification, they refused Chinese ratification instructions, and a battle resulted in which the Chinese drove off the foreigners. During the battle, the US commodore accompanying Minister John Ward, the American envoy, had his forces, with Ward's approval, join with the British in fighting the Chinese. Ward nonetheless followed the Chinese instructions for treaty ratification and managed to exchange ratification. The British and French returned in force in 1860 and marched to Peking before setting forth new conditions in the treaties of 1860 that also benefited the United States. [25]

US policy in China supported stronger Chinese government efforts after 1860 that worked within the confines of the Treaty System and accepted Western norms while strengthening the Chinese government, economy, and military. American Frederick Townsend Ward had led a foreign mercenary force paid by Chinese merchants to protect Shanghai during the Taiping Rebellion, and he later worked with Chinese authorities in leading a Chinese force that helped crush the rebellion. Americans supported the newly established Chinese Imperial Maritime Customs Service. This foreign-managed customs service had its roots in Shanghai in the 1850s during the years of threat posed by the Taiping Rebellion; it emerged as a unique Chinese-foreign enterprise (more than four hundred foreign employees in 1875) that preserved the Chinese government's access to an important and reliable source of revenue. The US government saw its interests well served by cooperating amicably with Britain and France as they worked collaboratively with a newly reformist Chinese government seeking to strengthen China along Western lines. The American Civil War weakened American military presence in China and prompted US policy to place a premium on avoiding disputes with Britain and France that might lead the European powers to be more inclined to support the secessionist South.[26]

Anson Burlingame, US minister to China 1861–67, symbolized American collaboration with other foreign powers and with China in promoting Chinese reforms and greater outreach to advanced Western countries. After leaving his position as minister, Burlingame accepted a Chinese offer to lead a Chinese delegation to observe and have talks with leaders of the West. The trip was moderately successful, meeting acceptance notably in America and England. The so-called Burlingame Treaty was signed during the delegation's visit to the United States in 1868. Among other provisions in the treaty, the United States said it would not interfere in the internal development of China, China recognized the right of its people to emigrate, and the United States gave Chinese immigrants the right to enter the United States. At the time, there were more than one hundred thousand Chinese in the United States. Many had come with the support of American business interests and their national and local US government backers seeking reliable labor for the rapid development of the American West.[27]

Unfortunately, American society showed deep prejudice against Chinese that eventually spread to other immigrants from Asia. Ironically, this came at a time when a wide range of elements in the United States generally welcomed the hundreds of thousands of immigrants coming annually to the United States from Europe. There emerged in the 1870s a broadly based exclusion movement in the United States that was a dominant feature in US relations with China for decades to come. This widespread US movement was grounded in prejudice and fear of Chinese workers amid sometimes difficult economic times in the United States. Showing blatant racism against Chinese, Americans took legal and illegal actions, including riots and the murder of hundreds of Chinese in the United States, to stop Chinese immigration to the United States. In September 1885, mobs of white workers attacked Chinese in Rock Springs, Wyoming, killing twenty-eight in an outburst of burning, looting, and mayhem. State governments and the national government passed an array of laws and the US courts made a variety of decisions that singled out Chinese immigrants for negative treatment and curbed the legal rights of Chinese residents and Chinese citizens in the United States. In 1888 the Scott Act restricted Chinese laborers' entry and denied them reentry into the United States. In 1892 the Geary Act stripped Chinese in the United States, whether citizens or not, of substantial legal rights, requiring them to obtain and carry at all times a certificate showing their right to reside in the United States. Without such proof, the punishment was hard labor and deportation. The movement broadened to include all Asians. The National Origins Act of 1924 barred new Asian immigration.[28]

Chinese officials in the Chinese legation in Washington protested US discrimination and persecution of Chinese and endeavored to reach agreements with the US government that would assure basic protection of Chinese rights. They repeatedly found US actions in violation of treaty obligations and other agreements. US violations seriously undermined diplomatic relations between the two countries in the 1890s. US mistreatment of Chinese people in the United States also prompted patriotic merchants, students, and others to organize anti-American movements. The 1905 boycott closed several coastal Chinese cities to US goods for several months. Nevertheless, the US exclusion movement persisted and grew.

Adding to the friction in Sino-American official relations were the tensions caused by expanding US and other foreign missionary activities in China and the resulting antiforeign backlash in China. Attacks against Chinese Christians and their missionary leaders became common occurrences in the latter part of the nineteenth century, prompting American and other Western governments to press the Chinese government for strong remedial actions, and prompting foreign officials to take actions on their own, including the use of foreign gunboats, in order to protect their interests and citizens. The Chinese authorities repeatedly found themselves caught between competing pressures. On the one hand were the strong American and other foreign pressures to protect missionaries and Chinese Christians. On the other hand was the strong need to preserve the support of the local Chinese gentry class, whose cooperation was essential for the maintenance of local governance in the minimally staffed Chinese administration at the grassroots level. The gentry often tended to see the foreign missionaries as posing social, political, and ideological challenges to the Chinese elite, and they frequently took steps to foster antiforeign sentiment against them by the broader Chinese society.[29]

Illustrating the marked shift toward the negative in official US attitudes toward China from the comparatively benign and somewhat paternalistic views of Anson Burlingame was the change in approach of Charles Denby, who served as American minister in China (1885–98). A loyal Democrat appointed by the first Grover Cleveland administration, Denby stayed as US minister through the end of the second Cleveland administration. Initially favoring a temperate position in seeking cooperation with Chinese officials seen as moving toward reform, Denby came later to the view that Chinese government incompetence and weakness endangered American and other missionaries and opened China to unchecked ambitions by outside powers. He saw little alternative to the United States' joining coercive foreign powers in order to protect US interests.[30]

Chinese official disappointment and frustration with the United States were reflected in the experience of Li Hung-chang (Li Hongzhang) (1823–1901). Dominating Chinese foreign policy in the last third of the nineteenth century, this senior regional and national leader and commissioner of trade in northern China repeatedly employed the past practice of Chinese leaders in using initiatives toward the United States in an effort to offset pressures on China from other powers. And, as in those earlier episodes, he found the US response wanting and became increasingly cynical about the utility of appealing to the United States for support.[31]

As in the case of earlier episodes of Chinese efforts to use the United States against more aggressive foreign powers, Li's view was based on the judgment that the United States posed little threat to Chinese territories or tributary states, while its commitment to commerce provided common ground in US-China relations that could be used by Chinese officials to win American support against more grasping and aggressive foreign powers. Li was forced to deal with the growing source of friction between the United States and China posed by US immigration policy discriminating against Chinese. Initially, he endeavored to deal with this issue through negotiation.

Li sought US assistance in dealing with Chinese difficulties with Japan over the Liu-ch'iu (Ryukyu) Islands in the 1870s. President Ulysses S. Grant favored a cooperative US policy toward China and was a personal friend of Anson Burlingame, the prominent proponent of cooperative China-US relations. After leaving office, Grant traveled to Asia in 1879 and was encouraged by Li to intercede with Japan on China's behalf regarding a dispute over the Liu-ch'iu (Ryukyu) Islands. Grant also received a promise from the Chinese government to negotiate treaty restrictions on Chinese immigration into the United States. Li later sought US endorsement of Chinese claims in Korea in the face of Japanese pressure there in the 1880s. He also sought US mediation in a growing dispute with France over Vietnam in the 1880s. All these initiatives achieved little of benefit to China. By July 1894 Li sought US good offices to avoid a war with Japan over Korea only after exhausting other options. Li then endeavored to rely on Russia and other European powers to deal with Japanese demands after the Japanese defeated China in 1895. Unlike other Chinese officials, including his senior colleague Chang Chih-tung (Zhang Zhidong), Li did not emphasize the option of turning to the United States for meaningful assistance in the period of demands by Russia, Japan, and other imperial powers for major territorial and other concessions from China at the turn of the nineteenth century.[32]

US-CHINA RELATIONS AMID FOREIGN DOMINATION, INTERNAL DECLINE, AND REVOLUTION IN CHINA, 1895–1941

China's unexpected defeat by Japan in the Sino-Japanese War of 1894–95 led European powers to join Japan in seeking exclusive spheres of influence and commercial and territorial rights in China. Alarmed that US interests in free commercial access to China would be jeopardized, US officials formulated a response that led to the so-called Open Door Notes of 1899 and 1900. The notes sought the powers' agreement that even if they established special spheres in China, they would not discriminate against foreign trade or interfere with customs collection. They underlined US interests in preserving equal commercial access to China and the preservation of the integrity of the Chinese Customs Service, a crucial source of revenue for the struggling Chinese government. [33]

Though generally unenthusiastic about the US initiatives, most concerned powers offered evasive and qualified responses, but all in effect endorsed the principles in the Open Door Notes. As the United States and other foreign powers dispatched troops to crush the Boxer Uprising and lift the siege of foreign legations in Peking, the United States in July 1900 sent a second round of Open Door Notes that expressed concern for preserving Chinese sovereignty. The foreign powers went along with the notes.

US policy makers repeatedly referred to the US Open Door policy following the issuing of the Open Door Notes. The William H. Taft administration in 1910 interpreted the policy to extend beyond equal trade opportunity to include equal opportunity for investment in China. The Wilson administration in 1915 reacted to the Japanese Twenty-One Demands against China by refusing to recognize such infringements of the Open Door policy. The related principles concerning US support for the territorial integrity of China were featured prominently in the Nine Power Treaty of the Washington Conference in the Warren G. Harding administration in 1922, and in the nonrecognition of Japanese aggression in Manchuria during the Herbert Hoover administration in 1932. The Harry Truman administration sought Soviet Union leader Joseph Stalin's promise that the Open Door policy would be observed in the Soviet-influenced areas of Manchuria following the Soviet military defeat of Japanese forces there in 1945. In general, American political leaders dealing with China throughout the twentieth century tended to refer to the Open Door policy in positive terms, as a US attempt to prevent China from being carved up into commercially impenetrable foreign colonies. Chinese interpretations often emphasized that Americans were more concerned about maintaining their own commercial access and were prepared to do little in practice in supporting Chinese sovereignty. The historical record tends to support the Chinese interpretations. [34]

Most prominent in US policy toward China in the tumultuous period of the Open Door Notes was John Hay. Secretary of state under President William McKinley and, after McKinley's assassination in 1901, President Theodore Roosevelt, Hay strove to preserve US commercial access to China and other interests amid widespread foreign encroachment on the weakened Qing dynasty. Responding to the unexpected Japanese defeat of China in 1895 and European powers' extortion of leaseholds and concessions in the following three years, Hay used the work of State Department China expert William Rockhill and his British colleague from the Chinese Imperial Maritime Customs Service, Alfred Hippisley, as the basis for official US messages sent to all foreign powers concerned with China in September 1899.[35]

The first Open Door Notes were followed by the crisis associated with the Boxer Uprising. A grassroots antiforeign insurrection in northern China, known as the Boxers, came to receive support from some Chinese officials, and by 1899 and 1900 it was carrying out widespread attacks against foreign missionaries and Chinese Christians. As the movement grew, it received the support of the Qing court, though regional leaders in most of China did not support the Boxers. The insurgents occupied Peking and Tientsin, besieging foreign legations and settlements. About twenty thousand foreign troops were mustered, including thousands of Americans, to end the siege and put down the insurgents. They ended the siege of Tientsin in July and of Peking in August 1900. Many troops stayed, carrying out punitive expeditions.[36]

As the United States and other foreign powers dispatched troops to crush the Boxer Uprising and lift the siege of foreign legations in Peking, Hay in July 1900 sent a second round of Open Door Notes in which he expressed concern for preserving Chinese sovereignty. He depicted local Chinese authorities as responsible for law and order and the safety of foreigners in China. This helped the United States and other powers continue to work constructively with regional Chinese leaders in central and southern China who were maintaining law and order, and focus their anti-Boxer suppression more narrowly, in northern China.

Though Hay tried to reduce the large size of the foreign indemnity demanded of China, the United States took its $25 million share of the $333 million indemnity China was required to pay the foreign powers under terms of the Boxer Protocol signed in September 1901, and the United States stationed troops along with other powers in northern China under terms of the protocol. While continuing to work in support of China's territorial integrity and equal commercial access to China, Hay responded to US pressures to obtain a coaling station in China by making a perfunctory and ultimately vain effort in December 1900 to acquire such a station on the China coast.[37]

Meanwhile, as Russia endeavored to consolidate its hold in Manchuria, and Japan and Great Britain worked together against it, ultimately forming an alliance in 1902, Hay attempted to secure US interests with a new Sino-

American trade treaty and a request for opening two new treaty ports in Russian-dominated areas of Manchuria. Russia at first resisted Chinese acceptance of the US request but decided to withdraw its opposition when it was clear to them that Americans or other foreigners, notably Japanese, would not settle in the ports.[38]

Though Li Hung-chang and his increasingly skeptical view of the utility of overtures to the United States for Chinese interests remained salient in Chinese foreign-policy decision making until his death in 1901, simultaneously, an important force often arguing for closer Chinese coordination with the United States came from Chang Chih-tung (1837–1909). A powerful Chinese official, well entrenched as governor-general in the provinces, Chang endeavored in the period after Japan's defeat of China in 1895 and subsequent European powers' extortion of concessions to cooperate with the United States as a power opposing seizure of Chinese territory. Though he supported China's reliance on Russia after the defeat by Japan in 1895, he came by 1898 to seek the support of Britain and the United States, viewing them as commercial powers with substantial interests in blocking seizures of Chinese territory by Japan, Russia, and others.[39]

That year, he entrusted an American consortium to build the Hankow-Canton railway. The US business group was known as the American-China Development Company. Organized in 1895 and representing US railway, banking, and investment interests, the company received from the Chinese government in 1898 a concession to build and operate a railway between the two Chinese cities. The company demanded and received better terms from the Chinese government in a supplementary agreement in 1900.[40]

Chang made overtures to the United States during and after the Boxer Uprising, seeking US mediation with the foreign powers and US assistance in moderating the foreign reaction to the crisis. Chang sought, without much success, US help in limiting the size of the foreign indemnity and in dealing with Russian military occupation of Manchuria after the Boxer Uprising. He subsequently became disillusioned with the American consortium for the Hankow-Canton railroad. Some of the American shareholders sold interest in the company to a Belgian syndicate, which by 1904 controlled five of seven seats on the company's board of directors. Chang and the Chinese government then sought to buy back the concession, and the US government encouraged efforts by American investors to restore American control to the company. In the end, American shareholders, having restored American ownership of the company, gained considerable profit by selling their interests in the railway concession back to the Chinese government in 1905.

Chang's frustration with the United States also was seen as he intervened at several points with the Chinese central government and the US government, emphasizing strong antipathy among Chinese patriots over the US exclusion of Chinese in the late nineteenth and early twentieth centuries.

During the anti-American boycott of 1905, prompted heavily by Chinese resentment over US restrictions on Chinese immigration, Chang privately advised President Theodore Roosevelt to ease the US restrictions.[41]

American officials also were active in the late nineteenth and early twentieth centuries, pressing the Chinese government to protect American and other missionaries and their converts, who were subjected to frequent attacks often fomented by Chinese local elites. The Boxer Uprising added greatly to the anti-Christian attacks and implicated the Qing government in the violence. Hundreds of foreign missionaries and thousands of Chinese Christians were killed. The violence against missionaries subsided but did not end. The Lien-Chou massacre of 1905 represented the most serious incident in US-China relations in the decade. The murder of five US missionaries in this southern Chinese city prompted President Theodore Roosevelt to consider the use of force in Canton, and American forces began gathering in Canton harbor. Roosevelt already was strongly critical of the prolonged anti-American boycott underway in China. Chinese officials ultimately took steps to punish those responsible for the massacre and to pay an indemnity.[42]

The Sino-American maneuvering over the Hankow-Canton railway was emblematic of an erratic pattern of American business and government interest in investment in China in railway and other development plans in the last fifteen years of Qing rule. Also reflected then was erratic Chinese interest in using such US involvement in efforts to offset foreign encroachment. The focus of interest for the United States and China came to rest in Manchuria, where Russia and especially Japan were consolidating spheres of influence. Prominent figures on the Chinese side in this issue were Tang Shao-yi, a governor in Manchuria, and the regional and emerging national leader of China, Yuan Shih-kai, both of whom sought such US support.[43]

A protégé of Li Hung-chang, Yuan emerged as the most important military and political leader in China in the early twentieth century until his death in 1916. His base of power was in northern China, and he was closely involved with efforts to stem the decline of Chinese influence and control in Manchuria in the face of Russian and Japanese advances. He supported the ways Tang Shao-yi and others approached the Theodore Roosevelt administration as they sought US support in order to counter Japanese expansion in Manchuria. Seeking good relations with the United States, he argued for the suppression of the anti-American boycott.[44]

Tang had studied in the United States and worked with Yuan and others in encouraging US government and business to become more involved with railway building in Manchuria as a means to counter Japanese expansion there. Tang sought support from US financial backers and officials in China. As US consul general in Mukden, Manchuria, during the Theodore Roosevelt administration, Willard Straight attempted to work with Tang and other Chinese officials to use US investments to counter Japanese domination in Manchuria. In 1908 Tang traveled to Washington, where he met with Secretary of State Elihu Root, who underlined the Theodore Roosevelt administration's lack of interest in confronting Japan in Manchuria by sharing with Tang the yet-unpublished Root-Takahira Agreement. This was an exchange of notes between Root and Japanese Ambassador Takahira Kogoro that underlined US commitment to the status quo in the Pacific region, including China; US desire to maintain friendly relations with Japan; and lack of US interest in considering any Chinese-inspired plan to challenge Japanese interests in Manchuria.[45]

US government policy on supporting railway building as a means to challenge other powers' encroachment and support Chinese influence in Manchuria shifted markedly for a time during the Taft administration, 1909–13. The president and Secretary of State Philander Knox tried to use schemes involving US investment in railways to prevent Russia and Japan from dominating Manchuria. A leading example of these plans was a proposed railway in Manchuria between the cities of Chinchow and Aigun. Willard Straight had left US government service and was working with Chinese officials and US and foreign backers to promote plans to build the railroad. Straight signed an agreement with Chinese authorities in Manchuria in October 1909 to have an American banking group finance the Chinchow-Aigun route. Before moving forward with the deal, the Chinese authorities in Peking awaited US efforts to deal with expected Japanese and Russian anger over this challenge to their spheres of influence in Manchuria. In this regard, Secretary of State Knox proposed a bold plan to neutralize or internationalize all railway projects in Manchuria. Japan and Russia rejected Knox's plan and warned against the Chinchow-Aigun railway. Chinese central government authorities temporized, and US investors showed little enthusiasm. The Taft administration's "dollar diplomacy" failed. The US administration subsequently adopted a more moderate stance emphasizing US cooperation with European powers, and ultimately Russia and Japan, in an international consortium dealing with loans to China. Ironically, Hsi-liang, the Chinese governor-general in Manchuria in the last years of the Qing dynasty, and his Qing dynasty colleagues chose this time to try to consolidate ties with the United States and to seek greater US support against Russia and Japan in Manchuria. However, Chinese government emissaries found the Taft administration now maintained a low profile regarding Manchuria.[46]

The pattern of US government policy on the one hand supporting an open door of international commercial access to China and Chinese territorial integrity, and on the other hand avoiding actions that would complicate US relations with salient foreign powers expanding in China, continued with the fall of the Chinese empire. In the thirty years from the end of the Qing dynasty in early 1912 to the attack on Pearl Harbor in late 1941, US policy and practice endeavored to stake out positions and formulate political measures designed to support Chinese sovereignty and integrity. But they did so while generally avoiding the risk of confrontation with imperial Japan, which emerged as the dominant power in East Asia after the pullback and weakening of European powers in the region with the start of World War I. US policy makers also were challenged by revolutionary movements and violent antiforeign sentiment sweeping China in the 1920s. They tended to adjust to these trends pragmatically, giving way to some of the Chinese demands and eventually establishing good working relations with the Nationalist Chinese government of Chiang Kai-shek, the dominant leader of China by the late 1920s.

Japan moved quickly to consolidate its position in China with the start of World War I. Allied with Great Britain and siding with the Allies in World War I, Japan occupied German concessions in China's Shantung province in 1914. In January 1915 Japan presented the Chinese government with five sets of secret demands that became known as the Twenty-One Demands. The demands were leaked, which compelled Japan to defer the more outrageous ones, but they resulted in May 1915 in Sino-Japanese treaties and notes confirming Japan's dominant position in Shantung, southern Manchuria, and eastern Inner Mongolia, and Japan's special interests in an industrial area in central China. US officials debated how to respond. Secretary of State William Jennings Bryan at first reaffirmed US support for China's territorial integrity and equal commercial access to China, but also acknowledged Japan's "special relations" with China. President Wilson subsequently warned that the United States would not accept infringements on its rights, and Bryan said the United States would not recognize infringements on US rights, Chinese sovereignty, or the Open Door policy. In a bid to expand US leverage, Wilson then reversed an earlier decision and supported American banks lending money to China through an international consortium as a means to balance Japanese expansion in China.

Not seriously deterred, Japan maneuvered to see that its position in Shantung province was secured by the Versailles Peace Treaty ending World War I. Like Japan, the Chinese government had aligned with the victorious allied powers. US and Chinese delegations worked closely at the peace conference to free China from restrictions on her sovereignty, and Chinese negotiators were particularly interested in regaining control of the former German concession in China's Shantung province. Nevertheless, Japan earlier had signed secret agreements with European powers that bound them to support Japan's claims to the Shantung leasehold, and the Chinese government's position was weakened by having agreed as part of the Twenty-One Demands in 1915 to accept German-Japanese agreement on the concessions. Robert Lansing, a counselor at the State Department during the early years of the Wilson administration, argued against confrontation with Japan in defense of China's integrity at the time of Japan's Twenty-One Demands in 1915. As secretary of state in 1917 he negotiated and exchanged notes with Japanese envoy Ishii Kikujiro that acknowledged Japan's "special interests" in China, even though Japan privately agreed not to seek privileges at the expense of other friendly powers in China. The notes were used by Japan as evidence of tacit US support for Japanese expansion in China. Though Lansing opposed President Wilson's decision at the Versailles Peace Conference in 1919 to accept the Japanese claim to the German concessions in China's Shantung province, Wilson felt compelled to accept Japan's claim to the former German concessions. The president's action gravely disappointed Chinese patriots. The provision in the treaty was a catalyst for demonstration in Peking on May 4, 1919, that led to both intellectual reform campaigns and radical, anti-imperialist movements that spread throughout China in following years and became known collectively as the May Fourth Movement.[47]

The United States after World War I took the lead in calling a major conference involving powers with interests in the western Pacific, including China but not the Soviet Union, to deal with relevant security issues. The result was the Washington Conference of 1921–22 that saw passage of a Nine Power Treaty supporting noninterference in Chinese internal affairs. US delegates working with others also succeeded in getting Japan to agree to withdraw from Shantung under terms of agreements at the conference. Nonetheless, the treaty and the conference results disappointed Chinese patriots heavily influenced by the strong nationalistic fervor that was growing in China, as they had no enforcement mechanisms and did nothing to retrieve the rights of sovereignty China had been forced to give up to foreign powers over the previous eighty years.[48]

Meanwhile, US policy makers were compelled to react to repeated acts of violence against Americans and other foreigners and their interests, as revolutionary political and military movements swept through China during the 1920s. By 1925 the foreign treaty port rulers and collaborating Chinese provincial rulers seemed to an increasing share of the Chinese public to constitute an evil partnership of "imperialism" and warlords. The rising Chinese Nationalist Party under Sun Yat-sen (d. 1925) and his successor Chiang Kai-shek was receiving substantial military and financial support and training from the Soviet Union and the international Communist organization known as the Communist International or Comintern. Soviet-backed Communist agents were instrumental in assisting the establishment of the Chinese Communist Party, which was instructed to align with Sun and Chiang's much larger Chinese Nationalist Party. These movements were compatible in seeing the evils of imperialism and warlords as enemies of Chinese nationalism. Chinese industrialists had prospered with the withdrawal of competition from Western enterprises and the rise in foreign demand during World War I. They were readier to take a stance against the foreigners in this period of revived foreign economic competition in China.[49]

In Shanghai early in 1925 union organizers were active and strikes increased, and at the same time merchants in the Chinese Chamber of Commerce protested against regulation and "taxation without representation" under the foreign-ruled Shanghai Municipal Council. An incident in Shanghai arising out of a strike against Japanese-owned textile mills led to an outburst of anti-imperialist and antiforeign demonstrations and sentiment. British-officered police under the authority of the foreign-ruled Shanghai Municipal Council killed thirteen demonstrators on May 30, 1925. There ensued a nationwide multiclass movement of protests, demonstrations, strikes, boycotts, and militant anti-imperialism. This May Thirtieth movement dwarfed all previous antiforeign demonstrations. In June a demonstration in Canton led to shooting between Nationalist Party cadets and Anglo-French troops, killing fifty-two Chinese. The resulting fifteen-month strike and boycott of Hong Kong crippled British trade with South China.[50]

In this revolutionary atmosphere, Chinese Communist Party organizations expanded membership rapidly. Consistent with guidance from the Joseph Stalin–dominated Comintern, the party remained in a wary united front with the larger Chinese Nationalists as Chiang Kai-shek consolidated his leadership and prepared to launch the Northern Expedition from the Nationalist base in Canton in 1926. The military campaign and attendant political agitation were designed to smash the power of the warlords, assert China's rights against imperialism, and reunify China. By 1927 the campaign had gained control of much of southern and central China.[51]

Advancing in Nanking in March 1927, some Nationalist forces attacked foreigners and foreign property in this city, including the American, British, and Japanese consulates. Several foreigners, including Americans, were killed. Looting and threats against foreigners did not stop until British and US gunboats began to bombard the attackers. The Americans joined the other powers in demanding punishment, apology, and compensation from the Nationalist authorities. The Nationalist authorities at the time were in turmoil with a power struggle for leadership that saw Chiang Kai-shek's forces kill several hundred Communist Party and labor leaders in Shanghai the day after the Nanking incident, foreshadowing the start of a broader and violent Nationalist campaign against Communists and other perceived enemies. Maneuvering within the Nationalist leadership resulted in Chiang Kai-shek's emergence as dominant leader in January 1928. US Secretary of State Frank Kellogg reacted with moderation and restraint to the violence and challenges to US and foreign rights in China. This helped facilitate US rapprochement with the Nationalist regime of Chiang Kai-shek once it consolidated power in 1928. In March 1928 Chiang's regime accepted American terms about the Nanking incident while the US government expressed regret about the gunboat bombardment.[52]

Imperial Japan felt threatened by rising Chinese nationalism and endeavored to consolidate its hold in Manchuria. Japanese agents assassinated the Chinese warlord in Manchuria and eventually took control of the territory under the guise of an independent state, Manchukuo, created in 1932 and recognized among the major powers only by Japan. US policy makers did not change their low-risk policy toward Japan despite Tokyo's blatant grab of Manchuria. Dealing with the disastrous consequences of the Great Depression, US President Hoover was reluctant to respond forcefully to Japan's aggression in Manchuria and its breach of US-backed security arrangements in the Nine Power Treaty of 1922 and the Kellogg-Briand Pact of 1928. With his secretary of state, Henry Stimson, in the lead, Hoover favored a moral stance of nonrecognition of the changes brought by Japan's aggression. This so-called Hoover-Stimson doctrine failed in 1932 as Japanese forces expanded their military aggression in China to include attacks on Chinese forces in Shanghai. The Hoover administration formally protested, sent additional forces to China, and appealed to the world not to recognize the Japanese aggression. The Japanese halted the assault on Shanghai and the League of Nations adopted a resolution of nonrecognition, but Japan created a puppet state of Manchukuo and withdrew from the League of Nations when it approved a report critical of Japan's actions. [53]

The Franklin D. Roosevelt administration continued a cautious stance in the face of Japanese aggression in China, though some administration officials showed sympathy and support for China. Harry Hopkins, a close adviser to President Roosevelt, was sympathetic to China's cause and provided a channel of communication between Chiang Kai-shek's administration and the US president. Secretary of the Treasury Henry Morgenthau endeavored to support the struggling Chinese Nationalist Party government against Japanese aggression. In 1934 the United States inaugurated, primarily for domestic reasons, a silver purchase program, which caused great turmoil in the Chinese economy as massive amounts of silver left China by 1935. In response, Morgenthau initiated a silver purchase program for Nationalist China, paying it hundreds of millions of dollars in gold and US dollars for 500 million ounces of silver. [54]

Even when Japan engaged in all-out brutal war against China in 1937, Washington showed sympathy to China but offered little in the way of concrete support. Responding to Japanese aggression against China and other military expansion, President Franklin D. Roosevelt in a speech on October 5, 1937, called for a quarantine of an "epidemic of world lawlessness." No specific US actions in Asia followed because the US government was not prepared to stand against Japan as it ruthlessly advanced in China. Indeed, Japanese aircraft in December 1937 sank the US gunboat *Panay* and machine-gunned its survivors in the Yangtze River. US officials accepted Japan's apology and compensation, not choosing to make this an issue of confrontation with Japanese aggression in China.[55]

Stanley Hornbeck, a senior State Department specialist on China, played important roles in advising and implementing US policy toward China during this period. A strong supporter of China, he also was realistic about Chinese weaknesses and capabilities in the face of Japanese power. He was involved in various efforts to provide US support for the Chinese Nationalist Party government and to resist Japanese aggression without directly confronting Japan. Those US efforts were slow in coming.[56]

As secretary of state in the Franklin D. Roosevelt administration in the years prior to World War II, Hornbeck's boss, Cordell Hull, shied away from support of China, then at war with Japan. He sought to avoid US involvement in an Asian war at a time of heightened tensions and war in Europe. Hull disapproved a plan supported by Treasury Secretary Henry Morgenthau to provide China $25 million in credits to purchase supplies in the United States, but President Roosevelt approved the plan while Hull was out of the country in December 1938. Hull resisted efforts to impose sanctions on Japan, but eventually the State Department in January 1940 announced that the United States would not renew a 1911 commercial treaty with Japan. This step allowed the United States subsequently to impose selective embargoes on the sale of strategic materials to Japan, leading to a US oil embargo in 1941.[57]

By this time, with the support of Treasury Secretary Morgenthau and others, President Roosevelt approved the formation of the American Volunteer Group, also known as the "Flying Tigers," to support the beleaguered Chinese Nationalist administration in the face of Japanese aggression. The group arose from plans by retired US General Claire Chennault and others that resulted in a secret presidential order allowing US pilots to resign their commissions and sign contracts with a firm whose operating funds came from the lend-lease air program, for the purpose of flying fighter planes transferred to the Chinese government under lend-lease. The lend-lease program was proposed by the president and approved by Congress in early 1941, and China became eligible to receive lend-lease aid on May 6, 1941. The Flying Tigers helped protect airspace over the Chinese Nationalist capital in China's interior city of Chungking and other Chinese Nationalist holdings against attacks by Japanese warplanes.[58]

Nongovernmental American interaction with China continued to focus on economic exchange and missionary-related activities, although educational exchange separate from missionary activities grew in importance. US trade with China increased to $290 million in 1929, worth almost half of the $692 million value of US-Japanese trade that year. As world trade contracted sharply with the Great Depression, the importance of US exports to Japan relative to US exports to China increased. In 1936, the year prior to the start of the Sino-Japanese War, US exports to China were valued at $47 million, while US exports to Japan were valued at $204 million. The balance of US economic interests appeared to reinforce continued strong isolationist tendencies in the United States to avoid involvement on the side of China in opposition to increasingly apparent aggression by Imperial Japan.[59]

Japanese atrocities in the war against China beginning in 1937 and Imperial Japan's subsequent alignment with Nazi Germany in 1940 hardened American public attitudes as well as those of US officials against Japan. Individual Americans with close ties to both the Chiang Kai-shek and Roosevelt administrations and a number of organizations such as the Committee for Non-Participation in Japanese Aggression advocated giving US aid to China. Thomas Corcoran, formerly a White House lawyer close to President Roosevelt, was among the group of several former federal officials paid by Chiang Kai-shek's agents to ensure stronger US support for the Nationalist government. Henry Luce, the child of Christian missionaries in China, created a powerful media enterprise in the United States centered on *Time* and *Life* magazines. Luce used these widely read publications to strongly support Chiang Kai-shek and his American-educated wife, Soong Mayling, hailing the nation-building struggles of the Nationalist Party government and its protracted resistance to Japanese aggression. The Committee to Defend America by Aiding the Allies and other groups and individuals worked against those in American politics who continued to adhere to a noninterventionist stance. The latter included the Women's International League for Peace and Freedom and the National Council for Prevention of War. The noninterventionist stance was buttressed by widespread feeling in the United States in the 1930s that the United States had mistakenly intervened in World War I on behalf of the privileges of a few, prompting peace activists to work to prevent repetition of such errors.[60]

The missionary response to China's problems in the early twentieth century went well beyond evangelical matters. Expanding from about a thousand American missionaries representing twenty-eight societies in China in 1900, the respective numbers increased by 1930 to more than three thousand missionaries representing sixty societies. Adjusting to the rise of nationalism in China, the emphasis now focused on making the Christian church in China indigenous, led by Chinese and at least partially self-supporting, with Americans assisting and advising. The YMCA had an emphasis on programs for literacy and social work and proved to be attractive to younger Chinese leaders. The North China famine of 1920–21 saw the creation of the China International Famine Relief Commission that by 1936 used more than $50 million in foreign donations to promote basics in rural development. An interdenominational Protestant conference in 1922 organized the National Christian Council that set to work on social issues in urban and rural China. James Yen, educated at Yale University and with the YMCA, used support from the Rockefeller Foundation to begin to spread literacy and practical education to rural China. [61]

American reformist ideas and influence were notable among the more moderate elements of the Chinese intelligentsia at the time. The latter tended to be foreign trained and to work in academic and scientific institutions. The dozen Christian colleges were coming under more Chinese control and relied on Chinese sources for more than half of their income, though a majority of their faculties were foreign trained. The big national universities also had staffs largely trained abroad, mostly in the United States. Such American influence also was evident in the various research institutes of the central government and the big Rockefeller-supported Peking Union Medical College. Supporting these trends, 2,400 Chinese students entered American universities between 1900 and 1920; and 5,500 did so between 1920 and 1940. They studied in 370 institutions and tended to major in such practical subjects as engineering and business. They returned to China as a new elite in Chinese business, academic, and government circles. [62]

Chapter Three

Relations during World War II, Civil War, Cold War

US-CHINA RELATIONS DURING WORLD WAR II AND CHINA'S CIVIL WAR

US Interests, Actions, and Perceptions

The Japanese attack on Pearl Harbor thrust the United States into a leadership position in China and in global affairs. American debates over international involvement and the long-standing US reluctance to assume costs and risks of leadership were put aside. President Franklin D. Roosevelt and his war cabinet enjoyed broad domestic support as they mobilized millions of American combatants and enormous contributions of equipment and treasure in working with and leading Allied powers in the largest war the world has ever seen. The coalition eventually defeated the Axis powers. US leaders and interests focused on effectively fighting the massive worldwide conflict and dealing with issues that would determine the postwar international order.

The United States emerged as the most important foreign power in China. However, waging war in China and dealing with complications there, notably the bitter rivalry between Chiang Kai-shek's Nationalist forces and the Communist forces under the direction of Mao Zedong, received secondary attention. Circumstances in China contrary to American plans and expectations also repeatedly forced US leaders to adjust strategies.[1]

Early American assessments that China would provide strong forces and reliable bases for the defeat of Japan proved unrealistic given the many weaknesses of Chiang Kai-shek's Nationalist armies, the inability of the United States to supply and train large numbers of Chinese forces on account of Japan's control of the main surface routes of supply, and the primacy

Chiang's Nationalists (KMT) and Mao's Communists (CCP) gave to their struggle with one another. The United States shifted focus to defeating Japan by advancing through the Pacific Islands; it strove to keep China in the war as a means to tie down the one million Japanese soldiers deployed to the country.[2]

The turning tide of the war with Japan caused US planners to look beyond generalities about China's leading role as a partner of the United States in postwar Asia to the realities of preparations for civil war in China possibly involving the United States and Soviet Union on opposite sides. Debate among US officials about how to deal with the Chinese Nationalists and the Chinese Communists and the postwar order in China eventually led to direct US arrangements with the Soviet Union, notably those negotiated at the Yalta conference of February 1945, and continued American support for Chiang's Nationalist government. In this context, US leaders encouraged negotiations and mediated between the Chinese Nationalists and Chinese Communists in order to avoid civil war and shore up China's position as a power in Asia friendly to the United States.[3]

Though they were repeatedly and deeply disappointed with the weaknesses and corruption of the Nationalist Chinese government, American officials tended to follow paths of least resistance when dealing with the dispute between the Chinese Nationalists and the Chinese Communists. US actions and policy choices reinforced existing American proclivities to back Chiang Kai-shek's Nationalists, who continued to enjoy broad political support in the United States. They avoided the difficult US policy reevaluation that would have been required for US leaders to position the United States in a more balanced posture in order to deal constructively with the Chinese Communists as well as the Chinese Nationalists. Though some American officials pushed for a more balanced US approach, others were suspicious of the Communists on ideological grounds and because of their ties to the USSR. There also was skepticism about the strength and prospects of the Communist forces. In the end, it appeared that moving American policy from support for Chiang Kai-shek's Nationalists would be too costly for American interest in shoring up a postwar Chinese government friendly to the United States. The drift and bias in US policy, strengthened by interventions of important US officials such as US presidential envoy and ambassador to China Patrick Hurley, foreshadowed the US failure in China once the Communists defeated the Chinese Nationalists on mainland China in 1949 and moved in early 1950 to align with the Soviet Union against the United States in the Cold War.[4]

Chinese Interests, Actions, and Perceptions

Having survived with enormous cost and deprivation four years of war with Japan, Chiang Kai-shek and his Nationalist government were relieved as the

United States entered the war with Japan in 1941. The eventual defeat and collapse of the Japanese empire seemed likely. The Nationalist government was prepared to cooperate with its new US ally in the war effort against Japan, but repeatedly it showed greater interest in using US supplies and support in order to prepare to deal with the opposing Communist forces and securing Nationalist leadership in postwar China. Chiang Kai-shek and his lieutenants sought to maximize the material, training, financial, and political support from the United States, while fending off repeated US requests for greater contributions by Nationalist armies in the war effort against Japan. When US officials in China repeatedly became frustrated with the lackluster support of the war effort from what was often seen as a corrupt, repressive, and narrowly self-serving Nationalist Chinese government, Chiang and his allies tried to outmaneuver them through such means as appeals to top US leaders and special US envoys sent to China, lobbying in Washington, and thinly veiled warnings that the Nationalists might seek accommodation with Japan.[5]

The Nationalists also resisted efforts by US officials in China to open direct American communication with and possible support for the Chinese Communist forces. Furthermore, Chiang and his government fended off repeated US calls for greater reform and accountability in the Chinese Nationalist government. They accommodated US mediation efforts to bridge the divide between the Nationalists and Communists. They found strong common ground with US mediator Patrick Hurley. US mediator George Marshall was much more critical of Chiang Kai-shek and Nationalist policies and actions. The Nationalists appeared to have little choice but to grudgingly go along with the humiliating arrangements imposed on them as a result of US-USSR negotiations at Yalta. Their future depended on preserving US support. They strove to continue this support without conditions that would compromise the goal of a Nationalist-ruled China in postwar Asia.[6]

The Chinese Communists under the leadership of Mao Zedong had strong and well-developed ideological and foreign policy leanings opposed to US policy in China and US leadership in world affairs. Their connections with the Soviet Union and the influence of the USSR on their approach to the United States also were significant. They endorsed the twists and turns of Soviet maneuvers in the early years of the war, and they followed Moscow's lead in an overall positive approach to the United States as it entered the war in 1941.[7]

Probably more important in Chinese Communist calculations were the realities of power in China. Like Chiang Kai-shek's Nationalists, the Communists under Mao foresaw the eventual defeat of Japan at the hands of the United States. The United States rapidly became the predominant power in East Asia, and in China it brought its power, influence, and aid to bear solely on the side of Chiang Kai-shek's Nationalists, who were determined to subordinate and suppress the Communists. For CCP leaders, there was a serious likelihood that the United States, because of growing association with Chiang Kai-shek, might use its enormous power against the CCP during the anticipated Chinese civil war following Japan's defeat.[8]

To counter this prospect, the Communists had the option of looking to their Soviet ally for support. But Moscow at that time was showing little interest in defending CCP interests against a challenge by US-backed Nationalist forces. The Communists saw that only at great risk could they ignore the change that had taken place in the balance of forces in China. Seeking to keep the United States from becoming closely aligned with Chiang Kai-shek against CCP interests, the Communists decided to take steps on their own to ensure that Washington would adopt a more evenhanded position. They strove to put aside historical difficulties with the United States and soft-pedaled ideological positions that might alienate Washington as they sought talks with US officials in order to arrive at a power arrangement that would better serve CCP interests in China.[9]

The United States chose to rebuff the Communist initiatives, leaving the CCP facing the likelihood of confrontation with a strong US-backed KMT army at the end of the Pacific war. Fortunately for the CCP, Moscow built its strength in East Asia during the final months of the war and the period following Japan's defeat, and the United States rapidly withdrew its forces from East Asia at the war's end. Later in the 1940s, the Communists obtained more support from the USSR, leading eventually to the Sino-Soviet alliance of 1950. Meanwhile, the Communist forces grew in strength while the larger Nationalist forces suffered from significant weaknesses including poor leadership and morale, paving the way to Communist victory against the US-supported Nationalists in 1949.[10]

Encounters and Interaction in the 1940s

It is hard to imagine a decade of more consequence for modern China and its relations with the United States than the 1940s. The US entry into World War II marked the beginning of the end of Japanese aggression in China and the Asia-Pacific. The stalemate between Japanese forces occupying the more well-developed eastern regions of China and the Chinese Nationalists and Chinese Communist forces holding out in China's interior eventually broke and ended under the pressure of the US-led war effort against imperial Japan. The end of the Japanese occupation of China opened the way to Chinese civil war and resolution of the decades-long conflict between Chinese Nationalist and Chinese Communist forces. As the leading foreign power in China, the United States wielded its influence in ways seen to accord with US interests and goals. At bottom, the US actions and policies did not mesh well with realities in China. The result by the end of the decade was a massive failure of US efforts to establish a strong China, friendly to the United States, in postwar Asia. [11]

The China theater was a secondary concern in the overall war effort, as the United States first focused on defeating Adolf Hitler and the Nazi-led forces in Europe. Initial expectations that China could be built up and play an active strategic role in the war effort, with Chinese armies under Chiang Kai-shek's leadership pushing back the Japanese and allowing China to become a staging area for attack on Japan, proved unrealistic. Chiang's Nationalist armies were weak, and the Americans were unable to provide large amounts of military equipment because Japan cut off surface routes to Nationalist-held areas of China. US strategists turned to an approach of island-hopping in the Pacific, with US-led forces coming from the south and east of Japan, taking island positions in step-by-step progress toward the Japanese home islands. The role for the Chinese armies in this strategy mainly was to stay in the war and keep the many hundreds of thousands of Japanese forces in China tied down and unable to reinforce Japanese positions elsewhere. [12]

The United States recognized Chiang Kai-shek and the Chinese Nationalist government as China's representative in war deliberations and insisted that Chiang's China would be one of the great powers that would lead world affairs in the postwar era. President Roosevelt strongly supported China's leading role and met with Chiang Kai-shek and British prime minister Winston Churchill at an Allied conference in Cairo in 1943 that determined, among other things, that territories Japan had taken from China would be restored to China. US aid in China flowed exclusively to Chiang and his officials. The commanding American general in the China theater, Joseph Stilwell, was appointed as Chiang Kai-shek's chief of staff. American contact with and understanding of the rival Chinese Communists were minimal. Mao Zedong's forces were cut off from American and other contact by a blockade maintained by Nationalist Chinese forces. There were American contacts with the Chinese Communist liaison office allowed in the Chinese wartime capital of Chungking. [13]

Chiang Kai-shek welcomed American support but constantly complained that it was insufficient. General Stilwell and many other US officials in China were appalled by what they saw in the poor governance of the Chinese Nationalist leadership, and the unwillingness of Chiang and his lieutenants to use US assistance against Japan as they focused on building capabilities to deal with the Chinese Communists. Stilwell and his American staff were interested in establishing relations with the Chinese Communist forces, who seemed more willing to fight Japan. Chiang resisted these American leanings. [14]

Despite widespread dissatisfaction with Chiang Kai-shek and the Chinese Nationalist government on the part of many American officials as well as media and other nongovernment American observers in China, Chiang Kai-shek maintained a positive public image in the United States. Publicists such as Henry Luce, who used *Time* and *Life* magazines, continued to laud the leadership of the courageous leader of China in the face of Japanese aggression. President Roosevelt's personal emissary to China, Lauchlin Currie, traveled to China in 1941 and again in 1942. He advised the US president to follow policies of strong support for Chiang Kai-shek and the Chinese Nationalists: The Chungking government should be treated as a "great power"; Chiang should be given greater economic and military support and should be encouraged to reform. In Currie's view and the views of other US officials in Washington, close US cooperation with Chiang would promote cooperation within China and ensure a more effective struggle against Japan. While President Roosevelt's private calculations regarding Chiang Kai-shek and the situation in China remain subject to interpretation, his actions and statements generally adhered to this kind of positive American orientation toward Nationalist China. [15]

Emblematic of broader support for the Chiang administration in the United States was the positive reception given to Madame Chiang Kai-shek when she toured the United States from November 1942 to May 1943. In February 1943 she delivered a stirring speech to the US Congress. She appealed for more American aid and higher US priority to the war effort in China. Roosevelt and his war planners were unwilling to change their focus on defeating Germany first, but the US Congress took steps to redress the grossly discriminatory US immigration policies against China. In 1943 it acknowledged China as an ally and amended exclusion provisions to permit 105 Chinese to immigrate annually. Initial steps also were taken to amend the various treaty provisions between the United States and China that supported unequal relations that were offensive to Chinese nationalism. In 1943 the administration signed a treaty surrendering American extraterritorial rights in China, and the Senate readily agreed. [16]

Some influential US military leaders, notably General Claire Chennault of the American Volunteer Group ("Flying Tigers") and the Army Air Force, were much more sympathetic to Chiang Kai-shek than Stilwell and his supporters. Chennault pressed for US military efforts that were supported by Chiang but opposed by Stilwell and his staff. He collaborated with and won Chiang's support for plans involving US use of Chinese Nationalist-defended air bases in China to attack Japanese positions and shipping with US bombers. Stilwell opposed the plans that diverted US supplies from his efforts to build Chinese armies in order to open ground supply routes to occupied China and for other use against Japan. Stilwell warned that once the US bombing attacks from Chinese air bases rose in Japan's war calculus as a result of Chennault's plan, the bases would be subject to Japanese ground attack and might be overrun because of weak Chinese Nationalist defenses for the bases. Indeed, presumably prompted at least in part by the US air attacks, Japanese forces in 1944 overran the weakly defended air bases and expanded more deeply into Nationalist-held areas, provoking a major crisis between Chiang and Stilwell and between the United States and its Nationalist allies.[17]

The Chinese Communists, for their part, took advantage of limited interaction with US officials, media, and nongovernment representatives in Chungking in order to build on the image they had already established through their brief encounters with American and other Western news personnel at the Communist base in Yenan in north China in the 1930s. Consistent with their approach to Edgar Snow and other American visitors in that period, the Communists emphasized the image of a relatively democratic and honest political administration, positive public support received by the Yenan leadership, and the CCP's reasonably benign attitude at that time toward free enterprise. In this way, they attempted to appeal to American ideals. At the same time, the Communist spokespersons tried to drive a wedge between Americans and Chinese Nationalists by criticizing what they viewed as the corrupt, oppressive, and totalitarian rule of the nationalist government. In line with their approach toward Snow and other visitors in the 1930s, the Communist officials did not disavow the CCP's ultimate Marxist-Leninist goals regarding the future of China but indicated that such objectives were to be achieved at the end of a long "democratic" period. They thus revealed to American officials and other representatives the image of a Chinese party worthy of US support, willing to compromise with Washington, and deserving of a share of power in China. In this context, heavy stress was placed on the Nationalists' unwillingness to share power as the prime cause for continuing Communist-Nationalist confrontation in China.[18]

The central role in CCP policy toward and interaction with the United States was played by senior Communist leader Zhou Enlai, the chief Communist representative in Chungking during World War II. In his frequent contacts with American officials and other US representatives, Zhou demonstrated repeatedly a preference for realistic exchange, unencumbered by ideological constraints or bitterness over past Chinese affronts at the hands of US "imperialism." He initiated a CCP proposal for the establishment of an American liaison mission to Yenan, cast doubt on Nationalist willingness to pursue the war against Japan, and attacked Chungking's legitimacy as the regime best serving the interests of the Chinese people. Zhou, along with visiting senior Communist military leader Lin Biao, in Chungking for negotiations with the Chinese Nationalists, appealed for US supplies so that the Communists could go on the offensive against Japan. They also promised close intelligence sharing with the United States regarding enemy activities near the Communist base areas. They condemned the Nationalists' passivity in the war effort while the Chiang Kai-shek forces reinforced their military blockade against the Communists.

Zhou Enlai's initiatives and subsequent interaction with American officials visiting Yenan on the part of Mao Zedong and other senior CCP leaders
reflected pragmatic actions to deal with potentially adverse circumstances.
The American entry into the war against Japan strengthened the position of
the Communists' adversary, Chiang Kai-shek, and raised the strong possibility that the United States would continue to side firmly with Chiang following the defeat of Japan and the establishment of a new Chinese administration. The relatively weak strategic position of the Chinese Communist forces
in China at the time and the low probability that the Soviet Union would take
decisive actions to protect the Chinese Communists from US-backed pressure from Chiang Kai-shek's Nationalists added to incentives for the CCP to
appeal to the United States for closer relations and support. [19]

The depth of the American–Chinese Nationalist alignment meant that the
Communists could have little hope of undermining the American-Nationalist
relationship. But by opening formal contacts with Americans through a US
liaison mission in Yenan or other means, the Communists would at least have
the opportunity to encourage the Americans to move away from Chungking
over the critical issue of the Chinese civil dispute. In particular, a formal
American mission in the Communist base area would allow CCP leaders to
present their case to the highest levels in Washington; it would enable Mao
and his group to scotch many ill-founded Nationalist allegations concerning
the Communist leaders and policies, which had heretofore enjoyed credibility with US policy makers. Further, formal ties with Washington would
enhance the Communists' ability to solicit US military supplies. The Communist leaders also seemed confident and proud of the economic, political,
and military situation in their base area; if their administrative achievements
could be shown to American officials, they would compare favorably with
the deteriorating situation in Nationalist-held areas. [20]

In early 1944 there was a formal US presidential request to Chiang Kai-
shek for the establishment of an American military observer mission in the
Communist-held areas of China. The proposal was grudgingly approved by
Chiang Kai-shek during the visit to China of American Vice President Henry
Wallace in June 1944. Amid the crisis caused by Japanese forces overrun-
ning US air bases in China and penetrating deep into previously Nationalist-
controlled territory, Chiang was in a weak position to resist the US request. [21]

American officials were not only interested in shoring up Chinese resistance to Japanese aggression and improving military coordination against
Japan with the Chinese Communists. By this time US officials were deeply
involved in plans for dealing with previously unanticipated divisions that
weakened China and posed the danger of Chinese civil war once Japan was
defeated. There was concern that the Chinese Nationalists might draw in the
United States on their side of the conflict and that the Chinese Communists
might draw in the Soviet Union on their side of the conflict. To deal with this

potentially dire situation warranted closer American interaction with, and understanding of, the policies and intentions of the Chinese Communist forces through the establishment of the US military observer mission to Yenan.[22]

Responding to Vice President Wallace's expressions of concern over the Chinese war effort and the Nationalist government's loss of public support, Chiang focused on American and especially Stilwell's responsibility. Chiang impressed the American visitor with his determination to remove Stilwell or to have the United States send a personal representative from Roosevelt to control Stilwell and give Chiang regular access to the president free from the interference of the Departments of War and State, which were seen as influenced by Stilwell and his supporters in the US embassy.[23]

Patrick Hurley, a prominent Republican who served as President Herbert Hoover's secretary of war, was a key figure in US policy toward the KMT and the CCP in 1944–45. His strong support for the Chinese Nationalists and accusations against opponents within the US government had lasting impacts on US relations with China. Hurley was sent to China as a special envoy by President Roosevelt in September 1944. Dealing with the major disputes then causing a crisis between Chiang Kai-shek and General Joseph Stilwell, Hurley sided with Chiang. Roosevelt recalled Stilwell in October 1944, appointing General Albert Wedemeyer as his replacement. Hurley was appointed as ambassador to replace Clarence Gauss, who shared Stilwell's negative opinions about Chiang and the Nationalists.[24]

In November 1944 Hurley traveled to Yenan and negotiated a Five-Point Agreement with Mao Zedong and his senior colleagues. Among other things, the agreement summarized Hurley's promises of equal treatment and US aid to the Communists in a coalition with the Nationalists. Returning to Chungking, he switched and sided strongly with Chiang Kai-shek in his demand that Communist forces be disbanded before the Communists could be brought into a Nationalist-led Chinese coalition government. Much of the US embassy staff in Chungking rebelled against Hurley by sending a collective message to Washington in early 1945 warning of the negative consequences of Hurley's alienation of the Communists and bias toward Chiang's Nationalists. The ambassador disputed the charges in a meeting with President Roosevelt, who supported Hurley, leading to transfers of dissident US staff from Chungking.[25]

As US ambassador, Hurley supported the Nationalist-Communist peace talks in Chungking in September 1945. Chiang Kai-shek, backed by Hurley and the Harry Truman administration, demanded the Communists surrender their forces and territory as a precondition for joining a coalition. Fighting spread in China, and the talks collapsed. Hurley, unsuccessful in urging a full US commitment to Chiang's cause, abruptly resigned as ambassador in November 1945, blaming pro–Chinese Communists in the State Department for thwarting US policy. After the Communist victory in China and the Chinese intervention in the Korean War, Hurley's charges provided a leading wedge for congressional investigators seeking to purge alleged pro-Communists and other security risks from among the ranks of the Chinese affairs specialists in the State Department and other agencies. [26]

US leaders worried about conditions in China and how they would affect the final stages of the war against Japan. They foresaw the inability of weak Chinese Nationalist forces to defeat the hundreds of thousands of Japanese forces in China as the war in the Pacific moved toward an end, and the danger of a Nationalist-Communist civil war in China that would drag in the United States and the Soviet Union on opposite sides. As a result of the so-called Far Eastern Agreement of the Allied powers at Yalta in February 1945, Soviet forces, not Chinese forces, would take on the main task of defeating Japanese armies concentrated in Manchuria and northern China. In compensation, Russian territory taken by Japan would be restored; Russian interests in Manchuria, including a naval base, would be restored; and Outer Mongolia would remain independent. The United States promised to obtain the concurrence of China's Nationalist government to provisions regarding Manchuria and Mongolia, which were claimed by China. The Soviet Union also expressed willingness to negotiate a friendship and alliance treaty with China's Nationalist government. The Far Eastern Agreement had negative implications for the Chinese Nationalist government, which was not consulted on the territorial concessions to the Soviet Union, and for the Chinese Communists, who appeared to be isolated from the Soviet Union. [27]

The broad outlines of US policy toward China prevalent in early 1945 persisted as Harry Truman became president upon the death of Franklin Roosevelt in April 1945, and as the war in the Pacific came to an unexpectedly quick end with Japan's surrender after the US atomic bomb attacks in August 1945. US policy strongly supported Chiang Kai-shek's Nationalist forces. US airplanes and other means were used to transport Nationalist forces to various parts of China to take the surrender of Japanese forces. The US government provided hundreds of millions of dollars of military equipment and other assistance. The rival Communists were urged to participate in peace talks and come to terms in a united Chinese government under Chiang's overall leadership. President Truman commanded that Japanese-controlled forces in China surrender their positions and arms to Chiang Kai-shek's representatives, not to Communist forces. [28]

The Soviet army entered the war in China and defeated Japanese armies. The Soviet Union signed a friendship treaty with Chiang Kai-shek's Nationalist government, as noted in the Far Eastern Agreement at Yalta. Seemingly isolated, the Chinese Communists agreed to join peace talks in Chungking in September where Chiang, backed by US Ambassador Hurley and the Truman administration, demanded the Communists surrender their armed forces and territory as a precondition for joining a coalition government under Chiang's leadership.

There was little consideration at high levels of US policy makers for a more evenhanded US approach to the Nationalist-Communist rivalry in China, though some American officials warned of the danger of civil war and were uncertain how the Chinese Nationalists, weakened by years of warfare and led by often corrupt and inept officials, would fare. As the peace talks deadlocked and Communist-Nationalist armed conflict spread in northern China in late 1945, it became clear to US planners that Chiang's forces would not defeat the Chinese Communists without a substantial commitment of US military forces. It was against this background that Ambassador Hurley pushed for an open-ended US commitment to Chiang Kai-shek, but Washington decision makers demurred and Hurley resigned.[29]

President Truman appointed General George Marshall as his personal representative to salvage the deteriorating situation in China. Marshall managed a few months of shaky peace, but they were followed by frequent fighting in Manchuria as Nationalist and Communist forces vied to take control as Soviet occupiers retreated. US aid continued to go exclusively to Nationalist-held areas and increased markedly in mid-1946. On July 1, 1946, Chiang Kai-shek ordered a nationwide offensive against the Communists. Marshall intervened, got Truman to stop US arms aid to Chiang, and Chiang agreed to US-Nationalist-Communist truce teams to prevent fighting in northern China. The fighting still spread, however, and soon became a full-scale war.[30]

The failure to avoid civil war in China did not lead to fundamental change in the broad framework of US policy in China. Even though the Nationalists appeared increasingly weak and inept, and seemed headed for defeat on the mainland by 1948, the Truman administration continued support for them and took no significant steps to reach out to the Chinese Communists. In 1948 the administration supported the China Aid Act providing $125 million for the failing Nationalist government in China. This was done in large measure to avoid resistance from many pro–Chiang Kai-shek congressional members regarding the administration's requests for funding the Marshall Plan for Europe and Japan. Prospects for positive US relations with the Chinese Communists were soured by years of one-sided US support for the Chinese Nationalists.[31]

Given what were seen by Truman administration officials as continued strong US congressional and other domestic constraints against abandoning Chiang Kai-shek and opening US contacts with Chiang's enemy, the Chinese Communists, the Truman administration officials allowed developments in China to settle the civil war in favor of the Chinese Communists. Over time, they hoped to find constructive ways for the United States to deal with the new Chinese Communist regime. There was strong debate in the administration as to whether the United States should allow Taiwan, the island off the Chinese coast where Chiang and his Nationalist forces retreated after their defeat on the mainland in 1949, to fall to the Communists. The policy decided upon was one of no intervention to protect Taiwan.[32]

Secretary of State Dean Acheson was known for his efforts to end US support for Chiang Kai-shek and his KMT regime. He sought publication of the famed "China White Paper." This lengthy (more than a thousand pages) document was issued by the US State Department in August 1949. It was critical of Chiang Kai-shek and his government for corruption and other failings as they lost the Chinese Civil War against the Chinese Communist forces. The report served to support the Truman administration's efforts to cut support for Chiang's Nationalists. It also deflected attention from US policy oversights and mistakes. The report was attacked by Chiang's Nationalists, Mao's Communists, and many US supporters of Chiang Kai-shek.[33]

Also during the last months of the Chinese Civil War on the Chinese mainland, Acheson instructed the US ambassador to Nanking, Leighton Stuart, to seek contacts with the Communist forces advancing on the Nationalist capital. Stuart stayed in the city after Nationalist forces retreated. He made contact with Huang Hua, a former student of his who was sent by the Communist leaders to investigate US intentions. Stuart was invited to meet Communist leaders setting up their new capital in Beijing, but President Truman was unwilling to support a plan to have the ambassador travel to Beijing for talks with the Communist rulers.[34]

The Chinese Communists, meanwhile, reinforced their victory in the civil war with the announcement that they would side with the Soviet Union in the emerging Cold War struggle with the United States and its non-Communist allies. Amid these grim developments for US interests in China, the administration endeavored to adopt a lower profile regarding China. US leaders anticipated Communist victory over Chiang's forces holding out in Taiwan and a subsequent long process of the United States working to build some semblance of workable ties with the new regime in China. The US military position in the region was weak as a result of the rapid US demobilization and withdrawal of forces following World War II. While the United States had shown strong military and political resolve following Pearl Harbor in defeating Japanese aggression and that of the Axis coalition, US leaders were only gradually coming to the realization of a need for continued strong military preparations and presence in Asia in order to deter new sources of expansion and aggression.[35]

CONFLICT AND CONTAINMENT

Chinese Interests, Actions, and Perceptions

Mao Zedong and his CCP-led fighters faced large challenges as they endeavored to consolidate their rule after defeating Chiang Kai-shek's Nationalist forces in the Chinese Civil War and establishing the People's Republic of China (PRC) on the Chinese mainland in 1949. China had been war-ravaged for decades and arguably had been without effective governance for more than a century. The Communists were a rural-based movement with decades of experience in guerrilla war. They also had decades of experience supporting administrative efforts in the Chinese countryside, but little experience in managing the complicated affairs of China's cities, its urban economy, or its national administration. Seeking needed technical and economic backing as well as guarantees and support for China's national security, the Maoist leadership endeavored to consolidate relations with the Soviet Union in an international environment heavily influenced by the United States, the main international supporter of its Chinese Nationalist adversary, and American-associated states influential in Asian and world politics.[36]

Taken together, these circumstances and determinants led to a strong current in analyses of Chinese relations with the United States that emphasized Chinese imperatives of consolidation and development domestically and reactions internationally to perceived threats and occasional opportunities posed by circumstances involving the United States. In particular, as the Cold War spread from Europe and came to dominate international dynamics in Asia for several decades beginning in the late 1940s, Chinese relations with the United States were seen as dominated in the 1950s and 1960s by Chinese efforts to deal with what emerged as a massive US-led military, economic, and political containment of China. Chinese interactions with the United States in this period often were assessed in terms of Chinese reactions to perceived threats posed by the strength and actions of the United States and associated powers.[37]

Heading the list of strengths that the Maoist leaders brought to bear as they began national leadership in China were the CCP's broad experience in political organization and related social and economic mobilization, and a strong revolutionary ideology. Mao Zedong and supporting leaders were committed to seeking revolutionary changes in China and in international affairs affecting China, and they had the determination and ability to move Chinese people along these paths. This set of determinants and circumstances led to another strong current in analyses of Chinese relations with the United States, one that emphasized the importance of the Chinese leadership's determination to challenge and confront the United States and its allies and associates in Asia as the Chinese Communist leadership sought to promote revolutionary change in Asian and world affairs. The analyses also showed a related tendency of the Chinese leadership to exploit episodes of confrontation with America as means to mobilize greater support within China for the often revolutionary changes sought there by the Maoist leadership. [38]

Assessments of the record of the Maoist period show a complicated mix of imperatives both revolutionary and more conventional—of security and nation building—that drove Chinese decision making. Adding to the mix was the emergence of the dominant role of Mao Zedong and his strong-man rule, which came to determine Chinese decision making with particular regard to Chinese foreign relations—notably, relations with the United States and the Soviet Union. One consequence was the ability and the actual tendency of China to shift direction dramatically in foreign affairs. China's strong alignment with the Soviet Union in 1950 and break with Moscow ten years later exemplified the kinds of major shifts in China's foreign policy on issues important to the United States during this period. [39]

For their part, Chiang Kai-shek and the Chinese Nationalists appeared at the end of their struggle when they retreated to Taiwan after defeat on the Chinese mainland in 1949. Given the Truman administration's decisions to cut ties with the Nationalists and await opportunities to build relations with the triumphant Chinese Communists, it appeared to be only a matter of time before Communist forces would overwhelm the Nationalists on Taiwan. Those Nationalist leaders and officials who were less than fully committed to Chiang Kai-shek and the Nationalist cause and had options other than joining Chiang on Taiwan tended to follow those alternative paths and settled in Hong Kong, the United States, or other safer locations. The two million Chinese who fled the mainland to Taiwan included leaders and officials who were loyal to Chiang and strongly anti-Communist, and large numbers of officials, soldiers, and dependents who had few other options. [40]

The outbreak of the Korean War and the subsequent US policy of containment against expansion of Chinese Communist power and influence dramatically reversed the fortunes of Chiang and his associates on Taiwan. They sought to use the new circumstances to strengthen support from the United States and to consolidate their power in Taiwan. On this basis, they endeavored to go beyond US efforts to contain Communist China by striving to lead efforts to roll back Communist rule on the mainland. [41]

US Interests, Actions, and Perceptions

At the start of the Cold War, Asia seemed secondary in US strategy. The United States demobilized rapidly after World War II. US forces occupied Japan and US naval and air forces patrolled the western Pacific, but overall, US military capabilities appeared unprepared for significant action in Asia. When the Korean War broke out unexpectedly, the United States abruptly reversed practice and began what became massive commitments of military power and related assistance to stop the spread of perceived communist expansion in Asia. Long-standing US interest in sustaining a balance of power in East Asia favorable to the United States, as well as ongoing US interests in fostering free economic access to the region and the spread of American values there, now were seen to require the United States to undertake the leading role in bearing the major costs, risks, and commitments associated with a system of containment that came to dominate US policy in Asia in the 1950s and the 1960s and to determine the course of American policy toward China during this period.[42]

Dominating the US foreign policy calculus toward China and other East Asian countries were strategic concerns with shoring up the regional balance of influence against Communist expansion in Asia. Strong efforts by the US government to mobilize domestic American support for the costs and risks associated with US leadership of the containment effort overshadowed private calculations of American leaders and strategists. The latter appeared to favor a more nuanced and flexible American approach that would have allowed for possible efforts to seek contacts and accommodation with Communist-ruled China. Eventually, US elites and supporting groups began to chafe publicly in the 1960s at what they saw as a counterproductive US tendency to try isolating China as part of the Cold War containment strategy in Asia. Their efforts to encourage greater US flexibility in dealing with the Chinese Communists failed in the face of strident Chinese opposition to the United States, a wide range of other adverse foreign influences at the start of China's Cultural Revolution in 1966, and the concurrent large increases in US combat forces fighting Chinese-backed Communist forces in Vietnam.[43]

Encounters and Interaction in the 1950s and 1960s

Neither the government of Mao Zedong nor the Truman administration sought or foresaw US-China war in early 1950. The Americans were surprised when North Korean forces, with the support of Soviet and Chinese leaders, launched an all-out military attack against South Korean forces in June 1950. The Chinese Communist leaders and their Korean and Soviet Communist allies apparently calculated that the better-armed North Koreans would attain victory quickly without provoking major or effective US military response. Thus, it was their turn to be surprised when the United States quickly intervened militarily in the Korean War and sent the Seventh Fleet to prevent Chinese Communist attack on Taiwan. US forces and their South Korean allies halted the North Korean advance and carried out an amphibious landing at Inchon in September 1950 that effectively cut off North Korean armies in the South, leading to their destruction.[44]

The string of miscalculations continued. With UN support, US and South Korean forces proceeded into North Korea. The Chinese Communists warned and prepared to resist them, but US leaders thought the warnings were a bluff. By November hundreds of thousands of Chinese Communist forces were driving the US and South Korean forces south in full retreat. Eventually, the Americans and their allies were able to sustain a line of combat roughly in the middle of the peninsula as the two armies faced off for more than two more years of combat, casualties, and destruction.[45]

Chinese Communist leaders also launched domestic mass campaigns to root out pro-American influence and seize control of US cultural, religious, and business organizations that remained in China. The United States began wide-ranging strategic efforts to contain the expansion of Chinese power and Chinese-backed Communist expansion in Asia. A strict US economic and political embargo against China; large US force deployments, eventually numbering between five hundred thousand and one million troops; massive foreign aid allocations to US Asian allies and supporters; and a ring of US defense alliances around China were used to block Chinese expansion and to drive a wedge between China and its Soviet ally. Meanwhile, led by often irresponsible congressional advocates, notably Senator Joseph McCarthy, congressional investigators in the early 1950s took aim at US specialists on China and Asia, discrediting those with moderate and pragmatic views about the Chinese Communists and endeavoring to silence those in or out of government who were less than uniform in opposing the Chinese Communists and supporting Chiang Kai-shek and the Chinese Nationalists.[46]

The Dwight D. Eisenhower administration used threats and negotiations in reaching an armistice agreement that stopped the fighting in Korea in 1953. American efforts to strengthen military alliances and deployments to contain Chinese Communist–backed expansion continued unabated. They faced off against enhanced Chinese efforts in the wake of the Korean armistice to strengthen support for Communist insurgents working against American-backed forces in French Indochina and direct Chinese military probes and challenges against the United States and their Chinese Nationalist allies in the Taiwan Strait.[47]

Mao Zedong and his CCP-led government continued their consolidation of control inside China, notably through mass campaigns led by Communist activists targeting landlords, the leading urban political and economic elites, and others deemed abusive or uncooperative with Communist goals. They prepared for major nation-building efforts with the support of their Soviet and Warsaw Pact allies to establish a governing structure, often along the lines of that of the Soviet Union, to rule Chinese civil administration, economic planning, military modernization, intelligence collection, and other endeavors. They sought means to tap into the surplus wealth being created in China's rural sector for investment in their planned expansion of China's industrial economy. After a brief period where peasants held land as a result of the mass campaign for land reform in rural China in the early 1950s, Chinese leaders saw the need to emulate the Soviet model and began to collectivize the land under government administration so as to better control the surplus rural wealth and to maximize its utility to the state's interests in promoting industrial development. The Soviet Union was providing more than a hundred major projects in assistance to Chinese industrialization and modernization, but they had to be paid for it. Collectivization of the land and concurrently greater state control of the urban economy along Soviet lines were chosen as the appropriate ways to deal with conditions in China while seeking economic modernization and development of the sinews of national and state power.[48]

These dramatic and massive shifts in domestic policy and direction occurred frequently in conjunction with crises and confrontations with the United States and its allies and associates around China's periphery in Asia. At one level, the Chinese determination to work against and confront the US-backed forces in Indochina and the Taiwan Strait reflected a deeply held determination to confound and wear down the American-fostered containment system. The Chinese Communist leadership held a strong revolutionary commitment to change the international order dominated by the United States and its allies and to support Communist-led forces struggling against this foreign imperialism.[49]

The US effort also directly threatened China's national security and sovereignty, often in graphic and severe ways. The Eisenhower administration threatened China with nuclear attack in order to push it toward an armistice in Korea, and the US government used the threat of nuclear attack at other times in the face of perceived Chinese provocations in the 1950s. Mao Zedong's China had no viable defense against US nuclear weapons and put top priority on developing Chinese nuclear weapons to deal with such repeated US intimidation. At the same time, the Chinese Communist leaders also were seen to continue to use the crisis atmosphere caused by confrontations with outside threats posed by the United States and its allies as a means to strengthen their domestic control and their mobilization of resources for advancement of nation building and administrative competence.[50]

Defeat of US-backed French forces in Indochina led to the 1954 Geneva Conference and accords that formalized French withdrawal from Indochina. After the conference, US policy worked to support a non-Communist government in South Vietnam, backing the regime when it resisted steps toward reunification set forth in the Geneva accords. The United States also deepened and broadened defense and other links with powers in Southeast Asia in order to check Chinese-backed Communist expansion in the region.[51]

President Eisenhower and Secretary of State John Foster Dulles were wary of Chiang Kai-shek and Chinese Nationalist maneuvers that might drag the United States into a war with the Chinese Communists over Taiwan. Chiang Kai-shek's Nationalists used the fortuitous turn of fate caused by the Korean War to consolidate their rule in Taiwan; and with American support they rapidly built Taiwan's military forces with the objective of eventually taking the battle to mainland China. The political atmosphere inside the United States was very supportive of Chiang and his harsh anti-Communist stance. The so-called China lobby supporting Chiang and his Nationalist government included liberals as well as conservatives in such respected organizations as the Committee of One Million, which opposed Communist China taking China's seat in the United Nations. US military and economic assistance to Chiang Kai-shek and the Nationalist forces on Taiwan expanded dramatically, and there was little public objection by the American government to Chiang's repressive authoritarian rule. [52]

Though Dulles and other leaders of the US government were privately unsure of the wisdom of such a close and formal US commitment to Chiang's Nationalists, Washington eventually brought Taiwan into the web of formal military alliances that provided the foundation of the US containment system against Chinese-backed Communist expansion in Asia. The United States and Nationalist China signed a bilateral defense treaty in December 1954. [53]

The People's Republic of China reacted with harsh rhetoric and military assaults against Nationalist Chinese–controlled islands off the coast of the Chinese mainland. The new and potentially very dangerous military crisis involving the United States and China so soon after the bloody conflict in Korea was not welcomed by Great Britain and other US allies, nor by some US congressional leaders and other elites. The US administration firmly backed the Chinese Nationalists and their Republic of China (ROC). US forces helped Nationalist forces on some exposed islands to withdraw as the Taiwan Strait crisis of 1955 continued, raising renewed fears of US-China war. [54]

Against this background, the Chinese Communist government's stance against the United States moderated. The reasoning appeared related to a shift in Soviet policy toward the West following Stalin's death in 1953. The incoming Soviet leaders were more interested than the now-dead Soviet dictator in arranging advantageous modus vivendi with Western powers in Europe. While they continued to give some public support to their Chinese ally in its dispute with the Chinese Nationalists and the United States, they also signaled Soviet wariness about getting involved in Asian conflicts by playing down the applicability of the Sino-Soviet alliance to Asia, where Soviet commentary implied China was to bear the major responsibility for dealing with the United States and its allies and associates. At the same time, the Chinese government also began to try to broaden productive economic and diplomatic ties with countries in nearby Asia and in Europe, and Chinese leaders found that their hard-line, confrontational behavior in the Taiwan Strait was counterproductive for this effort. Washington, for its part, had not sought to escalate military tensions with China, which complicated US efforts to work with European and Asian allies in exploring Soviet moderation and building lasting alliance relationships to contain communist expansion in Asia.[55]

Thus, Beijing by early 1955 was faced with an increasingly counterproductive campaign over Taiwan, a potentially dangerous military confrontation with Washington, lukewarm support from its primary international ally, and increased alienation from world powers now being wooed by the Chinese government. In this context, Chinese leaders understandably chose to shift to a more moderate stance when presented with the opportunity afforded by the American offer in mid-January 1955 of a cease-fire regarding the armed conflict in the Taiwan Strait. Beijing responded to the US proposal with criticism but indirectly signaled interest in the offer by gradually reducing Chinese demands concerning Taiwan.[56]

Chinese Premier Zhou Enlai used the venue of the Afro-Asian Conference in Bandung, Indonesia, in 1955 to ease tensions and call for talks with the United States. Chinese leaders at the time attempted to engage in high-level dialogue with the United States. How serious the Chinese were in pursuing their avowed interest in such engagement with the United States was never shown, as the Chinese overtures met with a nuanced but firm rebuff from the United States. Secretary of State Dulles was wary that direct talks with the PRC would undermine Chiang Kai-shek's Nationalist government on Taiwan. Though Dulles privately showed an interest in splitting China from alignment with the Soviet Union, the strategy called for maintaining a tougher US stance against China than the comparatively accommodating US stance toward the USSR. On the other hand, Dulles faced congressional and Allied pressures to meet with the Chinese, so he agreed to low-level ambassadorial talks that began in Geneva in 1955.[57]

The two sides fairly expeditiously reached an agreement on repatriating detained personnel. The Chinese intended the agreement to lay the ground for higher-level talks with the United States. American officials from Dulles on down responded by using the wording in the agreement to make demands on the Chinese for release of detained US personnel, notably captured US spies, which they knew, through private conversations with Chinese officials at the ambassadorial talks leading up to the agreements, that China would not do. Washington soon charged Beijing with perfidy and disregard for agreements, souring the atmosphere in the talks. The US side also pressed hard for a Chinese renunciation of force regarding Taiwan. Chinese negotiators came up with various formulas to bridge differences between the United States and China over this issue; at least one was positively received by the US negotiators but was rejected by Washington. This issue came to stop progress in the talks, which were suspended for a time before resuming in Warsaw in 1958, when the two sides met periodically without much result. The talks did at least provide a useful line of US-PRC communication during times of crisis, as both sides strove to avoid serious military conflict. [58]

Dulles's private strategy of vigorously pursuing a containment policy against China favored a tougher US policy toward China than toward the Soviet Union. He endeavored thereby to force Beijing to rely on Moscow for economic and other needs the Soviet Union could not meet. In this and other ways, he hoped to drive a wedge between China and the USSR. [59]

In 1958 Mao Zedong's Communists used artillery barrages in an effort to challenge and halt the resupply of the Nationalist hold over the fortress island of Quemoy and other Nationalist-controlled islands located only a few miles off the coast of the Chinese mainland. The military attacks predictably created another major crisis and war scare, with the United States firmly supporting Chiang Kai-shek's forces and threatening nuclear attack. Chiang Kai-shek refused to consider withdrawal from the Quemoy fortress, where a large portion of his best troops were deployed as part of his broader military preparations to attack mainland China and reverse Communist rule.

The absence of landing craft and other preparations for an invasion suggested that Mao was testing Nationalist and US resolve regarding the offshore island and did not intend to invade Taiwan itself. The crisis atmosphere played into Mao's efforts at the time to use the charged atmosphere of the mass campaign to mobilize national resources for a massive "Great Leap Forward" in Chinese development. Later, foreign analysts argued persuasively that the domestic mobilization was a major Chinese objective in launching the military aggression on the offshore islands held by the Chinese Nationalists. Another line of analysis argued that the Chinese leader also used the confrontation with the United States to test Soviet resolve in supporting China in what was seen in China as a weakening Sino-Soviet alliance. [60]

The Chinese-Soviet alliance indeed began to unravel by the late 1950s, and 1960 saw a clear public break with the withdrawal of Soviet economic aid and advisers. US policy makers had long sought such a split. Nonetheless, they were slow to capitalize on the situation as China remained more hostile than the Soviet Union to the United States, and deepening US involvement in Vietnam exacerbated Sino-American frictions.

During the 1960 presidential election campaign, Senator John Kennedy criticized the "tired thinking" of the outgoing administration on issues regarding China; however, he said little about China once he assumed office in 1961. US domestic opposition, Chinese nuclear weapons development, Chinese aggression against India, and Chinese expansion into Southeast Asia were among factors that seemed to block meaningful US initiatives toward China. The administration took firm action in 1962 to thwart plans by Chiang Kai-shek to attack the Chinese mainland at a time of acute economic crisis in

China caused by the collapse and abject failure of the Great Leap Forward campaign. The staggering damage to China from the three-year effort saw the premature deaths of thirty million people due to starvation and nutrition deficits.[61]

Though publicly reserved about China policy, the Kennedy administration seemed to appeal to emerging American elite opinions seeking some moderation in the stern US isolation and containment of China. However, scholarship has shown there was strong private antipathy on the part of Kennedy administration leaders to China's development of nuclear weapons and support for Communist-led insurgencies in Southeast Asia. The administration's backing of Chiang Kai-shek in the United Nations also went beyond pledges under Eisenhower, with officials privately reassuring Chiang that the United States would veto efforts to remove Nationalist China from the United Nations. Kennedy was actively considering a visit to Chiang in Taiwan.[62]

The administration of Lyndon Johnson, 1963–69, saw US-Asian policy dominated by escalating US military commitment and related difficulties in Vietnam. There was some movement within the US government for a more flexible approach to China, consistent with growing signs of congressional and US interest-group advocacy of a US policy of containment without isolation toward China. But they came to little as China entered the throes of the violent and often xenophobic practices of the Cultural Revolution, and the American forces in Vietnam faced hundreds of thousands of Chinese antiaircraft, railway, construction, and support troops sent there. Johnson was anxious to avoid prompting full-scale military involvement of China in the Vietnam conflict. US diplomats signaled these US intentions in the otherwise moribund US-China ambassadorial talks in Warsaw, and Chinese officials made clear that China would restrain its intervention accordingly.[63]

By early 1968 the bitter impasse in Sino-American relations had lasted two decades and seemed unlikely to change soon. The net result of the twists and turns in Chinese domestic and foreign policy since the widespread starvation and other disasters caused by the collapse of the Great Leap Forward were years of violence and life-and-death political struggle among elites and other groups mainly in Chinese cities during the Cultural Revolution, which began in 1966 and did not end until Mao's death in 1976. At first, the sharply deteriorating domestic situation in the early 1960s caused Mao to retreat from regular involvement in administrative matters. His subordinates pursued more moderate and pragmatic policies designed to revive agricultural and industrial production on a sustainable basis without reliance on the highly disruptive and wasteful mass campaigns and excessive collectivization of preceding years. The economy began to revive, but the progress was marred in Mao's eyes by a reliance on the kinds of incentives prevalent in the "revisionist" practices of the Soviet Union and its allied states, and the controlling bureaucratic elites in those states seen as restoring the kind of un-equal and exploitative practices of capitalism. [64]

Mao found that two of the three main pillars of power and control in China, the CCP and the Chinese government, continued to move in the wrong direction. The third pillar of power and control, the Chinese military, was under the leadership of Lin Biao following the purge of Defense Minister Peng Dehuai, who dared to resist Mao's Great Leap policies during a leadership meeting in 1959. Lin positioned his leadership in support of Maoist ideals of revolution, equality, and service to the people. Indoctrination and involvement in civil society and affairs often took precedence over professional military training. The distillation of Mao's wisdom from volumes of selected works was distributed throughout the Chinese military and the broader masses of China in the form of a plastic-covered "little red book," *Quotations from Chairman Mao Tse-Tung*, published with a preface by Lin Biao. [65]

Mao was not prepared to break with his party and government colleagues until 1966. By that time he had become sufficiently opposed to prevailing administrative practices and tendencies. Also, he had built up enough support outside normal administrative structures to challenge and reverse what were later portrayed as a drift toward revisionism and the restoration of capitalism. Relying on his personal charisma, organizational support from military leaders like Lin Biao, security forces controlled by radical leaders like Kang Sheng, and various political radicals and opportunists, Mao launched his unorthodox efforts that saw the creation of legions of young Red Guards leading the attack against established authority in urban China. The result was confusion, some resistance from political and government leaders often unaware of Mao's commitment to the radical Red Guards and their allies, and ultimately mass purges and persecution of senior and lesser authorities amid widespread violence and destruction carried out by Red Guard groups. By 1968 numerous sections in cities in China had burned during clashes of rival Red Guard groups, and the party and government structure had collapsed. The military was called into the cities to restore order. With Mao's support, they proceeded to transport the millions of Red Guards from the cities and to disperse them into various areas in the Chinese countryside, where they were compelled to stay and work for the indefinite future. [66]

The disaster and disruption seen in domestic affairs was duplicated in the shift toward radicalism in Chinese foreign relations. The Chinese public split with the Soviet Union deepened and broadened in the 1960s. Beijing not only opposed the Soviet Union on ideological grounds but also strongly attacked Moscow's willingness to cooperate with the United States in international affairs. Chinese leaders saw the newly independent Asian and African states providing an important arena for struggle with Moscow as well as the United States. Though weak economically and having little to spare following the deprivations of the Great Leap Forward, China provided economic and military aid to left-leaning governments and provided training, military assistance, and financial support to armed insurgents struggling against colonial powers or right-leaning governments of developing countries.[67]

Chinese Premier Zhou Enlai visited Africa in 1964 and said it was "ripe for revolution." China endeavored to compete with the Soviet Union in support of various anticolonial insurgencies and to supply significant aid to African governments prepared to align closer to China than the Soviet Union or the West. In Asia, China strongly supported the Vietnamese Communist forces directed by the North Vietnamese government in Hanoi in the face of increased American military involvement in South Vietnam and other parts of Indochina. The Chinese government also organized and/or strengthened support for Communist-led insurgencies against governments in Southeast Asia that were seen by China as pro-American or insufficiently accommodating to Chinese influence and interests. The left-leaning Sukarno government of Indonesia, the largest country in Southeast Asia, was a focus of Chinese support until the military coup in 1965 smashed Communist and Chinese influence in the country through mass killings and arrests.[68]

Maoist China sacrificed conventional diplomacy in pursuing revolutionary fervor during the early years of the Cultural Revolution. The foreign minister and much of the senior foreign policy elite were purged. Ambassadors were recalled and forced to undergo extensive ideological retraining. Lower-level embassy officials often endeavored to show their loyalty to Mao and his revolutionary teaching by unauthorized demonstrations and proselytizing to often unreceptive and hostile foreign audiences. They and the staff of foreign policy organs in Beijing followed a radical line that alienated China from most foreign governments.

The nadir of Chinese diplomacy seemed evident in several developments in 1967. Huge Red Guard demonstrations were mobilized against the Soviet embassy in Beijing, which was kept under siege in January and February. Later in 1967 Red Guards invaded the Soviet Embassy's consular section and burned its files. When Moscow withdrew its diplomats' dependents in February 1967, some were beaten or forced to crawl under pictures of Mao Zedong on their way to planes to take them home. When Red Guard demonstrators in Hong Kong were arrested by British authorities for public disruption and disorder, a major crisis in Chinese-British relations ensued. A mob of thousands of Chinese surrounded British diplomatic offices in Beijing and set fires in the building. Escaping British diplomats came into the hands of the Chinese mob.[69]

The life-or-death struggles for power and attendant violent mass campaigns inside China, combined with militant Chinese policies in support of the Vietnamese and other Communist insurgencies in Southeast Asia and a rigid Chinese stance on Taiwan, Korea, and other issues, continued to divide

China and the United States. US leaders saw little prospect for any significant movement in relations with the PRC as they grappled with consuming preoccupations associated with the failing US effort against Communist insurgents in Vietnam.[70]

Chiang Kai-shek endeavored to deepen the alliance relationship with the United States but found the Johnson administration reluctant to take actions that might embroil China more deeply in the Vietnam War. Despite China's radical and xenophobic posture, the newly independent developing nations tended to be supportive of China being diplomatically recognized by them and by international bodies, notably the United Nations. Sentiment in the West also shifted somewhat in support of recognition of China, even if it came at the expense of past ties with Taiwan. France set the precedent by establishing ties with Beijing in 1964. The successful Chinese nuclear weapons test that year was followed by many more, underlining the rationale for formal relations with the Asian power.

As Chiang aged, he incrementally passed administrative authority to his son Chiang Ching-kuo, who focused less on plans for attacking the mainland and more on strengthening the economy and the KMT's support on Taiwan. The elder Chiang precluded compromise in the zero-sum competition with China for diplomatic recognition and representation in the United Nations. At one level, Taiwan seemed sure to lose this competition, but in 1968, with China in the midst of the Cultural Revolution and all its radical excesses, such losses seemed far off.[71]

Chapter Four

Rapprochement and Normalization

STRATEGIC IMPERATIVES OPENING US-CHINA RELATIONS

The roots of the contemporary, closely intertwined Sino-American relationship began in what appeared to be very adverse circumstances. Maoist China had descended through phases of ideologically driven excess in foreign and domestic affairs, reaching a point of unprecedented international isolation, ideological rigidity, and wariness in foreign relations bordering on xenophobia. The United States had more than five hundred thousand troops in Vietnam fighting a Communist-led adversary supported by China with supplies, financing, and provision of many thousands of Chinese troops. US leaders were particularly fearful of an escalation of the prolonged and increasingly unpopular conflict that would somehow bring China more directly into a war that they were unsure how to win under existing conditions. The US containment effort along China's periphery continued, as did US political isolation and economic embargo against the Beijing regime. Nascent US efforts to consider greater flexibility in relations with China ran up against Maoist hostility, disinterest, and contempt, and were overshadowed by the broad implications of the Vietnam quagmire.[1]

The dramatic turnabout leading to the opening in US-China relations at the end of the 1960s and early 1970s has been subject to some different scholarly interpretations. One view sees a flagging of Mao's revolutionary drive and vigor, opening the way for the Chinese leader to consider and ultimately pursue pragmatic understanding with the United States.[2] Another sees a reconfiguring in the US calculus of China's position in world politics and its implications for the United States. This view highlights the importance of an apparent trend whereby US leaders privately came to see China in the late 1960s as less threatening than in the past; eventually they came to view the Maoist regime as a potential asset in American strategy focused increasingly on dealing with a rising and threatening Soviet Union.[3]

Despite these and other divergent views, assessments of this period and the opening in Sino-American relations find it hard not to give primacy to interpretations, broadly in line with the realist school of thought in international relations (IR) theory, that focused on the acute strategic necessities of both the United States and China amid circumstances of regional and international order featuring a rising and powerful Soviet Union challenging their core national interests. Only the threat of nuclear war with a domineering Soviet Union at a time of acute Chinese internal disruption and weakness appears sufficient to explain the remarkable turnabout in China's foreign policy calculus and approach to the United States. Given China's size and the preoccupation Chinese rulers have long given to the tasks of managing the complicated internal affairs of this vast country, China historians and specialists of contemporary affairs often have given pride of place to Chinese domestic determinants in Chinese foreign policy. There was no better example during Maoist rule of the way domestic Chinese policies and practices determined Chinese foreign policy than during the violent and disruptive early years of China's Cultural Revolution. Moving Chinese leaders out of their self-initiated isolation probably would have taken many years under more normal circumstances. But circumstances in the late 1960s were far from normal, giving rise to the real danger of the Soviet Union militarily invading China, destroying its nuclear and other strategic installations, and forcing China to conform to Soviet interests.[4]

For their part, US leaders faced an unprecedented situation of Soviet military power seeming to reach parity with and in some critical areas surpassing that of the United States. The concurrent Vietnam quagmire drained American resources, and Moscow pumped up support for the Vietnamese Communist resistance, seeking to further weaken the United States and strengthen the changing balance of power in Asian and world affairs. Finding a way to break this trend and deal more effectively with the Vietnam situation became critically important issues in American politics.[5]

It was fortuitous that strong strategic imperatives, which drove Chinese and US leaders toward one another, developed at the same time. Otherwise, Maoist China in particular seemed positioned to continue resistance to the United States, while US interest in greater flexibility toward China appeared likely to be overwhelmed by opposing US interests and political inclinations.

There had been earlier occasions when one side or the other saw their interests served by a possible improvement in Sino-American relations. But it turned out that when one side showed some interest in improved contacts, the other rebuffed or ignored it. Thus, despite deeply rooted differences between the US government and Chinese Communist leaders on ideological, economic, and international issues, United States–Chinese Communist interchange since the start of World War II witnessed a few instances where one side or the other saw their interests served by reaching out and seeking reconciliation and better ties with the other party. The Chinese Communists in particular tried a moderate and accommodating approach to the United States in greeting the American Military Observer Group to Yenan in 1944, and in the initial ambassadorial talks following Zhou Enlai's moderate overture at Bandung in 1955. The Americans tried more tentative overtures to Beijing in 1949 and showed interest in more flexibility toward China by the 1960s. Unfortunately, these initiatives and overtures failed, as there were never occasions when both sides sought improved relations at the same time, until internal and international weaknesses in 1968 and 1969 drove the United States and China closer together in a pragmatic search for means to deal with difficult circumstances, which appears best understood through the realist lens of IR theory.[6]

ENCOUNTERS AND INTERACTION, 1968–89

Opening Contacts

Difficulties in the United States in 1968 were profound. It is hard to recall a one-year period since the start of the Cold War with so many shocking and adverse developments for American leaders and their constituents. The string of calamities and reversals began in January with the communist Tet Offensive throughout South Vietnamese cities. The assault often was carried out by Vietnamese who were thought to be supporting the American war effort. The US and Allied forces counterattacked against the guerrillas in their own ranks and elsewhere in the supposedly pacified cities of South Vietnam, killing many thousands, but the uprising and mass killings shattered the Lyndon Johnson administration's predictions of progress in the increasingly unpopular Vietnam War.[7]

US commanders called for two hundred thousand more US troops in addition to the more than half million US forces in the country. The vast majority of these American forces were draftees. They and their families and friends tended in growing numbers to question the purpose of the US commitment to Vietnam and the massive costs in terms of American casualties and economic and military support. Antiwar demonstrations in the United States grew in size and frequency. Protest marches of two hundred thousand or more along the Mall in Washington, DC, became more regular occurrences. Providing security for the White House compound adjoining the Mall became an increasing concern given the size of the demonstrations and the uncertainty over whether they would stay on the Mall or turn against the nearby White House.

The rising antiwar sentiment in the United States changed the course of the 1968 presidential election campaign. President Johnson's mandate appeared to collapse when he did poorly in the New Hampshire primary in February. He ran against Senator Eugene McCarthy, an otherwise unexceptional opponent who emphasized an antiwar platform. Johnson pulled out of the race and redoubled peace efforts in talks with the Vietnamese Communists in Paris.

Civil rights leader and antiwar proponent Martin Luther King Jr. traveled to Memphis in March in support of a strike by city trash handlers. While standing outside his motel, King was killed by a rifleman. The assassination set off a rampage of urban looting and burning that afflicted several American cities. Washington, DC, was closed for days as major parts of the city burned out of control. The fire service was prevented by snipers and mob violence. Order was restored only after the imposition of martial law by US Army combat troops.

Amid this turmoil over the Vietnam War and race relations in the United States, the contentious Democratic primaries reached a conclusion in California in June, where Senator Robert Kennedy won. Kennedy was critical of the conduct of the war and drew vast crowds of African Americans and others hopeful for government policies to heal fractured race relations in the United States. Like King three months earlier, Kennedy was assassinated, just after the California victory was secured.

With Kennedy dead, antiwar advocates gathered in Chicago in August to protest the likely selection of Johnson's vice president, Hubert Humphrey, as the Democratic standard-bearer. Chicago's Mayor Richard Daley and his police officers promised tough measures to deal with unauthorized demonstrations. They delivered on their promise: As American television audiences watched in shock, police officers clubbed and beat demonstrators, reporters, and others they deemed to be obstructing the smooth flow of the convention and nearby hotel receptions.

The Republicans at their convention that summer nominated Richard Nixon. In a political comeback after retreating from public life in the early 1960s, Nixon said he had a plan to deal with the Vietnam morass. He did not speak very much about an opening to China. Nixon won the election and took office amid unprecedented tight security for fear of violence from antiwar protesters and others. Upon entering office, Nixon moved quickly to begin what would turn out to be the withdrawal of more than six hundred thousand US troops from around China's periphery in Asia. In his first year in office, he announced what later was called the Nixon Doctrine, a broad framework for Asia's future without massive US troop deployments. One implication seemed to be the end of the US-backed containment of China. Nixon also made several mainly symbolic gestures to the Chinese government while pursuing vigorous efforts in secret to develop communications with the Mao Zedong leadership. [8]

Meanwhile, in China, Mao succeeded in removing political rivals in the early years of the Cultural Revolution, but at tremendous cost. Many burnt urban areas testified to widespread violence and arson among competing groups. The party and government administration were severely disrupted. Experienced administrators were often purged, persecuted, or pushed aside by proponents of radical Maoist ideals or political opportunists. Expertise in economics, development, and other fields essential to nation building came to be seen as a liability in the politically charged atmosphere of repeated mass campaigns. Political indoctrination and adherence to Mao Zedong Thought overshadowed education and training in practical tasks. [9]

Military forces called into Chinese cities in order to restore order duly removed millions of disruptive Red Guards and began to lead the process of reconstituting a party and government infrastructure on the basis of military-led rule. Not surprisingly in this context, Defense Minister Lin Biao and his People's Liberation Army (PLA) associates rose to new prominence in the Chinese hierarchy. Military representation in various party and government bodies was high. Not all military leaders were as supportive of the radical policies and practices of the Cultural Revolution as Lin Biao and his associates in the high command. Some experienced civilian and military cadre had survived in office. But they appeared in the minority in a leadership featuring factional chieftains like the Gang of Four, involving Mao's wife and three other extremist party Politburo members, and such luminaries as Mao's speechwriter and sometime confidant Chen Boda and security forces and intelligence operative Kang Sheng. [10]

Under these circumstances, China was not prepared for a national security shock. Chinese troops were engaged in domestic peacekeeping and governance. They also for many years followed Maoist dictates under the leadership of Defense Minister Lin Biao and eschewed professional military training in favor of ideological training and promoting popular welfare in China. Chinese military programs for developing nuclear weapons and ballistic missiles were excluded from the violence and disruption of the Cultural Revolution, but the PLA on the whole was poorly prepared to deal with conventional military challenges. [11]

In August 1968 the Soviet Union invaded Czechoslovakia and removed its leadership, putting in power a regime more compatible with Soviet interests. The Soviet Union also made clear that it reserved the right to take similar actions in other deviant Communist states. This view came to be known as the Brezhnev Doctrine, named after the Soviet party leader Leonid Brezhnev, who ruled from the mid-1960s until the early 1980s. Of course, Chinese leaders well knew that, from the Soviet perspective, there was no Communist state more deviant than China. Moreover, since Brezhnev's takeover, the Soviet Union had backed political opposition to China with increasing military muscle, deploying ever-larger numbers of forces along the Manchurian border and, as a result of a new Soviet defense treaty with Mongolia, along the Sino-Mongolian border. The Soviet forces, mainly mechanized divisions designed to move rapidly in offensive operations, were configured in a pattern used by Soviet forces when they quickly overran Japanese forces in Manchuria and northern China in the last days of World War II.[12]

The Sino-Soviet dispute had emerged in the late 1950s as an ideological dispute with wide implications. Fairly quickly it became a major issue in bilateral relations, notably with the abrupt withdrawal of Soviet assistance from China in 1960. At that time, the dispute broadened to include stark differences on international issues and how to deal with the United States. Chinese accusations of Soviet weakness in the face of the firm US stance against Soviet missiles in Cuba during the Cuban missile crisis of 1962 saw Soviet officials respond by accusing China of accommodating colonial "outhouses" held by Great Britain and Portugal in Hong Kong and Macau, respectively. Maoist China responded by reminding the world that imperialist Russia took by far the greatest tracts of Chinese territory by virtue of the so-called unequal treaties imposed on China by imperialist powers in the nineteenth and twentieth centuries. The Sino-Soviet debate now focused on competing claims to disputed border territories, against the background of new uncertainty over the legitimacy of the boundaries established by the unequal treaties. Sino-Soviet negotiations soon after Brezhnev took power, following the ouster of Nikita Khrushchev in 1964, failed to resolve border uncertainties, prompting the new Soviet leader to make the force deployments and arrangements noted above in order to deal with the Chinese disputes from a position of strength. With the declared Soviet ambitions under terms of the Brezhnev Doctrine and Moscow's military preparations, the stage was set for the border dispute to evolve into the most serious national security threat ever faced by the People's Republic of China (PRC).[13]

The combination of perceived greater threat and internal weakness caused a crisis and debate in the Chinese leadership that lasted into the early 1970s. Chinese leadership decision making in the Cultural Revolution was not at all transparent. Mao seemed to remain in overall command, but official Chinese media duly reflected competing views on how to deal with the new and apparently dangerous situation in relations with the Soviet Union.[14]

Some commentary, presumably encouraged by some Chinese leaders, favored reaching out to the United States as a means to offset the Soviet threat. In November 1968 the Chinese Foreign Ministry under Premier Zhou Enlai's direction called for renewed ambassadorial talks with the newly elected Nixon administration in a statement that was notable for the absence of the then-usual Chinese invective critical of the United States. The argument used in media commentary that proposed a reaching-out to the United

States was that the United States was in the process of being defeated in Indochina and was no longer the primary threat to China. It too faced challenge from the expanding USSR, and China could take advantage of the differences between the competing superpowers in order to secure its position in the face of the newly emerging Soviet danger.[15]

Other commentary, presumably backed by other Chinese leaders, strongly opposed an opening to the United States. These commentaries were associated with Lin Biao and his lieutenants, along with the radically Maoist leadership faction, the Gang of Four. They argued in favor of continued strong Chinese opposition to both the United States and the Soviet Union. Though weakened by the defeat in Vietnam, the United States could not be trusted in dealings with China. In particular, any sign of Chinese weakness toward either superpower likely would prompt them both to work together in seeking to pressure China and gain at its expense.[16]

The latter leaders held the upper hand in Chinese leadership councils during much of 1969. Chinese media rebuked and ridiculed the new US president as he took office. At the last moment Chinese leaders cancelled the slated ambassadorial talks in February. The Chinese authorities took the offensive in the face of Soviet military pressure along the border, ambushing a Soviet patrol on a disputed island in early March and publicizing the incident to the world. Far from being intimidated, Brezhnev's Soviet forces responded later in the month by annihilating a Chinese border guard unit, setting the stage for escalating rhetoric and military clashes throughout the spring and summer of 1969. The clashes were capped in August by an all-day battle along the western sector of the border that saw the Soviets inflict hundreds of casualties on the Chinese. Soviet officials followed with warnings to Americans, and other foreigners sure to relay the warnings to the Chinese, that the Soviet Union was in the process of consulting with foreign powers to assure they would stand aside as the Soviet Union prepared all-out attack on China, including the possible use of nuclear weapons.[17]

In the face of such threats and pressure, Chinese leaders were compelled to shift strategy. Zhou Enlai was brought forward to negotiate with Soviet leaders. It was clear that while negotiating with the USSR would temporarily ease tensions and the danger of war, China would not accept Soviet demands. Beijing now viewed the USSR as China's number one strategic threat. Seeking international leverage, it took measures to improve strained Chinese relations with neighboring countries and with more distant powers. It was nonetheless evident that, while helpful, these improvements would not fundamentally alter China's strategic disadvantage in the face of Soviet intimidation and threat. Only one power, the United States, had that ability. Zhou and like-minded officials in the Chinese leadership were encouraged that the United States was weakened by the Vietnam War and that it was also beginning to withdraw sizeable numbers of troops from Asia and dismantle the US military containment against China. On this basis, Beijing could pursue relations with Washington as a means to deal with the Soviet threat. However, Lin Biao and others continued to argue that both superpowers were enemies of China, and in the end they would cooperate to isolate and control China. [18]

The debate seemed to get caught up with the broader struggle for power in this period of the Cultural Revolution. Mao Zedong came to side with the view associated with Zhou Enlai. Repeated overtures by the Nixon administration to China ultimately succeeded in Sino-American ambassadorial talks being resumed in Warsaw in early 1970. China used the image of restored contacts with the United States in order to offset and undermine Soviet efforts to intimidate China. Chinese officials arranged for the meeting to be held in the secure area of their embassy in Warsaw. The usual venue, a palace provided by the Poles, was long suspected of being riddled with secret listening devices that would give the USSR and Warsaw Pact allies the full transcript of the US-China discussions. The Chinese diplomats also made a point of being unusually positive to Western reporters during the photo opportunity as American officials were welcomed to the Chinese embassy at the start of the official talks. As Chinese officials presumably hoped, Soviet commentary on the secret talks and improved atmosphere in US-China relations viewed the developments as complicating Soviet border negotiations with China and nuclear armament limitation talks with the United States. Soviet commentators even charged that Beijing, fearful of Soviet intentions, was seeking to come to terms with the United States in order to play one nuclear power against the other. [19]

The Nixon administration's expansion of the Vietnam War by invading Cambodia in spring 1970 caused China to cancel the talks and slowed forward movement. Mao highlighted a mass demonstration in Beijing on May 20, 1970, where he welcomed the Cambodian leader Norodom Sihanouk, who had been deposed by the pro-US Cambodian generals who worked with US-led invading forces. The Chinese chairman, in his last major public statement denouncing the United States, called on the people of the world to rise up against US imperialism and their "running dogs." Outwardly, it appeared that Mao was siding with the Chinese advocates of a harder line against the United States. However, clandestine US-China communication continued, as did the withdrawal of US forces from Vietnam and other parts of Asia, so that by October 1970 Mao was prepared to tell visiting US journalist Edgar Snow that Nixon could visit China. [20]

The shift in Mao's stance was accompanied by other moves that appeared to undermine the standing of Lin Biao and his radical allies in the Chinese leadership. A key radical leader, Chen Boda, dropped from public view in late 1970 in what later was shown to be intensified factional maneuvering leading up to the alleged coup plans by Lin and his allies. [21]

What role was played by differences over the opening to the United States in the life-or-death struggle in the Chinese leadership remains hidden by pervasive secrecy in Chinese leadership decision making. Emblematic of the significance of the opening to the United States in Chinese politics at the time was the unusual greeting of US National Security Adviser Henry Kissinger upon his arrival in Beijing on his secret mission in July 1971 to open US-China relations. The first Chinese official to greet Kissinger on arrival was not a protocol officer from the foreign ministry or some other appropriate official; it was Marshall Ye Jianying. Ye was one of the most senior Chinese military leaders. He survived the Cultural Revolution, advised Mao to use connections with the United States in the face of the Soviet threat, later played a key role in the arrest of the Gang of Four following Mao's death in 1976, and became president of China. His approach was close to that of Zhou Enlai and at odds with that of Lin Biao.[22]

The announcement of Kissinger's successful secret trip appeared to represent a serious defeat for Lin Biao and his allies in their debate with opponents on how to deal with the Soviet Union and the United States. The setback came amid rising pressures and adverse developments affecting the military leader. The stakes apparently were very high. Two months later, Lin and his wife, son, and close aides died as a result of an air crash in Mongolia as they were allegedly trying to escape China following a failed coup attempt against Mao and his opponents. The military high command in the PLA that had risen to power under Lin's tenure as defense minister were arrested, removed from power, and not seen again until they eventually were brought out for public trial along with Gang of Four and other discredited radical leaders in the years after Mao's death.[23]

Though nothing like the intense factional struggles of Maoist China, US leadership and popular opposition to an opening to China were feared by President Nixon and his top aides. In particular, it was clear to the American leaders that they would have to sacrifice US official relations with Taiwan in order to meet the conditions Chinese leaders set for establishing relations with the United States. How the Chiang Kai-shek government in Taiwan would react to this new adverse turn of fate was uncertain. The so-called China lobby, both supportive of Chiang and the Chinese Nationalists and strongly anti-Communist, had become a feature of American domestic politics for more than twenty years. Chiang and the lobby had particular influence among conservatives in the president's Republican Party. Nixon had close and personal ties with the lobby.[24]

President Nixon, National Security Adviser Kissinger, and the small group of top aides involved in the opening to China dealt with potential domestic opposition through secrecy and what arguably could be seen as deception. Their motives focused on the advantages for the United States in a new relationship with China with regard to handling the difficult process of reaching an acceptable peace agreement to end the US involvement in the Vietnam War and in dealing with the Soviet Union in arms limitation and other negotiations from a position of greater strength. A new order in Asian and world affairs featuring positive US-China relations seemed much less costly and more compatible for US interests than the previous US confrontation with and containment of China. President Nixon and his administration also seemed acutely aware that the political opportunity of an American opening to China could fall into the hands of a Democratic Party opponent, and they were determined to preclude such an outcome.[25]

For a time, it was difficult for scholars to construct the full picture of the Nixon administration approach to China because much of the record initially remained secret, and public pronouncements, memoirs, and other documents from administration leaders sometimes seemed very much at odds with what was actually the administration's policy and practice. It was clear that US leaders now centered their strategies and approaches in East Asia on improving relations with China, and that US relations with Taiwan would decline, though the scope and extent of the decline were left ambiguous. Relations with Japan and other East Asian allies and friends also appeared secondary and were sometimes viewed as declining assets or liabilities. Also clear was evidence that the United States sought, through the new relationship with China, a means to secure US interests following the failure of US military intervention in Vietnam and the rising danger posed by the expanding power of the Soviet Union in the Asian region as well as elsewhere. And the ambitions of the Nixon administration to use the dramatic opening to China to garner personal prestige at home and abroad and strong domestic political support in the run-up to the 1972 US presidential race seemed evident.[26]

The American people, their representatives in Congress, the media, and others with an interest were notably left in the dark for many years regarding the full extent of the US compromises on Taiwan carried out in the early contacts between Kissinger and Nixon and Chinese leaders. The Nationalist Chinese government was in a similar situation. The record reconstructed by scholarship shows that Kissinger met Chinese conditions involving a full break in US official relations with Taiwan and other interaction with Taiwan during his initial meetings with Zhou Enlai in 1971, and that Nixon backed these steps in his initial meetings with Chinese leaders the following year. These compromises were kept from public view and also kept from many US officials responsible for the conduct of US policy toward China and Taiwan, amid statements and actions by the administration indicating continued support for Taiwan and ambiguity about what the future course of US policy might be.[27]

On the basis of the compromises by Kissinger and Nixon, scholarship judges that the Chinese leadership could reasonably have concluded Taiwan would soon be theirs, as the United States would remove itself from involvement in the issue. Unfortunately, Nixon and his associates had only begun to build support in the United States and internationally for this dramatic change in policy. It was unclear whether majorities in the Congress, the media, public opinion, and the major political parties would accept it. Nixon and his aides avoided building this support as they focused on developing relations with China in secret on a foundation of compromises and accommodations poorly understood in the United States and abroad. They made a strong case that such secrecy was needed in order to avoid complications in the process of normalization. That argument would be followed by later US administrations with mixed success and some serious negative consequences for long-term US-China relations. Notably, Chinese expectations that Taiwan would soon be theirs and that the United States would remove itself from involvement in Taiwan were sorely and repeatedly tested by US actions demonstrating continued support for Taiwan, backed by American leaders often unaware of or opposed to the Nixon-Kissinger secret compromises on Taiwan.[28]

The July 1971 announcement of Nixon's trip to China came as a surprise to most Americans, who supported the initiative; Americans watched with interest the president's February 1972 visit to China. Supporting Kissinger's secret pledges in the July 1971 meetings in Beijing, Nixon privately indicated to Chinese leaders that he would break US ties with Taiwan and establish diplomatic relations with China in his second term. In the Shanghai Communiqué signed at the end of President Nixon's historic visit to China, both sides registered opposition to "hegemony" (a code word for Soviet expansion), laid out differences on a variety of Asian and other issues, and set forth the US intention to pull back militarily from Taiwan and to support a "peaceful settlement of the Taiwan question by the Chinese themselves." Subsequently, both sides agreed to establish US-China Liaison Offices staffed with senior diplomats in Beijing and Washington in 1973, despite the fact that the United States still maintained official relations with the Chinese Nationalist government in Taipei.[29]

Normalization of Relations

Progress toward establishing formal US-China relations, the so-called normalization of relations, was delayed in the mid-1970s on account of circumstances mainly involving the United States. A politically motivated break-in at the Watergate office complex in Washington, DC, and cover-up of the crime involved President Nixon in criminal activity. As congressional investigation led toward impeachment, Nixon resigned in August 1974. His promise to normalize relations with China in his second term ended with his resignation. President Gerald Ford privately reaffirmed Nixon's pledge to shift diplomatic recognition from Taiwan to China, but then he backtracked in the face of US domestic opposition and international circumstances. [30]

Chinese leaders for their part were preoccupied with Mao's declining health and subsequent death in September 1976, and the most important leadership succession struggle in the history of the People's Republic of China. The leadership turmoil in China at the time had seen Zhou Enlai die in January 1976. His purported successor, recently rehabilitated veteran leader Deng Xiaoping, gave the eulogy at the memorial service for Zhou and then disappeared from public view, purged from the leadership for a second time. The radical Gang of Four seemed to exert more influence for a time, but the demonstration of support for Zhou and his relatively moderate policies, in the form of thousands of Beijing people placing flowers and wreaths in his memory at the monument for revolutionary martyrs in the capital in April 1976, appeared to indicate that the days of radicalism were numbered. The death of senior military leader Zhu De in July 1976 preceded Mao's by two months, setting the stage for the struggle for succession, following Mao's death in September. [31]

That China had far to go in creating a foreign policy that dealt with the United States and other countries in the world in conventional and normal ways was underlined by the tragedy of an earthquake in July 1976 that demolished the industrial city of Tangshan, 105 miles southeast of Beijing, and severely damaged nearby areas including the capital and the major port and industrial city of Tianjin. It later was disclosed that hundreds of thousands of Chinese died in the quake and that the needs for relief were enormous. Nevertheless, in a remarkable and extremely damaging demonstration of Maoist "self-reliance," the radical leadership in Beijing at the time refused to acknowledge these needs or to allow foreign countries and groups to assist in efforts to save lives and reduce misery. [32]

A coalition of senior leaders managed to stop the Gang of Four from gaining power after Mao's death. The coalition included veteran cadre who had survived the Cultural Revolution and administrators who had risen to prominence during the turmoil but also endeavored to avoid the harm caused by excessively radical policies. The four radical leaders were arrested. After a few years, they were put on public trial in 1980, once the Communist Party leadership had sufficiently reunited and come to overall judgment about what was correct and incorrect behavior during the Cultural Revolution. Reaching such judgment was particularly time-consuming and difficult since Chairman Mao Zedong, still seen as the revered leader of China, was personally responsible for support of the radicals and so much of the turmoil they and others carried out during the Cultural Revolution. [33]

Following the arrest of the Gang of Four, leadership changes in China slowly evolved toward a reversal of the disruptive policies of the past and restoration to power of senior cadre committed to pragmatic reform in the interest of Chinese development and sustaining Communist rule in China. Deng Xiaoping was once again brought back to power. By the time of the third plenary session of the Eleventh Central Committee in December 1978, Deng was able to consolidate a leading position within the party, government, and military and to launch the economic and policy reforms that provided the foundation for China's recent approach to the United States and international affairs. Deng and his colleagues constantly were compelled to maneuver amid competing interests and preferences within the Chinese leadership and the broader polity in order to come up with changes they felt would advance China's wealth and shore up the legitimacy of the Chinese Communist Party, which had been severely damaged by the excesses and poor performance of the past.[34]

Not only were Chinese leaders preoccupied internally, but their priorities internationally in the latter 1970s were less focused on consummating normalization with the United States and more focused on dealing with Soviet intimidation and threat. The United States was weakened internally by Nixon's resignation, and the Ford government was hobbled by the president's pardon of Nixon. Ford was in a poor position to continue strong support for the struggling South Vietnamese government and the neighboring Cambodian government aligned with the United States. Strong Soviet assistance to Vietnamese Communist forces bolstered their efforts to take control of the south. The Cambodian regime collapsed, and Chinese-backed Khmer Rouge insurgents entered Phnom Penh in March 1975. The new regime immediately began carrying out their radical and brutal policies that would see the evacuation of the capital and the massive repression and deaths of more than one million Cambodians. North Vietnamese forces launched an all-out assault in South Vietnam. The Saigon regime disintegrated; the Americans and what Vietnamese associates they could bring with them fled in ignominious defeat; and the Communist forces barged through the gates of the presidential palace and occupied Saigon in late April.[35]

Chinese officials showed considerable alarm at the turn of events around China's periphery. Stronger efforts by the Soviet Union to use military power and relations with allies around China, like Vietnam and India, to contain and pressure the PRC mimicked the US-led containment effort against China earlier in the Cold War. Under these circumstances, Chinese leaders focused on shoring up US resolve and the resolve of other governments and forces seen as important in what China depicted as a united front against expanding Soviet power and influence in Asian and world affairs. The Chinese leaders appeared prepared to wait for the United States to meet Chinese conditions on breaking all US official ties with Taiwan, including the US-Taiwan defense treaty, before moving ahead with full normalization of PRC relations with the United States.[36]

Desiring to complete the normalization of US-China relations begun by President Nixon, President Jimmy Carter felt compelled to wait until after his success in spring 1978 in gaining Senate passage of a controversial treaty transferring control of the Panama Canal to Panama. A visit by Secretary of State Cyrus Vance to China in 1977 showed that Chinese leaders were not prepared for significant compromise on Taiwan. President Carter was aware that a complete ending of US official relations with Taiwan would alienate many in the US Senate, and he needed the support of these senators for the two-thirds Senate vote of ratification on the Panama Canal treaty. Once the Senate approved the Panama treaty in spring 1978, Carter moved forward expeditiously with normalization with China. [37]

National Security Adviser Zbigniew Brzezinski was in the lead in seeking rapid progress in normalizing US-China relations in 1978 and in subsequent steps to advance US-China relations as a means to counter Soviet power and expansion. Soviet and Soviet-backed forces had made gains and were making inroads that seemed at odds with US interests in different parts of Africa, the Middle East, Central America, and Southwest and Southeast Asia. Chinese officials were in the lead among international advocates in warning the United States to avoid the dangers of "appeasement" and to stand firm and work with China against the expanding Soviet power. Carter followed Brzezinski's advice over that of Secretary of State Cyrus Vance, who gave a higher priority to working constructively with the USSR, notably in order to reach US-Soviet arms control agreements. [38]

The process of US administration decision making followed the practices of the Nixon period. Like their Nixon-administration counterparts, the Carter administration leaders were concerned with the reactions of US supporters of Taiwan and others opposed to American normalization with China. To outmaneuver anticipated opposition and complications, Carter, Brzezinski, and their senior aides worked hard to preserve the secrecy of the negotiations with China. Though the broad direction of US policy was understood to be moving toward normalization with China, the process of the talks with Beijing and the content of US concessions were held back. The Carter administration agreement to normalize diplomatic relations with China would follow through in a public way on many of the secret agreements the US leaders had already made with China over Taiwan. Though some in the Carter administration were concerned with preserving important US ties with Taiwan after normalization, Brzezinski showed little interest, and Carter seemed contemptuous of congressional backers of Taiwan. Key Carter officials didn't expect Taiwan to survive the change in relations. [39]

The United States–China Communiqué announced in December 1978 established official US relations with the People's Republic of China under conditions whereby the United States recognized the PRC as the government of China, acknowledged that Taiwan was part of China, ended official US relations with the Republic of China (ROC) government on Taiwan, and terminated the US defense treaty with the ROC on Taiwan. Official US statements underscored US interest that Taiwan's future be settled peacefully and that the United States would continue sales of defensive arms to Taipei.[40]

US and especially Chinese leaders used the signs of improved US-China relations in the communiqué and during Chinese leader Deng Xiaoping's widely publicized visit to the United States in January 1979 to highlight Sino-American cooperation against "hegemony," notably a Soviet-backed Vietnamese military assault against Cambodia beginning in late December 1978. Returning from the United States, Deng launched a large-scale Chinese military offensive into Vietnam's northern region. Chinese forces withdrew after a few weeks but maintained strong artillery attacks and other military pressure against Vietnamese border positions until the Vietnamese eventually agreed to withdraw from Cambodia ten years later. Carter administration officials voiced some reservations about Deng's confrontational tactics against Soviet and Vietnamese expansionism, but Sino-American cooperation against the USSR and its allies increased.[41]

In pursuing normalization of relations with China, President Carter and National Security Adviser Brzezinski followed the pattern of secret diplomacy used successfully by President Nixon and National Security Adviser Kissinger in early interaction with China. Their approach allowed for very little consultation with Congress, key US allies, or the Taiwan government regarding the conditions and timing of the 1978 normalization agreement. In contrast to general US congressional, media, and popular support for the surprise Nixon opening to China, President Carter and his aides clearly were less successful in winning US domestic support for their initiatives. Many in Congress were satisfied with the stasis that developed in US-PRC-ROC relations in the mid-1970s and unconvinced that the United States had a strategic or other need to pay the price of breaking a US defense treaty and other official ties with a loyal government in Taiwan for the sake of formalizing already existing relations with the PRC. Bipartisan majorities in Congress resisted the president's initiatives and passed laws, notably the Taiwan Relations Act (TRA), that tied the hands of the administration on Taiwan and other issues.[42]

The Taiwan Relations Act was passed by Congress in March 1979 and signed by President Carter on April 10, 1979. The initial draft of the legislation was proposed by the Carter administration to govern US relations with Taiwan once official US ties were ended in 1979. Congress rewrote the legislation, adding or strengthening provisions on US arms sales, economic relations, human rights, congressional oversight, and opposition to threats and use of force. Treating Taiwan as a separate entity that would continue to receive US military and other support, the law appeared to contradict the US stance in the US-PRC communiqué of 1978 establishing official US-PRC relations. Subsequently, Chinese and Taiwan officials and their supporters in the United States competed to incline US policy toward the commitments in the US-PRC communiqué or the commitments in the TRA. US policy usually supported both, though it sometimes seemed more supportive of one set of commitments than the other.[43]

Running against President Carter in 1980, California Governor Ronald Reagan criticized Carter's handling of Taiwan. Asserting for a time that he would restore official relations with Taipei, Reagan later backed away from this stance but still claimed he would base his policy on the Taiwan Relations Act. The Chinese government put heavy pressure on the Reagan administration, threatening serious deterioration in relations over various issues but especially continuing US arms sales to Taiwan.[44]

Viewing close China-US relations as a key element in US strategy against the Soviet Union, Secretary of State Alexander Haig led those in the Reagan administration who favored maintaining close China-US relations and opposed US arms sales to Taiwan that might provoke China. For a year and a half, Haig and his supporters were successful in leading US efforts to accommodate PRC concerns over Taiwan, especially regarding US arms sales to the ROC, in the interest of fostering closer US-China cooperation against the Soviet Union. The United States ultimately signed with China the August 17, 1982, communiqué. In the communiqué, the United States agreed gradually to diminish arms sales, and China agreed it would seek peaceful reunification of Taiwan with the mainland. Subsequent developments showed that the vague agreement was subject to varying interpretations. President Reagan registered private reservations about the agreement, and his administration also took steps to reassure Taiwan's leader of continued US support.[45]

Looking back at the first decade of opening and developing US-China contacts leading to the normalization of relations, prevailing assessments follow a pattern that seems consistent with the perspective of realism in IR theory. They show a strong tendency on the part of US leaders to focus on relations with China as the key element in a new US approach to East Asian and world affairs. The war in Vietnam, the growing challenge of an expanding Soviet Union, the seeming decline in US power and influence in East Asian and world affairs, and major US internal disruptions and weaknesses seemed to support emphasis on a new US approach to China with important benefits for US foreign policy and other interests. US leadership attention focused on doing what was needed to advance the new China relationship and gave secondary attention to long-standing US allies and other close relationships in East Asia or manipulated them in ways that would accord with the China-first emphasis in US policy. Emblematic of this trend, Nixon's surprise announcement in July 1971 that he would visit China was so shocking and disturbing to the long-standing and more conservative China policy of the government of Prime Minister Eisaku Sato of Japan that it brought down the Japanese government. Available scholarship shows that Nixon deliberately withheld information of the American shift so he could "stick it to Japan" and show US frustration with Japan's trade and economic policies working against US interests.[46]

The US emphasis on China came with significant costs for the United States and US interests, though scholarship tends to depict the benefits of the US approach as justifying the costs.[47] Notably, US leaders came to overestimate the power, influence, and utility of China in assisting US efforts to withdraw from Vietnam and to shore up international opposition to Soviet expansion. By so doing, they gave advantage to China in negotiations over contentious US-China issues regarding Taiwan and other disputes. Seeking sometimes unattainable advantages from improved relations with China, US leaders sacrificed relations with an ally, Taiwan, and treated relations with Japan and other Asian allies and associates in ways that subordinated those relations to US interests in improving relations with China. They also sacrificed attention to those US values and interests in Asian and world affairs that were inconsistent with a pragmatic pursuit of better ties with China.

The elitist approach of US leaders followed a pattern of secret diplomacy and deal making that undermined the US administration's credibility with the Congress and significant segments of the US media and public opinion. It also undermined the constitutionally mandated shared powers the executive and legislative branches hold in the conduct of US foreign policy. This experience established an atmosphere of suspicion and cynicism in American domestic politics over China policy and set the stage for often bitter and debilitating fights in US domestic politics over China policy in ensuing years that on balance are seen not to serve the overall national interests of the United States.[48]

The Pan-Asian Approach of George Shultz and Chinese Accommodation

Amid continued strong Chinese pressure tactics on a wide range of US-China disputes, US policy shifted with Haig's resignation in 1982 and the appointment of George Shultz as secretary of state. Reagan administration officers who were at odds with Haig's emphasis on the need for a solicitous US approach to China came to the fore. They were led by Paul Wolfowitz, who was chosen by Shultz as assistant secretary of state for East Asian affairs; Richard Armitage, the senior Defense Department officer managing relations with China and East Asia; and Gaston Sigur, the senior National Security Council staff aide on Asian affairs and later assistant secretary of state for East Asian affairs. While officers who had backed Haig's pro-China slant were transferred from authority over China policy, the new US leadership contingent with responsibility for East Asian affairs shifted US policy toward a less solicitous and accommodating stance toward China, while giving much higher priority to US relations with Japan, as well as other US allies and friends in East Asia. There was less emphasis on China's strategic importance to the United States in American competition with the Soviet Union, and there was less concern among US policy makers about China possibly downgrading relations over Taiwan and other disputes.[49]

The scholarship on the US opening to China that began in the Nixon administration, reviewed above, focuses on powerful strategic and domestic imperatives that drove the United States and China to cooperate in a pragmatic search for advantage for their respective national and leadership interests. It underlines the primacy of China in American foreign policy in Asia while relations with Japan and other East Asian allies and friends remained secondary and were sometimes viewed as declining assets or liabilities.[50]

Some scholars, often using a cost-benefit analysis seen in the realist school of thought, discern an important shift in US strategy toward China and in East Asia more broadly beginning in 1982.[51] The reevaluation of US policy toward China under Secretary of State Shultz is seen to bring to power officials who opposed the high priority on China in US strategy toward East Asia and the world, and who gave much greater importance to US relations with Japan and other US allies in securing US interests amid prevailing conditions. The reevaluation on the whole is depicted as working to the advantage of the United States. It notably is seen to have added dimensions related to a changing balance of forces affecting Chinese security and other interests in Asian and world affairs, which prompted heretofore demanding Chinese leaders to reduce pressures on the United States for concessions on Taiwan and other disputed issues. The changes in Chinese policy helped open the way for several years of comparatively smooth US-China relations after a period of considerable discord in the late 1970s and early 1980s.

Other scholars also employ cost-benefit assessments, which are seen in the realist school of thought to explain the improvement in US-China relations at the time through analyses focused on the dynamics of US-China relations.[52] They discern US compromises and accommodations in negotiations and relations with China that assuaged Chinese demands and met Chinese interests over Taiwan and other issues. They tend to avoid analysis of how any shift in emphasis in US policy away from a focus on China and toward a greater emphasis on Japan and the East Asian region might have altered Chinese calculations and the overall dynamic in US interaction with China.

The analysis in the assessment detailed below supports the former view. It shows that the Chinese leaders grudgingly adjusted to the new US stance, viewing their interests best served by less pressure and more positive initiatives to the Reagan administration, seen especially in their warm welcome for the US president on his visit to China in 1984. Cooperative Chinese relations with the United States were critically important to the Chinese leadership in maintaining Chinese security in the face of continuing pressure from the Soviet Union and in sustaining the flow of aid, investment, and trade essential to the economic development and modernization underway in China—the linchpin of the Chinese Communist leadership's plans for sustaining its rule in China. Meanwhile, the Reagan leadership learned not to confront important Chinese interests over issues like Taiwan in overt and egregious ways, seeking to continue US military and other support for Taiwan in ways less likely to provoke strong Chinese reaction. Thus, the accommodations that characterized US-China relations in Reagan's second term in office were mutual, but they involved significant Chinese adjustments and changes influenced by the new posture toward China undertaken by Secretary of State Shultz and his colleagues.

In this author's assessment, the scholarship that portrays the improvement in US-China relations at that time as largely based on the dynamics of US-China relations seems too narrowly focused. In this scholarship, the United States is seen to make compromises in ways that accommodate Chinese interests and thus allow for smoother US-China relations. By limiting the focus to the dynamics of US-China ties, this scholarship seems to miss the importance of the shift in US emphasis during the tenure of George Shultz. Overall, that shift seems to have significantly enhanced US power and leverage over China in negotiations over Taiwan and other disputes and compelled China to make concessions on its part in order to ensure a positive relationship with the United States advantageous to Chinese interests. This changed dynamic, with the United States in a more commanding position vis-à-vis China, also was much more acceptable to congressional members, media, and others in US politics that had been alienated by the secrecy and perceived excessive US deference to China in the previous decade. It made executive-congressional relations over China policy much smoother than in the previous six years.

China's Shifting Strategic Calculus and the Importance of the United States

The significance of the shifts in American policy toward China and Asia undertaken during the tenure of Secretary Shultz and under the direction of such influential US officials as Wolfowitz, Armitage, and Sigur are shown below to be important for China's broader international calculations, influencing its approach toward the United States. Chinese foreign policy was strongly influenced by Chinese assessments in line with realist IR theory of the relative power and influence of the Soviet Union and the United States and the effects these had on key Chinese interests of security and development. Throughout much of the 1970s, China had been more vocal than the United States in warning of the dangers of expansion by the Soviet Union, seen as the greatest threat to China's security and integrity. Chinese officials and commentary depicted Soviet efforts to contain China in Asia through its military buildup and advanced nuclear ballistic missile deployments along the Sino-Soviet border, its deployments of mobile mechanized divisions in Mongolia, its stepped-up naval activity in the western Pacific along the China coast, its military presence in Vietnam, including active use of formerly US naval and air base facilities, and its ever-closer military relationship with India and growing involvement with and eventual invasion of Afghanistan. These Soviet actions were seen as part of a wider expansion of Soviet power and influence that China judged as needing to be countered by a united international front including China and led by the United States. [53]

For much of the 1970s, particularly after the resignation of President Nixon, Chinese officials and commentary saw the United States vacillate between a tough line toward the USSR and an approach seeking détente and accommodation with Moscow. Concern over US resolve toward Moscow saw China criticize Secretary of State Henry Kissinger for being too soft toward Moscow during the Ford administration, favoring instead the harder line advocated by Defense Secretary James Schlesinger. Carter administration officials like UN envoy Andrew Young, who took a moderate view toward Soviet-backed Cuban troop deployments and other Soviet expansion in Africa, were roundly criticized in Chinese media. More cautious official commentary registered reservations about Secretary of State Cyrus Vance's approach in seeking arms limitation talks with Moscow, while Chinese officials and commentary registered approval of National Security Advisor Brzezinski's tough anti-Soviet stance. [54]

Over time, and especially after the Soviet invasion of Afghanistan in late 1979, Chinese leaders began to recalculate the balance of forces affecting their interests and their respective approaches to the Soviet Union and the United States. The previous perceived danger that the United States would "appease" the Soviet Union and thereby allow Moscow to direct its pressure against China now appeared remote. Carter's last year in office and Reagan's initial stance toward the USSR saw a large increase in US defense spending and military preparations. Closely allied with the United States, European powers and Japan also were building forces and taking firm positions against the USSR. Meanwhile, increased complications and weaknesses affecting the power of the Soviet Union included problems of leadership succession, economic sustainability, and tensions in Poland and elsewhere in the Warsaw Pact. Faced with such adverse circumstances prior to his death in 1982, Brezhnev reached out with positive initiatives toward China, attempting to improve relations. [55]

Against this background, Chinese officials saw an ability to exert a freer hand in foreign affairs and to position China in a stance less aligned with the United States. The priority to stay close to the United States in order to encourage resolute US positions against Soviet expansion was no longer as important as in the recent past. Also, there were new opportunities to negotiate with Soviet leaders calling for talks. Beijing moved by 1981 to a posture more independent of the United States and less hostile toward the USSR. China's new "independent foreign policy" also featured a revival of Chinese relations with developing countries and in the international communist movement, which had been neglected in favor of emphasis on the anti-Soviet front in the 1970s.[56]

However, the shift in Chinese policy away from the United States and somewhat closer to the Soviet Union did not work very well. Chinese leaders continued to speak of their new independent foreign policy approach, but they seemed to change their international calculations based on perceptions of shifts in the international balance of power affecting China. By 1983, Chinese leaders showed increasing concern about the stability of the nation's surroundings in Asia at a time of unrelenting buildup of Soviet military and political pressure along China's periphery, and of serious and possibly prolonged decline in relations with the United States. They decided that the foreign policy tactics of the previous two years, designed to distance China from the policies of the United States and to moderate and improve Chinese relations with the Soviet Union, were less likely to safeguard the important Chinese security and development concerns affected by the stability of the Asian environment.[57]

The Chinese leaders appeared to recognize in particular that Beijing would have to stop its pullback from the United States for fear of jeopardizing this link, so important for maintaining its security and development interests in the face of persistent Soviet pressure in Asia. Thus, in 1983 Beijing began to retreat from some of the tactical changes made the previous two years under the rubric of an independent approach to foreign affairs. The result was a substantial reduction in Chinese pressure on the United States over Taiwan and other issues; increased Chinese interest and flexibility in dealing with the Reagan administration and other Western countries across a broad range of economic, political, and security issues; and heightened Sino-Soviet antipathy. Beijing still attempted to nurture whenever possible the increased influence it had garnered by means of its independent posture among developing countries and the international communist movement, but it increasingly sided with the West against the USSR in order to secure basic strategic and economic interests.[58]

A key element in China's decision to change tactics toward the United States was an altered view of the likely course of Sino-American-Soviet relations over the next several years. When China began its more independent approach to foreign affairs and its concurrent harder line toward the United States in 1981–82, it had hoped to elicit a more forthcoming US attitude toward issues sensitive to Chinese interests, notably Taiwan. Beijing probably judged that there could be serious risks of alienating the United States, which had provided an implicit but vital counterweight serving Chinese security interests against the USSR for more than a decade and was assisting more recent Chinese economic development concerns. But the Chinese seemed to have assessed that their room to maneuver had been increased because

- The United States had reasserted a balance in East-West relations likely to lead to a continued major check on possible Soviet expansion. Chinese worries about US "appeasement" of the USSR seemed a thing of the past.
- The Soviet ability to pressure China had appeared to be at least temporarily blocked by US power, the determination of various US allies to thwart Soviet expansion, and Soviet domestic and international problems. China added to Soviet difficulties by cooperating with the United States in clandestine operations supporting fighters resisting the Soviet occupation of Afghanistan.
- At least some important US leaders, notably Secretary of State Alexander Haig and his subordinates in the State Department, continued to consider preserving and developing good US relations with China as a critically important element in US efforts to confront and contain Soviet expansion.[59]

By mid-1983 China saw these calculations upset. In particular, the United States under Secretary of State Shultz adopted a new posture that was seen to publicly downgrade China's strategic importance. The adjustment in the US position occurred after the resignation of Haig, perhaps the strongest advocate in the Reagan administration of sustaining good relations with China as an important strategic means to counter the USSR. Secretary Shultz and such subordinates as Paul Wolfowitz were less identified with this approach. Shultz held a series of meetings with government and nongovernmental Asian specialists in Washington in early 1983 to review US Asian policy in general and policy toward China in particular. The results of the reassessment—implicitly but clearly downgrading China's importance to the United States—were reflected in speeches by Shultz and Wolfowitz later in the year.[60]

US planners now appeared to judge that efforts to improve relations with China were less important than in the recent past because

- China seemed less likely to cooperate further with the United States (e.g., through military sales or security cooperation against the Soviet Union at a time when the PRC had publicly distanced itself from the United States and had reopened talks on normalization with the USSR).

- At the same time, China's continued preoccupation with pragmatic economic modernization and internal development made it appear unlikely that the PRC would revert to a highly disruptive position in East Asia that would adversely affect US interests in the stability of the region.
- China's demands on Taiwan and a wide variety of other bilateral disputes, and the accompanying threats to downgrade US-China relations if its demands were not met, seemed open-ended and excessive.
- US ability to deal militarily and politically with the USSR from a position of greater strength had improved, particularly as a result of the large-scale Reagan administration military budget increases and perceived serious internal and international difficulties of the USSR.
- US allies, for the first time in years, were working more closely with Washington in dealing with the Soviet military threat. This was notably true in Asia, where Prime Minister Yasuhiro Nakasone took positions and initiatives underlining common Japanese-US concerns against the Soviet danger, setting the foundation for the close "Ron-Yasu" relationship between the US and Japanese leaders.
- Japan and US allies and friends in Southeast Asia—unlike China—appeared to be more important to the United States in protecting against what was seen as the primary US strategic concern in the region—safeguarding air and sea access to East Asia, the Indian Ocean, and the Persian Gulf from Soviet attack. China appeared less important in dealing with this perceived Soviet danger.[61]

Western press reports quoting authoritative sources in Washington alerted China to the implications of this shift in the US approach for PRC interests. In effect, the shift seemed to mean that Chinese ability to exploit US interest in strategic relations with China against the Soviet Union was reduced, as was US interest in avoiding disruptions caused by China and other negative consequences that flowed from a downgrading of China's relations with the United States. Chinese ability to use these facets in order to compel the United States to meet Chinese demands on Taiwan and other questions seemed less than in the recent past. Underlining these trends for China was the continued unwillingness of the United States throughout this period to accommodate high-level PRC pressure over Taiwan, the asylum case of Chinese tennis player Hu Na, the Chinese representation issue in the Asian Development Bank, and other questions. The Reagan administration publicly averred that US policy would remain constant whether or not Beijing decided to retaliate, or threatened to downgrade relations by withdrawing its ambassador from Washington, or some other action.[62]

Moreover, Chinese commentary and discussions with Chinese officials suggested that Beijing perceived its leverage in the United States to have diminished at the time. Chinese media duly noted the strong revival in the US economy in 1983 and the positive political implications this had for President Reagan's reelection campaign. China also had to be aware, through contacts with leading Democrats, notably House of Representatives Speaker Tip O'Neill, who visited China that same year, that Beijing could expect little change in US policy toward Taiwan under a Democratic administration. As 1983 wore on, the Chinese saw what for them was an alarming rise in the influence of US advocates of self-determination for Taiwan among liberal Democrats. In particular, Senator Claiborne Pell took the lead in gaining passage of a controversial resolution in the Senate Foreign Relations Committee that endorsed, among other things, the principle of self-determination for Taiwan—anathema to Beijing.[63]

Meanwhile, although Sino-Soviet trade, cultural, and technical contacts were increasing, Beijing saw few signs of Soviet willingness to compromise on basic political and security issues during vice-ministerial talks on normalizing Sino-Soviet relations that began in October 1982. And the Soviet military buildup in Asia—including the deployment of highly accurate SS-20 intermediate-range ballistic missiles—continued.[64]

In short, if Beijing continued its demands and harder line against the United States of the previous two years, pressed the United States on various issues, and risked downgrading relations, it faced the prospect of a period of prolonged decline in Sino-American relations—possibly lasting until the end of Reagan's second presidential term. This decline brought the risk of cutting off the implicit but vitally important Chinese strategic understanding with the United States in the face of a prolonged danger to China posed by the USSR.

The Chinese also recognized that a substantial decline in Chinese relations with the United States would have undercut their already limited leverage with Moscow; it probably would have reduced Soviet interest in accommodating China in order to preclude closer US-China security ties or collaboration against the USSR. It also would have run the risk of upsetting China's ability to gain greater access not only to US markets and financial and technical expertise but also to those of other important capitalist countries. Now that the Chinese economy was successfully emerging from some retrenchments and adjustments undertaken in 1981–82, the Western economic connection seemed more important to PRC planners. Yet many US allies and friends, especially Japan, were more reluctant to undertake heavy economic involvement in China at a time of uncertain US-China political relations. The United States also exerted strong influence in international financial institutions that were expected to be the source of several billions of dollars of much-needed aid for China in the 1980s.

China also had to calculate as well that a serious decline in US-China relations would likely result in a concurrent increase in US-Taiwan relations. As a result, Beijing's chances of using Taiwan's isolation from the United States to prompt Taipei to move toward reunification in accord with PRC interests would be set back seriously.

The deliberations of Chinese policy makers regarding maneuvers between the United States and the Soviet Union during this period remain shrouded in secrecy. Given the upswing in Chinese public as well as private pressure against the United States during the early years of the Reagan administration over Taiwan arms sales and many other areas of dispute, any backing away from a firm line toward the United States on Taiwan and other sensitive issues almost certainly represented a difficult compromise for those leaders who had pushed this approach in 1981–82.

Unlike in the case of the United States, there was no concurrent major change in China's foreign affairs leadership, which ultimately depended on the attentive direction of strong-man ruler Deng Xiaoping. Deng appeared to have a freer hand to shift policy in foreign affairs than in the complicated mix of domestic politics at the time. Thus, for example, he was able to decide to shelve the sensitive territorial dispute of the Diaoyu/Senkaku Islands during negotiations with Japan over a peace treaty in 1978 and he allowed the agreement on normalization of relations with the United States to go forward that year despite the US intention to continue arms sales to Taiwan. Deng endorsed the most sensitive clandestine Chinese arms sale on record—the transfer of more than thirty intermediate-range nuclear-capable ballistic missiles to Saudi Arabia in the early 1980s, at a time when China also was transferring nuclear weapons technology and assistance that allowed Pakistan to develop and test a credible nuclear deterrent in the 1990s. Against this background, Deng seemed to have the domestic political standing to carry out the adjustment and moderation in China's approach to the United States without serious negative implications. No matter what might have taken place behind the scenes in Chinese decision making with regard to policy toward the United States and the Soviet Union at the time, Chinese officials did in fact pull back from pressing American leaders. The routine harangues on Taiwan and other differences that greeted senior Reagan administration visitors on the initial meetings in Beijing dropped off. Chinese leaders worked harder to curry favor with President Reagan and his associates.[65]

Moderation toward the United States

Appearing anxious to moderate past demands and improve relations with the United States, the Chinese responded positively to the latest in a series of Reagan administration efforts to ease technology transfer restrictions—announced by Commerce Secretary Malcolm Baldridge during a trip to China in May 1983. The Chinese followed up by agreeing to schedule the long-delayed visit by Secretary of Defense Caspar Weinberger in September, and to exchange visits by Premier Zhao Ziyang, a Chinese senior leader, and President Reagan at the turn of the year. Not to appear too anxious to improve relations with China, Reagan administration officials were successful in getting Premier Zhao Ziyang to visit Washington for a summit in January 1984, before the US president would agree to go to China later that year.

Beijing media attempted to portray these moves as Chinese responses to US concessions and as consistent with China's avowed "independent" approach in foreign affairs and its firm stance on US-China differences over Taiwan and other issues. But as time went on, it became clear just how much Beijing was prepared to moderate past public demands and threats of retaliation over Taiwan and other issues for the sake of consolidating Sino-American political, economic, and security ties.[66]

- In 1981 Beijing had publicly disavowed any interest in military purchases from the United States until the United States satisfied China's position on the sale of arms to Taiwan. It continued to note that it was dissatisfied with US arms transfers to Taiwan after the August 1982 communiqué, which continued at a pace of more than $700 million a year; but it now was willing to negotiate with the United States over Chinese purchases of US military equipment.
- Beijing muffled previous demands that the United States alter its position regarding Taiwan's continued membership in the Asian Development Bank.
- China reduced criticism of official and unofficial US contacts with Taiwan counterparts. It notably avoided criticism of US officials being present at Taipei-sponsored functions in Washington. Beijing was even willing to turn a blind eye to the almost thirty members of Congress who traveled to Taiwan in various delegations in January 1984—coincident with Zhao Ziyang's trip to Washington. It even welcomed some of the members who traveled on to the mainland after visiting Taiwan.
- Beijing allowed Northwest Airlines to open service to China in 1984, even though the airline still served Taiwan. This was in marked contrast with the authoritative and negative Chinese position adopted in 1983 in response to Pan American World Airways' decision to reenter the Taiwan market while also serving the mainland.
- China reduced complaints about the slowness of US transfers of technology to China and about the continued inability of the administration to successfully push through legislative changes that would have allowed the Chinese to receive American assistance.[67]

China's greatest compromise was to give a warm welcome to President Reagan, despite his continued avowed determination to maintain close US ties with "old friends" on Taiwan. Visits by Speaker O'Neill and others made clear to China the importance of the China visit in serving to assist the US president's reelection bid in the fall. Chinese leaders also understood that the president was unlikely to accommodate China interests over Taiwan and some other sensitive issues during the visit. Indeed, Chinese reportage made clear that there was no change in the president's position on the Taiwan issue during the visit. Thus it appears that the best the Chinese hoped for was to try to consolidate US-PRC relations in order to secure broader strategic and economic interests, while possibly expecting that such a closer relationship over time would reduce the president's firm position on Taiwan and other bilateral disputes.

The Reagan administration, meanwhile, attempted to add impetus to the relationship by accommodating Chinese concerns through the avoidance of strong rhetorical support for Taiwan that in the past had so inflamed US-PRC tensions, and by moving ahead on military and technology transfers to the PRC. Nevertheless, when the US-China nuclear cooperation agreement, which had been initialed during the president's visit, became stalled because of opposition from nonproliferation advocates in the United States who were concerned about reports of China's support for Pakistan's nuclear weapons program, China went along with administration explanations of their inability to reverse the adverse situation with only minor complaint.[68]

In short, by mid-1984 it appeared that, at a minimum, Beijing was determined to further strengthen military and economic ties with the United States and to soft-pedal bilateral differences that had been stressed earlier in the decade. On the question of Taiwan, Beijing retreated to a position that asked for US adherence to the joint communiqué and accelerated reductions of US arms sales to Taiwan, but Chinese leaders were not prepared to make a significant issue of what they saw as US noncompliance unless they were seriously provoked. This meant giving lower priority to Chinese complaints about President Reagan's interpretations of the communiqué at odds with China's position and lower priority to Chinese complaints over the US president's continued strong determination to support US interests in helping the defense of Taiwan. The new Chinese position also meant downplaying Chinese criticism of methods used by the United States to calculate the value of arms sales to Taiwan at high levels, thereby allowing more than a half billion dollars of US sales to the island's armed forces for years to come. It also meant that China chose not to contest vigorously the ultimately successful maneuvers used by Taiwan and US defense manufacturers that allowed the United States to support, through commercial transfers of equipment, technology, and expertise, the development of a new group of more than one hundred new jet fighters, the so-called indigenous fighter aircraft, for the Taiwan air force.[69]

Continued Sino-Soviet Differences

China's incentive to accommodate the United States was reinforced by Beijing's somber view of Sino-Soviet relations. China appeared disappointed with its inability to elicit substantial Soviet concessions—or even a slowing in the pace of Soviet military expansion in Asia—during the brief administration of Yuri Andropov (d. 1984). Beijing saw the succeeding government of Konstantin Chernenko (d. 1985) as even more rigid and uncompromising. In response, China hardened its line and highlighted public complaints against Soviet pressure and intimidation—an approach that had the added benefit of broadening common ground between China and the West, especially the strongly anti-Soviet Reagan administration.[70]

The Sino-Soviet vice-ministerial talks on normalizing relations were revived in October 1982 following their cancellation as a result of the Soviet invasion of Afghanistan in late 1979. These talks were unable to bridge a major gap between the positions of the two sides on basic security and political issues. Beijing stuck to its preconditions for improved Sino-Soviet relations involving withdrawal of Soviet forces from along the Sino-Soviet border and from Mongolia (later China added specific reference to Soviet SS-20 missiles targeted against China), an end to Soviet support for Vietnam's military occupation of Cambodia, and withdrawal of Soviet forces from Afghanistan.[71]

In part to get around this roadblock, a second forum of vice-foreign-ministerial discussions began in September 1983. The discussions covered each side's views of recent developments in the Middle East, Central America, the Indian Ocean, Afghanistan, and Indochina; concerns over arms control, including the deployment of SS-20 missiles in Asia; and other questions. No agreement was noted.

Progress in both sets of talks came only in secondary areas of trade, technology transfers, and educational and cultural exchanges. Both sides attempted to give added impetus to progress in these areas coincident with the exchange of high-level Sino-American visits in early 1984. In particular, Moscow proposed and Beijing accepted a visit to China by First Deputy Prime Minister Ivan Arkhipov. The visit was timed to occur just after President Reagan's departure from China in early May 1984. It was postponed on account of rising Sino-Soviet frictions.

Chernenko's leadership went out of its way to publicize strong support for Mongolia and Vietnam against China, and underlined Soviet unwillingness to make compromises with China at the expense of third countries. Beijing also saw Moscow as resorting to stronger military means in both

Europe and Asia in order to assert Soviet power and determination against China and others. In February and March, the Soviet Union deployed two of its three aircraft carriers to the western Pacific; one passed near China in late February, on its way to Vladivostok. And in March, the USSR used an aircraft carrier task force to support its first joint amphibious exercise with Vietnam, which was conducted fairly close to China and near the Vietnamese port city of Haiphong. This followed the reported stationing of several Soviet medium-range bombers at Cam Ranh Bay, Vietnam, in late 1983—the first time Soviet forces were reported to be stationed outside areas contiguous with the USSR.

Meanwhile, the Chinese escalated their artillery barrages and other military pressure against the Vietnamese—taking their strongest action precisely at the time of President Reagan's visit to China in late April and early May 1984. Beijing at the same time escalated charges regarding the Soviet threat to Chinese security, especially via Vietnam, and attempted to establish publicly an identity of interests with both Japanese Prime Minister Nakasone, during a visit to China in March, and President Reagan in April–May, on the basis of opposition to Soviet expansion in Asia. The result was the most serious downturn in Sino-Soviet relations since the Soviet invasion of Afghanistan in late 1979.

THE SUCCESS OF THE US–PAN-ASIAN APPROACH TO CHINA

In sum, the record of developments in China's approach toward and relations with the United States and the Soviet Union in 1983 and 1984 show that the pan-Asian approach adopted by Secretary of State George Shultz and the senior officials responsible for Asian affairs during this period of the Reagan administration worked effectively in support of American interests in policy toward China in several important ways. It notably played into an array of concerns and uncertainties in Chinese foreign policy calculations and interests, causing the Chinese leaders to shift to a more accommodating posture toward the United States—a posture that played down issues that in the recent past had threatened, according to Chinese officials, to force China to take steps to downgrade US-China relations. US officials made sure their Chinese counterparts understood that the United States was no longer as anxious, as evident in the first decade of Sino-American rapprochement and normalization, to seek China's favor in improving Sino-American relations as a source of leverage against Moscow. The United States was increasingly confident in its strategic position vis-à-vis the Soviet Union, and had begun a process to roll back the gains the Soviets had made in the previous decade in various parts of the developing world. It was China that appeared to face greater difficulties posed by Soviet military buildup and expansion. China needed the US relationship as a counterweight to this Soviet posture, and it increasingly needed a good relationship with the United States to allow for smooth and advantageous Chinese economic interchange with the developed countries of the West and Japan and the international financial institutions they controlled.

Under the circumstances, the Chinese leaders grudgingly adjusted to the new US stance, viewing their interests best served by less pressure and more positive overtures to the Reagan administration, seen notably in their warm welcome for the US president on his visit to China in 1984. As noted above, some scholarship portrays the improvement in US-China relations at the time largely through dynamics in US-China relations. In general, the United States is seen to make compromises in ways that accommodate Chinese interests and thus allow for smoother US-China relations. By limiting the focus to the dynamics of US-China ties, this scholarship seems to miss the importance of the shift in US emphasis during the tenure of George Shultz. Overall, that shift seems to have significantly enhanced US power and leverage over China in negotiations over Taiwan and other disputes and compelled China to make concessions in order to ensure a positive relationship with the United States advantageous to Chinese interests. This changed dynamic, with the United States in a more commanding position vis-à-vis China, was much more acceptable to congressional members, media, and others in US politics that had been alienated by the secrecy and perceived excessive US deference to China in the previous decade. It set the stage for relatively smooth US domestic politics over China policy for the remainder of the Reagan administration.

Chapter Five

Tiananmen, Taiwan, and Post–Cold War Realities, 1989–2000

COLLAPSE OF US POLICY CONSENSUS AND EMERGING DOMESTIC DEBATE ON CHINA

Unexpected mass demonstrations centered in Beijing's Tiananmen Square and other Chinese cities in spring 1989 represented the most serious challenge to China's post-Mao leadership. Deng Xiaoping was decisive in resolving Chinese leadership differences in favor of hard-liners who supported a violent crackdown on the demonstrators and broader suppression of political dissent that began with the bloody attack on Tiananmen Square on June 4, 1989. Reform-minded leaders were purged and punished. [1]

Anticipating shock over and disapproval of the Tiananmen crackdown from the United States and the West, Deng nonetheless argued that the negative reaction would have few prolonged adverse consequences for China. The Chinese leader failed to anticipate the breadth and depth of US disapproval that would profoundly influence US policy into the twenty-first century. American public opinion of China's government dropped sharply. It has never recovered the positive views of the Chinese government that prevailed in the years prior to Tiananmen and has reflected a wary and negative view of China on the part of a majority of Americans almost thirty years later. The US media switched coverage and opinion of China, portraying the policies and practices of the Chinese rulers in a much more critical light than in the years leading up to Tiananmen. Almost thirty years later, American and Chinese specialists have continued to see US and Western media remaining focused on the negative in reporting and commentary that deals with the

Chinese government. US leaders were shocked by the brutal display of power by China's authoritarian leaders. Expectations of rapid Chinese political reform dropped; they were replaced by outward hostility at first, followed by often wary pragmatism about the need for greater US engagement with the Chinese government as it rose in prominence in Asian and world affairs. The US engagement was tempered by a private suspicion of the longer-term intentions of the Chinese rulers, which remained a prominent feature of US expectations of China well into the next century.[2]

The negative impact of the Tiananmen crackdown on the American approach to China was compounded by the unforeseen and dramatic collapse of communist regimes in the Soviet bloc and other areas, leading to the demise of the Soviet Union in 1991. These developments undermined the perceived need for the United States to cooperate pragmatically with China despite its brutal dictatorship, on account of a US strategic need for international support against the Soviet Union. The Soviet collapse also destroyed the strategic focus of American foreign policy during the Cold War. The ability of the US president to use Cold War imperatives to override pluralistic US domestic interests seeking to influence American foreign policy declined. A variety of existing and emerging American interest groups focused on China's authoritarian regime in strongly negative ways, endeavoring to push US policy toward a harder line against China. Meanwhile, Taiwan's authoritarian government at that time was moving steadily to promote democratic policies and practices, marking a sharp contrast to the harsh political regime in mainland China and greatly enhancing Taiwan's popularity and support in the United States.[3]

Taken together, these circumstances generally placed the initiative in US-China relations with US leaders and broader forces in the United States. Chinese leaders at first focused on maintaining internal stability as they maneuvered to sustain workable economic relations with the United States and other developed countries while rebuffing major US and other Western-led initiatives that infringed on Chinese internal political control or territorial and sovereignty issues involving Taiwan, Tibet, and Hong Kong. Leadership debate about how open China should be to promoting economic reform at home and how welcoming China should be to economic interchange with the West as it consolidated authoritarian rule at home appeared to be resolved following Deng Xiaoping's tour of southern China in 1992. Deng urged continued rigorous economic reform and opening to the benefits of foreign trade, investments, and technology transfer. Beginning in 1993, as the Chinese government presided over strong economic growth, and the US and other international attention that came with it, Chinese leaders reflected more confidence as they dealt with US pressures for change. However, the Chinese leaders generally eschewed direct confrontation that would endanger the critically important economic relations with the United States unless China was provoked by US, Taiwanese, or other actions.[4]

US policy in the decade after Tiananmen worked explicitly against the central interest of the Chinese leadership to sustain the rule of the Communist Party in China (CCP). Even when US government leaders emphasized a pragmatic policy of engagement with China's leaders, they often used rationales that the engagement would lead to the demise of the authoritarian CCP rule. US policy also increased support for Taiwan, for the interests of the Dalai Lama in Tibet, and for forces in Hong Kong seen as critical of Chinese government goals and threatening to the overall territorial integrity and sovereignty of China. The United States also was in the lead in criticizing a range of Chinese foreign policies; it was seen to be strengthening strategic and other pressures on China through the reinforcement of US military relations with Japan and other allies and the improvement of American military as well as political and economic relations with other nations around China's periphery. In response, Chinese leaders and broader public opinion saw US policy and intentions in a negative way.[5]

Over time, years of pragmatic Sino-American engagement policies and generally positive treatment of the United States in state-controlled Chinese media in the first decade of the twenty-first century resulted in an improvement in Chinese public opinion about the United States. Privately, Chinese leaders were reported to remain deeply wary and suspicious of the policies and intentions of the United States. Strong public Chinese antipathy toward the United States and US policy and practice toward China also showed from time to time, over sensitive issues or during times of crisis in US-China relations.[6]

Although American leaders held the initiative in relations with China during the years after the Tiananmen incident, they had a hard time creating and implementing an effective and integrated policy. Coherent US policy toward China proved elusive in the midst of contentious American domestic debate over China policy during the 1990s. That debate was not stilled until the September 11, 2001, terrorist attack on America muffled continued US concerns over China amid an overwhelming American concern to deal with the immediate, serious, and broad consequences of the global war on terrorism.[7]

In the aftermath of Tiananmen, President George H. W. Bush tried to keep China policy under his control and to move US relations with China in directions he deemed constructive. Yet he and his administration were repeatedly criticized by Congress, the media, and organized groups with differing interests in policy toward the PRC but with an agreed emphasis on a harder US approach to China. In this atmosphere, Bush's more pragmatic approach to China became a distinct liability for the president, notably during his failed reelection campaign in 1992.[8]

President Bill Clinton entered office on an election platform critical of the "butchers of Beijing." His administration developed a clear stance linking Chinese behavior regarding human rights issues with US trade benefits to China. Majorities in Congress and many nongovernmental groups and the media favored this position. However, the policy came under increasing pressure from other groups and their allies in both Congress and the administration who were strongly concerned with US business interests in relation to China's rising market. The opposition prompted President Clinton to end the policy of linkage in May 1994.[9]

The president's decision did not end the battle for influence over China policy on the part of competing US interest groups and their supporters in the Congress and the administration. Pro-Taiwan interests mobilized in early 1995 to change US policy in order to allow the Taiwan president to travel to the United States in a private capacity. After senior US officials assured China that no visa would be granted, President Clinton decided to allow the visit. His reversal triggered a major crisis and military face-off between the United States and China over Taiwan in 1995–96. There were periodic live-fire Chinese military exercises in the Taiwan Strait, including tests of short-range Chinese ballistic missiles, over a period of nine months beginning in mid-1995 and culminating in large exercises coincident with Taiwan's first direct election of its president in March 1996. The US government did little in public reaction to the exercises at first, but by 1996 senior US leaders privately, and eventually publicly, strongly warned Chinese leaders against them. In the end, the United States sent two aircraft carrier battle groups to the Taiwan area to face off against the perceived Chinese military provocations during the Taiwan presidential elections.[10]

Seeking to restore calm and avoid repetition of dangerous crises with China, the Clinton administration accommodated Chinese interests as US policy shifted to a strong emphasis on pragmatic engagement with China, highlighted by US-China summits in Washington and Beijing in 1997 and 1998, respectively. Through often difficult negotiations, the United States and China were able to reach agreement in late 1999, leading to China's entry into the World Trade Organization (WTO). Related to this accord, the Clinton administration secured congressional passage of a law granting China the trading status of Permanent Normal Trade Relations (PNTR) in 2000. The law removed the previous annual legal requirement for the president to publicly notify Congress of his intention to seek most-favored-nation (MFN) status for American trade with China, and for the president's notification to be subject to possible legislation of disapproval by Congress. That legal requirement provided the focus of annual and often raucous congressional debates over the pros and cons of harsher US measures against China in the years after the Tiananmen crackdown.[11]

Clinton's policy shift toward engagement with China met strong opposition in Congress and the media and among nongovernment groups pressing for a harder policy. As for China, the US bombing of the Chinese embassy in Belgrade in May 1999 saw the Chinese government react by directing mass demonstrations that destroyed or severely damaged US diplomatic properties in Beijing and other cities. Beijing leaders also openly debated their continued emphasis on engagement with the United States, eventually coming to the conclusion that shifting to a more confrontational Chinese approach against US "hegemonism" was not in the overall interests of the Chinese administration.[12]

Those seeking to use international relations (IR) theory to understand the complicated dynamics in American policy toward China in the decade after the Tiananmen suppression of 1989 are urged to avoid emphasizing just one theory. Instead, it is important to consider various schools of thought in order to contextualize various determinants and offer a comprehensive view of the complex situation.

Liberalism helps explain the massive disappointment and hostility directed at China's rulers by American elite and public opinion following the crackdown at Tiananmen. In particular, liberalism captures the previous widespread American belief that post-Mao China's movement toward freer-market economic policies and greater engagement with the West would be accompanied by social and political pluralism in line with liberal expectations. Those expectations were grievously undermined by the Tiananmen crackdown, resulting in the negative backlash in US opinion. Meanwhile, while President Clinton's motives remain unclear, he justified his policy reversal in seeking compromise and closer engagement with China after the Taiwan Straits crisis on the assumption that such engagement would lead to social and political pluralism, in line with liberal thinking. US companies keenly interested in the growing China market also justified their support for continuing MFN tariff status for China on the argument that sustaining MFN treatment for China would lead to growing Sino-US economic relations that in turn would result in political pluralism in China, as forecast by liberal theory.

Realism played an important role in the determination of President George H. W. Bush and his senior aides to sustain workable relations with China, as China was seen as a major power and one of increasing international importance. Unfortunately for coherence in US foreign policy, realism also influenced those calling for sanctions and punishment of China after Tiananmen. Many such advocates used the realist argument that the demise of the Soviet Union and other communist states meant that the United States no longer needed China's favor to offset the USSR and its allies. In this view, the reality of power in world affairs saw the US superpower ascendant, with little need to accommodate gross offenses like the Tiananmen suppression.

Constructivism helps explain the massive gap between the American identity and the Chinese identity that developed after Tiananmen. The bloody crackdown against unarmed demonstrators was anathema for most Americans, more than justifying rigorous sanctions and punishments in response. The American response focused directly on the most important priority of the Chinese government: the preservation of CCP rule. To counter the pressure, the Chinese rulers appealed to a well-developed sense of Chinese identity as a people and society of tremendous achievement that, in weakness since the nineteenth century, was subjected to various unfair modes of oppression by arrogant foreign powers. Beijing worked effectively to portray the strident American polemics and sanctions as the latest in a long series of foreign affronts going back to the first Opium War and the beginning of China's gross victimization at the hands of evil foreign powers.

Post–Cold War Imperatives and American Debate over China Policy

Understanding the changes in US policy toward China in the 1990s requires going beyond the Tiananmen crackdown and other immediate issues in US-China relations to assess the implications of the post–Cold War debate in US foreign policy. Because security issues and opposition to Soviet expansion no longer drove US foreign policy, economic interests, democratization abroad, and human rights were among concerns that gained greater prominence in American foreign policy. Various US advocacy groups and institutions interested in these and other foreign policy concerns also showed greater influence in policy making, including policy making with regard to China. Historically, such fluidity and competition among priorities had more often than not been the norm in American foreign policy making. As noted in chapters 2 and 3, Woodrow Wilson and Franklin Roosevelt both set forth comprehensive concepts of a well-integrated US foreign policy, but neither framework lasted long. The requirements of the Cold War were much more effective in establishing rigor and order in US foreign policy priorities. The influence of these requirements in driving US interest in rapprochement and normalization with China was described in chapter 4. By the 1990s, that era was over.

In its place was a changed array of forces influencing American foreign policy in general and policy toward China in particular. There was a shift away from the elitism of the past and toward much greater pluralism. This increased the opportunity for inputs by nongovernmental groups, including lobby groups with interests in foreign policy, notably policy toward China. [13]

The elitist model of American foreign policy making that prevailed through much of the Cold War included the following characteristics:

- Domination of the process by the executive branch, particularly by the White House, the State Department, and the Pentagon.
- Presidential consultation with a bipartisan leadership in Congress and mobilization through them of broad congressional support for the administration's foreign policy.
- Parallel consultations with a relatively small group of elites outside government, some of whom were specialists on the particular issue under consideration and others of whom had a more general interest in foreign policy as a whole.
- Mobilization of public support through major newspapers and television programs, other media outlets, and civic organizations. [14]

This process transformed in much more pluralistic directions and took on quite different characteristics following the 1980s:

- A much greater range of agencies within the executive branch became involved in foreign policy, with the rise of economic agencies (Commerce, Treasury, and US Trade Representative) of particular importance.
- A reallocation of power within the government, moving away from dominance by the executive branch and giving more power to Congress.
- Much greater participation of nongovernmental organizations including lobbying groups, which attempted to shape foreign policy to conform to their interests.
- Much less consensus within Congress and within the broader American public over the direction of US foreign policy.

Among divergent American views about foreign policy in the post–Cold War period were three discernable schools of thought. [15] The first school was in line with realism in IR theory and stressed the relative decline in US power and its implications for US ability to protect its interests abroad. It called for the United States to work harder to preserve important interests while adjusting to limited resources and reduced influence. This school of thought—reflected in the commentary of such leaders as George H. W. Bush, Henry Kissinger, and others—argued that these circumstances required the United States to work closely with traditional allies and associates. In Asia, it saw that not to preserve long-standing good relations with Japan and other allies and friends whose security policies and political-cultural orientations complemented US interests, was inconsistent with US goals. It urged caution in policy toward other regional powers—Russia, China, and India. All three countries were preoccupied with internal development issues and did not appear to want regional instability. All sought closer economic and political relations with the West and with other advancing economies. Washington would be well advised, according to this view, to work closely with these

governments wherever there were common interests. In considering US assets available to influence regional trends, proponents of this view called on
the United States to go slow in reducing its regional military presence. [16]

A second school of thought argued for major cutbacks in US international
activity, including military involvement, and a renewed focus on solving
domestic American problems. Variations of this view were seen in the writings of William Hyland, Patrick Buchanan, and other well-known commentators of the time, and in the political statements of the independent candidate
in the 1992 presidential election, Ross Perot. Often called an "America First"
or "Neo-isolationist" school, it also was in line with realism in IR theory,
though it stressed different elements than the first school of thought noted
above. Rather, it contended that the United States had become overextended
in world affairs and was being taken advantage of in the current world
security-economic system. It called for sweeping cuts in spending for international activities, favoring US pullback from foreign bases and major cuts
in foreign assistance and foreign technical-information programs. Some in
this school favored trade measures that were seen as protectionist by US
trading partners. [17]

A third school of thought seemed to combine elements of liberalism with
realism and a strong American identity in line with constructivism. It argued
for policy that would promote more vigorously US interests in international
political, military, and economic affairs and would use US influence to pressure countries that do not conform to the US-backed norms on an appropriate
world order. Supporters of this stance wanted the United States to maintain
military forces with worldwide capabilities, to lead strongly in world affairs,
and to minimize compromise and accommodation in promoting American
interests and values.

Those who supported this view perceived a global power vacuum, caused
mainly by the collapse of the Soviet empire, which allowed the United States
to exert greater influence. [18] In the immediate post–Cold War years, some
advocates of this third view were most vocal in pressing for a strong US
policy in support of democracy and human rights. They opposed economic or
trading policies of other countries seen as inequitable or predatory. They
pressed for a strong policy against proliferation of weapons of mass destruction. Members of this school also argued variously for sanctions against
countries that practiced coercive birth control, seriously polluted the environment, harbored terrorists, or promoted the drug trade. Proponents of this view
came from both the left and the right in the American political spectrum. In
Congress, they included conservative Republican Newt Gingrich and liberal
Democrat Nancy Pelosi, both of whom would serve as speaker of the US
House of Representatives.

As far as US policy toward China was concerned during the 1990s, advocates of the third group—proponents of active US leadership and internation-

al intervention—were forceful in calling for policies opposing Chinese human rights violations, weapons proliferation, and protective trade practices. They pressed Beijing to meet US-supported international norms and called for retaliatory economic and other sanctions. By contrast, the more cautious and accommodating first group believed that the advocates of strong assertion of US values and norms were unrealistic about US power and were unwilling to make needed compromises with the Chinese government in order to (1) protect and support US interests and regional stability and (2) avoid strategic enmity.[19]

As the decade wore on, it was unclear what approach to China would prevail in US policy. Some in the George H. W. Bush and Clinton administrations advocated a moderate, less confrontational policy of "engagement" with China, for fear that doing otherwise could, among other things, promote divisions in—and a possible breakup of—China, with potentially adverse consequences for US interests in Asian stability and prosperity. Impressed by subsequent growth in Chinese economic and national strength later in the decade, many US officials, business interests, and others sought opportunities in closer economic and other relations with China. They also promoted engagement in order to guide China's power into channels of international activity compatible with American interests.

A tougher approach was supported by US officials and advocates outside the US government who stressed that China's leaders were biding their time and conforming to many international norms in order to avoid difficulties as China built national strength. Once the Chinese government succeeded with economic and related military modernization and development, Beijing was expected to become even less inclined to sacrifice nationalistic and territorial ambitions for the sake of cooperation in engagement policies by the United States and the West. Given this reasoning, US leaders were urged to be firm with China, to rely on military power as a counterweight to rising Chinese power, to remain resolute in dealing with economic and security disputes with China, and to work closely with US allies and friends along China's periphery in dealing with actual or potential Chinese assertiveness. Senator John McCain was identified with this view.[20]

An even tougher US approach to China at the time was advocated by some leaders in the Congress along with commentators and interest group leaders who believed that China's political system needed to change before the United States could establish a constructive relationship with Beijing. China's Communist leaders were perceived as inherently incapable of participating in truly cooperative relationships with the United States. US policy should aim to change China from within while maintaining vigilance against disruptive Chinese foreign policy. Prominent congressional leaders such as Senator Jesse Helms, Representative Frank Wolf, and Representative Christopher Smith were associated with these views.[21]

Nongovernment advocacy groups interested in influencing China policy found fertile ground in the often acute debate in the 1990s over the proper American approach to China and the broader debate over the appropriate course of US foreign policy after the Cold War. The groups endeavored to muster recruits, gain financial support, and build coalitions by focusing on issues related to China policy. Their concerns focused on issues like human rights, trade disputes, weapons proliferation, and other topics. Competing coalitions of interest groups fought bitterly, especially during major crises such as the decisions of the Bush and Clinton administrations to grant MFN tariff treatment to China. [22]

In general, the organized American interest groups active in China policy following the end of the Cold War can be divided among those dealing with economic interests, specific values or causes, ethnic issues, and issues important to foreign governments and foreign economic interests. Within the economic realm, the National Association of Manufacturers, the Chamber of Commerce, and the Business Roundtable endeavored to promote such business concerns as foreign trade and investment beneficial to American companies. The Emergency Committee for American Trade worked successfully to ensure that the United States would continue nondiscriminatory trading relations with China. [23]

Often at odds with these pro-business groups were groups representing organized labor. They favored more trade restrictions; they often viewed Chinese exports to the United States as a threat to US jobs; and they also weighed in on a variety of social justice issues including human rights and labor rights and the use of prison labor to produce Chinese exports. [24]

A number of public interest or citizen groups have common concerns of a noneconomic or nonoccupational nature. Many of these organizations focus on a single issue or a small group of issues. Examples include groups concerned with independence or greater autonomy for Tibet (e.g., the International Campaign for Tibet); freedom for political prisoners in China (e.g., Amnesty International and Human Rights Watch); religious freedom and freedom from coercive birth control and abortions (e.g., the Family Research Council, very active in the 1990s); as well as those concerned with curbing Chinese practices that endanger the regional and international environment or that promote instability and possible conflict through the proliferation of weapons of mass destruction and related technology (e.g., the Wisconsin Project, prominent in the 1990s in its focus on egregious Chinese failings in the area of weapons proliferation). [25]

Ethnic groups have long been a key factor in American foreign policy. Although Chinese Americans represent around 1 percent of the US population, they have not become a unified ethnic bloc influencing US foreign policy. However, there have been instances when segments of this group have been active in the politics of US foreign policy making. Expatriate

Chinese students heavily lobbied Congress and the administration during the years immediately following the 1989 Tiananmen crackdown. Their influence waned as the students became divided over their goals regarding US policy toward China. A much more cohesive ethnic group has been the more than half million Americans who trace their family background to Taiwan. Taiwanese-Americans have formed a variety of organizations that have actively encouraged US foreign policy to respect Taiwan's separate status and autonomy from the mainland. Many of these groups are strong advocates of independence for the island.[26]

Foreign governments, foreign businesses, and other elites also work actively to influence US foreign policy. Government, business, and other leaders of Taiwan have been active for many years in pressing their points of view on the US government. With the break in official Taiwan relations with the US government in 1979, they have focused more effort to lobby the Congress. Reports have linked the Taiwan government and other groups supportive of Taiwan with sometimes large campaign contributions to US political candidates. Taiwan government and nongovernment entities also have been prominent in promoting academic, think tank, media, local government, and other research and exchanges that enhance goodwill and positive feelings between Taiwan and the United States.[27]

The mainland Chinese government, business leaders, and other elites were much less active on these fronts, though their efforts to influence US foreign policy continue to grow. Media and congressional reports in the 1990s focused on charges that the Chinese government clandestinely was funneling campaign contributions to US candidates. Chinese government and business leaders found they were more attractive to and influential with US officials and elites as a result of the rapid growth of the Chinese economy. Against this background, the Chinese government was successful in promoting regular exchanges with Congress. The Chinese government also worked closely with like-minded US business leaders and officials in sustaining vibrant economic interchange with the United States.[28]

Relations during the Bush and Clinton Administrations

Developments in US-China relations after the Tiananmen crackdown in 1989 and through the 1990s witness repeated cycles of crisis heavily influenced by the newly active domestic debate in the United States over American policy toward China. The first major turning point came during the George H. W. Bush administration with US reaction to Tiananmen and the concurrent ending of the Cold War and emergence of Taiwan democratization. The second turning point came with President Clinton's advocacy in 1993 and then his withdrawal in 1994 of linkage between Chinese human rights practices and the granting of nondiscriminatory US trade status to China. A third and more serious crisis resulted from Clinton's decision in 1995 to allow the Taiwan president to visit the United States; Chinese military demonstrations in the Taiwan area ultimately prompted the deployment of two US aircraft carrier battle groups to the area in 1996. In 1999, contentious negotiations over China's entry into the WTO, Chinese mass demonstrations following the US bombing of the Chinese embassy in Belgrade, and a crescendo of congressional opposition to and criticism of the president and his China policy represented a fourth period of crisis since 1989.[29]

What would turn out to be a twisted course of US policy in this decade at first saw President George H. W. Bush strive to preserve cooperative ties amid widespread American outrage and pressure for retribution and sanctions against the Chinese leaders. President Bush had served as the head of the US Liaison Office in China in the mid-1970s. He took the lead in his own administration (1989–93) in dealing with severe problems in US-China relations caused by the Tiananmen crackdown and the decline in US strategic interest in China as a result of the collapse of the Soviet bloc. He resorted to secret diplomacy to maintain constructive communication with senior Chinese leaders; while senior administration officials said all high-level official contact with China would be cut off as a result of the Tiananmen crackdown, President Bush sent his national security adviser and the deputy secretary of state on secret missions to Beijing in July and December 1989. When the missions became known in December 1989, the congressional and media reactions were bitterly critical of the administration's perceived duplicity.[30]

Bush eventually became frustrated with the Chinese leadership's intransigence and took a tough stance on trade and other issues, though he made special efforts to ensure that the United States continued MFN tariff status for China despite opposition by a majority of the US Congress, much of the American media, and many US interest groups newly focused on China. Reflecting more positive US views of Taiwan, the Bush administration upgraded US interchange with the ROC by sending a cabinet-level official to Taipei in 1992, the first such visit since official relations were ended in 1979. He also seemed to abandon the limits on US arms sales set in accord with the August 1982 US communiqué with China by agreeing in 1992 to a sale of 150 advanced F-16 jet fighters, worth more than $5 billion, to Taiwan. The president's motives for the sale were heavily influenced by a need to appear to be protecting US manufacturing jobs at the F-16 plant in Texas, a key state in the Bush reelection plan.[31]

Presidential candidate Clinton used sharp attacks against Chinese government behavior, notably the Tiananmen crackdown, and President Bush's moderate approach to China to win support in the 1992 election. The presidential candidate's attacks, though probably reflecting sincere anger and concern over Chinese behavior, also reflected a tendency in the US-China debate in the 1990s to use China issues, particularly criticism of China and US policy toward China, for partisan reasons. The president-elect and US politicians in following years found that criticizing China and US policy toward China provided a convenient means to pursue political ends. For candidate Clinton and his aides, using China issues to discredit the record of the Republican candidate, incumbent George H. W. Bush, proved an effective way to take votes from him. Once Clinton won the election and was in office, he showed little interest in China policy, leaving the responsibility to subordinates.[32]

In particular, Assistant Secretary of State for East Asia Affairs Winston Lord in 1993 played the lead administration role in working with congressional leaders, notably Senate Majority Leader George Mitchell, Representative Nancy Pelosi, who was a House leader on China and human rights issues, and others to establish the human rights conditions the Clinton administration would require before renewing MFN tariff status for China. The terms he worked out were widely welcomed in the United States at the time. However, Chinese government leaders were determined not to give in on several of the US demands, and they appeared to calculate that US business interests in a burgeoning Chinese economy would be sufficient to prevent the United States from taking the drastic step of cutting MFN tariff treatment for China and risking the likely retaliation of the PRC against US trade interests. US business pressures pushed Clinton to intervene in May 1994 to reverse existing policy and allow for unimpeded US renewal of MFN status for China.[33]

Pro-Taiwan interests in the United States, backed by US public relations firms in the pay of entities and organizations in Taiwan, took the opportunity of congressional elections in 1995, which gave control of the Congress to pro-Taiwan Republican leaders, to push for greater US support for Taiwan, notably for a visit by ROC president Lee Teng-hui to his alma mater, Cornell University. Under heavy domestic political pressure, President Clinton intervened again and allowed Taiwan's president to visit the United States despite the strenuous opposition of China.[34]

The resulting military confrontation with China in the Taiwan Strait involving two US aircraft carrier battle groups saw the Clinton administration eventually move to a much more coherent engagement policy toward China. The policy received consistent and high-level attention from the president and his key aides, and was marked by two US-China summit meetings in 1997 and 1998. By the end of the Clinton administration, progress included US-China agreement on China's entry into the WTO and US agreement to provide PNTR status for China. However, the new approach failed to still the vigorous US domestic debate against forward movement in US relations with China on an array of strategic, economic, and political issues.[35]

As in the case of Clinton's attacks on George H. W. Bush, many of the attacks on Clinton's engagement policy with China after 1996 were not so much focused on China and China issues for their own sake as on partisan or other concerns. Most notably, as congressional Republican leaders sought to impeach President Clinton and tarnish the reputation of his administration, they endeavored to dredge up a wide range of charges with regard to illegal Chinese fund-raising; Chinese espionage; Chinese deviations from international norms regarding human rights, nuclear weapons, and ballistic missile proliferation; and other questions in order to discredit President Clinton's moderate engagement policy toward China, and in so doing cast serious doubt on the moral integrity and competence of the president and his aides.[36]

The Clinton policy of engagement with China also came under attack from organized labor interests within the Democratic Party, some of which used the attacks on the administration's China policy as a means to get the administration to pay more attention to broader labor interests within the party. In a roughly similar fashion, social conservatives in the Republican Party used sharp attacks against the continuation of US MFN tariff status for China (a stance often supported by congressional Republican leaders) despite China's coercive birth control policies; they did this in part as a means to embarrass and pressure the Republican leaders to pay more positive attention to the various agenda issues of the social conservatives.

During the 1990s, congressional criticism of China and moderation in US policy toward China was easy to do and generally had benefits for those making the criticism. The criticism generated positive coverage from US media strongly critical of China, and it generated positive support and perhaps some fund-raising and electioneering support for the congressional critics by the many interest groups in the United States that focused criticism on Chinese policies and practices during that decade. The Chinese government, anxious to keep the economic relationship with the United States on an even keel, was disinclined to punish such congressional critics or take substantive action against them. More likely were Chinese invitations to the critical congressional members for all-expenses-paid trips to China in order to persuade them to change their views by seeing actual conditions in China. Finally, President Clinton, like President George H. W. Bush, often was not in a position to risk other legislative goals by punishing congressional members critical of his China policy.

As President Clinton and his White House staff took more control over China policy after the face-off with Chinese forces in the Taiwan Strait in 1996, they emphasized—like George H. W. Bush—a moderate policy of engagement, seeking change in offensive Chinese government practices through a gradual process involving closer Chinese integration with the world economic and political order. The US-China relationship improved but also encountered significant setbacks and resistance. The high points included the US-China summits in 1997 and 1998, the Sino-American agreement on China's entry into the WTO in November 1999, and passage of US legislation in 2000 granting China PNTR status. Low points included strong congressional opposition to the president's stance against Taiwan independence in 1998; the May 1999 bombing of the Chinese Embassy in Belgrade and Chinese demonstrators trashing US diplomatic properties in China; strident congressional criticism in the so-called Cox Committee report of May 1999, charging administration officials with gross malfeasance in guarding US secrets and weaponry from Chinese spies; and partisan congressional investigations of Clinton administration political fund-raising that highlighted some illegal contributions from sources connected to the Chinese regime and the alleged impact they had on the administration's more moderate approach to the PRC.[37]

China's calculus amid the varied initiatives from the United States in the decade after the Tiananmen crackdown is explained in more detail later in this chapter. It shows that Chinese leaders had long sought the summit meetings with the United States. Coming in the wake of Chinese meetings with other world leaders in the aftermath of the international isolation of China caused by the Tiananmen crackdown, the summit meetings with the US president were a clear signal to audiences at home and abroad that the Communist government of China had growing international status and that its position as the legitimate government of China now was recognized by all major world powers.[38]

The benefits for the United States in the summit meetings were more in question, though the Clinton administration justified these steps as part of its efforts to use engagement in seeking change in offensive Chinese government practices through a gradual process involving closer Chinese integration with the world economic and political order. US and other critics failed to accept this rationale and honed their criticism on what they viewed as unjustified US concessions to Chinese leaders. Heading the list were perceived concessions by the US president articulating limits on American support for Taiwan in the so-called Three No's. Speaking in Shanghai in June 1998 during his visit to China, President Clinton affirmed that the United States did not support Taiwan independence; two Chinas; or one Taiwan, one China; and that the United States did not believe Taiwan should be a member of an organization where statehood is required. The Clinton administration claimed the Three No's were a reaffirmation of long-standing US policy, but the president's action was roundly criticized in the Congress and US media as a new gesture made to accommodate Beijing and undermine Taipei.[39]

Progress in US negotiations leading to eventual agreement on China's entry into the WTO was not without serious difficulties and negative consequences. The United States took the lead among the WTO's contracting parties in protracted negotiations (1986–99) to reach agreements with China on a variety of trade-related issues before Chinese accession could move forward. Chinese premier Zhu Rongji visited Washington in April 1999, hoping to reach agreement with the United States on China's entry into the WTO. An agreement was reached and disclosed by the Americans, only to be turned down by President Clinton. The setback embarrassed Zhu and raised serious questions in the Chinese leadership about the intentions of President Clinton and his administration. Recovering from the setback, Zhu was able to complete the US-China negotiations in November 1999, paving the way for China's entry into the WTO in 2001. US legislation passed granting PNTR to China in 2000. This ended the need for annual presidential requests and congressional reviews with regard to China keeping normal trade relations tariff status, previously known as most favored nation tariff status. [40]

Making such progress in US-China relations was difficult because of incidents and developments affecting US-China relations and vitriolic US debate over the Clinton administration's China policy. Heading the list was the US bombing of the Chinese embassy in Belgrade, the most important incident in US-China relations after the Tiananmen crackdown. The reaction in China included mobs stoning the US embassy in Beijing and burning US diplomatic property in Chengdu, a provincial capital. Both governments re-stored calm and dealt with some of the consequences of the bombing, but China and the United States never came to an agreement on what happened and whether the United States explained its actions appropriately. [41]

Taiwan's president, Lee Teng-hui, added to Taiwan Strait tension, thus worrying American policy makers when he asserted in July 1999 that Taiwan was a state separate from China and that China and Taiwan had "special state-to-state relations." Chinese leaders saw this as a step toward Taiwan independence and reacted with strong rhetoric, some military actions, and by cutting off cross-strait communication links. [42]

Complementing difficulties abroad were the many challenges at home to the Clinton administration's moderate policy of engagement toward China. The US media ran repeated stories in the second term of the Clinton adminis-tration that linked the president, Vice President Albert Gore, and other ad-ministration leaders with illegal political fund-raising involving Asian do-nors, some of whom were said to be connected with the Chinese government. Congressional Republican Committee chairmen, Senator Fred Thompson and Representative Dan Burton, held hearings, conducted investigations, and produced information and reports regarding various unsubstantiated allega-tions of illegal contributions from Chinese backers in return for the Clinton administration turning a blind eye to Chinese illegal trading practices and Chinese espionage activities in the United States. [43]

More damaging to the administration and its engagement policy toward China was the report of the so-called Cox Committee. Formally known as the Select Committee on US National Security and Military/Commercial Con-cerns with the People's Republic of China, and named for its chairman, Republican Congressman Christopher Cox, the committee released in May

1999 an eight-hundred-page unclassified version of a larger, classified report. It depicted long-standing and widespread Chinese espionage efforts against US nuclear weapons facilities, allowing China to build American-designed advanced nuclear warheads for use on Chinese missiles that were made more accurate and reliable with the assistance of US companies. It portrayed the Clinton administration as grossly negligent in protecting such vital US national security secrets. The report added substantially to congressional, media, and other concerns that the United States faced a rising security threat posed by China's rapidly expanding economic and military power.[44]

CHINA POLICY DEBATE IN PERSPECTIVE: STRENGTHS, WEAKNESS, AND IMPORTANCE

Looking back at Tiananmen from the perspective of the end of the Clinton administration in 2000, it was fair to assert that the domestic American debate over China policy had emerged powerfully in the 1990s and would continue to have a primary influence in the American approach to China for the foreseeable future. The incoming George W. Bush administration in January 2001 adopted a policy toward China that was tougher and more consistent with the widespread criticism of the Clinton administration's more moderate engagement policy. Bush's approach calmed the critics for the time being. A more lasting and significant impact on the China policy critics came with the September 11, 2001, terrorist attack on America. Though not comparable to the strategic danger posed by Soviet expansion during the height of the Cold War, the new challenge of terrorism became the focus of US government, media, and interest group attention. Those in the United States who endeavored to use criticism of China and their attacks on moderation in US policy toward China had a much harder time getting the attention of officials, media, donors, and the general public. The China debate as a force that pushed US policy toward a significantly harder line against China basically was overwhelmed by perceived American requirements to focus on other issues related to the complicated US war on terrorism. As the danger of terrorism to the United States appeared to subside and the popularity of the Bush administration also declined, the domestic US debate over China began to revive again in the middle of the decade. But it remained a secondary force influencing American China policy. It was more a drag on forward movement and improvement in US relations with China than it was a significant determinant of a more negative and critical American policy toward China.[45]

Closer examination shows that the rapid and unforeseen decline in the salience of the American domestic debate about China policy during the first year of the George W. Bush administration reflects some important weaknesses of the critics and their arguments in favor of a tougher stance toward

China. In fact, a comparison of the US China policy debate in the 1990s with the US debate over China policy debate in the late 1970s and early 1980s appears to illustrate weaknesses in the resolve and approach of the critics in the later period. The resolve and commitment of critics seen in late-1970s and early-1980s episodes related to both the passage of the Taiwan Relations Act and resistance to perceived excesses in US accommodation of China at the expense of US relations with Taiwan, Japan, and other interests, appear strong. They seem notably stronger than the resolve and commitment on the part of many of the various individuals and groups seeking a tougher US approach to China after the Cold War. The comparison of the two periods of criticism of prevailing US policy leads to a conclusion that even though the number of critics and their supporters in the 1990s was larger and broader than those of critics in the late 1970s and early 1980s, the commitment of the leaders and followers was comparatively thin and expedient in the post–Cold War period.[46]

COMPARING THE US DEBATES ON CHINA: LATE 1970s/EARLY 1980s VERSUS POST–COLD WAR

Domestic debate and related domestic interests have sometimes been an important determinant pushing forward the direction of US policy toward China, including Taiwan and related issues. More often, they have been an obstacle slowing the momentum of US policy. From Richard Nixon through Jimmy Carter and into early Ronald Reagan, domestic factors generally were a brake slowing the policies led by the administration to move the United States away from ties with Taiwan and closer to the PRC. For several years following the end of the Cold War, they generally were a driver pushing US policy against China and toward closer ties with Taiwan, though they reverted to the status of brake during the second term of the Clinton administration.[47]

As noted in chapter 4, the debate in the Nixon-Reagan period (1972–83) involved important tangible costs and benefits for the United States. The US strategic posture vis-à-vis the Soviet Union and the future of Taiwan headed the list of the serious issues at stake for the United States. Reflecting deep uncertainty about US power and purpose in world affairs, US policy was prepared to make major sacrifices in order to pursue respective paths in the debate, and indeed US policy ultimately sacrificed official relations with Taiwan and took the unprecedented step of ending a defense treaty with a loyal ally for the sake of the benefits to be derived from official relations with the PRC, notably with regard to assisting the United States in dealing with expanding Soviet power.[48]

The major protagonists in the US domestic debate over policy toward the PRC and Taiwan in the Nixon-Reagan (1972–83) period argued their case mainly because they were sincerely concerned about the serious implications and consequences of the direction of US policy in this triangular relationship. Partisan interests and the influence of interest groups or constituent groups also played a role, but less so than in the US China policy debate of the 1990s. The fact that a Democrat-controlled Congress took the lead, in the Taiwan Relations Act and in other legislative actions, in modifying the perceived oversights and excesses of the Democratic Carter administration, which tilted in favor of Beijing and against Taiwan in the late 1970s and 1980, showed that partisan interests played a secondary or relatively unimportant role in the US domestic debate. Significantly, this pattern persisted even after the Democrat-controlled Congress rewrote and passed the Taiwan Relations Act in April 1979. Democratic senators and representatives remained active in resisting the Carter administration's continuing perceived "tilt" toward the PRC and away from Taiwan. Among notable critics and skeptics of the US policy at the time were such Democratic senators as Adlai Stevenson, John Glenn, Richard Stone, and George McGovern.[49]

The congressional opposition of the day did reflect an important element of institutional rivalry between the executive branch and the Congress that colored US domestic debate over foreign policy during this period. Congress appeared determined to protect its perceived prerogatives in US foreign policy, while US administration officials were equally determined to protect the prerogatives of the executive branch in foreign affairs.[50]

Although the US domestic debate became more prominent and important in influencing the course of US policy toward China and Taiwan and related issues after the Tiananmen incident and the end of the Cold War in the late 1980s and the early 1990s, major features of the debate were markedly different from the debate in the 1970s and early 1980s. The differences underlined that the resolve and commitment of the critics generally was weaker in the 1990s than in the 1970s.[51]

- US policy makers in the executive branch and the Congress were confident of US power and influence in the world, especially now that the Soviet empire had collapsed—a marked contrast from the strategic uncertainty that had underlined the US policy debate in the 1970s and early 1980s.
- In the 1970s, US officials faced and made major sacrifices in pursuit of US policy toward the PRC and Taiwan. The protagonists in the US China policy debate after the Cold War had little inclination to sacrifice tangible US interests for the sake of their preferred stance in the US-PRC-Taiwan triangle or other China policy–related questions. Thus, those in Congress, the media, and elsewhere in US domestic politics who were vocal in

seeking an upgrading in US treatment for Taiwan's President Lee Teng-hui—demanding he be granted a visa to visit Cornell University in 1995—largely fell silent when Beijing reacted to the visit with forceful actions in the Taiwan Strait that posed a serious danger of US-China military confrontation. The majority of congressional members who opposed the annual waiver that granted continued MFN tariff treatment to Chinese imports had no intention of seeking a serious cutoff of US-China trade. They often explained that they were merely endeavoring to send a signal, to the administration and to China, over their dissatisfaction with US and Chinese policies.

- Many were active in the US domestic debate for partisan or other ulterior motives—a marked contrast from the 1970s, when the foreign policy issues themselves seemed to be the prime drivers in the US domestic debate. Clinton used the China issue to attack the record of the Bush administration, only to reverse course after a time in office, returning to the engagement policy of the previous president. The strident rhetoric coming from Republican congressional leaders critical of the Clinton administration's engagement policy in its second term seemed to have similarly partisan motives. Labor-oriented Democrats used the China issue to discredit the pro-business leanings of the leaders of the Clinton administration, while social conservatives in the Republican Party focused in on China's forced abortions and suppression of religious freedom to embarrass their party leaders and prompt them to devote more attention to the social conservatives' political agenda in US domestic politics.[52]

- Reflecting the less serious commitment by critics in the 1990s was the fact that the US China debate notably subsided whenever the United States faced a serious foreign policy challenge. Thus, the vocal congressional debate over China policy stopped abruptly following the Iraqi invasion of Kuwait in 1990, and the Congress remained quiet about China throughout the US "Desert Shield" and "Desert Storm" operations. Once the war was over and the need for Chinese acquiescence in the United Nations over the US-led war against Iraq ended in 1991, the China debate resumed immediately, with many Democrats in Congress and elsewhere seeking to use the China issue for partisan purposes in order to tear down President George H. W. Bush's then-strong standing in US opinion polls regarding his handling of foreign affairs. As noted earlier in this chapter, the September 11, 2001, attack on America also dampened the US China debate, which was then focused notably on the threat to US interests posed by a rising China. After several months, media organs like the *Washington Times* and some in Congress resumed lower-key efforts to focus on the China threat, while pro-Taiwan groups tried to use the rebalancing of Bush administration policy in directions more favorable to China, by arguing for concurrent favorable US treatment for Taiwan.[53] These moves were small and of little consequence; they seemed to underline the weakness of US critics of China or advocates of policies opposed by China in a US foreign policy environment focused on dealing with terrorism-related issues. [54]

CHINESE PRIORITIES AND CALCULATIONS: MANAGING CRISIS-PRONE RELATIONS

Whatever their strengths and weaknesses, the shifts in US policy prompted by the US debate over China policy after the Cold War posed major and repeated challenges for Chinese leaders. Once it became clear to Chinese leaders that the strategic basis of Sino-American relations had been destroyed by the end of the Cold War and the collapse of the Soviet Union and that it would take a long time for political relations to return to more moderate engagement after the trauma of the Tiananmen incident, Chinese leaders worked throughout the 1990s to reestablish "normalized" relations with the United States on terms as advantageous as possible to China. With the US-China summits of 1997 and 1998, relations arguably were normalized, but they remained far from stable. Chinese leaders continued to give high priority to managing differences with the United States while benefiting from advantageous economic and other ties with the US superpower. [55]

Throughout the post–Cold War period, Chinese officials reflected varying degrees of suspicion regarding US intentions and remained well aware of fundamental ideological, strategic, and other differences with the United States. [56] In general, Chinese officials settled on a bifurcated view of the United States. This view held that US leaders would extend the hand of "engagement" to the Chinese government when their interests would be served, but that US leaders were determined to "contain" aspects of China's rising power and block aspects of China's assertion of influence in world affairs when such aspects were seen as contrary to US interests. The Chinese emphasis on cooperating with the "soft" US "hand of engagement" or defending against the "hard" US "hand of containment" varied. The general trend from 1996 to 2001, and after adjustments in US-China relations in 2001, was to give more emphasis to the positive and less emphasis to the negative on the part of both the Chinese and US administrations. [57]

Presidents George H. W. Bush and Clinton were clear about US differences with China in several key areas. Despite Chinese disapproval, the United States was determined to expend such a vast array of resources on defense that it would remain the world's dominant power, and the dominant military power along China's periphery in East Asia, for the foreseeable future. The United States would continue to provide support, including sophisticated arms, to Taiwan; and the United States endeavored to use growing government, commercial, and other nongovernmental contacts with China, as well as other means, to foster an environment that promoted political pluralism and change in the authoritarian Chinese communist system.

For its part, Beijing strove for a post–Cold War world order of greater multipolarity; China would be one of the poles and would have greater opportunity for advantageous maneuvering than in a superpower-dominated order. China strove for a gradual decline in US power and influence in East Asia and globally, and Beijing called for cutbacks in US military sales and other support to Taiwan in order to help create advantageous conditions for the reunification of the island with mainland China. Finally, CCP leaders were determined to maintain the primacy of their rule in the face of economic, social, and political challenges at home and abroad, including challenges supported by the United States.

A critical problem for Chinese leaders in dealing with the United States in the 1990s involved mixing their strategies and goals with those of the United States in ways advantageous to China. In general, the Chinese approach focused on trying to work constructively with US power, concentrating on areas of common ground, building interdependent economic relations, and minimizing differences wherever possible. This was difficult to achieve, especially when US policy concentrated on the stark differences between the United States and China over human rights, Taiwan, weapons proliferation, and trade issues. In some instances, Chinese officials chose to confront the United States with threats of retaliation if the United States pursued pressure tactics against China. For the most part, however, Chinese leaders bided their time, endeavoring to avoid complications that would ensue from protracted confrontation with the United States. At bottom, they believed that China's growing economy and overall international importance would steadily win over foreign powers to a cooperative stance and encourage politically important groups in the United States, especially business groups, to press for an accommodating US approach to China.

Following this general line of approach in the 1990s, Beijing managed to end the diplomatic isolation that stemmed from the Tiananmen crackdown, weakened the Clinton administration advocates of conditioning MFN tariff treatment of Chinese imports to the United States, and prompted the president to end this policy in 1994. With the Sino-American summits of 1997 and 1998, Beijing clearly established the Chinese leaders as legitimate and respected actors in world affairs.[58]

Chinese officials duly noted during the 1990s and later that they had few illusions about beneficent US policy toward China. But they repeatedly affirmed to Western specialists and others that they—whether they personally liked it or not—also saw Chinese interests best served by trying to get along with the United States. They cited the following reasons:[59]

- The United States remained the world's sole superpower. As such, it posed the only potential strategic threat to China's national security for the foreseeable future. A confrontation with such a power would severely test China's strength and undermine Chinese economic and political programs.
- As the world's leading economic power, the United States had markets, technology, and investment important for Chinese modernization. It also played an important role in international financial institutions heavily involved in China; Western financial actors and investors viewed the status of US relations with China as an important barometer determining the scope and depth of their involvement in China.
- Internationally, establishing cooperative relations with the United States facilitated smooth Chinese relations with Western and other powers that were close to Washington. Antagonistic US-China relations would mean that China would have to work much harder, and presumably offer more in the way of economic and other concessions, to win over such powers.
- The United States continued to play a key strategic role in highly sensitive areas around China's periphery, notably Korea, Japan, the South China Sea, and especially Taiwan. It controlled sea lanes vital to Chinese trade. Cooperative US-China relations allowed Beijing to continue to focus on domestic priorities with reasonable assurance that its vital interests in these sensitive areas would not be fundamentally jeopardized by antagonistic actions by the United States. Indeed, good US-China relations tended to increase Chinese influence in these areas.

On balance, the record of Chinese relations with the United States in the 1990s showed considerable achievement for China. Beijing reestablished extensive high-level contacts with the US administration and saw the end of most Tiananmen-related sanctions against China. By 1998, the Clinton administration appeared sincerely committed to pursuing a policy of generally accommodating engagement with China. Administration officials in the United States endeavored to work closely with the Chinese government to reduce differences over US world primacy, the American strategic posture in East Asia, US support for Taiwan, and Washington's support for political pluralism in China. Chinese officials took satisfaction in the fact that the improvement in relations resulted much more from shifts toward accommodation of China's rising power and influence by the US administration than from adjustments by the Chinese government in dealing with issues sensitive to the United States.

While assessments among Chinese officials differed regarding the status and outlook of US-China relations, the prevailing view in 1999 was one of caution. There remained plenty of evidence that US policy continued to have elements of containment along with the seemingly accommodating engagement. Political forces in the United States, many interest groups, and the media still lined up against Chinese interests on a range of human rights concerns, strategic issues, Taiwan, and economic questions. Many Chinese officials remained suspicious of the ultimate motives of some members of the Clinton administration as well. As a result, Beijing was privately wary as it continued to seek advantages by building cooperative relations. [60]

The Challenges of Shifting US Policies

The Clinton administration decision in 1993 to condition MFN status for China on China's progress in human rights issues posed a major problem for the Chinese leadership. It was met indirectly by the rapid growth of the Chinese economy, which attracted strong US business interest, and the interest in turn of many visitors from Congress and the administration concerned with the growth of the US economy and economic opportunity abroad. By early 1994, Chinese officials were well aware that proponents for continuing the human rights conditions on MFN treatment for China had become isolated in the administration and centered in the State Department. The private reservations held among senior officials in US departments concerned with business, notably the Treasury Department and the Commerce Department, about these conditions on China's MFN status had become clear through their earlier visits to China and through other interactions. Moreover, US business groups had moved into high gear in warning that conditions on MFN treatment could jeopardize US access to the burgeoning Chinese market. [61]

Sino-American disagreements over human rights conditions in China and MFN status rose sharply during Secretary of State Warren Christopher's March 11–14, 1994, visit to Beijing. [62] Before and during Secretary Christopher's visit, Chinese leaders appeared defiant in the face of US human rights requirements. Most notably, Chinese security forces detained prominent dissidents immediately prior to the secretary's visit and also detained some Western journalists covering interaction between Chinese dissidents and Chinese security forces. In public interchange during the secretary's visit, Chinese leaders strongly warned against US use of trade or other pressure to prompt changes in China's human rights policy.

This tough approach reflected a determination to rebuff overt US pressure seen as targeted against the priority Chinese leadership concern of sustaining CCP rule. It also reflected the fact that the secretary's trip coincided with the annual convening of the National People's Congress. That meeting was the focal point of dissident activism in Beijing, and Chinese leaders were determined to take a hard line toward those both at home and abroad who pressed for political change.

Perhaps of most importance, Chinese leaders calculated that the time was right to press the United States to alter its human rights policy, especially the linkage with MFN renewal. They saw the Clinton administration leaders divided on the issue. They saw members of the US Congress as much more supportive than in the recent past of maintaining MFN treatment for China. Congress was perhaps influenced, too, by the fact that while the United States had been debating the issue, countries that were political allies to the United States but economic competitors, like Japan, Germany, and France, had been sending high-level officials to China—underlining their willingness to help fill the vacuum should US-China economic relations falter with the withdrawal of MFN tariff treatment.[63]

Reflecting a calculus of costs and benefits along the lines of realism in IR theory, Chinese leaders adopted a tough stance during the Christopher visit. Those in the US government favoring linkage of MFN treatment and human rights conditions were further isolated, and US leaders were forced to change their policy or lose the considerable economic opportunities in the Chinese market. In the end, Chinese leaders were generally pleased with President Clinton's May 26, 1994, decision to "delink" MFN treatment to China from US consideration of Chinese human rights practices.

Subsequently, Chinese officials and commentators in official Chinese media were anxious for the United States and China to take advantage of the improved atmosphere in bilateral relations to push for more far-reaching and comprehensive progress in the US-China relationship.[64] Whatever hopes Chinese leaders held about advancing relations with the United States were dashed by President Clinton's reversal of past policy, permitting Taiwan's president, Lee Teng-hui, to make an ostensibly private visit to Cornell University in June 1995.

Beijing's tough military and polemical responses and the Clinton administration's eventual dispatch of carrier battle groups to Taiwan highlighted mixed lessons for China.[65]

On the positive side, Chinese officials claimed several achievements resulting from the PRC's forceful reaction to Lee Teng-hui's visit to the United States:

- It intimidated Taiwan, at least temporarily, preventing it from taking further assertive actions to lobby in the US Congress or elsewhere for greater international recognition. Pro-independence advocates in Taiwan also had to reassess previous claims that the PRC was bluffing in its warnings against Taiwan independence.
- It prompted second thoughts by some pro-Taiwan advocates in the Congress and elsewhere in the United States as to the wisdom of pursuing their agenda at that time. International officials seeking to follow the US

lead in granting greater recognition to Taiwan had to reevaluate their positions as well.

- It resulted in heightened sensitivity by the Clinton administration regarding China. This led to official reassurances to the PRC that US policy toward Taiwan would not deviate from past practice; it also led to an invitation for the Chinese president to visit the United States, a summit meeting long sought by Chinese leaders; and it led to tightly controlled management of significant developments in US policy toward China by the president and his senior advisers, who now sought to pursue an active engagement policy with China and to avoid significant deterioration of relations.

At the same time, Beijing appeared to have overplayed its hand in pressing the United States for pledges against Taiwan official visits to the United States and in pressing Taiwan's people to abandon Lee Teng-hui in favor of a leader more committed to reunification with the mainland. Beijing also appeared to recognize that it was not productive to continue strident accusations in official Chinese media during 1995–96 that the United States was attempting to contain China, or to shun dialogue with the United States.

Given China's perceived need to sustain a working relationship with the United States for the foreseeable future, Beijing officials tried, for example through President Jiang Zemin's meeting with President Clinton in 1995, to find and develop common ground while playing down differences. Whereas Beijing had appeared prepared in mid-1995 to freeze contacts with the Clinton administration, awaiting the results of the 1996 US elections, Beijing now appeared to have judged that endeavoring to work constructively with the current US government was in China's best interests. Also, Jiang Zemin told US reporters in October 1995 that lobbying Congress would be an important priority in the year ahead, and Chinese specialists also said that the PRC would put more effort into winning greater understanding and support from other US sectors, notably the media and business.[66] For its part, the Clinton administration continued strong efforts to avoid serious difficulties with China; to emphasize a policy of engagement with the PRC; and to seek high-level contacts, summit meetings, and tangible agreement with China on sensitive issues.

The events of the next two years in US-China relations were highlighted by the summit meetings of Presidents Jiang and Clinton in Washington in 1997 and Beijing in 1998. Despite the continued debate in the United States over the Clinton administration's new commitment to a policy of engagement with China, Chinese officials and specialists claimed to be confident that China's rising power and influence in world affairs, and its willingness to cooperate with the United States on issues of importance to both countries, made it unlikely that the US opponents of the engagement policy would have a serious, lasting impact on US-China relations.[67]

The events of 1997 and 1998 seemed to bear out the Chinese view. The US-China summit meetings capped the Beijing leaders' decade-long effort to restore their international legitimacy after the Tiananmen incident. The results redounded to the benefit of the presiding Chinese leaders, especially President Jiang Zemin. Jiang was anxious to carve out a role as a responsible and respected international leader as part of his broader effort to solidify his political base of support at home. Basically satisfied with the results of the smooth summit meetings with the US president, Beijing saw little need to take the initiative in dealing with continuing US-China differences like human rights, trade, and weapons proliferation. It was the US side that felt political pressure to achieve results in these areas.

Responding to repeated US initiatives to reach agreements at the summit meetings and elsewhere on these kinds of questions, Chinese officials took the opportunity to make demands of their own, especially regarding US policy toward Taiwan. At the same time, Beijing was willing marginally to improve human rights practices, and it curbed nuclear and cruise missile exchanges with Iran, for the sake of achieving a smoother and more cooperative US-China relationship.

In sum, despite strong and often partisan debate in the United States over policy toward China, Chinese officials were well pleased with the progress they had made in normalizing relations with the United States from the low points after the Tiananmen crackdown of 1989 and the confrontation over Taiwan in 1995–96. The progress had been made largely by changes in US policy toward China, and with few concessions by Beijing in key areas of importance to China. The summits of 1997 and 1998 represented the capstone of the normalization effort, in effect strongly legitimating the PRC leaders at home and abroad—a key Chinese goal after the Tiananmen incident. Once this was accomplished, Chinese leaders could turn to their daunting domestic agenda with more assurance that the key element of US-China relations was now on more stable ground.

At the same time, Chinese leaders had few illusions about US policy. They saw plenty of opportunities for continued difficulties. American behavior continued to be seen as fitting into the pattern of engagement and containment—the "two hands" of US policy seen by Chinese officials and specialists. The main trend in 1997 and 1998 was toward greater engagement, and China endeavored to encourage that. But there remained many forces in Congress, in the media, and among US interest groups that were prepared to challenge any forward movement in US-China relations. And the fact remained that although it was clearly in China's interest to cooperate with the United States under existing circumstances, the two countries continued to have fundamentally contradictory interests over the international balance of influence, the American strategic role in East Asia, US support for Taiwan, and American support for political change in China.[68]

Events in 1999, highlighted by the US bombing of the Chinese embassy in Belgrade, posed new challenges for Chinese leadership efforts to sustain workable economic and other ties with the United States while defending key Chinese interests of sovereignty, security, and nationalism. Chinese mob violence against US diplomatic properties was accompanied by a virulent leadership debate over how to deal with the United States that was not resolved for months. In the end, Chinese leaders decided their interests were best served by working with the US administration to restore calm and to continue US-China engagement that was beneficial to China.

Amid the contentious US presidential campaign of 2000, where policy toward China figured as an issue of some importance, senior Chinese officials told senior Clinton administration officials that China was intent on approaching the United States constructively, regardless of which candidate won the election. Such comment was seen by these US officials as supporting a coherent and consistent Chinese strategy toward the United States. This strategy appeared similar to that seen in 1997 and 1998 in that it accepted US leadership in world affairs and in Asian affairs and sought Chinese development in a peaceful international environment where the United States maintained primacy.[69]

However, the limitations, fragility, and apparent contradictions of this Chinese moderate approach toward the United States also were starkly evident. Whatever this strategy entailed, it did not show Chinese willingness to curb harsh commentary and the use of military force in challenging US power and influence in Asian and world affairs. Thus, Chinese officials and commentary in 2000 and until mid-2001 continued to be full of invective against the United States, opposing alleged US power politics, hegemonism, and Cold War thinking. China repeatedly criticized the United States over a variety of key foreign policy issues, such as US plans for national missile defense in the United States and theater missile defense abroad, NATO expansion, enhanced US alliance relations with Japan, and US policy and practices in dealing with Iraq, Iran, Cuba, and other countries.[70] Chinese aircraft and ships monitoring US surveillance aircraft and ships in international waters near China carried out dangerous maneuvers in apparent efforts to harass and deter the Americans from carrying out their objectives.

Chapter Six

Pragmatism amid Differences during the George W. Bush Administration

George W. Bush became president in 2001 with a reputation of toughness toward the People's Republic of China (PRC) but no clearly articulated policy. The new US administration's approach to the Chinese government was based in large measure on a fundamental uncertainty: China was rising and becoming more prominent in Asia and world affairs, but US leaders were unsure if this process would see China emerge as a friend or foe of the United States.[1] The administration dealt with this ambiguous China situation within a broader US international strategy that endeavored to maximize US national power and influence in key situations, including relations with China. This involved strengthening

- US military and economic power.
- US relations with key allies; those in Asia, Japan, South Korea, and Australia—received high priority.
- US relations with other power centers; the Bush administration was successful in moving quickly, before September 11, 2001, to build closer relations with the two major flanking powers in East Asia: Russia and India.[2]

In 2001 the new US president and his leadership team displayed a notably less solicitous approach to China than the one displayed by the outgoing Bill Clinton administration. As seen in chapter 5, the Clinton administration during its second term adopted an engagement policy toward China that received the top priority among US relations with Asia. The administration was anxious to avoid serious downturns in US-China relations over Taiwan and other issues; it also repeatedly sought negotiations with Beijing to develop "deliverables"—agreements and other tangible signs of forward movement in US-China relations. President Clinton, senior US officials, and US specialists repeatedly made clear that key objectives of growing US engagement with China were to enmesh China in webs of interdependent relationships with the United States, international organizations, world business, and others that would constrain and ultimately change Chinese policies and practices at home and abroad that were seen as offensive to or opposed to US interests. [3]

PRC bargainers used a prevailing atmosphere of strong, public Chinese criticism of US policies and warnings of Chinese actions against Taiwan in order to press for US concessions in areas of importance to them, notably regarding US relations with Taiwan. Chinese criticism of US policy had a broad scope involving Taiwan and a wide range of issues in US foreign and security policy including missile defense; NATO expansion; US-Japan security cooperation; US human rights policy; US efforts in the United Nations to sanction Iraq; and US policy toward Cuba, Iran, the Middle East, and other areas in the developing world. As noted in chapter 5, Clinton administration concessions fueled the white-hot US domestic debate over the proper direction of the US China policy. [4]

By contrast, the Bush administration lowered China's priority for US decision makers, placing the PRC well behind Japan and other Asian allies and even Russia and India for foreign policy attention. [5] This kind of downgrading of China's importance in US policy had last been carried out in the Reagan administration under the supervision of Secretary of State George Shultz. It appeared to be no accident that the key architects of the policy shift in 2001, notably Deputy Secretary of State Richard Armitage, were among key decision makers in the similar US shift in US China policy that began in 1983. Armitage and his key aides in the State Department and close associates in the National Security Council Staff were in the lead in moving US policy from the strong emphasis on compromising with China and doing what was necessary in order to preserve good relations with China in the latter years of the Clinton administration.

Following the crash between a Chinese jet fighter and a US reconnaissance plane over the South China Sea during the so-called EP-3 incident of April 2001, discussed below, the Bush administration did not resort to high-level envoys or other special arrangements that were used by the Clinton administration to resolve difficult US-China issues. It insisted on working through normal State Department and Defense Department channels that did not raise China's stature in US foreign policy. In an unusual step showing that the administration was speaking firmly with one voice during the incident, US officials were instructed to avoid all but the most essential contacts with Chinese officials in Washington and elsewhere. [6]

Bush administration interest in seeking negotiations with China in order to create "deliverables" and other agreements remained low. Its reaction to the EP-3 episode, markedly increased US support for Taiwan, and a new US focus on China as a potential threat showed Beijing leaders that the Bush government, while seeking to broaden areas of cooperation where possible, was prepared to see US-China relations worsen if necessary.

Chinese leaders by mid-2001 seemed to recognize that if US-China relations were to avoid further deterioration, it was up to China to take steps to improve ties. In a period of overall ascendant US influence in Asian and world affairs, Beijing saw its interests best served by a stance that muted differences and sought common ground. Chinese officials thus significantly adjusted their approach to the United States. They became more solicitous and less acrimonious in interaction with US officials. Chinese officials and media toned down public Chinese rhetoric against the United States. They gave some tentative signs of public PRC support for the US military presence in East Asia. The US side also signaled an interest to calm the concerns of friends and allies in Asia over the state of US-China relations and to pursue areas of common ground in trade and other areas with the PRC.[7]

US-China relations faced a crisis when on April 1, 2001, a Chinese jet fighter crashed with a US reconnaissance plane, an EP-3, in international waters off the China coast. The jet was destroyed and the pilot was killed. The EP-3 was seriously damaged but managed to make an emergency landing on China's Hainan Island. The US crew was held for eleven days and the US plane for much longer by Chinese authorities. Weeks of negotiations produced compromises that allowed the crew and plane to return to the United States, but neither side accepted responsibility for the incident.[8]

Many specialists predicted continued deterioration of relations, but both governments worked to resolve issues and establish a businesslike relationship that emphasized positive aspects of the relationship and played down differences. The terrorist attack on America in September 2001 diverted US attention away from China as a potential strategic threat. Chinese officials privately indicated that they sought a constructive relationship with the new US government, and in the process they publicly showed remarkable deference in the face of the Bush government's uniquely assertive stance on Taiwan as well as its strong positions on regional and national ballistic missile defense, expansion of US-Japanese defense cooperation, NATO expansion, and other sensitive security issues that had been focal points of Chinese criticism of the United States in the recent past. The Chinese leaders seemed preoccupied at home, notably focusing on a very important and somewhat irregular leadership transition and related issues of power sharing and development policy. Against this background, Chinese leaders worked hard to moderate previous harsh rhetoric and pressure tactics in order to consolidate relations with the United States.

The course of US-China relations became smoother than at any time since the normalization of those relations. US preoccupation with the wars in Afghanistan and Iraq and the broader war on global terrorism meant that US strategic attention to China as a threat remained a secondary consideration for American policy makers. Chinese leaders for their part continued to deal with an incomplete leadership transition and the broad problem of trying to sustain a one-party authoritarian political regime amid a vibrant economy and rapid social change. In this context, the two powers, despite a wide range of continuing differences ranging from Taiwan and Tibet to trade issues and human rights, managed to see their interests best served by generally emphasizing the positive. In particular, they found new common ground in dealing with the crisis caused by North Korea's nuclear weapons program beginning in 2002, and the Chinese appreciated Bush administration pressure on Taiwan's leader Chen Shui-bian to avoid steps toward independence for Taiwan that could lead to conflict in the Taiwan Strait.

It is easy to exaggerate the growing Sino-American convergence during the Bush administration. The antiterrorism campaign after September 11, 2001, saw an upswing in US-China cooperation, though China was somewhat tentative and reserved in supporting the US war against Afghanistan. President Bush's visits to Shanghai in October 2001 and Beijing in February 2002 underlined differences as well as common ground. The US president repeatedly affirmed his strong support for Taiwan and his firm position regarding human rights issues in China. His aides made clear China's lower priority in the administration's view of US interests as the Bush administration continued to focus higher priority on relations with Japan and other allies in Asia and the Pacific. In its first year, the Bush administration imposed sanctions on China over issues involving China's reported proliferation of weapons of mass destruction (WMD) more times than during the eight years of the Clinton administration. The Defense Department's Quadrennial Defense Review unmistakably saw China as a potential threat in Asia. American ballistic missile defense programs, opposed by China, went forward, and rising US influence in Southwest and Central Asia and prolonged military deployments there were at odds with China's interest in securing its western flank.[9] The Defense Department's annual reports on the Chinese military pulled few punches in focusing on China's military threat to Taiwan and to US forces that might come to Taiwan's aid in the event of a conflict with the PRC. The Bush administration's September 2002 National Security Strategy Report called for better relations with China but clearly warned against any power seeking to challenge US interests with military force.[10]

It was notable that China's increased restraint and moderation toward the United States came even in the face of these new departures in US policy and behavior under the Bush administration—namely, presidential pledges (in particular) along with military and political support for Taiwan, strong missile defense programs, and strong support for alliance strengthening with Japan and expanded military cooperation with India. In the recent past, such US actions would have prompted strong Chinese public attacks and possibly military countermeasures.

American leaders showed an increased willingness to meet Chinese leaders' symbolic needs for summitry, and the US president pleased his Chinese counterpart by repeatedly endorsing a "constructive, cooperative, and candid" relationship with China. Amid continued Chinese moderation and concessions in 2002 and reflecting greater US interest in consolidating relations and avoiding tensions with China at a time of growing US preoccupation with the war on terrorism, Iraq, and North Korea, the Bush administration broadened cooperation with China and gave US relations with China a higher priority as the year wore on. An October 2002 meeting between President Bush and President Jiang Zemin at the US president's ranch in Crawford, Texas, highlighted this trend. Concessions and gestures, mainly from the Chinese side dealing with proliferation, Iraq, the release of dissidents, US agricultural imports, Tibet, and Taiwan, facilitated the positive Crawford summit.[11] Meanwhile, senior US leaders began to refer to China and Jiang Zemin as a "friend."[12] They adhered to public positions on Taiwan that were acceptable to Beijing. They sanctioned an anti-PRC terrorist group active in China's Xinjiang region. The Defense Department was slow to resume high-level contacts with China, reflecting continued wariness in the face of China's ongoing military buildup focused on dealing with Taiwan and US forces that may seek to protect Taiwan, but formal relations at various senior levels were resumed by late 2002.[13]

Looking back, it appears that patterns of Bush administration policy and behavior toward China began to change significantly in 2003. American officials sometimes continued to speak in terms of "shaping" Chinese policies and behavior through tough deterrence along with moderate engagement. However, the thrust of US policy and behavior increasingly focused on positive engagement. China also received increasingly high priority in US policy in Asia and the world.

The determinants of the US approach now appeared to center on the Bush administration's growing preoccupations with the war in Iraq, its mixed record in other areas in the war on terror and broader complications in the Middle East, and wide-ranging international and growing domestic disapproval of Bush administration policies. The North Korean nuclear program emerged as a major problem in 2003, and the US government came to rely heavily on China to help manage the issue in ways that avoided major negative fallout for the interests of the US government. Although Asian policy did not figure prominently in the 2004 presidential campaign, Senator John Kerry, the Democratic candidate, used a televised presidential debate to challenge President Bush's handling of North Korea's nuclear weapons development. President Bush countered by emphasizing his reliance on China in order to manage the issue in accord with US interests. [14]

The Bush administration's determination to avoid trouble with China at a time of major foreign policy troubles elsewhere saw the president and senior US leaders strongly pressure Taiwan's government to stop initiating policies seen as provocative by China and possible causes of confrontation and war in US-China relations. [15] The strong rhetorical emphasis on democracy promotion in the Bush administration's second term notably avoided serious pressures against China's authoritarian system.

The US government's emphasis on positive engagement with China did not hide the many continuing US-China differences or US efforts to plan for contingencies in case a rising China turned aggressive or otherwise disrupted US interests. The United States endeavored to use growing interdependence, engagement, and dialogues with China to foster webs of relationships that would tie down or constrain possible Chinese policies and actions deemed negative to US interests. [16]

On the whole, the Chinese government of President Hu Jintao welcomed and supported the new directions in US China policy. The Chinese leaders endeavored to build on the positives and play down the negatives in relations with the United States. This approach fit well with the Chinese leadership's broader priorities of strengthening national development and Communist Party legitimacy that were said to require China to use carefully the "strategic opportunity" of prevailing international circumstances seen as generally advantageous to Chinese interests. As in the case of US policy toward China, Chinese engagement with the United States did not hide Chinese contingency plans against suspected US encirclement, pressure, and containment and the Chinese use of engagement and interdependence as a type of Gulliver strategy, discussed below, to constrain and tie down possible US policies and actions deemed negative to Chinese interests. [17]

As China expanded military power along with economic and diplomatic relations in Asian and world affairs at a time of US preoccupation with the war in Iraq and other foreign policy problems, debate emerged inside and outside the US government about the implications of China's rise for US interests. Within the Bush administration, there emerged three viewpoints or schools of thought, though US officials frequently were eclectic, holding views of the implications of China's rise from various perspectives. [18]

On one side were US officials who judged that China's rise in Asia was designed by the Chinese leadership to dominate Asia and in the process to undermine US leadership in the region. [19] A more moderate view of China's rise in Asia came from US officials who judged that China's focus in the region was to improve China's position in Asia mainly in order to sustain regional stability, promote China's development, reassure neighbors and prevent balancing against China, and isolate Taiwan. Officials of this school of thought judged that China's intentions were not focused on isolating and weakening the United States in Asia. Nevertheless, the Chinese policies and behavior, even though not targeted against the United States, contrasted with perceived inattentive and maladroit US policies and practices. The result was that China's rise was having an indirect but substantial negative impact on US leadership in Asia.

A third school of thought was identified with US Deputy Secretary of State Robert Zoellick, who by 2005 publicly articulated a strong argument for greater US cooperation with China over Asian and other issues as China rose in regional and international prominence.[20] This viewpoint held that the United States had much to gain from working directly and cooperatively with China in order to encourage the PRC to use its rising influence in "responsible" ways in accord with broad US interests in Asian and world affairs. This viewpoint seemed to take into account the fact that the Bush administration was already working closely with China in six-party talks to deal with North Korea's nuclear weapons development and that US and Chinese collaboration or consultations continued on such sensitive topics as the war on terror, Afghanistan, Pakistan, Iran, Sudan, Burma, and even Taiwan as well as bilateral economic, security, and other issues. Thus, this school of thought gave less emphasis than the other two on competition with China and more emphasis on cooperation with China in order to preserve and enhance US leadership and interests in Asia as China rose.

Bush administration policy came to embrace the third point of view. Senior US leaders reviewed in greater depth the implications of China's rise and the strengths and weaknesses of the United States in Asia. The review showed that US standing as Asia's leading power was basically sound. American military deployments and cooperation throughout the Asia-Pacific region were robust. US economic importance in the region was growing, not declining. Overall, it was clear that no other power or coalition of powers was even remotely able or willing to undertake the costs, risks, and commitments of the United States in sustaining regional stability and development essential for the core interests of the vast majority of regional governments.[21] Thus, China's rise—while increasingly important—posed less substantial and significant challenge for US interests than many of the published commentaries and specialists' assessments might have led one to believe.

On this basis, the US administration increasingly emphasized positive engagement and a growing number of dialogues with China, encouraging China to act responsibly and building ever-growing webs of relationships and interdependence. This pattern fit well with Chinese priorities regarding national development in a period of advantageous international conditions while building interdependencies and relationships that constrained possible negative US policies or behaviors.

Domestic criticism of US policy toward China declined sharply with the election of President Bush and Republican majorities in the Congress and the American preoccupation with the war on terrorism. As explained below, Bush's initially tougher posture toward China was in line with views of the vocal critics of Clinton administration engagement policies, and the president benefited from strong Republican leadership and discipline that kept Congress in line with the president's foreign policies. American politicians and interest groups seeking prominence and support in attacking Chinese policies and practices were overwhelmed with the shift in the country's foreign policy emphasis after the terrorist attacks of September 11, 2001. Domestic criticism of the president's management of an increasingly close engagement with China began to revive in 2005 as the war on terrorism wore on and the conflict in Iraq reflected major setbacks for the Bush administration. Economic and trade issues dominated the China policy debate. At the same time, congressional, media, and interest groups revived criticism of China on a variety of other issues involving, notably, human rights, international energy competition, and foreign relations with perceived rogue regimes.

Democrats led by long-standing critics of China won majority control of both houses of Congress in the November 2006 elections. Democratic Party candidates for the 2008 presidential election generally were critical of the Bush administration's free-trade policies, which saw the US annual trade deficit with China rise to more than $250 billion and coincided with the loss of good-paying manufacturing jobs in the United States. They also tended to take a tougher line than the US administration on human rights, Tibet, and other issues in US-China relations. In the face of American criticism of China and of US government moderation toward China, the Bush administration, some in Congress, and some US interest groups emphasized pursuit of constructive engagement and senior-level dialogues as means to encourage China to behave according to US-accepted norms as a "responsible stakeholder" in the prevailing international order and thereby show that the positives in US-China relations outweighed the negatives.[22]

Viewed from the perspective of international relations theories, the patterns of US administration and Chinese government approaches to one another during this period seem well explained through cost-benefit analyses associated with realism. The differences in interests and values remained, as did the very different identities of the two societies, but pragmatic leaders on both sides viewed carefully the power realities that they were attempting to change to their advantage. They weighed costs and benefits of emphasizing various differences and, on the whole, saw the benefit in pursuing paths of convergence of mutual interest.

PRIORITIES AND ISSUES IN US POLICY TOWARD CHINA

As seen in chapter 5, the US debates over policy toward China after the Cold War generally had more to do with developments in the United States, especially changes in US *perceptions* of Chinese government policies and behavior, than with changes in those Chinese policies and behavior. From one perspective, the Chinese authorities generally were following broadly similar policies in the post-Mao (d. 1976) period designed to build national wealth and power, maintain territorial integrity and achieve unification with Taiwan, enhance the leadership of the authoritarian Communist Party, and improve the economic livelihood and social opportunities for the Chinese people. Their challenge to US-supported norms regarding such subjects as human rights, weapons proliferation, environmental protection, the use of force to settle territorial disputes, and other sensitive issues continued to wax and wane over the years. They often posed serious problems for the United States and US interests, but on balance they became less serious at the outset of the twenty-first century than they were in the Mao period or even during much of the rule of Deng Xiaoping.[23]

However, the shock of the 1989 Tiananmen incident and the end of the Cold War fundamentally changed the way the United States dealt with China. A pattern prevailing into the twenty-first century saw the US administration generally continue to seek closer ties, including frequent high-level leadership meetings and various senior official dialogues, in order to develop areas of common ground while managing differences. The US administration and the Chinese government typically highlighted the many positive results from US-China cooperation and dialogue. These included cooperation in facilitating mutually advantageous trade and investment relations, cooperation in managing such regional crises and threats as the Asian economic crisis of 1997–98, the crises in 1994 and later (beginning again in 2002) over North Korea's nuclear weapons program, the 1998 crisis prompted by nuclear weapons tests by India and Pakistan, the global war on terrorism beginning in 2001, and the global economic crisis beginning in 2008. Under the rubric of engagement or cooperation, the US administration officials and their Chinese counterparts presided over an ever-increasing economic interdependence between the United States and China, supplemented by growing cultural and political contacts and developing military contacts.

In contrast, a variety of US groups were in the lead among US critics who applied pressure in the Congress, the media, and in other public discourse to encourage a firmer US policy designed to press the Chinese government to conform more to US-backed norms. As discussed in chapter 5, some of these groups and advocates had varied motives that related less to China and its government's behavior and more to partisan or other ulterior benefits these groups and advocates derived from taking a tough stand against Chinese practices. The influence of the critics was sometimes evident in debates within US administrations. It was reflected more clearly in the varying intensity and scope of congressional debate and criticism of administration China policy that generally emphasized positive engagement in the post–Cold War period. On the whole, such criticism and the negative impact it had on developing US-China relations was seen to decline along with the overall influence of Congress in determining American foreign policy in the twenty-first century. In particular, in the 107th Congress (2001–2), which coincided with the start of the George W. Bush administration, there was a marked decline in the scope and intensity of domestic American debate over China policy compared to those seen in the 1990s. There were several reasons for the decline. First, the early actions of the Bush government supported firmer policies toward China that were backed by many in Congress regarding Taiwan, Tibet, human rights, and security concerns. These actions helped calm the strong congressional debate over China policy that prevailed in the previous Congress. Second, partisan attacks on the US administration's engagement policy toward China also diminished as the Bush White House and the Congress both were controlled by a Republican Party leadership intent on showing unity and party discipline on China policy and other sensitive issues. [24] Third, US preoccupation with the war on terrorism, including the US-led military attacks on Afghanistan and Iraq, made it more difficult for US interest groups and other activists to gain the public and private attention in Congress and elsewhere that they seemed to need in order to pressure for changes in US policies toward China.

Congress and China Policy

To help grasp the scope and depth of the US domestic debate over China policy during the first decade of the twenty-first century, it is instructive to review the issues that were raised in debates, notably in the US Congress. Because of its receptivity to US domestic political movements and constituent pressures, Congress has remained a focal point for those US individuals and groups critical of China's policies and practices, who pressed for change in US policy toward China. The record of the post–Cold War debate in Congress over China policy is long and wide-ranging. It deals with clusters of sensitive issues involving human rights and democratic political values, security issues, economic questions, and sovereignty issues, especially regarding Taiwan and Tibet. Highlights of the issues considered in congressional debate and actions at the outset of the twenty-first century are noted below. They provide evidence of the broad range of American interests that were trying to influence policy toward China and the directions these interests wanted China policy to follow. In general terms, the pattern shows these groups often opposed improvements or other forward movement in US-China relations until the Chinese government changed its policies and practices more in accord with US-supported norms. The groups sometimes favored sanctions or other pressures to force the Chinese government to change, although US business interests and others with a strong economic stake in China often were successful in seeking to sustain constructive trade relations without such pressures.

After the intense US domestic debates over China policy in the 1990s, the overall impact of the groups and the actions of Congress served in the first decade of the twenty-first century more as a drag on forward movement in US-China relations than an impetus for tougher US policy toward China. There was little support for serious retrogression in key areas of US-China relations. And, as in the case of the 1990s, there was almost no support for a US policy that would lead to military confrontation or strategic containment of China.[25]

A high point of revived congressional pressure on the administration's China policy came with the inauguration of the Democratic Party–controlled 110th Congress in 2007; Democratic leadership continued with stronger majorities in control of the 111th Congress beginning in 2009, though the partisan incentive of the Democratic-led Congress to differ with the president, now Democratic leader Barack Obama, declined. Overall, while some during these years forecast major challenges to existing US China policy from domestic US critics in the Congress and those working through the Congress, the outcome was more in line with predictions of a much more mixed outlook with pressures for a tougher US China policy offset by important countervailing factors.[26]

Congress dealt with each of the policy priorities and issues noted below in a variety of ways, through press releases and statements reacting to US media stories highlighting negative Chinese practices, legislation, hearings, so-called dear colleague letters, formal letters to the administration, speeches in and out of Congress, and other means.[27]

Human Rights Issues

China's human rights abuses remained among the most visible and persistent points of contention in US-China relations in the post–Cold War period. China's human rights record presented a mixed picture, with both setbacks and minor improvements providing plenty of ammunition for US policy debate in the Congress and elsewhere. Among the more positive developments in China's human rights record, the Chinese government signed two key human rights agreements: the UN Covenant on Economic, Social, and Cultural Rights (October 27, 1997) and the International Covenant on Civil and Political Rights (March 12, 1998). The government also was allowing local, competitive elections in rural areas in China, and it implemented legislation to make political and judicial processes more transparent and to hold law enforcement officials more accountable for their actions.

Crackdowns against Dissidents and the Falun Gong Group   In 1999, American news accounts began to give wide coverage to reports that the Chinese government was arresting prominent activists and giving out harsh jail sentences for what most Americans considered to be routine and benign civil acts. On July 22, 1999, the government outlawed Falun Gong, a spiritual movement with an impressive nationwide organization in China, said to combine Buddhist and Taoist meditation practices with a series of exercises. The government arrested Falun Gong leaders, imposed harsh prison sentences, closed Falun Gong facilities, and confiscated Falun Gong literature. At that time, the Chinese government also cracked down on democracy activists trying to register a new independent political party, the Chinese Democracy Party. Promoters of the new party were convicted on subversion charges and given long prison sentences. [28]

Tibet and Xinjiang   Chinese officials also harshly suppressed dissents among ethnic minorities, particularly in Tibet and in the Xinjiang-Uighur Autonomous Region, in China's far west. In April 1999, Amnesty International issued a report accusing the Chinese government of gross violations of human rights in Xinjiang, including widespread use of torture to extract confessions, lengthy prison sentences, and numerous executions. Harsh Chinese suppression continued as the global war on terrorism saw the Chinese government brand dissidents in Xinjiang as terrorists with some links to al Qaeda and other international terrorist organizations. Although US administration officials warned, after September 11, 2001, that the global antiterror campaign should not be used to persecute Uighurs or other minorities with political grievances against Beijing, some believe that the US government made a concession to the PRC on August 26, 2002, when it announced that it was placing one small group, the East Turkestan Islamic Movement, on the US list of terrorist groups. [29]

A significant episode of anti-China activism and rhetoric in Congress accompanied public protests in the United States and harsh American and other Western media criticism of China's crackdown of dissent and violence in Tibet in 2008. Congressional leaders called for a boycott of the summer 2008 Olympic Games, but President Bush announced firmly that he would attend the games.

Chinese Prisons/Prison Labor   Prisons in China were widely criticized for their conditions, treatment of prisoners, and requirements that prisoners perform productive work. From the standpoint of US policy, one issue was the extent to which products made by Chinese prisoners were exported to the US market, a violation of US law. Meanwhile, periodic reports of Chinese security forces taking organs from executed prisoners and selling them on the black market prompted repeated congressional hearings, queries, and condemnations.[30]

Family Planning/Coercive Abortion   Controversies in US population planning assistance continued with regard to China's population programs. Abortion, and the degree to which coercive abortions and sterilizations occur in China's family planning programs, remained a prominent issue in these debates.[31]

Religious Freedom   US government reports including the Department of State's Annual Reports on International Religious Freedom and the report issued on May 1, 2000, by the US Commission on International Religious Freedom criticized Chinese government policies on religious practices. They provided a focal point for congressional hearings and statements. Although some foreign commentators noted recent moderation and even encouragement by Chinese officials regarding freer religious practices, the strong US criticism of China's record on religious freedom continued.[32]

Internet and Media Restrictions   The growth of Internet, cell phone use, and text messaging led to new Chinese regulations begun in 2005 that prompted some congressional hearings and other actions. A key issue was the extent to which US Internet firms collaborated with Chinese authorities in helping the latter control Internet use in China.[33]

Issues in Security Relations

US-China security and military relations never fully recovered after they were suspended following the 1989 Tiananmen Square crackdown. The EP-3 incident resulted in a temporary halt regarding most military contacts.

China's Military Expansion   Some officials in the George W. Bush administration, backed by officials in Congress, the media, and others, focused on China's military buildup with regard to a Taiwan contingency concerning US military intervention and involvement. They pressed for stronger US measures to deal with this situation, which in turn reinforced US-China military competition and complicated bilateral military relations.[34]

WMD Proliferation   The Bush administration, backed by many in the Congress, also took a tougher position against China's WMD proliferation.[35] One key security issue for the United States was China's record of weapons sales, technology transfers, and nuclear energy assistance, particularly to Iran and Pakistan.

Espionage   Beginning in the late 1990s, US media sources reported about ongoing investigations of cases of alleged Chinese espionage against the United States dating back to the 1980s. The most serious case involved China's alleged acquisition of significant information about the W-88, an advanced miniaturized US nuclear warhead, as a result of alleged security breaches at the Los Alamos nuclear science laboratory between 1984 and

1988. Another serious instance, first reported in late April 1999 by the *New York Times,* involved allegations that a Taiwan-born Chinese-American scientist, Wen Ho Lee, had downloaded critical nuclear weapons codes, called legacy codes, from a classified computer system at Los Alamos to an unclassified computer system accessible by anyone with the proper password. As noted in chapter 5, alleged Chinese espionage featured prominently in the 1999 Cox Committee report that was sharply critical of the US administration's counterespionage activities against China. [36]

Subsequently, US media focused attention on a complicated case involving an alleged Chinese double agent whose sexual relationship with senior FBI counterintelligence officers seemed to undermine the integrity of US government efforts to curb Chinese espionage. Suspicions of Chinese espionage were voiced in Congress when the State Department decided to purchase computers for use in classified communications from a Chinese company. The controversy caused the department to halt the purchase. [37] Developments later in the decade featured arrests and convictions of individuals illegally funneling advanced US technologies to China at the behest of Chinese government clandestine agents.

Economic Issues

Trade Deficit   Issues involving trade with China factored heavily into US policy debates. The US trade deficit with China surged from a $17.8 billion deficit in 1989 to around $100 billion in 2000. It more than doubled in the five following years and was $256 billion in 2008. [38]

Intellectual Property Rights   China's lack of protection for intellectual property rights (IPR) was long an issue in US-China relations and became more important in the 109th (2005–6) and 110th (2007–8) Congresses. According to calculations from US industry sources in 2006, IPR piracy cost US firms $2.5 billion in lost sales a year, and the IPR piracy rate in China for US products remained estimated at 90 percent. Backed by Congress, US administration officials repeatedly pressed Chinese officials to better implement IPR regulations. [39]

Currency Valuation   In recent years until 2005, the PRC pegged its currency, the renminbi (RMB), to the US dollar at a rate of about 8.3 RMB to the dollar—a valuation that many critics in Congress and elsewhere in the United States concluded kept the PRC's currency undervalued, making PRC exports artificially cheap and making it harder for US producers to compete. On July 1, 2005, the PRC changed this valuation method. The resulting slow appreciation in the RMB from this action was not sufficient to assuage US congressional concerns. [40]

Chinese Purchase of US Government Securities   A related concern was Chinese purchases of US Treasury bills and other US government securities as a means of recycling China's massive trade surplus with the United States while maintaining the relatively low value of Chinese currency relative to the US dollar. The Chinese investments seemed very important to the stability of the US economy. Some congressional and other US critics warned of US overdependence on this type of investment by China. [41]

Bid for Unocal   The bid of a Chinese state-controlled oil company to acquire the US oil firm Unocal in 2005 set off an uproar in Congress and the US media. The congressional debate over the alleged dangers of the transaction to US energy security was so intense that the Chinese firm withdrew the bid after two months. [42]

China's International Rise

A set of issues emerged in the 109th and 110th Congresses, focusing on the critical implications of China's economic growth and increasing international engagement and influence for US economic, security, and political interests in various parts of the world. To feed its growing needs for resources, capital, and technology, Chinese officials, businesses, and others successfully sought trade agreements; oil and gas contracts; scientific and technological cooperation; and multilateral security, political, and economic arrangements with countries around its periphery and throughout the world. China's growing international economic engagement was backed by China's increasing military power and went hand in hand with expanding Chinese political influence. China notably used unconditional economic exchanges and assistance to woo governments and leaders seen as rogues or outliers by the United States and other developed countries. Chinese practices undercut Western pressures on these officials and governments to improve governance in accord with Western norms. China's increased influence also extended to many key allies and associates of the United States and to regions like Latin America, where the United States exerted predominant influence. [43]

Sovereignty Issues: Taiwan and Tibet

Taiwan   Taiwan remained the most sensitive and complex issue in US-China relations. Beijing engaged in a military buildup focused on a Taiwan contingency involving the United States.

In 2001 the George W. Bush administration offered the largest package of US arms to Taiwan in ten years and allowed President Chen Shui-bian to tour more freely and to meet with congressional representatives during stopovers in the United States. President Bush publicly pledged to come to Taiwan's aid with US military power if Taiwan were attacked by mainland China. The steps were welcomed in Congress, but they deepened Beijing's judgment that the United States would remain at odds with China over the Taiwan issue for the foreseeable future.[44]

Beginning in 2003, as the Taiwan government of President Chen Shui-bian advanced pro-independence proposals that the Bush administration saw as destabilizing, the US president and his aides took steps to curb those potentially destabilizing actions. In general, these steps elicited only minor objections from the normally pro-Taiwan Congress.[45] Beginning in 2008, the calming of cross-strait tensions that resulted from Taiwan President Ma Ying-jeou's policies of reassurance toward China was welcomed in the administration and the Congress.

Tibet   The Dalai Lama long had some strong supporters in the US Congress and among other US opinion leaders, and these continued to put pressure on the White House to protect Tibetan culture and accord Tibet greater status in US law despite Beijing's strong objections.[46] The Tibet issue flared again in US-China relations in 2007. Congress awarded the Congressional Gold Medal to the Dalai Lama in a public ceremony. President Bush met the Dalai Lama during his visit to Washington, and Bush took part in the congressional award ceremony. China protested strongly.[47] Congressional leaders spoke out firmly against the Chinese crackdown on dissent and violence in Tibet in 2008.

China and the 110th Congress

The strong victory of the Democratic Party in the November 7, 2006, congressional elections underlined a broad desire of the American electorate for change in the policies and priorities of the G. W. Bush administration. In the House of Representatives, the Democratic Party moved from a deficit position of thirty seats against the Republican majority to an advantage of thirty seats over the Republicans, and in the Senate it erased the Republican Party's ten-seat advantage, gaining a one-seat majority.

The implications of the Democratic victory seemed serious for US policy in the Asia-Pacific and particularly for US policy toward China, the focus of greatest controversy in the US Congress regarding Asia-Pacific countries. The Democratic majority of the 110th Congress, led by opinionated and often confrontational leaders Representative Nancy Pelosi and Senator Harry Reid, pressed for change in a partisan atmosphere charged by preparations for the US presidential election of 2008. The Democratic majority was forecast to pursue strong trade and economic measures that, if successful, would seriously disrupt US economic relations with China and the free trade emphasis of the Bush administration. Mainstream commentator Thomas Friedman predicted a civil war in American politics over the massive US trade deficit and related economic issues with China. Democrats pushing more activist approaches regarding human rights and environmental initiatives added to anticipated serious complications in US relations with China. [48]

In contrast to such dire warnings, however, factors of power, priorities, politics, and personalities diluted the push for substantial change in US policy in Asia and toward China in particular. These factors resulted in a more balanced assessment of what the Democratic-led Congress could actually accomplish in changing US policies and practices in Asia. On the one hand, there were frequent episodes of congressional proposals, postures, and maneuvers regarding US policies and practices involving China. On the other hand, the impact of these congressional actions seemed not to change the course of US relations with China in major ways. Overall the experience supported the view that the equilibrium that emerged in relations between the US and Chinese governments would not be substantially challenged by the continuing US domestic debate over priorities in policy toward China. [49]

Power   The US Constitution gave the executive the leading role in foreign affairs. In the face of a determined president like George W. Bush, the Democratic-led Congress appeared to have only a few levers to force change in areas that impacted on US relations with Asia and especially China. Congress controlled government spending—the "power of the purse." This control could be used to block, redirect, or tailor administration requests for US government spending and US foreign assistance. The relevance of this issue to China was low, especially as official US aid was not allowed to go to China. Congressional opposition could hold up and possibly halt administration personnel appointments or policy initiatives needing congressional approval. In its last years, the Bush administration did not appear to anticipate major or controversial personnel changes regarding China, and broader Asia policy or substantial policy initiatives requiring congressional action.

Priorities   Newly empowered Democratic leaders in the House and Senate voiced varied priorities, and China policy was not high on the list. They tended to focus initially on such domestic issues as raising the minimum wage, controlling government spending deficits, strengthening job security for US workers, preserving Social Security, and providing limited tax relief for middle-class taxpayers. Finding ways to change the adverse course of the US-led war in Iraq dominated the foreign policy agenda.

Against this background, lower priority attention to China-related issues focused on finding ways to deal more effectively with the massive US trade deficit and perceived unfair Chinese trade and economic policies. Some Democratic leaders and members favored strong emphasis on human rights, labor conditions, and environmental concerns in governing US policy to China and other concerned Asian countries, but others did not.

Politics   The bruising fight among House Democrats leading to the selection of Representative Steny Hoyer as House majority leader over the wishes of Speaker-designate Nancy Pelosi was a reminder that the Democrats in the House of Representatives would not follow their leaders in lock-step as Republicans had done in recent years. Even if Speaker Pelosi wanted to push House Democrats to follow her past leanings to be tough in relations with China regarding human rights and trade, the makeup of the Democratic caucus and likely committee leadership strongly suggested less-than-uniform support. Conservative Democratic members increased as a result of the 2006 election and were reluctant to press too hard on human rights, environment, and other issues when important US business and security interests were at stake. Many Democratic members supported free trade and resisted what they saw as protectionist measures of Democratic colleagues against China. They were backed by polling data of the Chicago Council on Global Affairs, which showed that Americans were fairly comfortable with the economic rise of China.[50]

Personalities   Given loose Democratic leadership control, individual members in key committee assignments mattered in the Democratic-led Congress and its approach to China issues. Because they differed among themselves on key issues, they were likely to have difficulty coming up with united positions in pressing for meaningful change in Bush administration policies regarding China.[51] On the one hand, the public positions of House leader Pelosi and Senate leader Reid were tough on trade and related economic and human rights issues regarding China. Representative Sander Levin and some other members of the House Ways and Means Committee and other economic policy committees also favored a tougher US stance on trade issues with China. However, they were offset by committee moderates headed by the Ways and Means Committee's leading Democrat, Charles Rangel. In the Senate, the leading Democrat on the Finance Committee, Max Baucus, also held moderate views supported by others on the committee that eschewed protectionism.

Leading Democrats in the House Committee on International Relations had records of vocal opposition to human rights violations, notably by China's authoritarian administration. These meshed well with the views of Representative Pelosi but were at odds with the large number of Democratic members who joined various working groups designed to foster pragmatic exchanges with, and more informed and effective US policy toward, China. On balance, these groups moderated the congressional tendency to engage in "China-bashing" seen during annual congressional debates in the 1990s on China's trading status with the United States.

In sum, prevailing circumstances showed why US policy toward China would not change substantially as a result of the Democratic victory in 2006. China's massive trade and foreign exchange surpluses and perceived unfair currency and trading practices generated legislation and other actions to apply pressure on the Bush administration to toughen the US approach to

China, but they appeared to fall short of forcing significant protectionist measures against China. Despite congressional pressure, the Bush administration's Treasury Department consistently refused to have China labeled a currency manipulator in its periodic reports to Congress. An increase in congressional rhetoric and posturing against Chinese human rights violations and other practices offending US norms was balanced by growing congressional interest in working pragmatically with China in study groups and exchanges. Any congressional interest in pressing the Bush administration to increase support for Taiwan despite China's objections seemed offset by the turbulent political situation in Taiwan in the last years of the administration of President Chen Shui-bian and the fracturing of the Taiwan lobby in Washington as a result of partisan and divisive politics in Taiwan.

CHINESE POLICY PRIORITIES

Those endeavoring to understand the priorities that determined the PRC's foreign policy, especially its policy toward the United States after the Cold War and into the twenty-first century, have a wealth of books, articles, and other assessments and analyses by scholars and specialists in Chinese foreign policy. These works document ever-expanding Chinese interaction with the outside world through economic exchanges in an era of globalization, and broadening Chinese involvement with international organizations dealing with security, economic, political, cultural, and other matters. They demonstrate a continuing trend toward greater transparency in Chinese foreign policy decision making and policy formation since the beginning of the era of Chinese reforms following the death of Mao Zedong in 1976. As a result, there is considerable agreement backed by convincing evidence in these writings about the course and goals of contemporary Chinese foreign policy and how they affect the United States. [52]

In the post-Mao period, Chinese Communist Party (CCP) leaders focused on economic reform and development as the basis of their continued survival as the rulers of China. Support for economic liberalization and openness waxed and waned, but the overall trend emphasized greater market orientation and foreign economic interchange as critical in promoting economic advancement, and by extension, supporting the continued CCP monopoly of political power. For a time, the leaders were less clear in their attitudes toward political liberalization and change, with some in the 1980s calling for substantial reform of the authoritarian Communist system. Since the crackdown at Tiananmen in 1989, there was a general consensus among the party elite to control dissent and other political challenges, allowing for only slow, gradual, and often halting political change that can be closely monitored by the authorities. [53]

In foreign affairs, post-Mao leaders retreated from the sometimes strident calls to change the international system, and they worked pragmatically to establish relationships with important countries, especially the United States and Japan but also China's neighbors in Southeast Asia and elsewhere, who would assist China's development and enhance Beijing's overall goal of developing national wealth and power. The collapse of Soviet communism at the end of the Cold War posed a major ideological challenge to Chinese leaders and reduced Western interest in China as a counterweight to the USSR. But the advance of China's economy soon attracted Western leaders once again, while the demise of the USSR gave China a freer hand to pursue its interests, less encumbered by the long-term Soviet strategic threat. [54]

Against this backdrop and following the death of strong-man leader Deng Xiaoping in 1997, Chinese authorities led by the president and party chief, Jiang Zemin, were anxious to minimize problems with the United States and other countries in order to avoid complications in their efforts to appear successful in completing three major tasks for the year, involving (1) the July 1997 transition of Hong Kong to Chinese rule, (2) the reconfiguration of Chinese leadership and policy at the Fifteenth CCP Congress in September 1997, and (3) the Sino-American summit of October 1997. [55]

Generally pleased with the results of these three endeavors, Chinese leaders began implementing new policy priorities. At the top of the list was an ambitious multiyear effort to transform tens of thousands of China's money-losing state-owned enterprises (SOEs) into more efficient businesses by reforming them (e.g., selling them to private concerns, forming large conglomerates, or other actions). Beijing also embarked on major programs to promote economic and administrative efficiency and protect China's potentially vulnerable financial systems from any negative fallout from the 1997–98 Asian economic crisis and subsequent uncertainties.

Making collective leadership work was an ongoing challenge for China's top leaders. President Jiang Zemin gained in stature and influence, but his power still did not compare to that exerted by Mao Zedong and Deng Xiaoping. When it came time for Jiang and his senior colleagues to retire, there was a distinct possibility of a renewed struggle for power and influential positions by up-and-coming leaders. The leadership transition was handled cautiously, with Jiang slow to hand over control of military power to the new generation of party leaders headed by Hu Jintao. Once Hu assumed the leadership of the Chinese party, government, and military by 2004, he moved carefully in consolidating his leadership position. He seemed well aware that if a major economic, political, or foreign policy crisis were to emerge, leadership conflict over what to do, how to do it, and who should do it could be intense. Hu and his associates dealt with such major issues as the crisis caused by the outbreak of the so-called SARS epidemic in China in 2002–3 and the North Korean nuclear crisis beginning in 2003, with generally effective policies that endeavored to support the leadership's interest in preserving Communist rule in China. The results of the Seventeenth Congress of the CCP in October 2007 appeared to underline a continuing cautious approach to political change and international and domestic circumstances, one that was designed to reinforce Communist Party rule in China.[56]

There was little sign of disagreement among senior leaders over recent broad policy emphasis on economic reform, though sectors affected by reform often resisted strenuously. The ambitious plans for economic reform, especially reform of the SOEs, were needed if China's economy was to become sufficiently efficient to sustain the growth rates seen as needed to justify continued Communist rule and to develop China's wealth and power. China's entrance into the World Trade Organization (WTO) in 2001 strengthened the need for greater economic efficiency and reform.

The reforms also exacerbated social and economic uncertainties, which reinforced the government's determination to maintain a firm grip on political power and levers of social control. The repression of political dissidents and related activities begun in 1998 continued into the next decade and appeared likely to last for the duration of the economic reform efforts.

The results of the Seventeenth Party Congress in October 2007 strongly underscored the emphasis the Hu Jintao leadership gave to dealing more attentively than the Jiang Zemin leadership with the many negative consequences of China's rapid economic growth and social change. These negative consequences included glaring inequities between urban and rural sectors and coastal and interior areas; pervasive corruption by self-serving government, party, and military officials; environmental degradation; misuse of scarce land, water, and energy resources; and the lack of adequate education, health care, and social welfare for hundreds of millions of Chinese citizens. The Hu Jintao leadership emphasized using scientific methods to promote sustainable development conducive to fostering a harmonious Chinese order under the leadership of the CCP.[57]

Against this background, foreign affairs generally remained an area of less urgent policy priority. Broad international trends—notably at that time, improved relations with the United States—supported the efforts by the Chinese authorities to pursue policies intended to minimize disruptions and to assist their domestic reform endeavors. The government remained wary of the real or potential challenges posed by a possible economic crisis, by Taiwan, by efforts by Japan and the United States to increase their international influence in ways seen as contrary to Beijing's interests, by India's great power aspirations and nuclear capability, by North Korea's nuclear weapons development, and by other issues. The PRC voiced special concern over the implications for China's interests of actual and reported US plans to develop and deploy theater ballistic missile defense systems in East Asia and a national missile defense for the United States. Chinese officials also voiced concern over the downturn in US-China relations at the outset of the George W. Bush administration, but appeared determined to cooperate with the US-led antiterrorism campaign begun in September 2001.

Chinese leaders were seen to be focused on promoting China's economic development while maintaining its political and social stability. These efforts undergirded a fundamental determination of the CCP administration to be an exception to the pattern of collapsing Communist regimes at the end of the Cold War and to reinvigorate and sustain its one-party rule in China. Foreign policy was made to serve these objectives by sustaining an international environment that supported economic growth and stability in China. This was done partly through active and generally moderate Chinese diplomacy designed to reassure neighboring countries and other concerned powers—notably the United States, the dominant world power in Chinese foreign policy calculations. Chinese efforts tried to demonstrate that rising Chinese economic, military, and political power and influence should not have been viewed as a threat, but should have been seen as an opportunity for greater world development and harmony. In the process, Chinese diplomacy gave ever-greater emphasis to engagement and conformity with the norms of regional and other multilateral organizations as a means to reassure those concerned over possible negative implications of China's increased power and influence.[58]

Chinese foreign policy placed great emphasis on seeking international economic exchange beneficial to Chinese development. A large influx of foreign direct investment (FDI), foreign aid, foreign technology, and foreign expertise was critically important in China's economic growth in the post-Mao period. China became the center of a variety of intra-Asian and other international manufacturing and trading networks that saw China emerge as the world's second-largest trading nation and the largest consumer of a variety of key world commodities and raw materials. In stark contrast to the "self-reliant" Chinese development policies of the Maoist period, which severely restricted foreign investment and curbed Chinese economic dependence on the outside world, China now depended fundamentally on a healthy world economy in which Chinese entrepreneurs competed for advantage and promoted economic development as an essential foundation for continued rule of the CCP government.

At the same time, the world economy depended increasingly on China. Now a member of the WTO and other major international economic organizations, the Chinese government exerted ever-greater influence in international economic matters as a key manufacturing center for world markets and an increasingly prominent trading nation with a positive balance of trade and the largest foreign exchange reserves in the world.

Chinese nationalism and Chinese security priorities also remained important determinants in contemporary Chinese foreign policy. Communism was weakening as a source of ideological unity and legitimacy due to both the collapse of the Soviet Union and other communist regimes and the Chinese government's shift toward free-market economic practices. As a result, the CCP leaders placed greater emphasis on promoting patriotism among Chinese people. Patriotism and the nationalism it engenders supported the Communist government's high priority to prevent Taiwan independence and restore this and other territory taken from China by foreign powers when China was weak and vulnerable during the nineteenth and twentieth centuries. Chinese leaders were forthright in building advanced military power and voicing determination to take coercive measures to achieve nationalistic goals, especially regarding Taiwan, even in the face of opposition by the power of the United States and its allies and associates. More broadly, Chinese leaders endeavored to build what they called "comprehensive national power"—particularly economic, military, and political power—as China sought an as yet not clearly defined leading role as a great power in Asian and world affairs.

Meanwhile, Chinese leadership and popular attention focused with great national pride on China's hosting of the August 2008 Olympic Games. The Chinese government seemed determined to avoid actions at home or abroad that might complicate their successful Olympic Games. It used the occasion to showcase China's many positive accomplishments to audiences abroad and to reinforce the legitimacy and power of the Communist rule in the eyes of the Chinese people and international audiences.

BUSH'S LEGACY: POSITIVE STASIS IN US-CHINA RELATIONS

The positive stasis in US-China relations that emerged in the latter years of the George W. Bush administration met the near-term priorities of the US and Chinese governments. Converging US and Chinese engagement policies tried to broaden common ground; they dealt with differences through policies fostering ever closer interchange that included respective strategies designed to constrain each other's possible disruptive or negative moves.

A pattern of dualism in US-China relations arose as part of the developing positive stasis. The pattern involved constructive and cooperative engagement on the one hand and contingency planning or hedging on the other. It reflected the mix noted above of converging and competing interests and prevailing leadership suspicions and cooperation.

Chinese and US contingency planning and hedging against one another sometimes involved actions like the respective Chinese and US military buildups that were separate from and developed in tandem with the respective engagement policies that the two leaderships pursued with each other. At the same time, dualism showed as each government used engagement to build positive and cooperative ties while at the same time seeking to use these ties to build interdependencies and webs of relationships that had the effect of constraining the other power from taking actions that opposed its interests. While the analogy is not precise, the policies of engagement pursued by the United States and China toward one another featured respective "Gulliver strategies" that were designed to tie down aggressive, assertive, or other negative policy tendencies of the other power through webs of interdependence in bilateral and multilateral relationships. Thus the positive stasis in US-China relations was based on an increasing convergence of these respective engagement policies and Gulliver strategies. Of course, the fact remained that these Gulliver strategies reflected underlying suspicions and conflicting interests that featured prominently in the calculations of both the US and Chinese administrations as they interacted with one another. [59]

Sustaining the positive stasis in US-China relations was based on the fact that neither the Chinese leadership nor the US administration sought trouble with the other. Both were preoccupied with other issues. Heading the list of preoccupations for both governments was dealing with the massive negative consequences of the international economic crisis and deep recession begun in 2008. Other preoccupations of the outgoing Bush administration included Iraq, Afghanistan, Pakistan, Iran, broader Middle East issues, North Korea, and other foreign policy problems that came on top of serious adverse economic developments.

The global economic decline added to Chinese leaders' preoccupations in dealing with the results of the October 2007 Seventeenth CCP Congress and the Eleventh National People's Congress in March 2008. Those meetings and subsequent developments showed a collective leadership, with Hu Jintao first among equals but not dominant, that continued to debate appropriate ways to meet a wide variety of pressing economic, social, political, and other issues at home and abroad. The leaders sought with only mixed results those lines of policy and action that avoided major cost and risk to China's ruling party leadership while endeavoring to promote Chinese development and the stability of one-party rule. There remained uncertainty about the major leadership transition expected at the Eighteenth Congress in 2012—a serious matter in an authoritarian political system like China's. [60]

The US and Chinese governments worked hard to use multiple formal dialogues, high-level meetings and communications, and official rhetoric emphasizing the positive in the relationship in order to offset and manage negative implications from the many differences and issues that continued to complicate US-China relations. Neither leadership publicly emphasized the major differences over key policy issues regarding economic, military, and political questions.

Both governments registered close collaboration over North Korea's nuclear weapons program. They worked in parallel to manage the fallout from

Taiwan's President Chen Shui-bian's repeated efforts to strengthen Taiwan's sovereignty and standing as a country separate from China. Chen's moves provoked China and were opposed by the United States. The US and Chinese governments supported Taiwan's new president, Ma Ying-jeou, who pursued an overall easing of Taiwan-China-US tensions over cross-strait issues. Meanwhile, much more limited collaboration between China and the United States influenced such international hot spots as Sudan, Iran, and Myanmar/ Burma, with leaders on both sides speaking more about Sino-American cooperation than Sino-American differences over these sensitive international questions.[61]

Unfortunately for those hoping for significantly greater cooperation between the United States and China, dramatic increases in cooperation seemed absent because of major conflicting interests and disputes over a wide range of issues. Cautious US and Chinese leaders seeking to avoid trouble with one another had a hard time overcoming these obstacles. Some disputes were at times hard to control, resulting in surprising upsurges in US-China tensions, such as strident criticism in Congress and the media on Beijing's crackdown on dissent in Tibet prior to the start of the 2008 Olympic games.

As noted in chapter 1, China's many disagreements with the United States can be grouped into four general categories of disputes, which have complicated US-China relations for years. China's moderation toward the United States since 2001 reduced the salience of some of these issues, but they remained important and were reflected in Chinese policies and actions. The risk-averse Hu Jintao leadership appeared to have little incentive to accommodate the United States on these sensitive questions.

The four categories, again, are: (1) opposition to US support for Taiwan and involvement with other sensitive sovereignty issues, including Tibet and disputed islands and maritime rights along China's rim; (2) opposition to US efforts to change China's political system; (3) opposition to the United States playing the dominant role along China's periphery in Asia; and (4) opposition to many aspects of US leadership in world affairs. Some specific issues in the latter two categories include US policy in Iraq, Iran, and the broader Middle East; aspects of the US-backed security presence in the Asia-Pacific; US and allied ballistic missile defenses; US pressure on such governments as Burma, North Korea, Sudan, Zimbabwe, Cuba, and Venezuela; US pressure tactics in the United Nations and other international forums; and the US position on global climate change.[62]

As noted in chapter 1 and earlier in this chapter, US differences with China continue to involve clusters of often contentious economic, security, political, sovereignty, foreign policy, and other issues.[63] Given the many foreign and domestic problems they faced, the outgoing Bush administration was disinclined to take dramatic steps forward in relations with China. Such steps probably would have required compromises unacceptable to important

US constituencies and partners abroad. It was more advantageous to follow and reinforce the recent equilibrium along generally positive lines in US policy and relations toward China.

Against this background, the outlook for US relations with China at the end of the Bush administration seemed focused on sustaining the positive equilibrium developed during the Bush years. One force for significant negative change seemed to be US domestic debate over China. In its last years, the Bush administration was preoccupied with many issues and appeared tired and reactive. It had a harder time in its waning days in controlling the consequences of a broad range of US interest groups and commentators that were sharply critical of various Chinese government policies and practices. Such groups and critics also became more active and prominent as they endeavored to influence the policy agenda of the new US administration as it came to power. They sought to push forward their various proposals before the incoming government set its policy agenda.

Meanwhile, there remained uncertainty on how lasting China's recent moderate and cooperative approach toward the United States would be. Chinese pronouncements and a variety of foreign specialists often depicted China's approach as based on a strategic decision by Chinese leaders seeking long-term peace and development and offering lasting reassurance to the United States, Japan, and other states with which Beijing had strongly differed over the years. Others saw China's recent moderate approach as dependent on circumstances. In particular, they suspected that the rise of Chinese power and its overall economic and military capabilities were likely to result in a less accommodating and tougher Chinese posture on the salient differences that continued to divide China and the United States. Developments in Sino-US relations during the Obama administration and especially with the ascendance of strong-man Chinese leader Xi Jinping seemed to support the reasoning behind the latter scenario.[64]

Chapter Seven

Barack Obama, Donald Trump, and Xi Jinping

Pragmatism Falters amid Acrimony and Tensions

With the outset of the US administration of President Barack Obama in January 2009, it appeared that the crisis in US-China relations after the Cold War and the Tiananmen crackdown had evolved during the first decade of the twenty-first century into a positive relationship that for a time seemed likely to continue. Converging US and Chinese engagement policies broadened common ground while the governments dealt with differences through dialogues. Neither the Chinese leadership nor the US administration sought trouble with the other. Both were preoccupied with other issues.

Heading the list of preoccupations for both governments was dealing with the massive negative consequences of the international economic crisis and deep recession begun in 2008. Other US preoccupations included Iraq, Afghanistan, Pakistan, Iran, broader Middle East issues, North Korea, and other foreign policy problems that came on top of serious adverse economic developments. The global economic decline added to Chinese leaders' preoccupations in dealing with uncertain leadership succession and ongoing debate about a number of contentious domestic and international problems.

However, long-standing differences between the two countries were not significantly changed as a result of pragmatic engagement. They began to worsen at the turn of the decade and grew in prominence over the following years. China's moderation toward the United States since 2001 had reduced the salience of some of these issues, but they remained important and were reflected in Chinese policies and actions. The risk-averse Hu Jintao leadership appeared to have little incentive to accommodate the United States on sensitive questions. Rather, his government took steps beginning in 2009 that challenged and tested the resolve of the incoming US administration of Barack Obama. Those challenges were met with the Obama administration's measured resolve and broader policy of American engagement with the Asia-Pacific as seen in its signature rebalance policy, also known as its "pivot" to Asia. China reacted negatively; its challenges and assertiveness on differences with the United States reached new heights with the rise to power of Xi Jinping and bold foreign policy moves that accompanied his domineering strong-man rule of China.

As noted in the previous chapter, the four categories of Chinese differences with the United States remained as follows: (1) opposition to US support for Taiwan and involvement with other sensitive sovereignty issues, including Tibet and disputed islands and maritime rights along China's rim; (2) opposition to perceived US efforts to change China's political system; (3) opposition to the United States playing the dominant role along China's periphery in Asia; and (4) opposition to many aspects of US leadership in world affairs.[1]

Explanations varied as to why China put aside past efforts to reassure the United States and instead undertook its more assertive and often coercive actions in areas of difference with the United States. Chinese commentators tended to see a starting point in the rising challenges in US-China relations as the Obama government's rebalance policy that was announced in late 2011. The new US approach emphasized strong and positive US engagement with China, but it also called for stronger American diplomatic, security, and economic relationships throughout the region, which many Chinese commentators saw as encircling and designed to contain and constrain China's rising influence in Asia.[2]

Obama government officials and many other Americans tended to see the origins of Chinese greater assertiveness and challenges to the United States coming from altered Chinese views of power realities between the two countries and in Asian and world affairs. The US-initiated international financial breakdown and massive recession added to perceived American weaknesses derived from declining American strength notably due to draining wars in Iraq and Afghanistan. On the other hand, China emerged from the economic crisis with strong growth, flush with cash and more confident in its state-directed growth model as opposed to the now deeply discredited American free-market approach. Under these circumstances, Chinese elite and popular opinion looked with increasing disapproval on the cautious and reactive approach of the Hu Jintao government. In foreign affairs, accommodating the United States and regional powers over long-standing Chinese interests involving Chinese security, sovereignty, and other sensitive issues seemed overly passive and misguided. Though Hu's approach was in line with Deng Xiao-ping's instruction that China should keep a low profile in foreign affairs and focus on domestic development, opinion in China now favored a more robust and prominent Chinese international approach. The result was an evolution of greater boldness, activism, and considerable use of coercion, generally short of using military force, in employing Chinese economic, political, and military power to meet the broad goals in what incoming leader Xi Jinping called the "China Dream." The goals involved China unified with disputed territories under its control and with a stature unsurpassed in Asia as a leading world power.[3]

The explanations of rising challenges and tensions in US-China relations over the time frame delineated above tended to use the lens of realism in international relations theory. The United States was seen in decline while China was rising. For Chinese commentators who saw containment in the Obama administration's rebalance policy, the US actions were motivated by America trying to sustain its leading position in the face of rising Chinese power and influence. For American observers, the catalyst for the rising tensions and challenges in the relationship came from more powerful China now putting aside past restraint and flexing its new muscles in pursuit of long-standing ambitions involving key differences with the United States.

Constructivism played a role in some assessments of the rising tensions and acrimony in US-China relations in recent years, especially as China continued to develop a strong sense of identity based on the nationalism of an aggrieved power with an exceptional sense of self-righteousness seeking to remedy past injustices. And the United States had its constructed identity of exceptional righteousness as well, making compromise between the two nations over sensitive issues more difficult. Liberalism figured in the recent developments by showing the failure perceived in the United States of economic interchange and close diplomatic and nongovernment engagement favored by liberals as sources of stability and cooperation in relations to actually lead to mutual accommodation and greater collaboration as the main trend in the relationship. Indeed, developments in recent years showed that Americans saw economic interchange with China as working against their interests, an increasingly adverse situation that required strong remedial measures by the US government. The liberal view that closer American engagement in reaching mutually acceptable agreements with China would lead to closer relations seemed belied by the 2016 US presidential campaign rhetoric of Obama administration Secretary of State Hillary Clinton, leading Republican candidate Donald Trump, and many other candidates. They argued that America had to be constantly vigilant in watching Chinese implementation of economic and other agreements, as Beijing was not to be trusted and had a record of manipulating and gaming accords to its advantage, at the expense of the United States.[4]

US differences with China continued to involve clusters of often contentious economic, security, political, sovereignty, foreign policy, and other issues. Economic issues became more prominent: The growing inequities seen in the United States with regard to America's economic relationship with China's ever more powerful economy included a massive trade deficit, Chinese currency policies and practices, US dependence on Chinese financing of US government budget deficits, and Chinese national security and industrial espionage and abuse of intellectual property rights.

Security issues became more prominent in the United States with the buildup of Chinese military forces and the threat they posed to US interests in Taiwan and the broader Asia-Pacific. China was increasingly assertive in using security forces backed by its robust military presence and other coercive means to expand influence at expense of neighbors in disputed territory in the East China Sea and the South China Sea. Its actions seriously undermined American interests in regional security and the US leadership role as a security guarantor in the Asia-Pacific.

Political issues included China's controversial record on human rights, democracy, religious freedom, and family planning practices. Sovereignty questions involved disputes over the status of Taiwan, Tibet, Xinjiang, Hong Kong, and Chinese claims to disputed islands and maritime rights along China's rim. Foreign policy disputes focused on China's support for such "rogue" states as North Korea, Sudan, Myanmar/Burma, Iran, Cuba, Zimbabwe, and Venezuela; and on Chinese trade, investment, and aid to resource-rich and poorly governed states in Africa that undermined Western sanctions designed to pressure these governments to reform.

Meanwhile, China's new boldness in foreign affairs saw Beijing create and lead a variety of international economic, political, and security organizations that challenged existing US-backed bodies, stressed norms more in line with China's objectives, and underlined US international leadership. The broad Chinese challenge seemed to sharpen with ever closer Chinese collaboration with Russia under President Vladimir Putin as Russia pursued blatant land grabs and military incursions among other egregious affronts against the international order supported by the United States.[5]

As in the past, these many areas of acrimony and friction developed in tandem with a wide range of cooperation between the two governments and societies. Economic interaction and deepening ties between the elites and peoples had major positive impacts. Relations between the two militaries, a heretofore weak link in US-China ties, made substantial progress. The two governments continued and advanced cooperation on a variety of international issues, including climate change, nuclear security, and various accords, which were highlighted notably during periodic meetings of groups like the G-20 dealing with issues in global governance. President Obama and President Hu Jintao and President Xi Jinping had several lengthy summits and numerous other meetings that announced progress in the multifaceted Sino-American relationship. The biannual senior dialogues between the two countries produced long lists of more than two hundred accomplishments in efforts to advance Sino-American cooperation. Many were the results of intensely focused collaboration by different agencies and departments of the two governments.

Such progress in the relationship gave support to liberals who argued that the overall relationship was changing for the better due to increased contacts and the impact of trade and economic interdependence. Constructivists also highlighted the common ground between the United States and China over issues like climate change, nuclear security, and other issues of international governance as reflecting positive learning by leaders on both sides and conducive to progress and mutually advantageous development. Meanwhile, realists needed to weigh the importance of these various areas of cooperation against the rising differences in the relationship, in charting recommended courses for the way ahead.[6]

At a practical level, whether the pragmatic engagement in US-China relations that developed during the tenure of the George W. Bush–Hu Jintao governments would continue depended heavily on the choices of Chinese and US leaders, especially regarding the major differences between the two countries. What the record over the next decade showed to this writer and many but certainly not all American specialists was that China's repeated policy choices sought advantage at the expense of the United States and others, as it endeavored to rectify the key differences it had with those countries. Those policy choices were supported by Chinese judgments of greater Chinese strengths and declining US influence and resolve and by a uniquely self-righteous and aggrieved Chinese nationalism fostered by the government, which provided an important moral imperative for China to seek advantage at the expense of others. The main counterarguments to the above assessments came from those American officials and specialists who judged that the recent negative trends and frictions were exaggerated, and they did not take enough account of China's legitimate concerns nor correctly weigh the differences against the many benefits that continued to flow from the Sino-American relationship. Indeed, as Obama government officials left office, they offered private assessments to American specialists that the administration had been remarkably successful in charting a course between US-China differences and common ground that redounded to the overall benefit of the United States. Other American specialists acknowledged the rising tensions and differences but judged that American myopia about China's concerns obscured what they saw as needed compromise where the United States would "meet China half-way" in seeking mutually advantageous outcomes.[7]

What the recent record does show clearly is that at times in the past, even as recently as the first two years of the George W. Bush administration, assertive Chinese proclivities to seek rectification of differences with America and others were held in check by effective and resolute US countermeasures. As discussed in chapter 6, the perception in China and actual reality of US economic, military, and political strength and determination to use it at that time influenced Chinese leaders to shift to a stance that focused on reassuring the United States that China's rise would not challenge the United States. And as seen in chapter 6, the Bush government's ability to employ such countermeasures declined as it came to depend heavily on China and faced enormous preoccupations at home and abroad.

The Obama government also remained preoccupied with other problems at home and abroad and gave a high priority to sustaining smooth relations with China despite growing differences. The Obama administration's approach to Beijing stressed transparency and predictability, with any change coming only after careful deliberations that usually resulted in incremental adjustments in policy. Linkage—using US policy in one area to influence Chinese policy in another—was not used. The result was that Chinese leaders could easily assess the likely reaction of the United States to China's increased assertiveness and probes seeking to advance control in disputed territory, economic advantage at US expense, cooperation with Russia against American concerns, and other initiatives sensitive to US interests. The likelihood of substantial changes adverse to Chinese interests seemed low, thereby weighing China's calculus in favor of the assertiveness and probes at American expense.[8]

The 2016 American election campaign made it evident that American discourse was shifting away from the optimistic outlook of Obama government officials and other specialists emphasizing the positive accomplishments in the relationship and the need for greater compromise with China. Democratic Party front-runner Hillary Clinton registered the broadest-ranging indictment of Chinese infringements on American interests. She warned against China's incremental advances to the detriment of the United States, promising to confront Beijing as it endeavored to maneuver in duplicitous ways and "game" the United States over various issues. Her rhetoric captured growing frustrations in the United States as China advanced its influence at American expense.[9]

Republican presidential candidate Trump had a narrower set of complaints against China, giving a high priority to negotiating more advantageous economic deals for America. During the election campaign, Chinese specialists judged that observers in China as well as the United States had adopted a more negative view of relations, highlighting salient differences seen from both sides. They disliked both the Democratic and the Republican nominees but judged that Beijing would be better off with a Trump government than a Clinton government.[10] They were taken up short when President-elect Trump, reflecting the views of key staff members in his administration and among Republicans in Congress, showed unusual support for Taiwan and questioned the US one-China policy as well as Chinese economic policies and expansion of control in the disputed South China Sea. After inauguration, the president reaffirmed the one-China policy and conducted a businesslike series of meetings with President Xi Jinping at the US leader's Florida resort, establishing negotiation frameworks for advancing relations and dealing with problems. The problems remained unresolved and highly prominent, raising tensions in the US-China relationship. [11]

COMPETITION CHALLENGES POSITIVE ENGAGEMENT

A major theme in President Obama's initial foreign policy was to seek the cooperation of other world powers, including China, to deal with salient international concerns such as the global economic crisis and recession, climate change, nuclear weapons proliferation, and terrorism. He and his team made vigorous efforts to build common ground with China on these and related issues. China's leaders offered limited cooperation; they focused much more on their own interests than the need for global responsibility urged by President Obama. Chinese officials suspected that added global responsibilities would hold back China's economic development and modernization. [12]

More worrisome, Chinese actions and assertions in 2009 and 2010 directly challenged the policies and practices of the United States, as follows:

- Chinese government patrol boats confronted US surveillance ships in the South China Sea. The Chinese government took the position, opposed by the United States and the majority of concerned world powers, that China had the right to regulate the movement of military naval and air vehicles in the Exclusive Economic Zone (EEZ) along China's rim. A coastal state's EEZ generally extends from the edge of its territorial sea (twelve nautical miles from its coast) to a distance of two hundred nautical miles from its coast.
- China challenged US and South Korean military exercises against North Korea in the Yellow Sea. Such exercises had occurred in the past and in 2010 they were initiated in response to North Korean provocations in the sinking of a South Korean warship that resulted in the death of forty-six sailors and the shelling of a South Korean island that resulted in South Korean military and civilian casualties.
- Chinese treatment of US arms sales to Taiwan and President Obama's meeting with the Dalai Lama in 2010 was harsher than in the recent past. In both cases the Obama government had delayed these US actions that conformed to past American practice until after the president's first visit to China in November 2009, hoping not to undermine the emerging coopera-

tive atmosphere in his administration's relationship with China. The more strident Chinese response came as a surprise to the United States.

- Chinese officials threatened to stop investing in US government securities and to move away from using the US dollar in international transactions.
- The Chinese government for a time responded very harshly to American government interventions in 2010 that (1) urged collective efforts to manage rising tensions in the South China Sea, and (2) affirmed, during Sino-Japanese disputes over East China Sea islands, that while the US took no position on the sovereignty of the islands, the US-Japan alliance did provide for American support for Japan in areas under its control, including the disputed islands in the East China Sea controlled by Japan but claimed by China. [13]

The Obama government reacted calmly and firmly to what Secretary of State Clinton referred to as "tests"—that is, this manifestation of new assertiveness by China. It gave no ground on any of the Chinese demands. It made clear to the Chinese government and the world that the United States was prepared to undertake military measures needed to deal with the buildup of Chinese forces targeting Americans and American interests in the Asia-Pacific. US officials also helped move China to curb North Korea's repeated provocations by warning privately as well as publicly that the United States viewed North Korea's nuclear weapons development as not just a regional issue nor a concern for global nonproliferation, but as a direct threat to the United States. [14]

The US government also found that prominent Chinese assertiveness and truculence with the United States and neighboring Asian countries over maritime, security, and other issues prompted Asian governments to be more active in working more closely with the United States and in encouraging an active US presence in the Asia-Pacific. Their interest in closer ties with the United States meshed well with the Obama government's broad effort begun publicly in late 2011 to "pivot" and "re-engage" with the countries of the Asia-Pacific, ranging from India to the Pacific Islands. [15]

The Obama government leaders from the president on down articulated the outlines of a new emphasis on what was called the American "rebalance" policy in the Asia-Pacific that was welcomed in the region but criticized by China. [16] The significant elements of the policy, many of which competed with China, included the following:

- The Obama government's priority international attention would focus on Asia-Pacific following US military pullbacks from Iraq and Afghanistan.
- The government was determined to maintain force levels and military capabilities in the Asia-Pacific region despite expected substantial cutbacks in US defense spending.

- More widely dispersed US forces and basing/deployment arrangements indicated rising importance of Southeast Asia and the Indian Ocean in support of long-standing American priorities, including those in Northeast Asia.
- The dispersal of US forces and a developing US air/sea battle concept provided a means to counter growing "area denial" efforts in the Asia-Pacific region, used mainly by China.
- Strong emphasis on US pursuit of free trade and other open economic interchange, notably through the multilateral Trans Pacific Partnership (TPP) arrangements was in competition with less liberal regional arrangements supported by China that excluded the United States.
- Significantly enhanced and flexible US diplomatic activism both bilaterally and multilaterally in pursuing American interests in regional security and stability, free and open economic exchange, and political relations and values involving human rights and accountable governance often were at odds with Chinese interests and positions.

At the same time, the US government took pains to reemphasize repeatedly the importance of across-the-board close and positive US engagement with China. US officials well understood that a zero-sum competition with China in the Asia-Pacific would fail, as the vast majority of those countries did not want to choose between good relations with China and good relations with the United States.[17]

The prominence and initial success of the rebalance almost certainly influenced the Chinese leadership's most significant changes in Chinese foreign relations since the death of Deng Xiaoping. Deng had stressed that China should bide its time in foreign affairs and focus on domestic modernizations. However, after the 2008 economic crisis and subsequent recession, China's comprehensive national power was rising remarkably as the United States and its allies faced protracted problems at home and abroad. Against that background, Beijing shifted to an assertive foreign policy exacerbating long-standing Chinese differences with the United States and others that was more in line with the China-centered nationalism prevalent in Chinese elite and public opinion. The shift came about with the transition from the comparatively weak and risk-averse collective leadership of Hu Jintao to the strong-man rule carried out by Xi Jinping, who took over leadership of the communist party in 2012.[18]

Xi Jinping's Challenges to America

The record of Chinese policy and behavior under the rule of President Xi shows repeated choices that have placed other foreign and domestic priorities above his avowed but increasingly hollow claims to seek a positive relationship with the United States. These actions made it increasingly clear that in Xi's view, positive US ties would come on condition of America avoiding opposition to new priorities in Chinese foreign relations under President Xi. Those priorities focused notably on Asia, where China's rising prominence seemed to provide a basis for more assertive actions challenging the United States.[19]

By putting the United States "on notice" that the United States had to give way to China's practices at odds with US interests, the Xi government eventually prompted President Obama and his government to be, by 2014, much more vocal in issuing often strident complaints. As President Xi ignored the complaints, leaving it to the foreign ministry to reject them, frustration within and outside the US government grew. There was toughening of behavior in some areas, with tensions rising in particular in nearby Asia. A significant debate emerged inside and outside the government, with those favoring a tougher policy toward China in the ascendance.[20]

Xi Jinping began the process of changing Chinese policies with major implications for the United States as he prepared to take control of Communist Party and state power in 2012. The caution and low profile of the previous leaders were viewed with disfavor. Chinese policies and practices became much more active, assertive, and bold. Xi received enormous publicity from Chinese propaganda and media outlets; his image as a decisive leader prepared to act strongly in the face of American and other criticism was welcomed by Chinese opinion, both public and elite. Chinese reassurance and restraint in dealing with the United States and others were played down since, according to officials in China, they had conveyed Chinese weakness to Asian rivals and the United States. The subsequent string of Chinese actions and initiatives, listed here, were truly impressive:[21]

- The government orchestrated the largest mass demonstration against a foreign target ever seen in Chinese history (against Japan over disputed islands in September 2012). It followed with intense political, economic, and security pressure on Japan unseen since World War II.
- China used coercive and intimidating means to extend control of disputed territory at neighbors' expense, notably in the disputed South China Sea. Chinese officials dismissed and rebuffed US and other complaints that their actions upset regional stability.
- Chinese advances were supported by ever-expanding Chinese capabilities backed by the impressive and growing economic and military power of China. The Chinese military capabilities were arrayed against and focused on the American forces in the Asia-Pacific region.
- Russian President Putin's shift against the United States and the West coincided with Xi's rise to power. The Russian and Chinese leaders increasingly converged most prominently on the desire to serve as a counter-

weight to perceived US preponderant influence and to constrain US power. China saw Russia as a useful counterweight to US power, and Russia valued Sino-Russian cooperation for the same reason. They worked separately and together to complicate and curb US power and influence in world politics, economy, and security. They supported one another in their respective challenges to the United States, allies, and partners in Europe, the Middle East, and Asia. These joint efforts also involved diplomatic, security, and economic measures in multilateral forums and bilateral relations involving US adversaries in North Korea, Iran, and Syria. The two powers also supported one another in the face of US and allied complaints about Russian and Chinese coercive expansion and other steps that challenged regional order and global norms and institutions backed by the United States.[22]

- Despite increasing US complaints, the new Chinese government continued manipulative economic practices, cyber theft, and reluctance to contribute regional and global common goods.
- China used its large foreign exchange reserves, massive excess construction capacity, and strong trading advantages to develop international banks and to support often grandiose Chinese plans for Asian and global infrastructure construction, investments, loans, and trade areas that excluded the United States and countered American initiatives and support for existing international economic institutions.
- Xi Jinping tightened political control domestically in ways grossly offensive to American representatives seeking political liberalization and better human rights conditions in China.

Official Chinese media highlighted Xi's leadership; he was depicted in glowing accounts directing multifaceted Chinese initiatives abroad with confidence and authority in pursuit of his broad vision of a unified, powerful, and internationally respected China—what Xi and the Chinese publicists called the "China Dream." Complaints by neighbors, the United States, and other powers concerned with the negative impacts of Xi's actions were rebuked or scorned.[23]

Obama and Xi's China: Measured Resolve, Limited Impact

President Obama proved to be less than fully effective in dealing with the various challenges posed by Xi Jinping's policies and practices. His administration gave top priority to supporting the overall positive US approach to engagement with China. Differences usually were dealt with in private consultations. Even if they seemed important, they were kept within carefully crafted channels and not allowed to "spill over" and impact other elements in the relationship. Thus, the Obama government eschewed "linkage"—that is, the seeking of US leverage to get China to stop behavior offensive to the United States by linking the offensive Chinese behavior to another policy area where the United States would threaten actions adverse to important Chinese interests.

The administration tended to focus on the success of US-China cooperation on such global issues as climate change, where recent shifts in Chinese domestic energy efficiency and pollution policies made Chinese priorities more in line with those of the Obama government and thus facilitated US-China agreement. Meanwhile, various American government department representatives had a wide range of cooperative interactions with their Chinese counterparts. They understood that, contrary to the practice of the Obama government, the Chinese government was prone to link—specifically, to punish the American or any other offending foreign government with adverse action in a policy area important to that government, in retaliation against actions by the American or other foreign government that China deemed offensive. Rather than risk China cutting off their department's positive interchange, these US officials tended to favor the Obama government's approach of giving top priority to the positive overall relationship and managing differences within narrow channels and usually with private talks.[24]

Critics of the Obama government's approach argued that its reticence failed to dissuade China to stop offensive behavior undermining important American interests. They averred that Beijing could easily read the US government's caution and take incremental steps forward and at odds with US interests without much worry about negative consequences. They identified particularly with the 2016 US election campaign rhetoric and the admonitions of Hillary Clinton in her avowed determination to halt the incremental Chinese advances made by Beijing as it "gamed" the United States on economic, security, and political issues important to the United States.[25]

The Obama government's reticence despite deepening frustration with China's advances at American expense showed during summit meetings in Washington in September 2015 and March 2016.[26]

The international nuclear security summit in Washington from March 31 to April 1, 2016, featured positive interaction between President Obama and President Xi. Both leaders pledged increased international nuclear security; and both promised to sign the Paris Agreement on climate change on April 22, the first day the United Nations accord would be open for government signatures. The agreements were central elements of the outgoing US president's historical legacy. Consistent with past practice, other issues, including growing differences over the South China Sea, were handled largely behind closed doors during one of only two one-on-one meetings President Obama held with a foreign counterpart during the summit.

The cooperative atmosphere in US-China relations had deteriorated in the previous two years, and forecasted tensions over key differences seemed accepted in Washington as unavoidable consequences of America's need to protect important interests from negative Chinese practices.[27] However, President Obama also seemed to clarify the priority of South China Sea disagreements with China; his administration's actions showed that the president judged that this most prominent area of bilateral differences had not reached a level where it would be allowed to spill over and negatively affect other sensitive areas in the relationship, like Taiwan, or jeopardize the cooperation with China that the United States sought.

As reviewed above, President Obama rarely criticized China during his first six years in office. However, he became outspoken from 2014 on about Chinese behavior. President Xi ignored the complaints, which were dismissed by lower-level officials. Ignoring Obama's complaints, President Xi repeatedly emphasized a purported positive "new model of major country relations" with the United States; American critics increasingly saw Xi playing a double game at America's expense.[28]

After a strained US-China summit in Washington in September 2015, Obama had less to say about China. Rather, he and his administration took stronger actions, exemplified by the following:

- Much stronger pressure than seen in the past to compel China to rein in rampant cyber theft of American property.
- Much stronger pressure than seen in the past to compel China to agree to international sanctions against North Korea.
- China's continued militarization of disputed South China Sea islands followed President Xi's seemingly duplicitous promise, made during the September summit, not to do so. In tandem came much more active US military deployments in the disputed South China Sea, along with blunt warnings by US military leaders of China's ambitions.
- More prominent cooperation with allies Japan, the Philippines, and Australia, along with India and concerned Southeast Asian powers that strengthened regional states and complicated Chinese bullying.
- US action in March 2016 halted access to American information technology that impacted China's leading state-directed electronics firm ZTE. The company reportedly had earlier agreed, under US pressure, to halt unauthorized transfers to Iran of US-sourced technology, but it then clandestinely resumed them.
- The US rebuked negative Chinese human rights practices in an unprecedented statement to the UN Human Rights Council in March 2016 that was endorsed by Japan, Australia, and nine European countries.

However, the impact of the actions was less than appeared at first. The public pressure regarding cyber theft and Chinese support for sanctions against North Korea subsided once bilateral talks on cyber theft began and

China went along with tougher UN sanctions against North Korea. Cutting off ZTE was reversed after a few days of secret consultations. Much later, during the early Trump administration, came the news that the United States had negotiated a punishment with ZTE that required payment of a fine of more than $1 billion.[29] The rebuke in the Human Rights Council turned out to be a one-time public occurrence. Meanwhile, the so-called Taiwan issue in Sino-American relations became more sensitive following the landslide election in January 2016 of Democratic Progressive Party (DPP) candidate Tsai Ing-wen and a powerful majority of DPP legislators. Avoiding actions that might "rock-the-boat," the Obama government eschewed controversy and emphasized constructive cross-strait dialogue.

In sum, the Obama government's greater resolve against China's challenges seemed to end up focusing on one issue area: the South China Sea disputes and related American maneuvering with Japan, Australia, India, and some Southeast Asian nations, in response to China's destabilizing and coercive measures. Defense Secretary Ashton Carter and Pacific Commander Admiral Harry Harris repeatedly spoke of China's "aggressive" actions and what Harris called Chinese "hegemony in East Asia." They and other defense officials pointed to US military plans "to check" China's advances through deployments, regional collaboration, and assistance to Chinese neighbors. American officials also expected a Chinese defeat in a ruling later in the year (noted below) at the arbitral tribunal at the Permanent Court of Arbitration in The Hague, that undermined the broad and vague Chinese claims used to justify expansion in the South China Sea.

As seemed likely at the time, the opportunistic and incremental Chinese expansion in the South China Sea continued. From China's perspective, the benefits of Xi's challenges continued to appear to outweigh the costs. Notably, President Xi was viewed in China as a powerful international leader, while President Obama appeared weak. China's probing expansion and intimidation efforts in the East China Sea ran up against firm and effective Japanese efforts supported strongly by the United States; and they were complicated for Beijing by China's inability to deal effectively with provocations from North Korea. The opportunities for expansion in the South China Sea were greater, given the weaknesses of governments there. And adverse judgment in July 12 in the case at The Hague was effectively dismissed by Beijing, with the United States offering few public objections to China's flaunting its egregious opposition to the legally binding ruling.

What these developments showed was that the Obama government's efforts to counter China in the South China Sea were significant. However, it was obvious to Beijing and anyone else paying attention that they were carefully measured to avoid serious disruption in the broader and multifaceted US-China relationship. The American government signaled that such measured resolve was likely to continue to the end of the Obama government, and it did. The Obama administration favored transparency and predictability in Sino-American relations. Unpredictability was generally not favored, notably by US officials responsible for managing US-China relations, in part because of all the work involved in managing uncertainty. Unfortunately, smooth policy management seen as fostered by the predictability and transparency of Obama policy allowed the opportunistic expansionism of China to continue without danger of serious adverse consequences for Chinese interests.

CHINA ISSUES IN THE 2015–16 US ELECTION CAMPAIGN

The ongoing American debate about China policy figured prominently in the US presidential election campaign. Going into the campaign, debates over US policy in the Asia-Pacific focused heavily on perceived US weaknesses in the face of growing challenges from China. Notably, rising China's prominent leader Xi Jinping was prone to coercive strong-man tactics at home and abroad that kept his opponents and competitors off balance and on the defensive. In the Asia-Pacific, the Chinese authorities created an environment of increasing tensions that was seen in China and elsewhere to benefit Xi at the expense of his opponents and competitors, including the United States, heretofore relied on as the region's stabilizer and security guarantor.

As the US election campaign progressed, this broad concern with China remained active, but it was overshadowed by strong debate on two sets of issues: international trade and the proposed TPP accord, and candidate Trump's controversial proposals on burden sharing among allies, nuclear weapons proliferation, and North Korea. Criticism of the TPP received broad bipartisan support and posed increasingly serious obstacles to US government approval of the pact. Trump's controversial proposals were unpopular and were opposed by senior Republicans in Congress along with many others. Mr. Trump avoided bringing them up in the immediate aftermath of the US election.[30]

China Policy

University of Virginia's Batten School Dean Harry Harding and other specialists detected a broad sense of American disappointment at the apparent failure in long-standing US efforts to constructively interact with China's leaders in expectation that those leaders would conform more to international norms in line with American interests. Instead, they found an ever more powerful Chinese state under the often bold leadership of President Xi Jinping seeking unfair advantage at America's expense and posing ever larger challenges to important US interests.[31]

Relevant 2015–16 Election Debates

Though most presidential candidates voiced harsh criticism of Chinese policies and behavior, the mix of strong differences and positive engagement
seen in the Obama administration's policy toward China was reflected in the
candidates' similarly mixed policy recommendations. The contenders' views
also were in line with American public opinion that, on balance, disapproved
of the Chinese government but ranked China lower than in the recent past as
an economic threat and viewed China's military as less threatening to US
interests than terrorism, nuclear weapons development in North Korea and
Iran, various conflicts in the Middle East, climate change, refugee flows, and
infectious diseases.[32]

Hillary Clinton's discourse on China showed a general theme of injustice.
China was seen as manipulative, as it maneuvered for selfish gains at the
expense of US international interests and American workers. Clinton underlined her past record and continued resolve to rectify various wrongs, abuses,
unfair practices, and China's threatening of allies. Key themes in her campaign included holding China accountable for egregious behavior, opposing
Chinese military intimidation and unfair economic practices, and supporting
human rights in China.[33]

Bernie Sanders focused primarily on trade and how China's development
had come at the cost of American workers. He opposed international trade
treaties in general and with China in particular, because he said they led to
job losses in the United States and the weakening of labor unions. Sanders
also advocated working with China to curb fossil fuel consumption and address global climate change.[34]

Ted Cruz said the best way to approach China was to emphasize US
military and economic might. He cited former President Ronald Reagan's
"peace through strength" approach toward the Soviet Union during the Cold
War as a model for contemporary US-China relations. On human rights,
Cruz joined other senators in petitioning for a plaza outside the Chinese
embassy in Washington to be named after Liu Xiaobo, a human rights activist and 2010 Nobel laureate who was then imprisoned in China.[35]

John Kasich was moderate about China. He advised, "We don't seek
confrontation with China. But then why would we?"[36] Marco Rubio's well-
developed approach to China was much tougher than what he saw as the
"disaster" of Clinton's tenure as secretary of state and the failed engagement
policy of President Obama.[37]

According to Donald Trump, the main problem the United States had
with China was that we weren't using our power to influence them. The
source of our power over China, according to Trump, was our economic
strength. Overall, Trump was not hostile to or confrontational with China,
having said, "We desire to live peacefully and in friendship with Russia and

China. We have serious differences with these two nations . . . but we are not bound to be adversaries." Trump tended to avoid discussing China as a national security threat. He averred that issues with China could be dealt with through negotiations, using American strengths as leverage.[38]

Implications

US policies dealing with China were seen as not working in several important areas. However, China was not seen as an enemy by the candidates or American public opinion. Most of the candidates, including leaders Hillary Clinton and Donald Trump, favored tougher policies, with Trump focused on seeking leverage in negotiations centered on economic issues, while Clinton's broader scope of concern included salient national security and human rights problems. The overall upshot of all the discussion of China in the campaign was moderate controversy over proposed remedies, with the possible exception of sometimes strident warnings against Trump's threat to impose 45 percent tariffs on Chinese imports to the United States.

Officials and specialists in Beijing saw negatives with both Hillary Clinton and Donald Trump. Like many Americans, they were frustrated with the downward trend in US-China relations and judged that trend would worsen at least to some degree if Clinton were elected. Some in Beijing nonetheless voiced confidence that mutual interests and highly integrated US-China government relationships would guard against relations going seriously off track. Chinese derision of Trump earlier in 2016 shifted to seeking advantage, given the candidate's disruption of US alliances along China's rim and emphasis on seeking common ground with China through negotiations. Overall, a common view was that China could "shape" President Trump to behave in line with its interests, as Donald Trump was seen as less ideological and more pragmatic than Hillary Clinton.[39]

Discerning the Trump Administration's Approach to China

President-elect Trump sharply broke with past practice in December 2016 by accepting a congratulatory phone call from Taiwan President Tsai Ing-wen. He reacted promptly to Chinese criticisms with blunt public complaints about unfair Chinese economic policies and military expansion in the disputed South China Sea. He also publicly questioned US government support for a policy of one China that included Taiwan. The phone call was facilitated by representatives in the president-elect's entourage and Republican Party leadership, who favored an American policy toward Taiwan that was less deferential to Beijing. The *New York Times* among other mainstream media depicted the move negatively as dangerously broadening the ongoing frictions in US-China relations amid substantial hardening of US policy toward China to include sensitive issues involving Taiwan.[40]

President-elect Trump's controversial actions regarding Taiwan and the one-China policy at least temporarily upset Chinese forecasts of smoother sailing with Donald Trump than with Hillary Clinton. President Trump eventually was persuaded to publicly reaffirm support for the American one-China policy during the US president's first phone conversation with President Xi on February 9. Xi reportedly refused to speak with President Trump until he made this reaffirmation. The scope and effect of President Trump's support for the US one-China policy remained vague to many observers, especially given his concurrent ambiguous treatment of other sensitive US commitments involving the so-called two-states solution for Israelis and Palestinians.[41]

As noted in chapter 1, the president-elect showed President Xi and his lieutenants, in a few gestures and blunt messages to the media and on Twitter, that the new US leader was capable of a wide range of actions that could surprise Chinese counterparts with serious negative consequences.[42] Meanwhile, some elements of the administration's policy seemed to work strongly against Chinese interests. President Trump not only moved away from election rhetoric critical of Japan and its unfair trade policies and inadequate defense burden sharing. He and his administration's defense and foreign policy leaders went to extraordinary measures to show solidarity with Japanese Prime Minister Shinzo Abe, who was treated to a summit meeting at the White House and a weekend of golf with the president at his Florida resort. The positive treatment included warm support, according to Prime Minister Abe, for Abe's controversial overtures to the Vladimir Putin government in Russia, an initiative that might have been followed by President Trump and was viewed with suspicion in Beijing.[43]

President Trump held meetings at the Florida resort with Chinese President Xi Jinping two months later. The meetings marked progress in setting up frameworks for advancing relations and dealing with differences. They did not have statements of mutual support and solidarity as were seen in the Japan visit, thereby reflecting a more distant and businesslike approach in US-China relations. The Trump-Xi summit sandwiched in the US president's abrupt decision on and prompt launching of a large-scale cruise missile attack on the Syrian government airbase that was involved in Syria's latest use of outlawed chemical weapons against its civil war opponents. As China supported the Syrian government as Beijing was urging a negotiated solution to the conflict, the forceful US action showed determination to pursue American interests despite Chinese sensitivities.[44]

Noted in chapter 1 was the intense Trump government pressure on China to use its economic leverage to curb North Korea's nuclear weapons development. While stoking widespread fears of conflict on the peninsula, President Trump stressed his personal respect for President Xi. He promised Beijing easier treatment in negotiations on the two countries' massive trade imbalance and other economic issues. The crisis over North Korea for several weeks put a premium on US interaction with China. Planned arms sales to Taiwan, freedom-of-navigation exercises in the South China Sea, and other US initiatives that might complicate America's search for leverage to stop North Korea's nuclear weapons development were put on hold or delayed.[45] It was against this background that President Trump told the media in April 2017 that he would not accept another phone call from Taiwan's president until he had discussed the matter with President Xi.[46]

Showing a remarkable inclination to change American policy in ways that complicated Chinese efforts to seek the advantageous stability it desired in relations with the United States, President Trump in June expressed disappointment with China's efforts to curb North Korea's nuclear weapons. What followed were US freedom-of-navigation exercises in much faster sequence than in previous months in the disputed South China Sea, an announced major US arms sales package for Taiwan, strong public statements from Secretary of Defense James Mattis and Secretary of State Rex Tillerson in support of American military and other commitments to Taiwan, substantial US sanctions against a Chinese bank and Chinese individuals seen by the United States as aiding North Korea to circumvent international sanctions against its nuclear weapons program, and sharper US government criticism of Chinese human rights practices. Administration officials privately indicated that tougher trade and other policy measures were to come, demonstrating American resolve against Chinese actions seen as opposed to US security, economic, and other interests.[47]

Another key element in the Republican Party platform that was strongly supported by President Trump and his administration leaders was a major increase in defense spending that would allow for a marked increase in the presence of US forces in the Asia-Pacific. The main obstacle to this goal, which was very much at odds with Chinese interests, was legislation restricting such discretionary funding by representatives in the administration and the Congress who required offsetting cuts or using other means to allow for a rise in defense spending beyond available revenue.[48]

The new US administration's approach to trade, investment, and related issues toward China remained ambiguous and arguably conflicted. Officials appointed as leaders of the Commerce Department, the Special Trade Representative office, and the White House National Trade Council were known to be sharply critical of China on economic issues, whereas the leaders of the Treasury and State Departments and the director of the White House Economic Council came from backgrounds strongly supporting globalization and openness in American trade and investment policies. The latter at times were reported to be backed by the president's adviser and son-in-law, Jared Kushner.[49]

Chinese officials stressed their opposition to Hillary Clinton because she was "ideological" in her criticism of China on human rights and related issues. They expected Trump to be less ideological. Given that the Trump government did not have a senior adviser with strong views on China in this policy area, the Chinese calculations appeared to be correct.[50]

Going forward, the zigs and zags in 2017 US policy toward China foreshadowed greater uncertainty and probably greater tensions. For its part, the Xi Jinping government avoided for the moment the more egregious kinds of challenges (e.g., island-building in the disputed South China Sea) that it posed for the Obama government. President Trump was distracted, but he had considerable power and he proved to be much less restrained than President Obama had been in using American power against China in pursuit of his objectives. Xi Jinping's China still sought to advance its power and influence at American expense, but it seemed determined to avoid a confrontation of major consequence. How Beijing would balance between these objectives going forward and how the Trump government would manage its various imperatives in dealing with China were not at all clear. What was clear was that the long-standing differences between the two powers were getting more public scrutiny at the highest levels in both countries. Such scrutiny raised tensions without showing mutually accepted paths to resolution.

Chapter Eight

Security Issues in Contemporary US-China Relations

In the course of US normalization with China since the late 1960s, security issues moved from being the main source of converging interests between the United States and China to the main source of divergence and mutual distrust between the two countries. Throughout the entire period, security issues have never been uniformly positive or negative for the relationship; their implications usually have been mixed. However, the broad pattern shows important convergence of Sino-American security interests against the Soviet Union in the period from the late 1960s through the early 1980s. This convergence can be explained using the lens of realism in international relations (IR) theory, with both the United States and China putting aside important differences in pragmatically seeking advantage in mutual collaboration against a common adversary. US-China security ties were cut drastically after the 1989 Tiananmen crackdown. This US step can be explained in part by liberalism in IR theory, with the United States asserting strong opposition to China's affront to American liberal norms involving human rights and democracy. Constructivism in IR theory helps explain what happened next. In response to US assertion of its liberal values, the Chinese government put much greater emphasis on strongly conditioning Chinese opinion to support a Communist Party–led China. Each side reinforced an identity of its state and society with divergent values and norms, complicating compromise and collaboration up to the present. The United States and China did restore businesslike security ties and developed common ground on a variety of international security questions. These positive elements were offset by differences on a range of security issues. The differences arose against a background of changing Asian and international power relations caused in part by China's rising power and prominence in international affairs, and particularly by

China's strong military modernization focused on Asian issues of key concern to the United States. China's growing military role in Asia was supported by expanding Chinese nuclear and unconventional attack capabilities and espionage directed at the United States. The pattern in the 2010s has seen China employing its increasing power and acting more boldly and assertively to change the regional and international status quo, supported by what it sees as a declining United States. Against the background of strong national identities with many antagonistic values and norms that can be understood by constructivism, the maneuvering of the two powers in the post–Cold War period can be assessed using realism, with both sides seeking advantage amid changing power realities in Asia and the world.

CONVERGENCE AGAINST THE SOVIET THREAT

As discussed in chapter 4, the United States and China aligned together after decades of intense Cold War conflict and confrontation because of common security interests in the face of an expanding threat posed by the Soviet Union. Maoist China was racked by factional leadership disputes and committed to radical domestic and foreign policies and practices, but the Chinese leadership saw the need and wisdom of working closely with the United States in the face of the pressure China was receiving from the USSR. The Nixon administration and later US governments were prepared to put aside or play down a long list of American differences with China over foreign policy, economics, and values, in order for American foreign policy to prioritize the development of a new opening to China for the benefit of US interests in Asian and world affairs—interests that were challenged in particular by expanding Soviet power.[1]

Both governments judged they had a lot at stake in how they worked together and in parallel to deal with security dangers posed by the Soviet Union. China was particularly vocal in complaining repeatedly in the 1970s and early 1980s that the United States was not firm enough in dealing with Soviet expansion or that the United States was too interested in bilateral agreements with Moscow that would benefit the United States but have adverse consequences for China. It took years for Chinese leaders to overcome a previous assumption that the United States would be more likely to cooperate with the Soviet Union against Chinese interests than to cooperate with China against the USSR. American leaders were concerned during this period with the possibility of a Sino-Soviet rapprochement and the negative impact this would have on US foreign policy and security. They worked hard to keep China on the US side in an international arena seen heavily influenced by trilateral US-USSR-China relations.[2]

The Shanghai Communiqué of 1972 and other official statements of both China and the United States during the 1970s and early 1980s made clear the large number of security as well as economic, political, and other issues that continued to divide the two countries. Despite secret US concessions to China over Taiwan at the start of the Sino-American normalization process, the slow pace of US withdrawal from official relations with Taiwan and the continued US commitments to the island government remained at the center of a set of key differences between the United States and China that were of fundamental importance to China. The United States was disappointed with China's position regarding the US war in Vietnam. Chinese leaders seemed from the American perspective to straddle the fence in opening closer relations with the United States while continuing support for the Vietnamese Communists fighting Americans in Indochina.[3]

The two powers were at odds over the Korean Peninsula, where they were on opposite sides, China supporting Kim Il-song's North Korea and the United States sustaining a strong alliance with and large military presence in South Korea. The close US alliance with Japan and China's avowed fear of revived Japanese "militarism" were important sources of differences between the United States and China, though China and Japan quickly normalized their relations in 1972, and China seemed more concerned in this period in shoring up Japanese resolve to join with the United States and China in struggling against the danger posed by the expanding Soviet Union. Elsewhere in international politics, China's influence was comparatively small, as Beijing was slowly rebuilding its international relationships tattered by the binge of self-righteous radicalism during the Cultural Revolution; Chinese leaders generally followed a path that focused opposition against the Soviet Union but also demonstrated strong differences with the United States. Chinese officials publicly opposed the two superpowers: the Soviet Union and the United States. The Chinese priority was building a strong international united front against expanding Soviet "hegemonism," but China continued to register strong differences with US policies in the Middle East, Africa, Latin America, and other parts of the developing world, as well as US positions in international organizations and American views on international economic and political issues.[4]

Balancing American security interests with China and the Soviet Union was a repeated challenge for US policy makers. The prevailing US tendency to "play the China card," to lean closer to China in seeking US advantage against the Soviet Union, remained controversial in American politics and government decision making. Secretary of State Cyrus Vance and critics in and out of government saw US interests better served by seeking negotiations and improved relations with the USSR through arms control and other agreements. China's actual utility in assisting the United States in dealing with the expanding Soviet power also seemed limited. What exactly China would do in assisting the United States in a security confrontation with the Soviet Union was subject to debate.[5] In addition, China's sometimes strident positions and provocative actions against the USSR or its allies raised the danger of military conflict that alarmed some US officials. For example, China's military invasion of Soviet-backed Vietnam in 1979 prompted numerous statements of disagreement from prominent Americans.[6]

How US support for China in the face of the common danger posed by the Soviet Union would impact other important US security issues remained controversial. The United States was reluctant to build close military ties with China; US arms sales to the Chinese government were not an option until the early 1980s. Not only were such sales and the closer US alignment with China seen as limiting US options in relations with the Soviet Union, but US arms sales to China also had implications for long-standing US allies and associates in Asia who remained wary of Chinese intentions and expanding military capabilities. Nonetheless, the Jimmy Carter administration and the early Ronald Reagan administration continued efforts to solidify US security and other relations with China on an anti-Soviet basis. The full extent of American security cooperation with China against the Soviet Union did not become clear until years later. It involved extensive Sino-American clandestine operations directed against Soviet forces occupying Afghanistan following the Soviet invasion of December 1979, and agreements allowing US intelligence agents to monitor Soviet ballistic missile tests from sites in China.[7]

TIANANMEN AND POST–COLD WAR DIVERGENCE

US sanctions against China in reaction to the Tiananmen crackdown focused heavily on the US-China military relationship. The George H. W. Bush administration suspended military-to-military contacts and arms sales to China. US legislation in February 1990 enacted into law sanctions imposed on US arms sales and other military cooperation. In April, China cancelled what had been the most significant US arms transfer to China, the so-called Peace Pearl program to upgrade avionics of Chinese fighter planes.[8]

The Bill Clinton administration began to revive military-to-military meetings with China. However, relations were marred by the Sino-American military face-off in the Taiwan Strait as a result of China's provocative military exercises there in 1995–96; the trashing of US diplomatic properties in China following the US bombing of the Chinese embassy in Belgrade in 1999; and, during the first months of the George W. Bush administration, the crash of the EP-3 US surveillance aircraft with a Chinese fighter jet in 2001.[9]

During this period, Congress stuck to a harder line toward China than the administration did. It passed into law strict limits on the types of military exchanges the United States could carry out with China, and it required reports on the purpose and scope of such exchanges. It also required classified and unclassified annual reports on the purpose and scope of China's military buildup and its implications for American interests. [10]

The US reaction to the Tiananmen crackdown and the shifts in US policy toward China and Taiwan as a result of the decline and demise of the Soviet Union and the emergence of newly democratic Taiwan raised fundamental security questions in China regarding the United States. Though US administrations continued with varying vigor to pursue engagement with China, US leaders repeatedly made clear their interest in American liberal values and sought to promote change in China's authoritarian political system. The top priority of the Chinese Communist Party (CCP) leadership was to preserve its rule in China, and the Chinese military and broader security apparatus focused on this task accordingly. As a result, Chinese security and other leaders came to view the US government and related nongovernment organizations and groups, notably the US media, which encouraged and fostered democratic change in China, as a fundamental threat to this key Chinese national security goal. [11]

The shift in American support for Taiwan also was seen in China as fundamentally at odds with Chinese national security objectives regarding preservation of Chinese sovereign claims and security. The fact that the Clinton administration, seen by Chinese officials as sometimes irresolute on security issues, sent two aircraft carrier battle groups to face off against Chinese forces in the Taiwan area at the height of the Taiwan Strait crisis in 1996 had important lessons for Chinese national security planners. From that time forward, Chinese security planners seemed to have little doubt that a key aspect of Chinese military preparations to counter Taiwan's moves toward independence must involve building the military capability to impede or deter US military intervention in a possible conflict between China and Taiwan. Meanwhile, the US threat to Chinese national security and sovereignty also took other concrete forms for China, as American leaders became more prominent in support for the Dalai Lama and his calls for greater Tibetan autonomy, and as they supported legislation and administrative actions pressing for democratic change and greater autonomy for Hong Kong as it passed from British to Chinese rule in 1997. [12]

TWENTY-FIRST-CENTURY DEVELOPMENTS: REASSURANCE FOLLOWED BY GROWING TENSIONS

China's foreign policy approach shifted in the first decade of the twenty-first century in order to take into account concerns over the possible negative reactions of the United States and other powers to China's rising international prominence and influence. More emphasis was given to reassuring China's neighbors, and new emphasis was given to reassuring the United States; all were told that China's rise would not affect their interests in adverse ways. Opposition to "hegemonism" (a code word used by China in the past to condemn the now-collapsed Soviet Union and used prominently by Chinese officials and media throughout the 1990s to condemn the United States) had been one of the two main stated goals in major Chinese foreign policy pronouncements for decades. It was dropped from major Chinese foreign policy statements, or it received only passing reference. In its place emerged a policy of reassurance with a strong focus on the United States. The process of this evolution and change in Chinese foreign policy took several years and culminated in a major foreign policy document, "China's Peaceful Development Road," released by the Chinese government in December 2005. A few years later, China's foreign policy goal was recast by party leader Hu Jintao, who stressed that China was seeking to promote a "harmonious world" as the Chinese government also strove to achieve greater harmony inside China. The net effect of the new emphasis on "harmony" reinforced Chinese efforts to reassure American and other foreign leaders concerned with the implications of China's rise.

As shown in chapter 7, the emphasis on reassuring the United States did not last. On the one hand, the Xi Jinping leadership came to power in 2012–13 and stressed a nonconfrontational and constructive framework for US-China relations known as a "new type of great power relationship." On the other hand, Beijing carried out a wide range of actions much bolder than under the previous Chinese president to advance the Xi government's avowed "China Dream," which involved policy choices that came at the expense of a broad range of American interests in the prevailing Asian and international order. Many Chinese and American observers saw the United States as weakened and in decline on account of the draining wars and security commitments involving Iraq, Afghanistan, Syria, and the Islamic State, and the protracted economic recession brought on by the American financial breakdown in 2008. Under these circumstances, China was seen opportunistically advancing its interests through bolder actions and initiatives—short of military confrontation—that came at American expense. The Barack Obama government endeavored to counter China's moves in part through its signature "pivot" to Asia, or "rebalance," policy. The policy was widely welcomed by China's neighbors concerned with Beijing's new assertiveness in the region. Beijing reacted negatively and countered with various military, economic, and diplomatic initiatives undermining US interests. President Obama eventually would complain repeatedly, but China for the most part went ahead with offensive actions. Chinese strong reassurance of the United States in the first decade of this century was now privately seen as having been a mistake—a sign of weakness that would not be repeated. [13]

Beginning in 2003, Chinese leaders entered a new stage in China's efforts to define China's approach toward its neighboring countries and what China's approach meant for the United States and US interests in Asia and the world. Premier Wen Jiabao addressed the topic of China's peaceful rise in a speech in New York on December 9, 2003. The exact purpose and scope of the new emphasis on China's "peaceful rise" became clearer over time. [14]

According to senior CCP strategists and other officials, Chinese motives rested on a leadership review of the negative experiences of China's past confrontations with the United States, Asian neighbors, and other powers, and the negative experiences of earlier rising powers, such as Germany and Japan in the twentieth century. They concluded that China could not reach its goals of economic modernization and development through confrontation and conflict. As a result, they incorporated and advanced the moderate features of China's recent approach to Asia and the world into their broader definition of China's peaceful foreign policy approach. [15]

A central feature of the new Chinese approach was a very clear and carefully balanced recognition of the power and influence of the United States. In the 1990s, the Chinese leadership often worked against and confronted US power and influence in world affairs. China resisted the US superpower–led world order, seeking a multipolar world of several powers where China would enjoy more influence and room for maneuver. By contrast, in the next decade, Chinese leaders reevaluated this approach and adopted a more pragmatic attitude to the continued unipolar world led by the United States. [16]

Greater pragmatism and a strong desire to offset views in the United States that saw rising China as a competitor and a threat prompted Chinese leaders and officials to narrow sharply their view of areas of difference with the United States. They avowed that most differences with the United States now centered on the Taiwan issue and US continued support for Taiwan. The wide range of other Chinese complaints about US hegemonism in the post–Cold War period was said to be reduced. This seemed to conform to actual Chinese practice, though at times there were strong rhetorical attacks in the Chinese media against US policies and practices not related to Taiwan. [17]

In this improved atmosphere, Chinese leaders sought to build closer ties with America. They wished to integrate China more closely in the Asian and world system, which they saw as likely to continue to be dominated by US power for many years to come. They pursued closer partnership with the US leaders and wanted to avoid taking steps that would cause the US leaders to see China as a danger or threat that would warrant a concerted US resistance to Chinese development and ambitions. At the same time, they were not abandoning their past differences with US hegemonism. They still disapproved of perceived US domination and unilateralism seen in US practices in

Iraq, US missile defense programs, US strengthening alliance relations with Japan, NATO expansion, and other areas that were staples in the repertoire of Chinese criticism of US practices in the 1990s. But Chinese officials were not prepared to raise such issues as significant problems in US-China relations, unless they impinged directly on core Chinese interests. As a result, most important Chinese criticism of US policy focused on issues related to disputes over Taiwan.[18]

According to Chinese officials and specialists, Chinese leaders pursued the peaceful approach because they needed the appropriate environment to deal with massive internal difficulties and to avoid creating foreign opposition as China developed greater economic and other power and influence. Chinese leaders were said to judge that China faced a period of "strategic opportunity" to pursue its important and complicated nation-building tasks without major distractions, and they wanted to assure that complications and distractions did not emerge in China's relations with the United States. The duration of this strategic opportunity was said to include the first two decades of the twenty-first century.[19]

An early indication of the weakness in Chinese reassurances to neighbors and the United States that China would invariably rise peacefully and harmoniously was seen in concurrent statements on China's national security strategy. There was a significant disconnect between China's national development policy and China's national security policy.[20] The pronouncements about China's peaceful rise and harmonious development made little or no reference to military conflict, the role of the rapidly modernizing People's Liberation Army (PLA), and other key national security questions. The broad outlines of Chinese national security policy were laid out in official Chinese documents and briefings.[21] They revealed Chinese leadership's strong concern about China's security in the prevailing regional and international order. This concern drove decades of double-digit percentage increases in China's defense budgets; it also placed China as Asia's undisputed leading military power and an increasingly serious concern to American security planners as they sought to preserve stability and US leadership in Asia.[22]

China's military growth increasingly complicated China's relations with the United States and some Asian neighbors, notably Taiwan and Japan. Leaders from the United States and some Asian countries were not persuaded by Chinese leadership pledges to pursue the road of peace and development. They saw Chinese national security policies and programs as real or potential threats to their security interests.[23]

Chinese national security pronouncements duly acknowledged that with the end of the Cold War, the danger of global war—a staple in Chinese warning statements in the 1970s and 1980s—ended. However, twenty-first-century Chinese national security statements rarely highlighted the fact that Chinese defense policy was being formulated in an environment less threatening to China than at any time in the last two hundred years.[24] Rather, they made clear that the United States remained at the center of the national security concerns of Chinese leaders.[25] Authoritative PLA briefings in 2008 presented growing US military power as the most serious complication for China's international interests, China's main security concern in the Asian region, and the key military force behind Chinese security concerns over Taiwan, Japan, and other neighbors.[26]

Chinese statements and the PLA buildup opposite Taiwan underlined that Taiwan for many years up to the present was the most likely area of US-China military conflict. The United States and its close ally Japan were portrayed as the principal sources of potential regional instability in Asia. Japan was explicitly criticized for various increased military activities and for its alleged interference in Taiwan.[27]

PLA and other Chinese officials registered strong determination to protect Chinese territory and territorial claims, including areas having strategic resources such as oil and gas. As discussed in more detail in chapters 9 and 10, Chinese-Japanese and other territorial conflicts involving energy resources in the East and South China Seas grew in scope and intensity in recent years, and they intruded ever more directly on these PLA priorities. Chinese concerns increased over US and allied forces controlling sea lines of communication, which were essential for growing Chinese shipping and increasing oil flows to China.[28]

The Obama government with some success continued the efforts of the George W. Bush administration to strengthen exchanges and dialogues between US and Chinese military leaders, which were the weakest set of links among the array of formal interchange between the two governments. As noted in chapter 7, the Obama government also became concerned about China's perceived assertiveness and its repeated public threats and use of coercion and intimidation regarding territorial claims involving neighboring countries and US interests in unimpeded transit through Chinese-claimed air and sea spaces. Encouraged by China's neighbors, the US government embarked on a new military strategy, announced in January 2012 as part of the US administration's "rebalance" policy in Asia, which emphasized American security, economic, and diplomatic reengagement with the Asia-Pacific region.

Though initial US military advances remained modest, US leaders pledged robust US military interchange with allies and associates throughout China's eastern and southern periphery, from the Korean Peninsula through Southeast Asia, Australia, New Zealand and the Pacific Islands, and into the Indian Ocean and its central power, India. They said that with the US military withdrawal from Iraq and planned withdrawal from Afghanistan, the United States would reposition military assets and expand defense ties with many of China's neighbors, and the proportion of US warships in the Asia-Pacific region would rise from 50 percent to 60 percent of the US war fleet.[29]

China's criticism of US initiatives made clear to specialists at home and abroad a forecast of greater strategic competition for influence between the United States and China—competition that would deepen the security dilemma at the heart of the pervasive distrust between the leaders of both countries. Indeed, as discussed in chapter 7, the bold and assertive initiatives of the Xi Jinping government, which began in 2012–13

- departed from China's previous reassurance efforts under President Hu Jintao (2002–12).
- used wide-ranging coercive means short of direct military force to advance Chinese control in the East and South China Seas at the expense of neighbors and key American interests.
- advanced China's military buildup targeted mainly at the United States in the Asia-Pacific region.
- increased military, economic, and political pressure on Taiwan's government.
- rebuffed efforts for stronger pressure on North Korea's nuclear weapons development while sharply pressuring South Korea's enhanced US-supported missile defense efforts.
- cooperated ever more closely with Russia, as both powers increasingly supported one another as they pursued, through coercive and other means disruptive of the prevailing order, their revisionist ambitions in respective spheres of influence, taking advantage of opportunities coming from weaknesses in the United States, Europe, the Middle East, and Asia.
- used foreign exchange reserves and massive excess industrial capacity to launch various self-serving international economic-development programs and institutions to undermine US leadership and/or exclude the United States.
- continued cyber theft of economic assets, intellectual property rights (IPR), and grossly asymmetrical market access, investment, and currency practices; also intensified internal repression and tightened political control—all with serious adverse consequences for US interests.

As noted earlier, beginning in 2014, usually reserved President Obama complained often. President Xi tended to publicly ignore the complaints; he emphasized a purported "new great power relationship" with the United States to American critics who were skeptical of his intentions.

MILITARY MODERNIZATION THROUGH THE MID-2010s: IMPLICATIONS FOR THE UNITED STATES

From the perspective of American defense planners and strategists, the Chinese military buildup since the 1990s has focused in considerable part on strengthening a capability to impede and deny US forces access to the Taiwan area in the event of a China-Taiwan military conflict or confrontation. The scope of this "anti-access" effort seemingly has broadened: Chinese military capabilities have grown to include the South China Sea and East China Sea, where Chinese security forces have endeavored to expand control and influence at the expense of other claimants and in the process have challenged and confronted US naval vessels and military aircraft and undermined US regional influence. Related challenges have appeared in Chinese efforts to counter US dominance in space and to use cyber attacks and other unconventional means to erode US military capabilities.[30]

As noted in earlier chapters, the United States has a fundamental interest in sustaining naval and other access to the Asia-Pacific region. And since the Japanese attack on Pearl Harbor, it has undertaken the obligations of leadership in sustaining a favorable balance of power in the region in order to protect that access and other American interests. The conflicts of the Cold War allowed for equilibrium to emerge in East Asia and the western Pacific where—in general terms and with some notable exceptions—the United States sustained dominance along the maritime rim of East Asia and the western Pacific, while continental Asia came to be dominated by China. Almost twenty years ago, this stasis was labeled the "Geography of Peace" by IR specialist Robert Ross.[31]

As of 2017 the situation has changed substantially. China has long chafed under superpower pressure along its periphery. Its military modernization gives top priority to upgrading power projection by air and naval forces along its maritime borders. While the United States seemed satisfied with the stasis Ross discussed at the end of the 1990s, American concern with Chinese anti-access efforts now grows in tandem with the increasing Chinese military capabilities to carry out the broadening scope of their anti-access goals.[32]

Key security issues involving Taiwan and other nearby contested territories, Chinese one-party rule, sovereignty, and resistance to superpower presence along China's periphery provide the foundation for Chinese security differences with the United States and help explain the suspicion and wariness that characterizes contemporary Sino-American relations. Of course, as explained in chapter 6 and chapter 7, prevailing discourse between the US and Chinese governments has tried to emphasize the positive for a variety of mainly pragmatic reasons important to the respective interests of the two governments. Security differences tend to be dealt with in dialogues concerning US-China military contacts and security issues in Asian and world affairs. [33]

The two governments also have developed considerable common ground on important security issues. China used to be seen by the United States as an outlier regarding issues of proliferation of weapons of mass destruction (WMD) and related delivery systems. Into the 1990s, China passed nuclear weapons technology and missile systems to Pakistan and engaged in suspicious nuclear technology cooperation and missile development and sales with Iran and other nations deemed hostile to the United States. Under pressure from the United States and reflecting recalibration of Chinese foreign policy and national security priorities, China moved to a position much more consistent with American interests on WMD proliferation. [34] The United States and China at times have shown cooperation and common ground along with significant differences in dealing with North Korea's nuclear weapons and ballistic missile programs and the danger they pose for stability on the Korean Peninsula and elsewhere. [35] China also has worked cooperatively and in parallel with the United States in dealing with international terrorism since the terrorist attack on America in September 2001, in managing tensions between nuclear-armed Pakistan and India in South Asia, and in managing crises precipitated by pro-independence initiatives by Taiwanese president Chen Shui-bian (2000–2008). China has endeavored to moderate and then support Western-backed efforts in the UN Security Council to curb Iran's suspected nuclear weapons development program. It also has been among the most active participants in sending security forces abroad as UN peacekeepers and, more recently, in contributing to the UN peacekeeping budget. [36]

Trends and Prospects in Military Modernization

Overall, Chinese defense acquisition and advancement have reflected broad ambitions for Chinese military power. While they have appeared to focus recently on dealing with US forces in the event of a Taiwan contingency, these forces can be used by Chinese leaders as deemed appropriate in a variety of circumstances, including the territorial disputes along China's rim that have received higher priority in recent Chinese foreign relations.

Salient Chinese defense acquisitions and modernization efforts include the following: [37]

- Research and development in space systems to provide wide-area intelligence, surveillance, and reconnaissance, and the development of antisatellite systems to counter the surveillance and related efforts of potential adversaries; development of cyber attack and means of defense; development of electronic warfare capabilities

- Cruise missile acquisitions and programs that improve the range, speed, and accuracy of Chinese land-, air-, and sea-launched weapons
- Ballistic missile programs that improve the range, survivability (through mobile systems in particular), reliability, accuracy, and response times of tactical, regional, and intercontinental-range weapons to augment or re-place current systems; development of ballistic missiles with warheads capable of targeting naval surface combatants
- Construction and acquisition of advanced conventional-powered subma-rines with subsurface-launched cruise missiles and guided torpedoes, and nuclear-powered attack and ballistic missile submarines to augment or replace older vessels in service
- Development and acquisition of more capable naval surface ships armed with advanced antiship, antisubmarine, and air-defense weapons
- Air force advances, including hundreds of modern multirole fighters, ad-vanced air-to-air missiles, airborne early-warning and control system air-craft, aerial refueling capabilities, and unmanned aerial vehicles
- Air-defense systems involving modern surface-to-air missiles and air-de-fense fighters
- Improved power projection for ground forces, including more sea- and airlift capabilities, special operations forces, and amphibious warfare ca-pabilities
- Research and development of defense information systems, and improved command, control, communications, and computer systems
- Increase in the tempo and complexity of exercises in order to make the PLA capable in joint interservice operations involving power projections, including amphibious operations

The Chinese advances mean that no single Asian power can come close to matching China's military power on continental Asia. With the possible ex-ception of Japan, no Asian country will be capable of challenging China's naval and air power in maritime East Asia. Should Beijing choose to deploy naval and air forces to patrol the sea lines of communications in the Indian Ocean, only India conceivably would be capable of countering China's pow-er.

Looking to the future, it is possible to bound the scope of China's military buildup. Available evidence shows that it is focused on nearby Asia. A major possible exception is the long-range nuclear weapons systems that target outside Asia, notably the United States. China has used these to deter the United States and other potential adversaries by demonstrating a retaliatory, second-strike capability against them. Other challenges with implications beyond nearby Asia involve cyber attack and antisatellite weapons.[38]

The objectives of the Chinese military buildup seem focused first on Taiwan, preventing its move toward independence and assuring that China's sovereignty will be protected and restored. More generally, Chinese forces can be deployed to defeat possible threats or attacks on China, especially China's economically important eastern coastline. Apart from conflict over Taiwan, Chinese forces are designed to deal with a range of so-called local war possibilities. These could involve territorial disputes with Japan, Southeast Asian countries, or India, or instability requiring military intervention in Korea.

Meanwhile, the Chinese military plays a direct role in Chinese foreign policy, which seeks to spread Chinese international influence, reassure neighboring countries and others of Chinese intentions, and nurture an international environment that will allow China to rise in power and influence without major disruption. This role likely will involve continued active diplomacy by Chinese military officials, increased numbers of military exercises with Asian and other countries, some Chinese arms sales to and training of foreign military forces, and more active participation by Chinese national security officials in regional and other multilateral security organizations, some created or fostered by China. [39]

The Chinese military is on course to continue a transformation from its past strategic outlook, that of a large continental power requiring large land forces for defense against threats to borders. The end of the threat from the Soviet Union and the improvement of China's relations with India, Vietnam, and others have eased this concern. China is likely to move away from a continental orientation, requiring large land forces, toward a combined continental/maritime orientation, requiring smaller, more mobile, and more sophisticated forces capable of protecting China's inland and coastal periphery. Unlike the doctrine of protracted land war against an invading enemy prevalent until the latter years of the Cold War, Chinese doctrine probably will continue its more recent emphasis on the need to demonstrate an ability to strike first in order to deter potential adversaries and to carry out first strikes in order to both gain the initiative in the battlefield and secure Chinese objectives.

To fulfill these objectives, Chinese forces will need, and will further develop, the ability to strike or respond rapidly, to take and maintain the initiative in the battlefield, to prevent escalation, and to resolve conflict quickly and on favorable terms. Chinese military options will include preemptive strikes and the use of conventional and nuclear forces to deter and coerce adversaries. Chinese forces will expand power-projection capabilities, giving Chinese forces a solid ability to deny critical land and sea access (for example, Taiwan Strait) to adversaries, and providing options for force projection farther from Chinese borders. [40]

To achieve these objectives, Chinese conventional ground forces will evolve, consistent with recent emphasis, toward smaller, more flexible, highly trained, and well-equipped rapid-reaction forces with more versatile and well-developed assault, airborne, and amphibious power-projection capabilities. Special operations forces will play an important role in these efforts. Navy forces will build on recent advances with more advanced surface combatants and submarines having better air defense, antisubmarine warfare, and antiship capabilities. Their improved weaponry of cruise missiles and torpedoes, an improved naval air force, and greater replenishment-at-sea capabilities will broaden the scope of their activities and pose greater challenges to potential adversaries. Air forces will grow with more versatile and modern fighters, longer-range interceptor/strike aircraft, improved early warning and air defense, and longer-range transport, lift, and midair refueling capabilities.

These forces will be used increasingly in an integrated way consistent with an emphasis on joint operations that involves more sophisticated command, control, communications, computers, intelligence, and strategic reconnaissance (C4ISR), early warning, and battlefield management systems. Improved airborne and satellite-based systems will improve detection, tracking, targeting, and strike capabilities, as well as enhanced operational coordination of the various forces.

Chinese strategic planners are sure to build on the advantages Chinese strategic missile systems provide. While estimates vary, it appears that Chinese plans call for more than 1,500 short-, medium-, and intermediate-range, solid-fueled, mobile ballistic missiles (with a range under four thousand miles), and short-range cruise missiles, with increased accuracy, and some with both nuclear and conventional capabilities. China is also modernizing a small number of longer-range nuclear missiles capable of hitting the continental United States, and has developed a submarine-launched nuclear missile that would broaden Chinese nuclear options. Chinese nuclear missiles will have smaller and more powerful warheads with multiple independently targeted reentry vehicles or multiple reentry vehicle capabilities. The emphasis on modern surveillance, early warning, and battle management systems with advanced C4ISR assets seen in Chinese planning with regard to conventional forces also applies to nuclear forces.

These advances will build on China's existing military abilities. They pose a long list of serious concerns for the United States, as well as Taiwan, Japan, and some other Chinese neighbors, and an overall strategic reality of increasing Chinese military power that influences the strategic outlook of most Chinese neighbors. The existing military abilities include the following:

- The ability to conduct intensive, short-duration air and naval attacks on Taiwan, as well as prolonged air, naval, and possibly ground attacks. China's ability to prevail against Taiwan is seen as increasing steadily, especially given lax defense preparedness and political division in Taiwan. Massive US military intervention is viewed as capable of defeating a

Chinese invasion, but Chinese area denial capabilities could substantially impede and slow the US intervention.

- Power-projection abilities to dislodge smaller regional powers from nearby disputed land and maritime territories, and the ability to conduct air and sea denial operations for two hundred miles along China's coasts.
- Strong abilities to protect Chinese territory from invasion, to conduct ground-based power projection along land borders against smaller regional powers, and to strike civilian and military targets with a large and growing inventory of ballistic missiles and medium-range bombers armed with cruise missiles.
- Limited ability to project force against the territory of militarily capable neighboring states, notably Russia, India, and Japan.
- Continued ability to deter nuclear and other attacks from the United States and Russia by means of modernized and survivable Chinese nuclear missile forces capable of striking at these powers.

As China's military capabilities continue to grow more rapidly than those of any of its neighbors, and as China solidifies its position as Asia's leading military power, the situation clearly poses serious implications for, and some complications in, China's foreign policy. Many neighboring officials and those in the United States, sometimes publicly but more often privately, remain concerned for several reasons.

The history of the use of force in Chinese foreign policy provides little assurance to Americans or others that China's avowed peaceful emphasis will be sustained. The Chinese government has resorted to the use of force in international affairs more than most governments in the modern period.[41] The reasons have varied.[42] China's growing stake in the international status quo and its dependence on smooth international economic interchange are seen to argue against Chinese leaders' resorting to military force to achieve international objectives. At the same time, the rapid development of Chinese military capabilities to project power and the change in Chinese doctrine to emphasize striking first to achieve Chinese objectives are seen to increase the likelihood of Chinese use of force to achieve the ambitions and objectives of the Chinese government. Against this background, it is not surprising that an active debate continues in the United States and elsewhere about Chinese national security intentions and whether they will override the Chinese government's public emphasis on promoting peace and development in Chinese foreign affairs. Prudence argues for increased US defense preparations in the face of China's rise. Those American efforts continued, notably under the rubric of the Obama government's reengagement with the Asia-Pacific region, and they reinforced long-standing Chinese suspicions that the positive hand of US engagement was accompanied by the negative hand of US containment. Deeply rooted Chinese suspicions of US intentions and policies continue to be reinforced.

From five years or so into this century, Chinese and American security officials have tended to register their reservations and concerns in dialogues or less prominent briefings and statements. Chinese concerns and differences with the United States on security issues involve a long list of US security activities that are seen to underline a US security posture opposed to China. They include:

- US statements and actions seen by China to show that the United States viewed China as a potential adversary, that it sought to change China's authoritarian political system, and that it endeavored to complicate and hold back China's rising international role
- Perceived US support for Taiwan independence, US refusal to support Taiwan's reunification with China, and US use of Taiwan as a "card," a source of leverage, in negotiations with China
- US support for leaders and groups in Tibet and Xinjiang that undermine Chinese sovereignty
- US force deployments and defense arrangements in the Asia-Pacific region that are seen to surround China with adverse strategic pressures and to prompt China's neighbors to contest more actively with China over territorial disputes
- A strengthened US-Japan alliance directed at countering rising China
- A US nuclear weapons strategy that sees China as an enemy
- US, Japanese, and South Korean missile defense efforts that are seen as or are in fact targeted against China's growing ballistic missile capabilities
- A US-backed Western arms embargo against China

Forecasts of Chinese military strengths and their challenges to the United States differ because of variables involving political, economic, and other developments and because of possible upturns or downturns in Sino-American relations. Nonetheless, the United States and China have become more competitive; China's economy is catching up with and is widely seen to surpass that of the United States in the next decade. Against that background, more attention is focused on China's robust military buildup targeted along its periphery and on what forces the United States, still the world's largest military power, can bring to bear to offset negative impacts from China's military rise.

The debate in the United States on what to do about China's rise features a range of specialists who see the implications of China's military strengthening as a demand for substantial changes in US policy. On one side are those arguing in support of US Defense Department stance that in the event of an armed confrontation with China, the United States should be ready to attack China with air and sea forces that would destroy and disrupt Chinese forces—otherwise the Chinese forces would strike at US and allied combatants in areas along China's periphery.[43] This so-called air-sea battle concept calls for US forces to be prepared to attack Chinese sensors, radars, targeting systems, and/or weapons in order to break links in the Chinese process of finding the US or allied target and striking it. This offensive posture is seen as likely to lead to a broader and very destructive US-China war, and so other specialists call for an American response to a confrontation with China that would involve an American and allied blockade of major shipping routes to China. The blockade would seek to destroy Chinese shipping and supporting naval vessels but avoid direct attack on Chinese territory.

On the other side are specialists who judge that it is futile for the United States to endeavor to preserve its leading position in Asia through military primacy.[44] Given the rapid increase in Chinese military power and the worldwide commitments of US forces, the United States is advised to seek an agreement with China on a balance of power in the region that both find acceptable. A challenge facing this proposal is persuading China, which has in recent years seen significant advance in its control of contested territories and its related influence in Asia, to set aside its assertiveness in seeking its vision of the China Dream in favor of an accommodation with the United States, a power seen on the decline and thus far ineffective in checking China's advances along its periphery.

President Trump, China, and the Crisis over North Korea's Nuclear Weapons

As noted in chapter 6, China's approach to nuclear weapons proliferation changed markedly after the Cold War. Beijing sometimes reluctantly but steadily conformed more to international norms supported by the United States. There was considerable cooperation and common ground between the two powers in dealing with this issue with regard to Iran and, notably, North Korea. Nevertheless, North Korea continued to develop and test its nuclear weapons and ballistic missile delivery systems despite UN sanctions supported by the United States and China. The development reached a point at the end of the Obama administration and the start of the Donald Trump administration where North Korea was anticipated to soon have the ability to launch a nuclear strike against the continental United States.[45]

The Trump administration conducted a policy review and announced that if North Korea could not be persuaded to stop its nuclear weapons development, the United States would take unspecified unilateral actions. The resulting crisis featured intense consultations among US and allied leaders. It also was a centerpiece in the April 2017 summit between President Trump and President Xi Jinping. President Trump listened to President Xi's explanation of China's concerns with the North Korean situation. China opposed the North Korean nuclear weapons program, but it put a high value on maintaining stability in this important neighboring area. It favored negotiations and avoiding confrontation. Against that background, President Trump publicly and repeatedly appealed to China to use its leverage as North Korea's neighbor and main economic partner to compel North Korea to change its policy and halt its nuclear weapons program. In these appeals, the US president voiced his respect for the Chinese leader. He also indicated that progress on the North Korean issue would lead to US moderation in dealing with trade issues with China.[46]

In June 2017 there was still no resolution to the crisis. North Korea continued its testing of delivery systems despite UN sanctions against them. Its commitment to nuclear weapons development seemed undiminished. There were reports that China was tightening restrictions on economic interaction with North Korea, but there also were reports that Chinese businesses had managed to circumvent such restrictions despite Beijing's avowed commitments to economic sanctions that it established to persuade North Korea to stop its nuclear weapons program.[47]

Chapter Nine

Economic and Environmental Issues in Contemporary US-China Relations

The rapid growth of the Chinese economy and close integration of Chinese development into the global economy have been the most salient accomplishments of the reforms pursued by Chinese leaders since the death of Mao. China's economic modernization has had a staggering impact on the lives of Chinese people. It is the foundation of the legitimacy of the ruling Chinese Communist Party, the source of China's growing military power, and the main reason for China's international prominence in the early twenty-first century. The implications of Chinese economic development also have had negative features at home and abroad, notably regarding trade disputes and environmental protection. [1]

As the world's leading economy, source of foreign investment and technology, and leading importer of Chinese products, the United States has had an important influence on, and in turn has been influenced in important ways by, China's economic advance and integration into existing international economic structures and agreements. The burgeoning Sino-American economic relationship had a positive effect on relations between the two countries. In the post–Cold War period, it replaced the strategic cooperation between the United States and China against the Soviet Union that had provided the key foundation of US-China cooperation in the 1970s and 1980s. The two world economies became increasingly interdependent. They were so important for each country's development that by the first decade of the twenty-first century, signs of serious economic dispute or confrontation between the great economic powers had profound impacts on world markets detrimental to the well-being of each country. [2]

The rapid growth of China's economy and US-China economic relations were driven by forces of international economic globalization. The overall process has had profound effects, both positive and negative, on broad swaths of public and elite opinion, economic and other interest groups, and political leaders in both societies. On the whole, China's rapid growth and rise to great power status as a leading world economy have shown the process in recent years as highly beneficial to China's interests. The Chinese government has generally avoided major initiatives that have the potential to disrupt existing economic relationships seen as largely beneficial for its interests.[3]

Complaints and initiatives to change existing economic relations have come in recent years largely from the US side of the Sino-American relationship. They were particularly prominent for mainly political reasons in the wake of the Tiananmen crackdown, when the US administration and the Congress considered whether to place conditions on the United States' provision of most-favored-nation trading status to China. Those efforts ended in US agreement with China on China's entry into the World Trade Organization (WTO) and the passage of US legislation granting China permanent normal trade status in 2000.[4]

More recent US complaints reflect a wide range of US interests and constituencies disadvantaged by perceived unfair negative aspects of the massive US-China economic relationship. They are supported by varying numbers of congressional members and generally less vocal officials in the US government. The US administration has followed a pattern of dealing with such economic and trade disputes through a variety of bilateral discussions and dialogues with Chinese counterparts. The Chinese government favors this approach in dealing with these and other issues. It reacts negatively to American public pressure or US policy initiatives on trade and related economic issues that it tends to see as protectionist or otherwise adverse to Chinese interests. Chinese officials also were openly critical of US financial management and other policies that negatively affected China's economy in the global financial crisis and recession beginning in 2008.[5]

For many years, periodic US complaints and initiatives on economic and trade issues caused public disagreements with China as the United States pressed for change and China resisted US demands on various economic questions. Against the background of continuing negative if not alarmist US public opinion on the threat China's economic practices posed for the United States came more recent hardening in US attitudes. Strident charges against Chinese economic practices were featured in the rhetoric of the leading candidates of both political parties during the 2016 US presidential election campaigns. President Donald Trump's victory was based on a promise to right glaring economic wrongs with China. American organizations usually moderate in dealing with China were sharply critical of Chinese economic practices.[6]

Many US experts and government leaders came to see as incorrect their past expectation, consistent with the liberal school of international relations (IR) theory, that growing trade and economic interchange would prompt China to conform more to international economic practices in line with American interests. What they found, as explained in a prominent report by the Asia Society in February 2017, was that Chinese practices reinforced, from a decade earlier, state-directed "zero-sum, mercantilist trade and investment policies that are highly . . . damaging to US commercial and economic interests."[7] This darker view of Chinese economic behavior was more in line with the realist school of IR theory. Using that lens, China was seen deliberately eschewing economic reforms that would open China more to investment and trade advantageous for the United States and other developed countries. The Chinese government practiced a form of "state capitalism" that used its control of bank lending and important state-owned enterprises (SOEs) and its influence over China's dynamic private sector to carry out industrial policies designed to advance a wide range of protected segments of the Chinese economy; and in this way, China eventually acquired advanced technology from abroad in a high-priority effort to create national industries that would prevail in the China market and international markets at the expense of American and other international competitors.[8]

Whether this growing realist view of economic relations with China would result in strong US countermeasures or have a broader impact on overall US policy toward China remained uncertain at the outset of the Trump administration. On the one hand, it could mesh with growing American concern over China's international assertiveness at the expense of neighbors and US interests in the Asia-Pacific region and concern over China's increased domestic repression of civil society and individual rights to support an overall tougher US policy toward China. On the other hand, many important American companies have a large stake in continuing to work constructively with China. And they have important connections with senior leaders of the Trump government and the Congress. Meanwhile, the willingness of the US government to pressure China on salient economic issues may be overshadowed by need to cooperate with Beijing on other more immediately important issues, such as North Korea.[9]

CHINA'S ECONOMIC IMPORTANCE

Since the beginning of economic reforms following the death of Mao Zedong in 1976, China has been the world's fastest-growing major economy. From 1979 to 2014, the average annual growth rate of China's gross domestic product (GDP) was about 10 percent. By 2010 China became the world's second-largest economy, after the United States. In 2011 it became the largest manufacturer, surpassing the United States. In 2012 it became the world's largest trader. China also has become the second-largest destination of foreign investment, the largest holder of foreign exchange reserves, and the largest creditor nation.[10] Several predictions said that China was on track to surpass the United States, the world's largest economy, in the next decade.[11]

Chinese growth rates declined steadily from 12.8 percent in 2012 to 6.7 percent in 2016. Chinese foreign trade growth stopped and overall trade was less in 2016 than in 2015. In 2013 Chinese leaders began a wide range of more than sixty sets of mainly economic reforms to deal with existing or anticipated economic weaknesses involving the inefficient practices of SOEs and the state banking system, resource and energy scarcities, massive environmental problems, and China's strong dependence on the health of the global trading economy, which stalled in the financial crisis and recession begun in 2008.[12] Active foreign direct investment (FDI) in China continued, and growing Chinese investment abroad surpassed China's FDI in 2015 and later years.[13]

Economists generally attribute much of China's rapid economic growth to two main factors: large-scale capital investment, financed by large domestic savings and foreign investment; and rapid productivity growth. The two factors appear to have worked together during the reform period,[14] though decline in productivity has prompted recent economic reforms seeking higher efficiency in the economy.

In foreign affairs, the growing importance of the Chinese economy was manifested most notably by the growth in economic interchange between China and countries throughout the world, notably the United States. Most important in this regard was the growth of trade and foreign investment in China. International trade played a key role in increasing Chinese influence around the world and in enabling China to import the technology, resources, food, and consumer goods needed to support economic growth, to finance China's military buildup and other aspects of its national power, and to maintain the legitimacy of the Communist Party government. Greater Chinese access to foreign markets also enabled China to attract foreign investment. Foreign-affiliated companies played a key role in generating economic growth and employment and in the manufacture of world-class products. China's joining the WTO in 2001 added to reasons for strong foreign investment in China, which in turn boosted the size of Chinese foreign trade. Chinese exports and imports in 2004 were both more than twice as large as those just three years earlier, in 2001.[15]

For many years, about half of Chinese foreign trade was so-called processing trade, where a commodity crosses China's border, perhaps several times, before the final product is produced and the value of each cross-border transfer is duly registered in Chinese import and export figures. In 2012 the level of processing trade was said to be 34.8 percent of the value of Chinese foreign trade, down from a level of 44 percent in 2011. Some other more recent estimates have been higher. In effect, such processing trade results in a good deal of double-counting in Chinese import and export figures, which tends to exaggerate the actual size and importance of Chinese foreign trade. This consideration aside, the fact remains that the internationally recognized figures for Chinese exports surpassed those of the United States in 2007.[16]

Though China has sometimes run trade surpluses and sometimes run trade deficits in the reform period since the late 1970s, in the past two decades (as of 2017) China has run only trade surpluses. The surplus grew to about $300 billion in 2008, declined somewhat after that, and rose again to reach $500 billion in 2016. The US global trade deficit in these years was enormous, amounting to more than $700 billion for several years. It was $500 billion in 2016; China was the lion's share of that deficit with a US merchandise trade deficit with China valued at $350 billion. Merchandise trade surpluses and large-scale foreign investment saw China accumulate the world's largest foreign exchange reserves. The value of the reserves reached more than $3 trillion in the past six years.[17]

In assessing China's major trading partners, it is important to keep in mind differences between Chinese trade data and those of some of its major trading partners. The differences exist because a large share of China's trade (both exports and imports) passes through Hong Kong, which reverted back to Chinese rule in July 1997 but is treated as a separate customs area by most countries, including China and the United States. China treats a large share of its exports through Hong Kong as Chinese exports to Hong Kong for statistical purposes, while many countries, including the United States, that import Chinese products through Hong Kong generally attribute their origin to China for statistical purposes.

As a result, trade data from the United States showed that the importance of the US market to China's export sector was much higher than was reflected in Chinese trade data. Based on US data on Chinese exports to the United States, and Chinese data on total Chinese exports, it was estimated that Chinese exports to the United States as a share of total Chinese exports grew from 15 percent in 1986 to 33 percent in 2004 and then declined in following years, amounting to 18 percent of Chinese exports in 2015.[18]

Reflecting the importance of foreign investment in the Chinese economy and trading relationships, a high level of Chinese exports was from foreign-funded enterprises in China. According to Chinese data, about half of its trade was conducted by such enterprises. The largest share of these enterprises was owned by investors from Hong Kong and Taiwan, as well as growing numbers of investors from South Korea, Japan, the United States, and Southeast Asia. Some of the foreign entrepreneurs shifted their labor-intensive, export-oriented firms to China to take advantage of low-cost labor and other cost benefits. A significant share of the products made by such firms was exported to the United States. Chinese data indicated that the share of China's exports produced by foreign-invested enterprises in China rose from 2 percent in 1986, to 41 percent in 1996, to 57 percent in 2004, and to 58.5 percent in 2005. In 2014 foreign-invested enterprises accounted for 46 percent of Chinese exports and 46 percent of China's imports. Such foreign firms dominated China's high-technology exports.[19]

China's abundance of cheap labor made it internationally competitive in many low-cost, labor-intensive manufactures. As a result, manufactured products constituted an increasingly large share of China's trade. Meanwhile, a large share of China's imports, such as raw materials, components, parts, and production machinery, was used to manufacture products for export. For example, China imported cotton- and textile-production machinery to produce textile and apparel items. A substantial amount of China's imports comprised parts and components that were assembled in Chinese factories and then exported. Major products in these efforts included consumer electronics and computers.[20]

Viewed in comparison to the United States, the world's top economy, the recent growth of Chinese trade was impressive.[21] In 1995, US total trade was $1.39 trillion or five times that of China's $281 billion. In 2007 US total trade of $3.116 trillion was 1.4 times that of China's $2.175 trillion. China became a major trading nation and an increasingly competitive rival to the United States in more industries. Given the rise of international supply chains, China's economy also complemented that of the United States in certain areas. US companies joined many other foreign firms in relying on China to manufacture products designed, advertised, and distributed by the home (American-based) part of the multinational corporation; or they manufactured in the United States using Chinese components; or they produced components in the United States for assembly in China.

In 2011 US merchandise trade was $3.745 trillion and the merchandise trade of China (not including Hong Kong or Macau) was $3.641 trillion. In 2012 China's merchandise trade valued at $3.87 trillion surpassed that of the United States valued at $3.82 trillion, making China the world's largest trading nation.[22] As this trend developed, Chinese trading partners were seen as possibly inclined to rely more on China than on the United States both as a market for exports and a source of imports. However, such a shift was offset by the fact—well illustrated in the international economic crisis beginning in 2008–9—that Chinese trade and the trade of Asian and other countries linked with production chains focused on China—depended very heavily on exports to the United States and the European Union.[23]

The scope of Chinese trade grew commensurate with its rapidly increasing size. China for several years surpassed the United States in overall trade with Northeast Asia, Southeast Asia, Australia/Oceania, Africa, and Brazil.[24]

China's rising trade prominence in international markets went hand in hand with the rise in China's importance as a destination for and source of FDI. As much of Chinese trade was done by foreign-invested enterprises in China, China was in the lead among developing countries in receiving foreign investment. Annual utilized FDI in China reached $116 billion in 2011; the figure was $118 billion in 2016.[25]

At the same time, Chinese companies beginning in recent years have been urged by the Chinese government to increase what had been more limited Chinese investment abroad. It remained difficult to measure the extent and importance of these investments and their significance for data on foreign investment into China. In recent years, more than half of Chinese overseas investment was shown in Chinese data to go to Hong Kong, the Cayman Islands, and the British Virgin Islands. The accounting rules in these locales were such that they were seen to provide tax havens and to allow Chinese firms to seek advantage by investing there, and from those locations to send investment back into China.[26]

With government support came strong growth in outbound Chinese investment. China was the world's fifth-largest foreign investor in 2010, with outbound Chinese investment valued at $59 billion.[27] According to UN data, China provided $101 billion in investment in 2013; it ranked as the third-largest source of global FDI that year. The stock of China's outward FDI through 2013 was estimated at $512 billion. In 2016 China's outbound investment was valued at $161 billion.[28] How much of these flows were to tax havens, how much they involved finance and nonfinance investment, and other uncertainties remained to be determined, though the rise of China's importance as an international investor was clearly growing rapidly.[29]

China's foreign aid remains difficult to assess, given a lack of official and reliable data. The *China Statistical Yearbook 2003–2006* released an annual aid figure of $970 million, but specialists judged that this did not include loans, a main form of Chinese aid. A 2007 US study judged that China's annual aid ranged in value between $1.5 billion and $2 billion.[30] Studies that inventoried various reports of loans, state-sponsored investment, and other official Chinese financing came up with much larger figures, though aid specialists judged that much of these efforts would not qualify as aid and that it was difficult to determine when and whether reported aid and loan pledges were ever actually made and disbursed. The wide range of Chinese financing at times involved interest-free or concessional loans, but it also involved trade and investment agreements, including arrangements whereby Chinese loans were to be repaid by commodities (e.g., oil) produced as a result of the development financed with China's help.[31]

The Chinese government's first white paper on foreign aid was released in April 2011; it provided an overall figure of China's cumulative foreign assistance and data on other trends, but not enough information to determine the cost of Chinese assistance to specific countries or during specific times. The second Chinese white paper on foreign assistance was issued in 2014; it offered better information focused on the three-year period 2010–12. China provided $14.4 billion in grants, interest-free loans, and concessional loans in that period.[32]

China also was important as a recipient of considerable foreign assistance. Because of the difficulties in assessing the costs and scope of Chinese assistance efforts and the varied and complicated channels of foreign assistance to China, there remained considerable uncertainty as to what degree China was a net provider of foreign assistance. Some estimates saw China receiving each year international assistance valued at more than $6 billion.[33] The *Economist* in January 2015 reported that "as recently as 2010 it [China] was still a net recipient of foreign assistance."[34]

GLOBAL ECONOMIC CRISIS AND RECESSION: IMPLICATIONS AND ISSUES

Although Chinese financial institutions were not believed to have heavily invested in US subprime securities, the global economic crisis that began in the US financial sector in 2008 had a major impact on China's economy. China's leading trading partners, the United States, the European Union, and Japan, were pushed into a deep recession exacerbated by a major crisis in world credit markets that markedly slowed lending needed for growth. Chinese trade and foreign investment coming to China declined; the overall rate of growth of the Chinese economy also declined. The Chinese government implemented a two-year, $586 billion stimulus package, mainly dedicated to infrastructure projects. Interest rates were cut repeatedly as were real estate taxes. The government increased export tax rebates for textiles, garments, toys, and other export products hard hit by the decline in foreign demand for Chinese products. It endeavored to revise tax policies and provide financial support to domestic firms.[35]

China's international role in the crisis developed cautiously. Some Chinese and Asian commentators at first asserted that China and its neighbors could confidently ride out the economic crisis in US and Western markets. They appeared in retreat by the end of 2008 as the impact of the financial turmoil and recession in America and Europe began to have a major effect on China and the region's trade, manufacturing, currency values, and broader economic stability.[36]

Like its Asian neighbors, the Chinese government also was cautious in taking the lead in international financial arrangements and commitments that could involve significant risks for the Chinese economy in what increasingly appeared to be a period of prolonged adverse international economic conditions.[37] On the whole, Chinese leaders stuck to the position that China's top priority in the crisis was to sustain growth at home. Despite China's continued large cumulative trade and current account surpluses, the Chinese government took steps to keep the value of its currency low relative to the US dollar and some other currencies, and to stimulate export growth through tax changes and other measures. These steps helped Chinese export manufacturers, but they seemed to work to the disadvantage of China's international trade competitors in Asia and elsewhere. Meanwhile, despite sometimes prominent Chinese criticisms of the existing international economic order in the World Bank, the International Monetary Fund (IMF), and the WTO—the existing order was said to have disadvantaged developing countries and supported the primacy of the US dollar—Chinese government investors, for the time being at least, continued to see their interests best served by heavy investment of their foreign exchange reserves in US Treasury securities.

Over time, world leaders including American and Chinese leaders acknowledged a strong need for fundamental restructuring in the global economy. The US and Chinese economies were the world's largest, with China's rapidly growing GDP valued in nominal terms in 2011 at $7 trillion and the US economy valued at $15 trillion. In terms of purchasing power parity (PPP), China's GDP was valued at $11.3 trillion and the US GDP at $15.1 trillion. There was broad recognition that the United States needed more disciplined economic policies that would curb its massive current account deficit, and China needed to reduce its dependence on exports and infrastructure and move toward more domestic consumption. Acrimonious US debate on how to deal with US government budget deficits as well as economic and trade policies continued with mixed and uncertain results through the 2012 election campaign and into the second term of the Barack Obama administration. China signaled its shift toward greater domestic consumption in a five-year economic plan begun in 2011. The IMF reported some advance in domestic consumption in China in 2011, though consumption as a percentage of GDP remained low. Official and media commentary on both sides featured criticism of the other for not doing enough in dealing with perceived dangerous and unsustainable global economic imbalances.[38]

As discussed in chapter 7, a significant longer-term implication of the crisis was related to Chinese views of American leadership and power. Chinese officials and commentators had long debated the resiliency and decline of American international leadership. The US economic crisis came from gross negligence and mismanagement by American firms with weak government oversight. In the eyes of Chinese observers, the previously admired US economic model was discredited. And the economic crisis along with a prolonged gridlock in American governance and protracted wars in Southwest Asia added to a Chinese perception of overall US weakness and decline. Against that background, Beijing's reliance of its state-directed elements in

China's hybrid capitalist economic policies was reinforced, despite US criticism. And China's willingness to challenge a weakened and preoccupied United States on long-standing disputes and more recent disagreements in US-China relations appeared stronger. As seen in chapter 7, that new willingness to challenge the United States showed in early Chinese testing of the incoming Obama government with regard to Taiwan, Tibet, and various other economic and political issues. Such challenges would emerge with considerable fanfare under the strong-man rule of party leader and President Xi Jinping beginning in 2012.

TRADE AND RELATED ECONOMIC ISSUES

The context of controversy in US-China economic relations in the second decade of this century rests heavily on growing American perception of China as a "state capitalist" economy employing government-directed means, seen as egregiously unfair by critics, in order to manipulate and outmaneuver American firms as China seeks global leadership in key international industries. Earlier US engagement with China, premised on the expectation that increased trade and investment would lead China to liberalize its economy along lines favored by the United States, has been seen as failing. What has emerged is a determined economic competitor using a wide variety of state-led industrial development and trade policies and practices that come at the direct expense of the United States and other economies. [39]

US Trade Deficit with China

The US trade deficit with China has continued to grow in recent years; it leveled off in 2008, declined somewhat in 2009, but then rose again, reaching record levels of $273 billion in 2010, $296 billion in 2011, and $315 billion in 2012. The merchandise trade deficit with China was $367 billion in 2015 and $347 billion in 2016. It was the largest with any country or group of countries. [40]

Offsetting to a small degree the negative implications of the merchandise trade deficit is a surplus in US service trade with China. In 2016 China was the United States' fourth-largest services trading partner at $69.6 billion, the third-largest services export market at $53.5 billion, and the eleventh-largest source of services imports at $16.1 billion. The United States ran a $37.3 billion services trade surplus with China, which was the largest services surplus of any US trading partner. [41]

The enormous deficit has been accompanied by long-standing complaints voiced by the major candidates in the 2016 US presidential election campaign, many in Congress, the media, and interest groups in the United States who focus on the massive trade gap as a key indicator that China's economic and trade policies are unfair and disadvantageous for the United States. Chinese officials publicly and privately resent US attempts to "politicize" the trade deficit, which Chinese trade figures show as significantly less than shown by US trade figures, largely because of the way China counts its exports to Hong Kong that are actually going to the United States. They tend to see the American complaints as "protectionist" efforts by special interests in the United States that have been disadvantaged by international economic trends associated with economic globalization. They tend to find little fault in Chinese policies or practices, and view American criticisms of China as unjustified.[42]

US exports to China grew markedly in recent years albeit from a relatively low base; they were small compared with massive US imports from China. The US merchandise sold was wide-ranging, including leading goods categories of aircraft and parts, oil seeds and grains, motor vehicles, semiconductors and electronic components, and waste and scrap. Chinese merchandise sold to the United States tended to move from low-value consumer products of past years to more advanced technology products, like communications equipment, computer equipment, miscellaneous manufactured commodities, semiconductors and other electronic components, followed by apparel and footwear. An important dimension of the recent increase in US imports of Chinese manufactured goods is the movement in production facilities from other Asian countries to China. Various manufactured products that used to be made in Japan, Taiwan, Hong Kong, South Korea, and Southeast Asian nations and then exported to the United States are now being made in China (in many cases by foreign firms in China using components and materials imported from foreign countries) and exported to the United States. Such processing trade, noted earlier, often does not provide much overall value for the ultimate exporter, China.[43]

The diversity of Chinese products sold to the United States includes agricultural exports. The United States long viewed China as a major market for US agricultural goods, and US farmers sold $20 billion in products to China in 2015.[44]

Chinese "State-Capitalism" and Its Implications for the United States

The practices of the state-directed Chinese economy include extensive networks of trade and investment barriers, financial support, and indigenous innovation policies that seek to promote and protect domestic sectors and firms deemed by the government to be critical to the country's future economic growth; widespread government-directed cyber theft of US trade, technology, and other economic secrets; selective implementing of WTO obligations; government-led financial policies that promote high savings and allow surpluses favoring state-guided industries; and a history of managing exchange rate policy to the advantage of China and the disadvantage of the United States, among others. [45]

US government agencies and many others argue that the Chinese government's intervention in various sectors through industrial policies has increased in recent years. The central and local Chinese governments promote industries deemed crucial to the country's future economic development by using various means that critics judge to be grossly out of line with international norms, such as subsidies, tax breaks, preferential loans, trade barriers, foreign investment restrictions, discriminatory regulations and standards, export restrictions, technology transfer requirements imposed on foreign firms, public procurement rules that give preferences to domestic firms, and weak enforcement of intellectual property rights. [46]

China's state sector centers on SOEs, which account for more than 40 percent of China's nonagricultural GDP. A wide range of industries where Beijing has decided that the state should dominate include autos, aviation, banking, coal, construction, environmental technology, information technology, insurance, media, steel and other metals, oil and gas, power, railways, shipping, telecommunications, and tobacco. The state-controlled banks provide generous funding for SOEs in various sectors selected by the government. [47]

"Indigenous Innovation"

A major focus of the government's attention since 2008 has been to transform China from a global center for low-technology manufacturing into a major center for innovation by the end of this decade and a global innovation leader by 2050. Concurrently, Beijing seeks to reduce sharply the country's dependence on foreign technology, notably that sold by advanced US firms that lead in these fields. This stress on so-called indigenous innovation means that China curbs foreign sales in the China market while Beijing acquires advanced technology through coercing American and other foreign high-technology firms seeking access to the China market to share their advanced technology with favored Chinese companies. Beijing also seeks such advanced technology through cyber and human industrial espionage, and the acquisition of generally smaller high-technology foreign firms to gain access to their advanced techniques for the benefit of the protected Chinese enterprise, while allowing no such acquisition of Chinese firms by foreign companies. [48]

Technology Transfer Issues

Related to the broader US concerns with China's "indigenous innovation" comes concern about coerced technology transfer. When China entered the WTO in 2001, it agreed that foreign firms would not be pressured by government entities to transfer technology to a Chinese partner as part of the cost of doing business in China. However, many US firms argue that this is a common Chinese practice, although this is difficult to quantify because US business representatives often appear to try to avoid negative publicity regarding the difficulties they encounter doing business in China out of concern over retaliation by the Chinese government. In addition, Chinese officials reportedly pressure foreign firms through oral communications to transfer technology (e.g., as a condition to invest in China), but they avoid putting such requirements in writing to evade being accused of violating WTO rules. In 2011 then US Treasury Secretary Timothy Geithner charged that "we're seeing China continue to be very, very aggressive in a strategy they started several decades ago, which goes like this: you want to sell to our country, we want you to come produce here. If you want to come produce here, you need to transfer your technology to us." Thirty-three percent of the respondents to a 2012 AmCham China survey reported that technology transfer requirements were negatively affecting their businesses. [49]

Restrictions on Information and Communications Technology

For the past ten years, many US and other foreign business groups have registered increasing concerns over a continuing stream of Chinese laws and regulations on information and communications technology products and services that have the effect of limiting foreign companies' access to this important Chinese market. Several proposals say that critical information infrastructure should be "secure and controllable," an ambiguous term that has not been precisely defined by Chinese authorities. Other proposals lay out policies to promote indigenous information and communications technology industries or require foreign firms to hand over proprietary information. Overall, such requirements could have a significant impact on US firms, which exported $12 billion of these kinds of services to China in 2015. Summarizing US concerns, the Commerce Department said the Chinese requirements would cause long-term damage in American efforts to participate in China's information and communications market valued at $465 billion in 2015. [50]

Intellectual Property Rights (IPR)

For more than two decades, the United States, along with Japan and other developed countries, has been pressing China to abide by internationally accepted IPR guidelines. Episodic progress was repeatedly upset by new developments of Chinese infringements that disadvantaged US firms and angered senior US officials. Most recently and discussed in more detail below, China's use of cyber attacks to steal American commercial technology and other know-how prompted usually reticent President Obama and his advisers to sharply criticize China and to publicly sanction a few of those responsible. The US administration pressed hard for China to engage in senior-level talks and seek agreements on how to curb the offensive Chinese practice.

Steps to protect IPR go back to the early 1990s. In 1991 the United States threatened to impose $1.5 billion in trade sanctions against China if it failed to strengthen its IPR laws. Although China later implemented a number of new IPR laws, it often failed to enforce them, which led the United States to threaten China once again with trade sanctions. The two sides reached a trade agreement in 1995, which pledged China to take immediate steps to stem IPR piracy by cracking down on large-scale producers and distributors of pirated materials and prohibiting the export of pirated products; to establish mechanisms to ensure long-term enforcement of IPR laws; and to provide greater market access to US IPR-related products.[51]

Under the terms of China's WTO accession, China agreed to immediately bring its IPR laws into compliance with the WTO agreement on Trade-Related Aspects of Intellectual Property Rights (TRIPS). Chinese officials repeatedly highlighted advances in improved IPR protection in China and the Office of the United States Trade Representative (USTR) stated on a number of occasions that China made great strides in improving its IPR protection regime, noting that it passed several new IPR-related laws, closed or fined several assembly operations for illegal production lines, seized millions of illegal products, curtailed exports of pirated products, expanded training for judges and law enforcement officials on IPR protections, and expanded legitimate licensing of film and music production in China.[52]

However, the USTR continued to indicate that much work needed to be done to improve China's IPR protection regime. Business groups in the United States continued to complain about significant IPR problems in China, especially in terms of illegal reproduction of software, retail piracy, and trademark counterfeiting. According to a US International Trade Commission report in 2011, US intellectual property–intensive firms that conducted business in China in 2009 lost $48.2 billion in sales, royalties, and license fees because of IPR violations in China. The Congressional Research Service estimated in 2009 that counterfeits accounted for 15 to 20 percent of all products made in China and accounted for 8 percent of China's GDP. China's enforcement agencies and judicial system often lacked the resources or the will needed to vigorously enforce IPR laws; convicted IPR offenders generally faced minor penalties. In addition, while market access for US and other foreign IPR-related products improved, high tariffs, quotas, and other barriers continued to hamper US exports; such trade barriers were believed by US analysts to be partly responsible for illegal IPR-related smuggling and counterfeiting in China. In addition, China accounted for a significant share of imported counterfeit products seized by US Customs and Border Protection officers ($110 million, or 62 percent of total goods seized, in FY-2011 and $1.1 billion, or 88 percent of total goods seized, in 2015).[53]

Following a long list of US government measures to prompt the Chinese government and Chinese businesses to respect American IPR and to adhere to obligations undertaken in bilateral agreements and multilateral commitments, the USTR in 2008 stated in a report that its top IPR protection and enforcement priorities involved China and Russia. Among other charges, the USTR meshed its complaint with an ongoing controversy over the safety of products imported from China by stating that Chinese counterfeit products, such as pharmaceuticals, electronics, batteries, auto parts, industrial equipment, and toys "pose a direct threat to the health and safety of consumers in the United States, China, and elsewhere."[54]

US firms contend that IPR piracy in China has worsened despite Chinese government agreements to strengthen IPR enforcement and stamp out major piracy concerns. American and other foreign businesses charge that poor IPR protection is one of the most significant obstacles for doing business in China. Some of their senior representatives have maintained that China's lax enforcement of IPR regulations is part of a deliberate Chinese government effort to use IPR theft as part of broader efforts to advance China's ambitions to become a major producer of capital-intensive and high-technology products.

In government testimony in 2010, a representative of the US Chamber of Commerce offered a graphic indictment in charging that Chinese IPR policies were part of a coherent and government-directed, or at least government-motivated, strategy to lessen China's perceived reliance on foreign innovations and IP. He charged, "China is actively working to create a legal environment that enables it to intervene in the markets for IP, help its own companies 'reinnovate' competing IPR as a substitute to American and other foreign technologies and potentially misappropriate US and other foreign IP as components of its industrial policies and internal market regulations. . . . The common themes throughout these policies are: (1) undermine and displace foreign IP; (2) leverage China's large domestic market to develop national champions and promote its own IP, displacing foreign competitors in China; and (3) building on China's domestic successes by displacing competitors in world markets."[55]

Cybersecurity Issues

Leaders of the US Intelligence Community and their congressional overseers warned for several years that China's use of human agents for industrial, economic, and national security espionage was complemented by a massive Chinese use of cyber espionage targeting information, held by American companies, that would be useful in advancing China's goal of innovation and leadership in key economic areas. This issue eventually prompted substantial US action. On May 19, 2014, the US Department of Justice issued a thirty-one-count indictment against five members of the Chinese People's Liberation Army (PLA) for cyber espionage for commercial advantage against five US firms and a labor union. This marked the first time the federal government initiated such action against state actors. On April 1, 2015, President Obama issued an executive order authorizing certain sanctions reportedly targeting Chinese cyber thieves. Shortly before Chinese President Xi's state visit to the United States in September 2015, press reports indicated that the Obama administration was considering the imposition of sanctions against Chinese entities over cyber theft, possibly doing so even before the arrival of President Xi in Washington later that month. China sent a high-level delegation to Washington, DC. It held four days of talks with US officials over cyber issues. The result of the talks allowed President Xi and President Obama to announce at their summit that they had reached an agreement on cybersecurity. The agreement stated that neither country's government would conduct or knowingly support cyber-enabled theft of IP, trade secrets, and related information, with the intent of providing competitive advantages to companies or commercial sectors. They set up a high-level dialogue mechanism to address cybercrime. The first meeting was held in December 2015 in Washington, DC; the second was held in Beijing in June 2016. Both resulted in signs of progress in a complicated and usually secret area of international relations. [56]

WTO Implementation Issues

An important benchmark in Chinese leaders' embrace of economic globalization and interdependence was the decision to join the WTO under terms requiring major concessions from China to its international trading partners. On September 13, 2001, China concluded a WTO bilateral trade agreement with Mexico, the last of the original thirty-seven WTO members to have requested such an accord. On September 17, 2001, the WTO Working Party handling China's WTO application announced that it had resolved all outstanding issues regarding China's WTO accession. China's WTO membership was formally approved at the WTO Ministerial Conference in Doha, Qatar, on November 10, 2001. On November 11, 2001, China notified the

WTO that it had formally ratified the WTO agreements, which enabled China to enter the WTO on December 11, 2001.[57]

Under the WTO accession agreement, China set forth various concessions and actions to accommodate the interests of its major trading partners. It agreed to:

- Reduce the average tariff for industrial goods to 8.9 percent and for agricultural goods to 15 percent; most tariff cuts were to come by 2004.
- Limit subsidies for agricultural production to 8.5 percent of the value of farm output and end export subsidies for agricultural exports.
- By 2004, grant full trade and distribution rights to foreign enterprises (with some exceptions).
- Provide nondiscriminatory treatment to all WTO members; foreign firms in China were to be treated no less favorably than Chinese firms for trade purposes; price controls would not be used to provide protection to Chinese firms.
- Implement the WTO's standards on IPR seen in the organization's TRIPS agreement.
- Accept a twelve-year safeguard mechanism, available to other WTO members in cases where a surge in Chinese exports cause or threaten to cause market disruption to domestic producers.
- Fully open the Chinese banking system to foreign financial institutions by 2006; joint ventures in insurance and telecommunications would be permitted, with various degrees of foreign ownership allowed.[58]

The subsequent record of implementation of the Chinese agreement with the WTO was a source of considerable criticism from the United States and some others among China's major trading partners. These criticisms, in turn, prompted Chinese government complaints. As a result of burgeoning Chinese exports of a variety of manufactured products, the United States, the European Union, and others imposed restrictions on Chinese imports of these products that met with vocal complaints from the Chinese government. Surges in Chinese exports involving agricultural products were a frequent source of complaint from some of China's Asian trading partners, who tried to restrict the imports in ways that antagonized the Chinese authorities.[59]

The US government took the lead among WTO members in reaching the agreements leading to China's joining the organization. It viewed the US market as by far China's largest export market and had a growing concern over the unprecedented US trade deficit with China. As a result, it maintained a leading role in measuring Chinese compliance with WTO commitments, and its complaints met with dissatisfaction and criticism from the Chinese government.[60]

The USTR issued annual reports assessing China's WTO compliance, as did prominent US nongovernmental organizations such as the US-China Business Council. These reports tended to give China mixed evaluations. On the one hand, China was seen making significant progress in meeting such commitments as formal tariff reductions; on the other hand, the reports raised a host of concerns involving quotas, standards, lack of transparency, and protection of IPR, all of which were seen to impact negatively on US trade interests. As time went on, the US government reports highlighted evidence of trends toward a more restrictive trade regime. The USTR's 2015 report on China's WTO compliance summarized US concerns over China's trade regime as follows:

> Many of the problems that arise in the US-China trade and investment relationship can be traced to the Chinese government's interventionist policies and practices and the large role of state-owned enterprises and other national champions in China's economy, which continue to generate significant trade distortions that inevitably give rise to trade frictions. [61]

The specific priority areas of US concern identified in the report dealt with IPR, Chinese industrial policies disadvantaging US firms, restriction on services provided by US companies in the China market, restrictions on US agricultural products sold to China, inadequate transparency in the production and announcement of Chinese laws and regulations, and restrictions working against US firms in licenses and related matters.

The United States has utilized the WTO dispute settlement mechanism on a number of occasions to address China's alleged noncompliance with its WTO commitments. It brought twenty-one dispute settlement cases against China (or more than half of the total number of cases against China brought by all WTO members through January 2017). The United States generally prevailed in these cases; several were resolved before going to a WTO panel. China in turn has brought more dispute settlement cases against the United States than any other WTO member: ten (or two-thirds of all cases against the United States). Several Chinese complaints were against US antidumping and countervailing duty measures. In December 2016 China initiated a dispute resolution case against the United States for its continued treatment of China as a nonmarket economy for the purpose of calculating and imposing antidumping measures. [62]

The December 2011 USTR report highlighted the following areas of concern regarding China's obligations for WTO membership: (1) enforcement of IPR; (2) industrial policies, including concerns over so-called indigenous innovation, explained above; (3) lack of transparency in China's agricultural market; and (4) government discrimination thwarting US firms seeking to operate in China's service sector. [63]

US businesses have expressed strong concern about Chinese industrial policies that limit market access for non-Chinese goods and services and promote Chinese industries that compete with US and other firms in international markets. The American concerns have been brought up repeatedly by senior US officials in various dialogues with China, and some issues have been addressed by Chinese officials.[64] Nevertheless, US businesses remain concerned that the continued heavy direct and indirect involvement of elements of the Chinese state in the creation and strengthening of government-supported companies will result in practices that only allow foreign companies to work in China in restricted ways; the ways often require close cooperation with government-favored Chinese enterprises, including the sharing and ultimate loss of foreign technological and other advantages to Chinese competitors.[65]

China's Currency Policy

Criticism in the United States over China's currency policy emerged against the background of the massive and growing US trade deficit with China and complaints from US manufacturing firms and workers over competitive challenges posed by Chinese imports that benefit from the Chinese currency's value relative to the US dollar. Unlike most advanced economies, China does not maintain a market-based floating exchange rate. Between 1994 and 2005, China pegged its currency, the renminbi (RMB) or Yuan, to the US dollar at about 8.28 Yuan to the dollar. In July 2005, China appreciated the RMB to the dollar by 2.1 percent and moved to what it called a "managed float," based on a basket of major foreign currencies, including the US dollar. In order to maintain a target rate of exchange with the dollar and other currencies, the Chinese government maintained restrictions and controls over capital transactions and made large-scale purchases of US dollars and dollar assets. At that time and continuing in following years, many US policy makers, business leaders, union representatives, and academic specialists charged that China's currency policy made the RMB significantly undervalued relative to the US dollar. Estimates of undervalue ranged from 15 to 40 percent. The American critics maintained that China's currency policy made Chinese exports to the United States cheaper and US exports to China more expensive than they would have been if exchange rates were determined by market forces. They complained that this policy particularly hurt several US manufacturing sectors (such as textiles and apparel, furniture, plastics, machine tools, and steel), which were forced to compete against low-cost imports from China. The Chinese currency policy was seen by the American critics to add to the size and growth of the US trade deficit with China. Responsive to these complaints, representatives in Congress introduced numerous bills in recent years designed to pressure China to either significantly appreciate its currency or let it float freely in international markets. As the 2012 Republican presidential candidate, Mitt Romney pledged to take strong action against Chinese currency "manipulation."[66]

According to the Bank of China, from July 2005 to July 2009, the dollar-Yuan exchange rate went from 8.27 to 6.84, an appreciation of 21.1 percent. Because of the impact of the global economic crisis beginning in 2008, the Chinese government halted appreciation of the Yuan relative to the dollar from July 2009 to June 2010 in order to limit the impact of the sharp decline in global demand for Chinese products.[67] Currency appreciation was resumed in June 2010, although at a slower pace than in previous years. From June 2005 through July 2015, the RMB appreciated by 35.3 percent on a nominal basis against the dollar.[68]

On August 11, 2015, China's central bank announced new measures regarding the market-orientation of its daily central parity rate of the RMB. Over the next three days, the RMB depreciated against the dollar; it went from 6.12 Yuan to 6.40 Yuan. From July 2015 to mid-December 2016, the RMB depreciated by 13.6 percent against the dollar. Possible reasons for this turn of events included the following: Some viewed the Chinese currency's depreciation as a reflection of China's slowing economy; others judged that the Chinese economy may have been weaker than acknowledged by the government, so the depreciating thus might have been a deliberate policy to boost economic growth at the expense of China's trading partners.[69]

In any event, experts continued to differ strongly on the RMB's valuation against the dollar and other currencies. The IMF had criticized the low value of the Yuan in the past, but it said in May 2015 that the currency was no longer undervalued.

The US Department of the Treasury said in April 2015 that the RMB remained "significantly undervalued." Treasury's October 2015 report noted that China had intervened heavily in exchange rate markets from July to September 2015. It noted that market forces were currently pushing the RMB downward, but it concluded that the RMB remained "under its appropriate mid-term valuation."[70]

The first Treasury report on exchange rates under the Trump administration, issued on April 14, 2017, did not conclude that China (or any country) had manipulated its currency, noting that the Chinese government over the past year or so had intervened heavily to prevent rapid RMB depreciation (as opposed to trying to prevent RMB appreciation, which often occurred in the past). Adding to such indications that Chinese manipulation of its currency value for the sake of gaining trade advantage against the United States was no longer considered—at least for now—an important issue in United States was the change in President Trump's view of the issue. During the 2016 presidential election campaign, Donald Trump was outspoken in criticizing Chinese manipulation of the value of RMB for the sake of trading advantage over the United States, but he told the *Wall Street Journal* in April 2017 that he had changed his mind and no longer viewed China as such a currency manipulator.[71]

INVESTMENT ISSUES

China's investments in US assets can be broken down into two categories: holdings of US securities (e.g., US Treasury securities, US government agency securities, corporate securities, and stocks) and FDI. China's holdings of US public and private securities are significant and constitute the largest category by far of Chinese investment in the United States. These securities include US Treasury securities, US government agency (such as Freddie Mac and Fannie Mae) securities, corporate securities, and equities (such as stocks). China's investment in public and private US securities totaled $1.84 trillion as of June 2015, making China the second-largest holder after Japan. US Treasury securities, which help the federal government finance its budget deficits, are the largest category of US securities held by China. China's holdings of US Treasury securities increased from $118 billion in 2002 to $1.24 trillion in 2014 but fell to $1.06 trillion in 2016, making China the second-largest foreign holder of US Treasury securities after Japan. China's holdings of US Treasury securities as a share of total foreign holdings rose from 9.6 percent in 2002 to a historic high of 26.1 percent in 2010, but this level has since fallen, dropping to 18 percent in 2016.[72] Meanwhile, US holdings of Chinese securities are comparatively small. The US government estimated the value of such holdings (mainly equities such as stocks) at $107 billion in 2015. This was comparable to US holdings in Brazil and represented a very small percentage of total US holdings of foreign securities.[73]

Regarding bilateral FDI, China's FDI in the United States remained small until China recently and rapidly expanded investment abroad. In part because much Chinese investment in the United States comes via tax havens, estimates of the size of Chinese investment in the United States vary. The US government said the amount was $5.8 billion in cumulative investment through 2010. In 2015 China ranked as the twelfth-largest investor in the United States, with investment that year amounting to $5 billion and the stock of cumulative investment valued at $14.8 billion. Private estimates of Chinese investment are higher. US FDI in China declined during the recession in 2009 but grew by $9.6 billion in 2010 for a cumulative figure of $60.4 billion. In 2015 the respective figures were $7.3 billion and 74.6 billion. While the overall value of US investment in China is relatively low, amounting to about 10 percent of US investment in the Asia-Pacific region, the investment is very important for certain US companies seeking investment and sales in China. China has the world's largest mobile phone network and hundreds of millions of mobile phone users; it is the largest market for commercial aircraft outside the United States; it has the largest number of Internet users in the world; and more recently China became the world's largest market for new cars. US firms invest substantially in China as they endeavor to expand to meet the needs of these Chinese markets. [74]

Chinese Holdings of US Securities

As noted above, China remains a large foreign holder of US Treasury securities, and thus a large foreign financier of the US federal budget deficit. It held $1.17 trillion in US Treasury securities in May 2012 and $1.11 trillion in October 2016; its share as part of foreign holdings of US Treasury securities has declined recently, representing 18.5 percent in October 2016. On one hand, US government leaders and other Americans encourage Chinese investment in such US securities as a means for the United States to meet its investment needs and to fund the large US federal budget deficit. On the other hand, US policy makers at times have raised concerns that the Chinese investment could give China increased leverage over the United States on major economic or other issues. For example, some Chinese officials have been reported to suggest that China could dump (or threaten to dump) a large share of its holdings in order to prevent the United States from imposing trade sanctions against China. Other Chinese officials judged that China should diversify its investments of its foreign exchange reserves away from dollar-denominated assets to those that offer higher rates of return. The global economic crisis beginning in 2008 heightened US concerns that China might reduce its US assets holdings. [75]

Practices a few years later seemed to support the arguments of those who judged that China's holdings of US debt didn't provide much practical leverage over the United States. They argued that, given China's economic dependency on a stable and growing US economy, and its substantial holdings of US securities, any attempt to try to sell a large share of those holdings would likely damage both the US and Chinese economies. Such a move could also cause the US dollar to sharply depreciate against global currencies, which could reduce the value of China's remaining holdings of US dollar assets. Responding to a congressional reporting requirement, the Department of Defense in 2012 came down strongly in favor of this skeptical view of Chinese leverage that would result from holding US government securities. It said, "Attempting to use US Treasury securities as a coercive tool would have limited effect and likely would do more harm to China than to the United States. As the threat is not credible and the effect would be limited even if carried out, it does not offer China deterrence options, whether in the diplomatic, military, or economic realms, and this would remain true both in peacetime and in scenarios of crisis or war." [76]

Growing Chinese Investment in the United States and Restricted US Investment in China

With Chinese investment in the United States on the rise, the American debate on the perceived pros and cons of the investment has intensified. On one side are many US specialists and advocates who judge that greater Chinese FDI in the United States will create new jobs for US workers and have an overall beneficial economic impact on US interests. As Chinese investment abroad is growing rapidly, they urge more efforts in order to attract increased foreign investment in the United States. On the other side are American specialists and critics who assess that Chinese investment is geared toward unfair, state-directed industrial policies designed to improve the competitive position of Chinese firms through mergers and acquisition of US technology. They see Chinese firms as directly or indirectly controlled by Chinese officials bent on acquiring US economic assets in a drive to outperform the United States in higher-valued industries and services. There also is a growing concern of China using investment to gain access to secret US national security technology. [77]

Reinforcing these arguments are rising American concerns over growing restrictions on American and other foreign investments in China. The restrictions especially involve the many highly protected sectors of the Chinese economy that are being developed by the state as "national champions," which are seen as designed to dominate the Chinese and international markets at the expense of America's leading firms in advanced production and technology. Such practice reinforces the view that China's growing acquisitions of high-technology American and other foreign firms are part of an overall industrial strategy that comes at the expense of the United States. [78]

OPTIONS FOR US POLICY ON TRADE AND INVESTMENT

Whether the rising American concerns over trade and investment issues will result in significant change in American policy remains uncertain. One clear result of the overall hardening of American attitudes on economic issues with China has been to weaken the US-China convergence on economic interests that served as an important positive ballast for the relationship in the past. [79]

Although the Chinese government obviously sees China benefiting greatly from the development of US-China economic relations in recent decades, it also has numerous complaints about American trade and economic practices. They include US restrictions on Chinese acquisition of US high technology, US refusal to treat China as a market economy under WTO rules, the complications posed by what is seen as the United States politicizing and exaggerating various economic disputes with China, and the faulty American leadership that resulted in the massive international financial crisis and recession beginning in 2008.[80]

Going forward, it is quite possible that US administration leaders—as in previous US governments—will see overall US interests with China best served through a process that deals with economic disputes through high-level dialogue that avoids sharp negative changes in policy. The Trump administration has a number of senior officials who favor a tougher stance toward China on trade issues than seen in previous governments, but they may be offset by administration leaders who are less inclined to take negative economic actions for reasons related to US economic interests or to America's broader need for a cooperative policy with China.

If tougher American measures toward China are supported, they are likely to follow paths that will involve such steps as increasing the number of dispute settlement cases brought against China in the WTO, threatening to impose trade sanctions against China unless it addresses policies (such as cyber theft of US trade secrets) that hurt US economic interests, and making greater use of US trade remedy laws (such as antidumping and countervailing measures) to address China's "unfair" trade practices. Restrictions on Chinese acquisitions of high-technology US firms are probable parts of this mix.[81] The wide range of experts contributing to the 2017 Asia Society report on China policy saw major weaknesses in existing US economic policies toward China and called for across-the-board efforts involving the United States and allied countries to pressure China for needed changes through direct application of sanctions, tougher application of existing laws, and bilateral and multilateral negotiations with China.[82]

ENVIRONMENT AND CLIMATE CHANGE ISSUES

The George W. Bush administration was notorious among environmental activists concerned with global warming and climate change. Under the leadership of President Bush, the US government took the lion's share of domestic and international criticism for policies and practice seen as at odds with growing international efforts supported by various developed and developing nations to curb environmental pollution, greenhouse gas emissions, and global climate change. Emblematic of Bush administration policies and of the reasons for international and domestic criticism of those policies was the US government's refusal to support the Kyoto Protocol on climate change.[83]

China's rapid economic development has been accompanied by massive air and water pollution and greenhouse gas emissions; the country has emerged as the number-one emitter of greenhouse gases. China's poor record in reversing environmental degradation associated with its rapid economic development and in curbing the rapid growth of greenhouse gas emissions from Chinese power plants, factories, and other sources has been widely acknowledged even by Chinese leaders. But for many years, Chinese policies and practices failed to generate much friction between the Chinese government and a US administration under constant international and domestic attack for its alleged passive or even hostile approach to key aspects of international efforts to curb global warming, climate change, and related environmental degradation.[84]

This situation began to change dramatically with the approach of the US presidential and congressional elections of November 2008. All the US presidential candidates and the vast majority of congressional contenders promised to shift US policy regarding environmental degradation and climate change. In fact, the shift began in earnest in 2009, setting the stage for Americans and others concerned with environmental pollution and climate change to view Chinese policies and practices in a new, more attentive, and more critical light.[85]

The incoming Obama government chose to build on mechanisms inherited from the outgoing Bush administration and engaged in bilateral dialogues with Chinese counterparts seeking forward movement on environmental and climate change issues. Others, in Congress, the US media, and among a wide range of American activists associated with global warming and environmental issues, tended to be more vocal and critical regarding China's environmental record. As the United States moved to take action on environmental protection and climate change, American officials, especially in Congress, and public opinion were often explicit in expecting no less of China.[86]

Against the backdrop of prominent policies and efforts by senior Chinese leaders beginning in the 1990s to curb environmental damage and limit adverse consequences of economic development such as greenhouse gas emissions and climate change, the Chinese government over the past ten years undertook a new series of steps in order to improve efficiency in the use of energy, curb environmental damage, and check possible damage to China's international standing as a responsible actor in world affairs. During that time frame, it remained hard to gauge how well these steps would work in actually curbing environmental damage associated with Chinese development, in offsetting international attention to China's negative record in areas of pollution and climate change, and in avoiding serious disputes with the Obama government more sensitive than the previous US government to issues of environmental degradation and to China's important role in those matters.[87]

The Obama government seemed to seek to avoid major friction with China as it sought common ground on important issues like global economic revival, North Korea's nuclear weapons development, and terrorist threats and instability in Southwest Asia. And China's recent emphasis on improving the efficiency of China's energy use reduced to some degree the gross waste involved in Chinese consumption of coal and other resources. Nevertheless, Chinese carbon emissions continued to rise dramatically. In 2010 China's total carbon dioxide emissions rose by 10 percent, marking a doubling of the country's CO_2 emissions since 2003.

Moreover, the United States and China continued to stress different approaches to international climate change negotiations, producing frequent frictions, notably in the international climate change summit at Copenhagen in December 2009. Disagreements centered on the relative responsibilities of developed and developing countries for addressing climate change. China, along with many other developing countries, long argued that developed nations bear the major share of the historical responsibility for climate change and continue to have far higher levels of emissions per capita, so they alone should be subject to legally binding commitments to reduce emissions. Developing countries' reductions should be voluntary. Chinese officials viewed attempts to force developing countries to accept legally binding emissions targets as an attempt to restrict those countries' rights to develop. In the United States, the Congress and the Obama administration indicated that the United States would not accept legally binding commitments, such as the Kyoto Protocol, to reduce US emissions, without binding commitments from other major emitters, starting with the world's current leading emitter, China.[88]

While the US and Chinese governments cooperated on energy efficiency and clean energy projects, the trajectory of rapidly growing CO_2 emissions and other pollution and resource use in China posed problems for Sino-American cooperation on the environment. China's growing negative impact on the environment still involved a massively wasteful use of energy in the production of goods and services and the associated burgeoning greenhouse gases coming from China.[89] In China, the vast majority of greenhouse gas emissions come from power generation and other support for industrial production. That production has focused more on heavy industry and high energy-consuming products. The situation is worsened because Chinese industrial production remains much more inefficient than more developed economies, despite gains in efficiency in recent years.[90]

As noted above, Chinese leaders since the 1990s have shown sensitivity to environmental practices in China and the consequences of China's rapid growth for the Chinese and world environment. On the one hand, they have worked hard to avoid being considered an international laggard on environmental practices while, on the other, they have tried to avoid environmental obstacles to the rapid development of China's economy. On the positive side, Chinese leaders have taken serious steps to deal with worsening environmental conditions in China. Premier Li Peng, a political hard-liner who played a key role in the Tiananmen crackdown of 1989, was particularly instrumental in putting ecology on the political map in China. Laws were passed on air, water, solid waste, and noise pollution. Enforcement mechanisms were bolstered, and funds for cleanup, inspection, education, and enforcement increased repeatedly in the 1990s.[91]

In January 1999, a top environmental official announced that China would boost spending on "green" projects to 1.5 percent of GDP between 1997 and 2000. Altogether, in 1996 to 2000, plans called for investing almost $60 billion in environmental programs. State-owned banks and the State Environmental Protection Agency (SEPA) in 1997 announced that no loans would be issued to seriously polluting firms; in 1996 some sixty thousand enterprises—mostly rural factories with no environmental safeguards—were shut down. In January 1997, Beijing set up a national center to disseminate environmentally sound technology; and on March 1, 1997, the government announced the adoption of five new sets of international environmental protection standards.

Despite good intentions at the top, Beijing had serious problems, especially compliance and follow-through with funding and implementation of promised programs. In the late 1990s, China had only about twenty thousand enforcement officials nationwide to inspect industrial firms throughout the country; enforcement authority remained weak and fragmented; and penalties were anemic. Local officials tended to judge proposed projects by the number of jobs they created and the revenue they generated rather than by the environmental damage or good they did.[92]

With close to 10 percent annual growth and massive foreign investment focused on manufacturing, China faced enormous environmental problems in the twenty-first century. Demand for electric power grew rapidly and was met predominantly by coal-fired plants. Autos clogged roads in and between major cities. Air pollution went from bad to worse. Efforts to develop hydropower using dams on China's rivers were controversial as the projects displaced large numbers of people and had major environmental impacts on people in China and other countries downstream from the new dams. Serious depletion of water resources in northern China was exacerbated by water pollution, pervasive throughout China.[93]

The Hu Jintao leadership gave more emphasis than its predecessors to the need for sustainable development in China. However, the results remained mixed as in the past. Official Chinese media and Chinese officials noted significant improvement in water pollution levels in some Chinese rivers during the Tenth Five-Year Plan (2001–5), but not in others. Efforts to curb air pollution included 182 projects to reduce sulfur dioxide emissions, and closures of more than six thousand heavily polluting enterprises. Air pollution levels were said to have improved in some cities, but sulfur dioxide remained a major problem.[94]

As of 2017 it can be said that in recent years, there was notable progress reported in greater efficiency in energy use, but Chinese officials sometimes were cautious in predicting improvements, especially with the projected rapid rise of automobile use in China, along with the pollution and land, water, and natural resource use associated with China's rapid economic growth. The nation still lacks a powerful national body that is able to coordinate, monitor, and enforce environmental legislation. The devolution of decision-making authority to local levels has placed environmental stewardship in the hands of officials who frequently are more concerned with economic growth than the environment. Meanwhile, the deficiency of capital and the lack of will to promote the massive spending necessary to reverse several decades of environmental damage indicated that environmental restoration would be problematic in the near future.[95]

The international consequences of China's environmental problems are varied and usually negative. Dust storms from eroding land in northern China pollute the atmosphere in Korea and Japan, leading to popular and sometimes official complaints and concerns. Air pollution from China affects locales to the east as far away as the Pacific coast of the United States. Chinese dams on the Mekong River negatively impact the livelihood of people in Cambodia and Vietnam, complicating official relations. Extensive international and especially American publicity regarding China's poor environmental record makes US opinion less patient with Chinese government explanations that China, as a developing country, should not be held to strict environmental standards. As a result, China's image in the United States declined.[96]

Facing such circumstances, the Obama administration made energy and climate cooperation one of the highest items on its agenda with China. On emissions reduction, the Obama administration worked collaboratively with China and used US-China presidential summits to push Beijing toward stronger international climate commitments. Prior to the December 2015 COP-21 Paris climate negotiations, all parties to the UN Framework Convention on Climate Change were expected to put forward post-2020 targets in the first half of 2015. Those targets, once combined, would form the framework for a new global climate deal. President Obama took the initiative to reach out to President Xi Jinping, and the two were able to reach agreement in 2014 on targets to be announced in Paris in 2015, thereby substantially adding to international momentum in support of environmental reforms to meet the dangers of climate change.[97]

Whatever positive impact this accord made on US-China relations at the time was undermined by the election of President Trump and an administration antagonistic to or disinclined to support international climate change efforts. Under these new circumstances, concern over Chinese environmental policies figures much less in US government policy calculations, either positively or negatively. Some in the Congress and many more among the media and nongovernment groups have a negative view of China's impact on the global environment, but their focus is diverted to contending with the new US administration.[98]

Chapter Ten

Taiwan and East Asian Maritime Disputes in Contemporary US-China Relations

There is much to support the judgment of experts on both sides of the Taiwan Strait and in the United States that the so-called Taiwan issue in US-China relations is sui generis, encompassing a unique set of elements that stand on their own as they influence the US-China relationship in negative and positive ways. Thus, past editions of this volume duly treated Taiwan as the subject of a separate chapter. Nevertheless, as reviewed in chapter 7, the serious challenges to US interests posed by President Xi Jinping's assertive and expansionist behavior in the disputed East China Sea to the north of Taiwan and the South China Sea to the south of Taiwan represent a leading cause of hardening US attitudes toward China by the US administration, Congress, the media, and various elite and public opinion outlets. That hardening did not spill over to change the Barack Obama administration's tightly managed relations with Taiwan that carefully avoided serious controversy with China. Nevertheless, the 2016 election campaign saw the Republican Party and its winning candidate, now President Donald Trump, repeatedly chastise President Obama's perceived weakness in foreign affairs. The criticism included the Obama government's alleged weakness in dealing with China over disputes in the East and South China Seas and other issues, and in that context the Republican Party platform and prominent Republicans registered stronger American support for Taiwan. As noted in chapter 7, President-elect Trump temporarily upended the Obama government's discreet handling of Taiwan by having a phone conversation with Taiwan's president; and when rebuked by China, Trump criticized Chinese expansion in the South China Sea and questioned adherence to the American one-China policy. He later reverted—perhaps again temporarily—to handling Taiwan matters in ways that would not grossly offend Beijing.

Against that background, this chapter first assesses long-standing Taiwan issues and their impact on US-China relations; it then assesses the serious differences that have emerged between the United States and China caused by recent unprecedented tension over territorial disputes in the East China Sea and the South China Sea that surround Taiwan.

Given the rising tensions amid recently more serious differences over various aspects in US-China relations, the issues examined in this chapter regarding Taiwan and the maritime disputes probably are best understood using a realist lens in international politics: seeing China and the United States engaged in an often zero-sum competition for influence. Of course, realism could result in negotiations leading to compromises that would markedly improve relations, say, for example, if the Trump government in economic negotiations with China saw such progress for US interests that it was prepared in turn to substantially reduce US support for Taiwan. Advocates of liberalism in international relations theory might see such an outcome as reflective of the importance of economic engagement and economic engagement as reflective of the salience of their perspective in recent US-China relations. Meanwhile, the constructivist perspective seems more likely than not to perceive that the strong nationalistic identities being built in China, Taiwan, and other nearby states as factors that make significant compromise over territorial and related disputes more difficult, which adds to the prevailing trend of competition and distrust.

TAIWAN ISSUES AND CONTEMPORARY
US-CHINA RELATIONS

The governments in China and the United States approved improvements in cross-strait relations carried out by Taiwan President Ma Ying-jeou (2008–16). This unusually positive trajectory followed more than a decade of repeated crises in cross-strait relations brought on by China's harsh reactions to movement toward self-determination and independence by Taiwan's leaders, who looked to the United States for support in the face of Chinese pressure. Ma's eight years of engagement with and accommodation of China ended with the landslide election as president of his long-standing opponent, Tsai Ing-wen, who pledged to avoid further compromise with Beijing over sensitive cross-strait issues while seeking greater autonomy for Taiwan. [1]

Even during the improving cross-strait relations under President Ma, the interests, policies, and practices of the United States and China have remained at odds over Taiwan in important ways. Notably, the Chinese authorities continue an impressive buildup of military forces targeting Taiwan and

American forces that they believe will come to Taiwan's assistance in the event of conflict over Taiwan. The Americans carefully monitor the Chinese buildup as they prepare forces to counter and destroy Chinese combatants that would impede US response in a Taiwan conflict. The military strengthening on both sides underlines the position of Taiwan as one of only a few world areas where the world's number-one and number-two powers could come to blows, with devastating implications for them and international affairs.[2]

The history of the normalization of US-China relations shows the United States giving ground on US relations with Taiwan in seeking to foster beneficial US relations with China. Yet, the United States has tended to side with Taiwan, which remained in strong competition with China until Ma's election in 2008, and faced renewed pressure from Beijing with the election of President Tsai and her less accommodating posture toward China. The result was repeated efforts by both countries to move forward in developing US-China relations while dealing with often mixed results with differences over Taiwan. Seemingly successful understandings and agreements have been compromised and reversed; both sides have periodically resorted to military, diplomatic, and economic pressures to support their goals; the result has been mutual wariness and suspicion.[3]

A new situation fostering détente and cooperation in cross-strait relations and in US relations with China over Taiwan emerged with the election of Ma Ying-jeou in March 2008. His administration followed moderate policies and sought to reassure China, marking a sharp contrast with the intense Taiwan-China competition that had prevailed up to that time. Ma was reelected in 2012 and continued positive engagement with China. The result was a significant easing of cross-strait tensions that affected US-China relations, though often competing and conflicting US and Chinese interests and policies regarding Taiwan—notably the respective arms buildups focused on Taiwan—remained.

As explained in chapter 4, the process of normalization of US-China relations saw Henry Kissinger and Richard Nixon privately pledge to meet firm Chinese demands about ending US official relations with Taiwan in return for the perceived strategic and other benefits the United States would gain from the breakthrough in official relations with China. To avoid controversy in American domestic politics and in US interaction with Taiwan and other concerned powers, these commitments remained hidden from the American public, the Congress, most officials in the Nixon government, Taiwan, and other foreign governments. The US-China normalization process stalled on account of Nixon's forced resignation over the Watergate scandal. Unaware of the Kissinger-Nixon secret commitments, American public opinion and mainstream views in Congress supported continuing US ties with Taiwan while moving ahead with China.

The Jimmy Carter administration endeavored to complete the normalization of diplomatic relations and eventually met most Chinese demands on ending US official ties with Taiwan. China seemed basically satisfied, though Carter's insistence on continuing some US arms sales to Taiwan after breaking official relations remained an outstanding dispute. The backlash in the United States severely complicated the Carter understanding with China. Bipartisan congressional leaders rewrote the administration's proposed bill governing future unofficial relations with Taiwan, passing the Taiwan Relations Act, which underlined continued strong US interest in protecting Taiwan from Chinese pressure and sustaining close economic, arms sales, and other ties with Taiwan.

Ronald Reagan highlighted his record of support for Taiwan in defeating Carter in the 1980 presidential election. Strong Chinese pressure against the seeming reversal of US policy resulted in a compromise over US arms sales to Taiwan in a Sino-American communiqué in 1982. Whatever Chinese expectations continued about the United States withdrawing from Taiwan diminished further with concurrent US efforts to support Taiwan in international organizations, to transfer to Taiwan the technology and expertise to produce its own jet fighters, and to increase high-level US officials' meetings with Taiwan counterparts. American officials from Reagan on down saw US interests well served by preserving a balance in American relations with Taiwan and China where Taiwan would be sufficiently supported by the United States through military and other means that it would not feel compelled to come to terms with China on reunification or other issues seen as adverse to Taiwan's interests. Reagan's successor, George H. W. Bush, continued this approach, notably by sending the first US cabinet member to visit Taiwan and by transferring more than $5 billion of advanced jet fighters to Taiwan in a deal that was widely seen to have undermined the understandings reached in the 1982 communiqué with China.

As discussed in chapter 5, Sino-American interaction over the issues associated with Taiwan became much more complicated as democracy and a strong movement toward self-determination emerged in Taiwan in the post–Cold War period. The American antipathy to China following the Tiananmen crackdown added to the shift in American attitudes against China and in favor of Taiwan. American attraction to growing democracy in Taiwan overshadowed US attention to the profound implications for China of moves by Taiwan's democratic leaders toward greater separation from China. The moves were popular among many Taiwanese people and their supporters in the United States but were fundamentally at odds with China's concerns over sovereignty and nationalism.

The clash of Sino-American interests reached a high point with the military crisis in the Taiwan Strait in 1995–96, caused by Chinese military reaction to President Bill Clinton's unexpected reversal of US policy in granting

Taiwan's President Lee Teng-hui a visa in order to visit the United States and give a speech at his alma mater, Cornell University. Following the face-off of US and Chinese forces in the Taiwan area in 1996, China's strong political pressure against Taiwan and its US supporters continued along with concerted Chinese efforts to build up military forces in the Taiwan area designed to coerce Taiwan, prevent its movement toward permanent separation from China, and deter US military efforts to intervene. American policy reflected a complicated mix of efforts to preserve a balance of power favorable to the United States and Taiwan and thereby deter China's coercive pressures, on the one hand, while trying to dampen pro-independence initiatives in Taiwan and thereby reassure China regarding US commitment to a one-China policy, on the other.

The period from the Lee Teng-hui visit to the United States in 1995 until the end of the administration of President Chen Shui-bian in 2008 featured repeated episodes of escalating tensions in US-China relations regarding Taiwan. They usually were prompted by actions by Taiwan's government, often in reaction to escalating coercive pressure from China, to move in directions seen by China as supporting Taiwan's independence. As indicated in chapters 5 and 6, the Clinton and George W. Bush administrations had a hard time in efforts to deter the two sides from provocative actions, to calm tensions when one side or the other took steps that worsened cross-strait relations, and thereby to sustain the broad American interest in preserving peace and stability in the Taiwan area.

The election of Ma Ying-jeou as president of Taiwan in 2008 significantly reduced cross-strait tensions and the salience of the Taiwan issue in Sino-American relations. Ma reversed the policies and practices of his immediate predecessors that were seen by China as moving Taiwan toward independence of China. He put aside the zero-sum competition that had generally prevailed in Taiwan-China relations for sixty years. He opened Taiwan to much greater interchange with China that made the Taiwan economy more dependent than ever on close and cooperative relations with China. China reciprocated with policies and practices designed to foster closer ties and build closer identity between Taiwan and the mainland. US policy makers in the Bush and Obama administrations warmly welcomed the moderation of cross-strait tensions.[4]

The domestic foundations of Ma's positive engagement with China remained unsteady. Vocal oppositionists continued attacking as they grew in political prominence. Domestic opinion in Taiwan turned against closer ties with China, and mass demonstrations opposed agreements seen as making Taiwan more dependent on China. Ma's overall approval rating plummeted and his Nationalist (or Kuomintang, KMT) party lost the presidential and legislative elections in 2016 by such wide margins that it was questionable how soon it would revive as a leading force in Taiwan politics. The incoming

Tsai Ing-wen administration promised to sustain the status quo in cross-strait relations as it refused Chinese demands and pressures to accommodate Chinese interests. Beijing gradually increased negative military, diplomatic and economic pressures with an eye to weakening Taiwan and thereby eroding domestic support for the Tsai government. [5]

Why Cross-Strait Relations Improved, 2008–16

The relevant context of cooperation and easing of tensions in cross-strait relations in this period is the tumultuous period dating from President Lee Teng-hui's visit to the United States in 1995 to the end of the administration of President Chen Shui-bian in 2008. Tensions in cross-strait relations and the perceived danger of conflict in the Taiwan area rose dramatically in the mid-1990s, lasting until the election of Ma Ying-jeou. In the end, Taiwan voters and US policy makers reacted strongly against the extremes of Taiwan's leaders in this period, establishing the momentum behind an improvement of relations. China welcomed and endeavored to influence this turn of events.

Taiwan's President Lee Teng-hui surprised Chinese leaders by gaining permission from the United States to visit Cornell University in 1995. Lee's international activism and the US role in it were seen in China as fundamental challenges to Chinese interests, and Beijing responded harshly, notably with a series of military exercises in the Taiwan area during a nine-month period leading up to Taiwan's presidential election in March 1996. The Clinton administration became seriously concerned with the need to reassure China of US intentions toward Taiwan while deterring China from using force. Prior to Taiwan's presidential election, the United States deployed two aircraft carrier battle groups to the region. [6]

Tensions rose again following Lee Teng-hui's declaration in an international media interview in 1999 that he viewed cross-strait relations as a relationship between two separate states, an implicit challenge to China's one-China principle, which considers Taiwan to be part of China. China's top leaders warned Taiwan voters against choosing the Democratic Progressive Party (DPP) candidate, Chen Shui-bian, in the 2000 presidential elections, given that Chen and his party had a long record supporting self-determination for Taiwan, an anathema to China. In spite of such objections, Chen won the election. He made little progress with China, which chose to work with the KMT and its political allies, who controlled the legislature and opposed many of Chen's initiatives. [7]

Chen's reelection campaign in 2003–04 featured a series of appeals to Taiwanese nationalism and autonomy from China, which Chinese leaders again saw as direct challenges to their national interests. The Bush administration initially was very supportive of Taiwan but US leaders from the president on down came to see Chen's actions as dangerously provocative, and they turned against him. As the Chen administration wound down its term in office with a reputation for poor governance and rampant corruption as well as with low approval ratings, Chen carried out a variety of controversial policies and practices treating Taiwan as a state separate from China. These steps usually were seen as provocative by China and by the Bush administration, with the US government weighing in publicly against measures it saw as upsetting the stability in the Taiwan Strait. The Chen administration's relations with the United States eventually reached a point where the United States began restricting stopovers for Chen's transits on trips abroad to locales as far away from Washington as possible.[8] The administration was loath to move forward with arms sales, senior-level contacts, or other initiatives that would appear to be supporting Chen.

China duly registered public opposition to Chen's initiatives but placed more emphasis on working in consultation with the Bush administration to deal with Chen's maneuvers. Beijing strengthened the impressive military buildup focused on Taiwan and deepened Taiwan's economic interdependence with the mainland. Looking beyond the Chen administration, Chinese officials built increasingly positive connections with the KMT and other opposition political leaders and broader segments of Taiwan business elites and other opinion leaders.[9]

Chen's maneuvers and their negative consequences for cross-strait and Taiwan-US relations, along with the Taiwanese president's apparent deep personal involvement in corruption scandals, undermined the attractiveness of DPP candidates in legislative elections in January 2008 and the presidential election in March 2008. The result was a landslide victory for KMT candidates. The party gained overwhelming control of the legislature, and new president Ma Ying-jeou received a strong mandate to pursue policies of reassurance and moderation in cross-strait relations.[10] The United States and China both welcomed this new policy direction.

President Ma had an agenda emphasizing reassurance of China that his government would not move Taiwan toward independence; it was based on closer economic, social, and other contacts across the strait. Ma and his colleagues in Taiwan and their counterparts in China emphasized that progress would be easier in building closer and mutually advantageous economic and social ties. Issues of security and sovereignty posed by the growing Chinese military buildup opposite Taiwan and Taiwan's desire for greater international participation would be harder to resolve.[11]

On the whole, the improvements in cross-strait relations were rapid and impressive. Admittedly, the Chinese government took no significant action to reduce its military presence directly opposite the island. Likewise, Ma was reluctant to engage in talks with China on a possible peace agreement, while arguing that discussion of reunification would have to await developments after his term in office. Nonetheless, the security situation in the Taiwan Strait entered a period of relaxation of tensions as both Beijing and Taipei emphasized enhancing people-to-people contacts and expanding economic ties. A major development was the 2010 free trade agreement (FTA) between China and Taiwan, known as the Economic Cooperation Framework Agreement (ECFA), which provided privileged access to Chinese markets and other economic benefits for important constituencies in Taiwan.[12]

The numerous cross-strait agreements increased face-to-face interaction between Taiwan and Chinese authorities after decades of no direct dealings. The agreements were between ostensibly unofficial organizations—Taiwan's Straits Exchange Foundation (SEF) and China's Association for Relations Across the Taiwan Strait (ARATS). They required officials of the two governments to deal with each other on transportation, food safety, financial regulation, law enforcement, and other issues. In effect, three channels of communication became active between Taiwan and Chinese authorities: the SEF-ARATS exchanges; exchanges between the leaders of the Chinese Communist Party (CCP) and Taiwan's KMT; and widening government-to-government coordination and cooperation on a variety of cross-strait issues. Many of the agreements, interactions, and understandings focused on managing the large-scale trade and investment between Taiwan and China.[13]

Meanwhile, the Ma Ying-jeou government achieved a breakthrough in convincing China to allow Taiwan to participate in the annual World Health Assembly (WHA) meeting as an observer, using the name "Chinese Taipei." Other evidence of progress in China-Taiwan relations regarding Taiwan's participation in international affairs was the diminishment of what had been intense competition between the two countries for international recognition.[14]

The Bush administration welcomed the efforts of the Ma government and China's positive response as stabilizing and beneficial for all parties concerned. After the United States turned aside an initiative by President-elect Ma to visit for talks with US officials prior to his inauguration, Ma made no other such requests and worked hard to keep his transit stops in the United States discreet in ways that would not complicate US relations with China. High-level contacts occurred between the United States and Taiwan in quiet and private ways that avoided upsetting China, while ongoing US military consultations with and advice to Taiwan's armed forces continued.[15]

The Bush administration delayed until close to the last minute approval of a large arms sales package for Taiwan, which at $6.5 billion was the largest approved by the Bush government. Initial generous offers from the United States during Bush's first year in office were repeatedly delayed and whittled down on account of partisan bickering and funding delays for many years in Taiwan. This was followed by US reluctance to provide arms that would appear to support Chen Shui-bian's perceived provocative stance toward

China. The package in 2008 represented about half of what Taiwan requested and did not include sixty-six F-16 fighters that Taiwan had been trying for years to buy from the US government. Nonetheless, China strongly criticized the arms sale and suspended military contacts with the United States until mid-2009.[16]

The Obama administration also welcomed the new stability in cross-strait ties and appeared to be relying on Ma and his team to continue to manage cross-strait ties in positive ways that would not cause Taiwan to rejoin the already crowded list of US policy priorities needing urgent attention.[17] The Obama government followed through with a $6 billion arms package for Taiwan in 2010. Although the package did not include F-16 fighters, it still prompted sometimes strident public complaints along with limited substantive retaliation from China. Later US arms sales included another large arms package worth more than $5 billion in 2011 that proposed significant upgrades in the capabilities of Taiwan's existing F-16 fighters.[18]

Recent Developments

The thirteen-year (1995–2008) experience with tense cross-strait and US-Taiwan-China relations reinforced a strong tendency in the US government to manage issues with Taiwan in ways that avoided major friction with what was viewed as a much more important relationship with China. The strength of that tendency was seen during the escalation in recent years of US-China frictions over a range of security, economic, and political issues, which from the American side were seen as caused by the newly assertive actions of Chinese party leader and President Xi Jinping, who was elected in 2012. The Obama government showed a pattern of very deliberative and transparent foreign policy making that in the case of China saw gradual escalation of rhetorical criticism and eventually some serious actions to deal with disputes with China. The pattern showed that specific differences and disputes with China were dealt with separately; they were not linked to other issues in US-China relations or to the overall state of the relationship, which continued to be portrayed by the president and his advisers in a positive and optimistic way, with priority given to areas of increased constructive engagement and a credit-worthy foreign policy legacy for President Obama. Under these circumstances, Taiwan policy was not allowed to change in ways that could seriously aggravate Beijing.

For example, as noted in chapter 7, President Obama for many years rarely criticized China, but China's practices under the rule of President Xi Jinping prompted a remarkable rhetorical and to some degree substantive hardening in US government policy. The president's wide-ranging and often sharp criticism notably did not include Taiwan. Rather, the president and his administration continued to adhere to an approach inherited from the George

W. Bush administration that Taiwan issues should be handled in ways that avoided serious negative consequences for American policy toward China. Thus, the president's signature rebalance policy in the Asia-Pacific region was repeatedly and sometimes harshly criticized by China. The Obama government nonetheless went ahead with a wide range of initiatives with Japan, The Philippines, Vietnam, and other areas around Taiwan, but initial administration statements about the policy failed to even mention Taiwan. In response to various queries, the administration began stating routinely that Taiwan was included in the rebalance policy, though it avoided discussing any details of what the United States and Taiwan were doing, presumably to avoid offending the People's Republic of China in ways seen as adverse to administration interests.[19]

US officials highlighted progress in relations with Taiwan that involved cooperation on global issues, increased official interchanges at levels somewhat higher than in the recent past, and assisting Taiwan membership in international bodies and other matters that were deemed less likely to prompt frictions with China. They avoided taking sides, including during her candidacy in 2015-2016, against President Tsai Ing-wen, a member of the DPP, which refuses to endorse the view of one China demanded by Beijing. The Obama government had voiced reservations about Tsai's cross-strait policy during her failed 2012 election campaign against Ma Ying-jeou. US officials encouraged both Beijing and Taipei to avoid provocations, seek constructive communications, and reach compromise formulas or understandings that would avoid a break in cross-strait interchange detrimental to peace and stability.[20]

US policy toward Taiwan continued to be challenged by new circumstances. For one thing, the Taiwan voters' deepening wariness of Ma Ying-jeou's approach to China supported President Tsai and her DPP colleagues' firm stance in protecting their view of Taiwan's sovereignty in the face of Chinese pressure. Military tension in cross-strait relations rose with Chinese naval combatants, including China's aircraft carrier and air force bombers carrying out exercises in areas surrounding Taiwan. China cut off SEF-ARATS talks and curbed other formal or informal contacts with Taiwan officials. It curbed the active flow of Chinese mainland tourists to Taiwan. It broke with the so-called diplomatic truce in place at the time and established relations with two African countries that previously had official relations with Taiwan.[21]

Beijing eschewed close contacts with DPP leaders. It used continued close contacts with the now-weakened KMT to reaffirm China's main demand on cross-strait relations that the Tsai government had to affirm the so-called 1992 consensus. The consensus was used by the Ma Ying-jeou government and Beijing to provide a sense of agreement on China's insistence that what Beijing has called its one-China principle was recognized by both sides, thereby allowing China to go forward with improved cross-strait relations. Ma held a summit meeting with President Xi Jinping two months prior to the January 2016 presidential elections in Taiwan that reaffirmed both sides' commitment to the 1992 consensus. Though avoiding any abrupt changes in the cross-strait status quo she inherited from Ma, Tsai refused to meet China's demands on the 1992 consensus. The result reinforced Beijing's suspicion of her alleged pro-independence tendencies and prompted carefully applied increases in Chinese military, diplomatic, and economic pressure on Taiwan.[22]

While the Obama government stressed cross-strait communication to avoid serious instability, American critics of the administration's policy favored stronger support for Taiwan. They included Republican leaders in Congress, Republican-leaning think tanks, media, and interest groups, along with many Democrats and progressive think tanks, media, and interest groups advocating change that would allow for a US-Taiwan policy that was less deferential to China.[23]

Some Americans strongly urged US policy to deal with Taiwan for its own sake, rather than in a contingent way that was dependent on US interests with China. They opposed the US government intervention, by its voicing concern about Tsai Ing-wen's cross-strait policies in 2011, in Taiwan domestic politics. They favored more forthright American government support for Taiwan's entry into the Trans Pacific Partnership (TPP) multilateral economic agreement, more frequent US cabinet-level visits to Taiwan, and the sale of more advanced US military equipment to Taiwan; and they averred that strident American leadership complaints about Chinese bullying and intimidation of neighbors, using military and other coercive means, needed also to highlight and condemn China's two decades of massive bullying, coercion, and intimidation toward Taiwan.

A second group of Americans focused on using Taiwan's strategic location in opposition to what they saw as Chinese efforts to undermine the American strategic position around China's rim and achieve overall dominance in the region contrary to long-standing American interests. In their view, to counter such perceived efforts required a clear American strategy working with China's neighbors involving maritime control, and interdiction if necessary. Because of its location at the center of the so-called first island chain, Taiwan looms large in plans to counter Chinese expansion along its rim. The plans involve gaining the Taiwan government's cooperation in setting and monitoring sensors and other means of surveillance, preparing mobile units with antiship missiles to deploy to various locations in the first island chain, and preparing the use of mines and other means to deny access to Chinese ships and submarines.

A third group of Americans focused on the Xi Jinping government's coercive expansionism at American expense along China's rim and the other practices grossly at odds with US interests, to argue that America should take actions showing greater support for Taiwan as part of a cost imposition strategy to counter Xi Jinping's anti-American practices. In their view, the kinds of steps forward in US relations with Taiwan that were advocated by the previous two groups should be considered and used, as the United States endeavored to show Beijing that its various challenges to US interests would not be cost free and actually would be counterproductive for Chinese concerns on the all-important Taiwan issue. [24]

Meanwhile, the US election campaign of 2015–16 featured acrimony with China and some attention to Taiwan. A few Republican candidates and the Republican Party platform used the arguments of the three schools of thought described above in calling for change in policy toward Taiwan. Since before his stint as a presidential candidate, Senator Marco Rubio has been active in congressional measures to support Taiwan along the lines of the first group of critics noted above, who urge treating Taiwan for its own sake and without so much deference to Beijing. He frequently highlighted those initiatives during his campaign. He notably backed a US military buildup to ensure Taiwan's protection in the face of China's military power. He advised that US policy should be guided by historic American reassurances of support for Taiwan and not by reputed need to avoid exacerbating tensions with China over the issue. [25]

Senator Ted Cruz released a statement on the results of Taiwan's January 2016 presidential elections lauding Taiwan on ideological grounds as a beacon for democracy and inspiration to those in China and Hong Kong seeking freedom against the oppressive Communist government. [26]

Senator John McCain and other senators visited Asia in May–June 2016 to reassure US allies and partners of continued strong American regional engagement despite Trump's call for allies depending on US military protection to do more to offset the US costs or face American withdrawal. McCain and six of the visiting senators stopped in Taiwan to affirm support for recently installed President Tsai Ing-wen. The visit marked the first by the Chair of the Senate Armed Services Committee in twenty-six years and the largest group of US senators to visit Taiwan in ten years. [27]

Though Mr. Trump said little about Taiwan, Professor Peter Navarro, an Asia expert, used a byline as a policy adviser to Trump on Asian issues in publishing in July 2016 an extensive assessment of the importance of stronger US support for Taiwan; he employed the arguments of the three schools of thought noted above. [28]

Overall, the implications of the US election debates on policy toward Taiwan were limited. They showed little deviation from the arguments seen in the Congress and the media prior to and during the American campaign. How Hillary Clinton's promised hardening of policy on disputes with China would impact her approach to Taiwan remained undefined, though her senior staff member Jake Sullivan said in July 2016 that Hillary Clinton would not change Taiwan policy.[29] Candidate Trump devoted little attention to the issue.

Interviews in Taipei with officials and think tank experts in July 2016 showed concern that Taiwan would suffer if Trump followed through with pledges to negotiate major agreements with China as the Taiwan issue would likely be raised by the Chinese side in those negotiations. There also was worry in Taipei that candidate Trump's stance on demanding more payment from US ally Japan would seriously weaken the US ability to support Taiwan in the face of China's military intimidation. Observers in Taiwan appreciated the resolve shown by Senator McCain and his Senate colleagues to continue support for US allies and partners in Asia regardless of the results of the American presidential election. They were encouraged by interactions with Navarro when he visited Taiwan and by strong support for Taiwan registered in the Republican Party platform. There was broad worry among Taiwan observers on how they could advance Taiwan's importance in US administration's policy deliberations. In particular, the Taiwan government was preparing actively for future entry into the TPP and hoped the agreement would be approved by Congress, thereby allowing Taiwan to be supported for entry by the United States in the next round of membership for the body.[30]

Interviews with officials and specialists in Beijing in July 2016 registered low concern over the US election campaign and its implications for US policy toward Taiwan. Observers in Beijing saw negatives with both Hillary Clinton and Donald Trump. Like many Americans, they were frustrated with the downward trend in US-China relations and judged that trend would worsen at least to some degree if Clinton were elected. Some in Beijing nonetheless voiced confidence that mutual interests and highly integrated US-China government relationships would guard against relations going seriously off track. Chinese derision of Trump earlier in the campaign shifted to seeking advantage, given the candidate's disruption of US alliances along China's rim and emphasis on seeking common ground with China through negotiations. Overall, a common view was that China could "shape" President Trump to behave in line with its interests as Trump was seen as less ideological and more pragmatic than Clinton was. High-level interlocutors in Beijing judged that Hillary Clinton's tougher approach than Obama toward China would not involve major moves on Taiwan.[31]

The uncertainty surrounding US China policy under a Trump administration included the sensitive issue of Taiwan. As noted at the start of this chapter, although Donald Trump said little about Taiwan during the campaign, once elected he broke ranks with past practice and reflected the views of many Republican Party leaders and other Americans in publicly questioning past deference to Beijing over this matter of acute sensitivity to Chinese leaders. The outgoing Obama government reacted in part by halting a planned large US arms sale to Taiwan at the end of the US president's term. Subsequently, President Trump saw the wisdom of adhering to the conventional US policy and practice in dealing with Taiwan discreetly and in accord with the so-called American one-China policy. In a summit meeting with President Xi in April 2017, President Trump sought improved relations with China and an increase in Chinese pressure on North Korea as part of the Trump government's strong interest in international pressure on Pyongyang to halt its nuclear weapons development. He lavished repeated public praise on President Xi's integrity and leadership. In that context, planned US arms sales to Taiwan were postponed and a suggested second phone conversation with Taiwan's president was publicly rejected, as these activities could undermine Chinese support for the United States at such an important juncture.[32]

As of this writing, the durability of the trajectory in US administration policy toward Taiwan remains to be seen. Limited experience with President Trump's reversal of major policy positions in Asian and world affairs in his initial months in office has put observers in the United States, China, Taiwan, and elsewhere on guard for circumstances, moods, and other factors that could prompt further abrupt change. Trump is easily capable of seemingly minor actions such as tweets, phone calls, and remarks in interviews and at press conferences and rallies that in a few words will surprise leaders in China, Taiwan, and elsewhere with serious negative consequences. He values unpredictability and does not place the high value President Obama did on policy transparency, carefully measured responses, and avoidance of dramatic actions. He is much less constrained than the previous US administration by a perceived need to sustain and advance US-China relations. Like President Xi and unlike President Obama, President Trump does not eschew tension and presumably seeks advantage in tensions between the two countries. Also like his Chinese counterpart and unlike President Obama, he is prepared to seek leverage through linking his policy preference in one area of the relationship with policies in other areas of the relationship.[33]

EAST ASIAN MARITIME DISPUTES AND CONTEMPORARY US-CHINA RELATIONS

As reviewed in chapter 7, early Chinese tests of the Obama administration's resolve on sensitive issues in US-China relations reached a more assertive stage around the time of the Obama government's launching of its rebalance to Asia policy in 2011 and the ascendance to power of President Xi Jinping, strong-man ruler and Communist Party leader, in 2012. Following President Hu Jintao's last visit to the United States in January 2011 and concurrent reassurance of the United States and other concerned powers in statements about commitments to peace and development by authoritative Chinese foreign policy leaders, there was some anticipation that China would avoid the type of disruptive assertiveness at US expense that was seen in the first years of the Obama government. The hope was that China would return to the pragmatic cooperation with the United States that had marked most of the Hu Jintao government.[34]

Unfortunately, 2012 saw unprecedented demonstrations of Chinese power short of using military force in defense of Chinese claims to disputed territories in the South China Sea and the East China Sea. The measures were accompanied by official Chinese commentary that accused the United States of fostering the territorial disputes and using them to advance US influence in the Asian region to the detriment of China. The Chinese demonstrations of coercive power went well beyond established international norms and re-sulted in extralegal measures and in some cases in widespread violence and property destruction. They placed China's neighbors and concerned powers, notably the United States, on guard. They compelled the neighbors and the United States not only to consider methods of dealing effectively with Chi-nese pressures, but also to consider more carefully the wide range of differ-ences they had with China that might set off highly disruptive and assertive actions by the now second-ranking and rapidly growing power in world politics. The implications for regional order clearly took a negative turn in 2012.[35]

Subsequent developments in the East China Sea and the South China Sea saw no meaningful letup in China's determination to advance its disputed claims at the expense of neighbors and at the expense of the US position as security guarantor of the Asia-Pacific. China's interest in avoiding military conflict with the United States meshed with American priorities; senior US and Chinese leaders stayed in close contact with one another in an effort highlighted by China to search for a "new type of great power relationship" that would avoid conflict and manage tensions as China's rising power and expanding interests rubbed against American interests, policies, and prac-tices.

Competition for influence and advantage characterized US-China rela-tions over these disputes as well as many other issues during the remainder of the Obama government. As noted earlier, the Obama government was pleased overall with its record in dealing with China, including over the disputes in the maritime regions adjoining China's mainland. Many others saw reactive and overly restricted US responses to Chinese affronts that gave priority to other goals. A notable result was substantial setbacks and lost influence as the United States seemed weak and less than resolute in the face of determined Chinese expansion at others' expense.[36]

Amid rising frictions in US-China ties, President Obama was pressed by the sharp attacks on Chinese economic and security policies by Republican challengers in the 2012 presidential election campaign. He joined the fray with harsh rhetoric not seen in his presidential campaign in 2008. In the third presidential debate on October 22, veteran China specialist Donald Keyser noted that the president publicly referred to China for the first time as "an adversary" though the president went on to describe China as a "potential partner in the international community if it follows the rules." Highlighting his administration's rebalance policy of reengagement with countries in the Asia-Pacific region as a means to compete with China in security, economic, and other terms, the president went on to emphasize, "We believe China can be a partner, but we're also sending a very clear signal that America is a Pacific power, that we are going to have a presence there. . . . And we're organizing trade relations with countries other than China so that China starts feeling more pressure about meeting basic international standards."[37]

The Obama government's reengagement policy toward the Asia-Pacific indeed underlined a stronger American determination to compete more broadly for influence in the region.[38] The security aspects of the so-called rebalance policy or pivot to Asia received high-level attention by the president, secretary of defense, and secretary of state. They explained in speeches throughout the Asia-Pacific region and in the release of a defense planning document in January 2012 the purpose and scope of US redeployment of forces from the Middle East and other areas to the Asia-Pacific and the determination of the American leaders to sustain and advance US security relations and power despite anticipated cuts in overall US defense spending. Actual advances in US force deployments remained modest though the scope, tempo, and intensity of US military interactions with the region continued to grow.

American diplomatic activism in support of its interests was registered with an impressive advance in senior US leaders headed by President Obama traveling to the region and participating actively in bilateral relations as well as existing and newly emerging regional groupings that involved the United States. Problems impacting US interests in regional stability, freedom of navigation, and relations with allies and partners saw the American leaders take an active role in discussing ways to manage and hopefully ease tensions over sensitive sovereignty and security concerns in disputed maritime territories along China's rim.

As President Obama indicated in his remarks in the October 2012 debate, the United States also was more active in competing in support of its economic interests as part of the reengagement with Asia. A highlight of US interest was the proposed TPP free-trade accord involving the United States and countries on both sides of the Pacific in an arrangement seen as moving American interests forward in regional and international trade liberalization. The proposed agreement was viewed as competing with groupings favored by China that required less trade liberalization and that excluded the United States.

The Obama government's reengagement in Asia ran up against rising Chinese assertiveness and coercive and intimidating actions to protect and advance Chinese sovereignty and security interests in disputed territories along China's rim. The Chinese actions were influenced and strongly supported by patriotic elite and public opinion that viewed the US activism as a justification for China to take more coercive actions to protect and advance its interests. In effect, the US and Chinese initiatives represented the most important challenge or test of the durability of cooperative Sino-American engagement during 2012, and the testing would continue until the end of Obama's term.

The pattern of assertiveness showed remarkable features in defending Chinese disputed claims in the South China Sea and the East China Sea in 2012.[39]

Round One

The first round of Chinese assertiveness over territorial issues in 2012 involved the South China Sea. Following Chinese disagreement with the Philippines in April over the attempt of Philippine officers to arrest Chinese fishermen in disputed Scarborough Shoal in the South China Sea, Chinese authorities used impressive and extraordinary demonstrations of Chinese security, economic, administrative, and diplomatic power to have their way in the South China Sea, including the following:

- China employed its large and growing force of maritime and fishing security ships, targeted economic sanctions out of line with international norms and WTO rules, and repeated diplomatic warnings to intimidate and coerce Philippine officials, security forces, and fishermen to respect China's claims to disputed Scarborough Shoal.
- China showed stronger resolve to exploit more fully contested fishing resources in the South China Sea with the announced deployment of one of the world's largest (thirty-two-thousand-ton) fish-processing ships to the area and the widely publicized dispatch of a fleet of thirty fishing boats supported by a supply ship to fish in disputed South China Sea areas.
- China created a new, multifaceted administrative structure backed by a new military garrison that covered wide swaths of disputed areas in the South China Sea. The coverage was in line with China's broad historical claims, depicted in Chinese maps with a nine-dashed line and encompassing most of the South China Sea. The large claims laid out in Chinese maps also provided justification for a state-controlled Chinese oil company to offer nine new blocks in the South China Sea for foreign oil compa-

nies development that were far from China but very close to Vietnam. Against this background, little was heard in Chinese commentary of the more moderate explanation of Chinese South China Sea territorial claims made by a Chinese foreign ministry spokesperson on February 29, 2012, who said that China did not claim the "entire South China Sea" but only its islands and adjacent waters.

• Chinese authorities later prompted some alarm in the South China Sea when provincial authorities announced that Chinese maritime police patrols would board and hold ships carrying out illegal activities in the claimed Chinese areas of the South China Sea. And Vietnam and the Philippines as well as Taiwan joined India and other countries in condemning new Chinese passports that showed the South China Sea and other disputed areas along the rim of China as Chinese territory.

• China advanced cooperative relations with the 2012 Association of Southeast Asian Nations (ASEAN) chair, Cambodia, thereby ensuring that with Cambodia's cooperation, South China Sea disputes did not receive prominent treatment in ASEAN documents in the annual ASEAN Ministerial Meeting in April and later ASEAN-related meetings in November. A result was strong division in ASEAN on how to deal with China that resulted in unprecedented displays of ASEAN disunity at those meetings.

Chinese officials and official Chinese media commentaries endeavored to bound and compartmentalize the South China Sea disputes. Their public emphasis remained heavily on China's continued pursuit of peaceful development and cooperation during meetings with Southeast Asian representatives and those of other concerned powers including the United States. Thus, what emerged was a Chinese approach having at least two general paths:

1. One path showed to South China Sea claimants, notably the Philippines and Vietnam, who disputed Chinese territorial claims, and others in Southeast Asia, as well as to their supporters in the United States and elsewhere, how powerful China had become in disputed South China Sea areas; how China's security, economic, administrative, and diplomatic power was likely to grow in the near future; and how Chinese authorities could use those powerful means in intimidating and coercive ways short of overt use of military force in order to counter foreign "intrusions" or public disagreements regarding Chinese claims.

2. Another path forecast ever closer "win-win" cooperation between China and Southeast Asian countries, ASEAN, and others including the United States. It focused on burgeoning China–Southeast Asian trade and economic interchange and was premised on treatment of South China Sea and other disputes in ways that avoided public controversy

and eschewed actions challenging or otherwise complicating the extensive Chinese claims to the area. In this regard, China emphasized the importance of all concerned countries to adhere to efforts to implement the 2002 Declaration of the Conduct of the Parties in the South China Sea (DOC). It duly acknowledged recent efforts supported by ASEAN to reach the "eventual" formulation of a code of conduct (COC) in the South China Sea, implying that the process of achieving the latter might take some time.

In sum, China set forth an implicit choice for the Philippines, Vietnam, other Southeast Asian disputants of China's South China Sea claims, ASEAN, and other governments and organizations with an interest in the South China Sea, notably the United States. On the one hand, based on recent practice, pursuit of policies and actions at odds with Chinese claims in the South China Sea would meet with more of the demonstrations of Chinese power along the lines of path 1, above. On the other hand, concurrent Chinese leaders' statements and official commentary indicated that others' moderation and/or acquiescence regarding Chinese claims would result in the mutually beneficial development seen in path 2.

The Philippines, Vietnam, and other disputants of Chinese claims did not seem to be in an advantageous position in the face of Chinese power and intimidation. ASEAN remained divided on how to deal with China. And options of the United States and other concerned powers to deal effectively with the new situation of greater muscle short of military use of force in Chinese policies and practices regarding the South China Sea remained to be determined.

Round Two

The second round of Chinese assertiveness on sensitive sovereignty and security issues came with a dispute, more widely publicized at the time, with Japan over the Senkaku (Diaoyu) Islands.[40] Even more so than in the recent case in the South China Sea, China's response to a perceived affront by Japan involved a variety of extralegal measures sharply contrary to international norms. The Japanese government had endeavored to avoid a crisis prompted by Japanese politicians hostile to China who sought to buy three of the contested islands and develop them in ways sure to antagonize China. Instead, the Japanese government intervened and purchased the islands. The purchase triggered an extraordinary Chinese reaction. It included trade sanctions and failure to provide security of Japanese people and property in China. As large anti-Japanese demonstrations, fostered by well-orchestrated publicity efforts of Chinese authorities, emerged in more than one hundred Chinese cities, the security forces tended to stand aside as agitated Chinese demonstrators destroyed Japanese properties and manhandled Japanese citizens. The displays of violence were eventually mildly criticized by Chinese official media commentary, but the publicity organs of China were full of support of Chinese peoples' "righteous indignation" against Japan as the widespread violence spread throughout the country. Meanwhile, the Chinese authorities deployed maritime security forces and official aircraft, and took legal steps that showed Japan and other concerned powers that the status quo of Japan's control of the islands had changed amid continued challenge from China employing security forces and other means short of direct use of military force.

Chinese popular and elite opinion reacted positively to the Chinese actions in the South China Sea and the East China Sea. Chinese media continued to strongly criticize alleged US efforts to support American allies and partners against China and to exploit Chinese differences with neighboring countries in order to advance American influence in the Asia-Pacific region. Meanwhile, some Chinese officials also viewed approvingly the reaction of the US government to the crises in the disputed seas in 2012. They advised that the Obama administration leaders seemed less willing in 2012 to confront China on such assertive actions regarding territorial disputes, in contrast to what they saw as a more prominent and assertive US stance against Chinese interests regarding the territorial disputes in 2010.[41]

Overall, Chinese commentary and elite and public opinion had a strong stream arguing that China was successful in its muscular reactions to US allies, the Philippines and Japan, despite the widely touted US reengagement with the Asia-Pacific. It triumphed with effective use of often extralegal coercive measures to advance China's territorial claims and show firm resolve against perceived challenges. Some foreign and Chinese specialists also observed that unlike the debates and various policy options stressed in Chinese commentary during a period of assertiveness in 2009–10, the actions and commentary regarding the South China Sea and the East China Sea in 2012 showed effective coordination and little sign of debate even though the Chinese actions involved extraordinary use of coercion, intimidation, and extralegal means well beyond the pale of international norms said to be respected by the Chinese government.[42]

Subsequent developments in the East China Sea disputes saw the election of Liberal Democratic Party (LDP) leader Shinzo Abe as Prime Minister, defeating the discredited Democratic Party in elections in late 2012. Abe was firm in the face of Chinese pressure. Japan's experienced coast guard forces—backed by Japan's modern and well-trained naval and air forces—were up to the new challenges posed by China's coast guard fleet. The Obama government welcomed Abe's ascendance. America shifted from a mediating role to a tougher stance critical of China's coercive behavior.[43] The US position overlapped closely with Abe's defensive but firm stance toward China. China stridently attacked Abe as he sought support against Chinese pressures by strengthening defense at home and seeking support in visits to all members of ASEAN as well as India, Australia, and others. In contrast, President Obama, visiting Japan in April 2014, embraced close collaboration with Japan in Asia and underlined America's defense commitment to all areas under Japanese administrative control, including the Senkaku (Diaoyu) Islands. Prime Minister Abe's visit to the United States in April 2015 advanced defense cooperation and international coordination between the two allies. President Obama took the opportunity to rebuke China for "flexing its muscles" to intimidate neighbors and gain control of disputed territory.[44]

In sum, while China continued coast guard and naval and air intrusions, it had no success in trying to intimidate Japan, backed firmly by the United States. A highlight of Chinese assertiveness was Beijing's November 2013 announcement that it would establish an air defense identification zone (ADIZ) over the East China Sea to include the disputed Senkaku (Diaoyu) Islands. Outside of China, the ADIZ was widely interpreted as a challenge to Japanese administration of the Senkaku (Diaoyu) Islands. Washington weighed in strongly against China's actions.[45] The United States and Japan coordinated closely and at a high level in their individual and collective responses to the new situation. American officials expressed appreciation for Japan's measured response in what could have been a combustible situation.

Stymied in the East China Sea, Beijing found it easier to advance against weaker Southeast Asian states and a less resolute America. On the one hand, domestic nationalism and demands for a less deferential and more activist Chinese foreign policy drove Chinese policy. The Xi government's widely publicized policies met with domestic approval as they advanced Chinese South China Sea claims. Rapidly expanding Chinese military and paramilitary capabilities along with impressive oil rigs, fishing fleets, dredging machines, and construction abilities allowed and probably prompted China's leaders to expand in areas that were long claimed by China. China's advance also was in reaction to the Obama government's rebalance policy opposed by Beijing.

On the other hand, Xi's China married its tough policy on South China disputes with visionary publicity of China's proposed Silk Road Belt, Maritime Silk Road, and related proposals, including the still-forming Asian Infrastructure Investment Bank (AIIB) and related economic initiatives. In effect, China set forth a choice for the Philippines, Vietnam, other Southeast Asian disputants of China's South China Sea claims, ASEAN, and other governments and organizations with an interest in the South China Sea, notably the United States. Pursuit of policies and actions at odds with Chinese claims in the South China Sea would meet with more of the demonstrations of Chinese power seen in China's takeover of Scarborough Shoal from the Philippines in 2012, its deployment of an oil rig and a massive armada of defending ships near islands very sensitive to Vietnam in 2014, and its subsequent massive land reclamation for force projection in the far reaches of the South China Sea. At the same time, Southeast Asian and other neighbors' moderation and/or acquiescence regarding Chinese South China Sea claims would result in mutually beneficial development flowing from Chinese economic largess.[46]

The most notable advance of Chinese intimidating and coercing other claimants in the South China Sea came in 2014 and involved Vietnam. On May 2 China's abrupt deployment, in the disputed Paracel Islands of the South China Sea, of a forty-story oil rig along with a protecting armada of more than one hundred fishing, coast guard, and reportedly military vessels shocked the region and particularly Vietnam, the other main claimant to these islands. Concurrent disclosures showed large-scale dredging that created Chinese-controlled islands on previously submerged reefs in the disputed Spratly Islands, with China fortifying some of these sites for surveillance and power projection far from the Chinese mainland.[47]

The egregious Chinese advances demonstrated to audiences at home and abroad how far Beijing was prepared to go in confronting its neighbors, the United States, and other powers concerned with regional stability in order to advance its broad territorial claims in the South China Sea. The Chinese moves to defend and advance control in the South China Sea elicited uniformly positive treatment in Chinese media while Chinese leaders exuded confidence in facing predictable negative international reactions.

Nevertheless, probably unanticipated by Beijing's planners were mass demonstrations in Vietnam that turned violent, killing five Chinese and injuring many more while causing widespread damage to Chinese and other Asian-invested enterprises. Sharply critical rhetoric and moves at odds with Chinese interests by the United States, Japan, Australia, and some Southeast Asian countries also underlined deepening wariness and growing diplomatic and security measures directed at China. Chinese delegates at the annual Shangri-La defense forum in late May were on the defensive in the face of direct attacks on China led by the United States and Japan.

Against this background, China's removal of the rig and its protective fleet in mid-July, much earlier than expected, was widely interpreted outside China as designed to reduce tensions, at least for a time. China denied this interpretation. It nonetheless toned down harsh rhetoric while continuing to defend the rig deployment. High-level Sino-Vietnamese talks in Beijing on August 27 reduced bilateral tensions.

There was no easing of the disputes over Chinese dredging to create outposts for power projection in the far reaches of the South China. Those issues worsened and provided the focus on American and allied complaints at the 2015 Shangri-La defense forum.[48]

The regional reaction to the Sino-Vietnamese confrontation appeared to show unwillingness by most Southeast Asian countries to take a stand against China. The Philippines was very critical of Chinese actions and Manila collaborated with Hanoi in seeking options. The United States came into the lead of international critics of Chinese coercion; Japan and Australia usually weighed in supporting the American stand. However, most Southeast Asian countries remained on the sidelines.

In 2015 Xi Jinping's government entered its third year registering significant success in advancing control in the disputed South China Sea. China's bold tactics involving the massive dredging and rapid construction, shows of force involving large military exercises, deployments of China's impressive coast guard fleet, and movement of massed fishing vessels and large oil rigs warned weaker neighbors of China's power and determination to have its way. US Pacific Commander Admiral Harry Harris said in July that the dredging over the past eighteen months rapidly created three thousand acres of Chinese island territory, which is widely seen for military use and maritime control.

In early 2016 Chinese-Southeast Asian relations were dominated by China's unremitting expanding control in disputed territory in the South China Sea in the face of complaints, maneuvers, and challenges by a range of regional governments and concerned powers headed by the United States. At the top of the list of American-led challenges to Chinese expansion were military shows of force, expanded military presence, and freedom-of-navigation operations accompanied by strong rhetoric from American defense leaders warning of Chinese ambitions. China rebuked the American actions and pressed ahead with military deployments, construction of defense facilities, and island expansion. Beijing remained determined to gain greater control in the disputed sea despite earlier indications of moderation, notably President Xi Jinping's pledge not to militarize disputed territory made during his September 2015 summit in Washington. Reflecting the Obama government's careful management of South China Sea tensions with China, the rising tension did not spill over and impede the constructive outcome of the US-China summit on March 31, 2016. This served to reinforce various indications showing Southeast Asian governments and other concerned powers that Washington sought to avoid confrontation, as did Beijing though China was prepared to risk tensions with the United States caused by its expansion in the South China Sea.[49]

Against that background, when China reacted with harsh rhetoric and intimidating threats to the July 2016 decision of an international tribunal in The Hague ruling against China's South China Sea claims in a case brought by former Philippines President Benigno Aquino, the onslaught worked to China's advantage. The United States was in the lead among regional powers in calling for restraint and moderation, and no other regional country was willing to get out in front of Washington. In contrast to the high tempo of large-scale US and US-led naval exercises and other military maneuvers in the South China Sea prior to the decision, there were no US military actions signaling pressure on China in the weeks following the July 12 decision. Japan and Australia, important American allies in the Asia-Pacific and concerned with China's territorial expansion, joined the United States in restricting reactions mainly to official statements of approval of the tribunal's decision. The Philippines, a US ally and the initiator of the case, had come under a new government on June 30 and was much more interested in seeking common ground with China.[50]

In 2017 Chinese officials showed growing confidence and satisfaction that the cooling tensions in the South China Sea demonstrated increasing regional deference to Beijing's interests, while China's economic importance to Southeast Asia loomed larger in a period of anticipated international economic retrenchment. They remained alert to possible actions by the United States, Japan, Australia, and South China Sea claimant states that might upset the recent positive trajectory but generally saw those states preoccupied or otherwise unwilling to push back strongly against Chinese ambitions. The incoming Trump government seemed preoccupied with the Middle East and Russia; its main initiative in East Asia focused on working cooperatively with China to press North Korea to halt its nuclear weapons program. There was a notable decline in US freedom-of-navigation demonstrations and other US efforts to challenge China's expansion in the South China Sea. For the time being at least, the way seemed open to a steady Chinese consolidation and control of holdings and rights in the South China Sea, a Chinese-supported code of conduct in the South China Sea, Chinese diplomatic initiatives to promote closer ties and reduce regional suspicion of Chinese intentions, and an array of economic blandishments in line with Beijing's ambitious Silk Road programs.[51]

Chapter Eleven

Issues of Human Rights in Contemporary US-China Relations

Issues of human rights in US-China relations reflect a wide range of values dealing with economic, social, political, cultural, and other interests and concerns of groups and individuals. Differences over human rights issues have long characterized Sino-American relations. The differences have their roots in the respective backgrounds of the American and Chinese societies, governments, and peoples. Those backgrounds foster values that are often at odds.[1]

Such differences may be understood through the constructivist school of thought in the field of international relations, which sees national identity as an important determinant of international affairs. As discussed in chapter 1 and noted elsewhere, the governments and societies of China and the United States reflect a self-centered exceptionalism that comes from their very well developed national identities. The US identity has evolved over more than two centuries while China's has developed over millennia. Adding to this mix, the Communist Party (CCP)–ruled government of China, seeking to preserve its rule, works very hard to reinforce an identity based on China's past. Overall, these circumstances make it difficult for either power to compromise with the other on issues of values and norms that impact their respective deeply rooted identities.

Meanwhile, the school of thought of liberalism in the field of international relations can deepen understanding of a fundamental ingredient in the American incentive to engage positively with China despite wide differences, especially over values and norms. That is, America's engagement with China, especially after the Cold War, was premised on a commonly held assumption by liberals that economic change and integration of China with developed countries having free-market economies and pluralistic political systems would eventually lead to social and then political change toward pluralism and democracy in China. As discussed below, a major reason for a growing sense among Americans that US engagement with China is failing is the fact that many Americans previously optimistic that engagement with China would lead to change in China's political system and other norms and values in line with American norms and values have become more pessimistic about the possibility of this kind of change.

In general, since the opening of Sino-American relations in the early 1970s, the Chinese and American governments have endeavored to manage these differences in ways that do not block progress in other important areas of Sino-American relations. At times when one side or the other has focused high priority on human rights issues, as did the United States following the Tiananmen crackdown of 1989, US-China relations have tended to stall or retrogress. As US and Chinese leaders more often have devoted only secondary consideration to human rights differences, the obstacles posed by these issues for Sino-American relations have also been less significant.[2]

The importance of human rights differences between the United States and China has also been influenced by changes in policies and practices, especially on the part of China. In a broad sense, the United States has sought to prompt the Chinese authorities to adopt policies and practices in line with the international values and norms prevalent in modern developed countries of the West. The review of economic issues in chapter 9 and the examination of security issues in chapter 8 show how Chinese leaders have frequently seen their interests better served by conforming more to international norms in these areas. Economically, China's government has embraced many of the norms of the globalized international economy and has adapted comprehensively to economic market demands. A significant benchmark in this process was China's decision to join the World Trade Organization (WTO) with an agreement demanding extensive changes in Chinese economic policies and practices. Evidence of shortcomings of the process include rising complaints by Americans and others regarding China's failure to live up to WTO commitments. China's conformity to world norms in the security area has been slow but substantial, especially in areas involving such sensitive issues as the proliferation of weapons of mass destruction. Meanwhile, as China has grown in international power and prominence, it has endeavored to create new international norms in economic and security matters more in line with its interests and often at odds with US-backed norms.[3]

China's leadership also has endeavored at various times to appear more in line with international norms regarding issues affecting political power and processes in China. Chinese officials have engaged in a broad range of discussions, dialogues, and agreements with various countries and international organizations designed to advance political rights in line with world norms supported by the United States. China has signed international covenants dealing with economic, social, and political rights. Chinese leaders routinely pledge cooperation with other countries in promoting human rights. They have fostered reforms emphasizing the rule of law, greater transparency, and accountability; and promoting democracy and democratic decision making in handling various human rights concerns in China. At times, the progress of Chinese reform in these areas has encouraged some Chinese and foreign specialists to anticipate continued change leading to the transformation of China's authoritarian one-party political system.[4] However, other specialists in China and abroad see the Chinese leadership as following policies of adaptation and adjustment in the area of political reform and related human rights.[5] The reforms in these areas are seen as undermining neither Chinese leadership control of political power in China nor what is viewed as the overriding concern of Chinese leaders to sustain and strengthen one-party rule in China through authoritarian as well as more liberal means.

CHANGING IMPORTANCE OF HUMAN RIGHTS ISSUES, 1969–2017

It's hard to imagine two societies and governments with more different sets of values than the United States and Maoist China. The progress made in US-China reconciliation during the initial efforts of normalization begun by President Richard Nixon and Chairman Mao Zedong is a testament to the pragmatism of their respective leaderships. Other interests—notably each country's need for support in the face of rising Soviet power and other complications—overrode differences regarding political and other values that divided the United States and China.[6]

President Jimmy Carter rose to power on a platform pledging to devote more concern to American political values in the conduct of US foreign policy. He pledged to put aside the realpolitik calculations seen as prevalent in the policies of the Nixon and Gerald Ford administrations. This shift in policy resulted in divergence and confrontation between the United States and some authoritarian governments, but it had little effect on US relations with China. In the case of China, President Carter and his key aides pursued the pragmatic search for strategic leverage begun by Nixon; they did not allow differences over human rights and values to impede advances in relations, leading to the normalization of diplomatic relations in 1979.[7]

During the 1970s, there were signs of domestic debate and disagreement in both the United States and China over issues involving how the two countries differed with regard to values and human rights and the tendencies of the respective governments to give little overt attention to these differences in the pursuit of other interests. Leadership debate in China at the end of the Maoist period included disagreements over the alleged corrupting effect American and broader Western values would have on the prevailing authoritarian political order and social and economic structure of China. Removal of the radical Chinese leadership faction known as the Gang of Four following Mao's death in 1976 reduced the debate. Deng Xiaoping's return to power in 1978 coincided with a remarkable demonstration of freer speech in the posting of various proposals for reform, individual freedom, and democracy in Beijing's so-called Democracy Wall. After one year of publicizing proposals for sometimes radical reform, including some calling for the end of Communist rule in China, the Chinese leadership closed off this channel of free speech and arrested and imprisoned some prominent reform advocates.[8]

American public and elite opinion supported Nixon's opening to China and gave comparatively little attention to human rights issues in relations with China. A minority of media commentators, specialists, members of Congress, and other influential Americans called attention to President Carter's apparent double standard in pushing human rights issues in relations with various authoritarian governments, but not doing so in his administration's approach to China. The Democracy Wall caught the attention of the American and other foreign media and their audiences. As China opened to greater foreign contact and Chinese intellectuals were able to write about some of the searing experiences of Maoist rule, reporters, academic specialists, and other American and foreign commentators showed greater awareness of the enormous abuses of human rights in China and the wide gap between the United States and China over political and other values.[9]

The disclosures of human rights abuses in Maoist China and the closing of the Democracy Wall and arrests and imprisonment of prominent dissidents had little effect on the forward momentum in US-China relations. Deng Xiaoping's reform programs were widely seen in the United States and elsewhere in the West to be advancing the material well-being of Chinese people while curbing many of the capricious uses of authoritarian administrative power that had prevailed during the Maoist period. Broadly gauged human rights conditions in China were seen to be improving with post-Mao economic and political reforms and opening to greater international interchange. Some American officials, advocacy groups, and media commentators focused on the negative implications of China's continued Communist rule for imprisoned or otherwise suppressed political dissidents, and for religious and ethnic groups, notably Tibetan followers of the Dalai Lama. US supporters of democracy and self-determination for Taiwan also joined Americans pressing for continued US support for Taiwan's status separate from the control of China's Communist government. In contrast, President Ronald Reagan seemed to capture the generally more optimistic American view about trends in China during his remarks at the time of his official visit to China in 1984. Reagan approved of emerging capitalist economic development in China and tended to soft-pedal criticism of China's authoritarian political system, refer-ring to "so-called Communist China," a sharp contrast with his trademark criticism of the "evil empire" seen as prevalent in the Communist-ruled Soviet Union.[10]

The economic and political reforms in China in the 1980s saw continued Chinese debate over the implications of closer Chinese interchange with the United States and the West. American and broader Western values of indi-vidual freedom were widely seen in elite and public opinion in China as a threat to the Communist system in China. Conservatives railed against the danger of the so-called spiritual pollution from US political values and cul-ture that would undermine and weaken Chinese resiliency and power in the face of international forces, including the United States, that were often seen as unfriendly to China. The conservatives included key leaders in the old guard in the CCP hierarchy, and many other senior leaders said to be retired but who actually exerted great influence in Chinese decision making. The conservatives continued to influence the reformists leading the Chinese Communist government, forcing them to curb initiatives at home and abroad that might undercut the traditional power and prerogatives of Communist rule in China.[11]

The conservative leaders played a key role in support of the decision to suppress the demonstrators in Tiananmen Square in Beijing and in other Chinese cities in June 1989. Communist Party leaders advocating more mod-erate treatment of the demonstrators and continued political reform were removed from power. Over time, a Chinese leadership consensus emerged in favor of continued economic reform and outreach to the world for the benefit of Chinese modernization and development, on the one hand; and strong efforts, on the other hand, to sustain authoritarian political rule in China and to resist pressures and other influences coming from US and Western govern-ments and other advocates of political and other change that could lead to the end of CCP rule in China. With the demise of the Soviet Union, the main "threat" to China was seen to come from the United States and its allies. The US and other Western governments and a broad array of nongovernmental forces in these countries were seen to be pressing and undermining Commu-nist Party rule and endeavoring to weaken and constrain its influence in Asian and world affairs.[12]

A resumption of more moderate policies of engagement with China by the United States and other governments later in the 1990s helped reassure Chinese authorities of the intentions of those governments, and it diminished Chinese concern with the immediate threat of US and other pressure regard-ing human rights and American values. But the Communist authorities re-mained on guard against US values; they were diligent and generally effec-tive in suppressing political dissidents and perceived deviant religious organ-izations, ethnic groups, and other nongovernmental organizations (NGOs) and individuals. The latter organizations and individuals sometimes received support from individuals and groups, including some government-sponsored organizations, in the United States or other countries favoring change in China's authoritarian political system in line with American and broader Western values. [13]

The Chinese crackdown on the Tiananmen demonstrators and the emerging consensus in the Chinese leadership on the need for a continued hard line against political dissent and unauthorized religious and ethnic movements placed human rights issues in the forefront of American differences with China. For a period after the Tiananmen crackdown, human rights advocates seemed to have the initiative in setting US policy toward China. The George H. W. Bush administration was on the defensive, endeavoring to preserve key elements of the US partnership with China despite the ending of the Cold War and the perceived diminished importance of China as a counterweight to the now sharply declining Soviet Union. Congressional leaders for a few months gave top priority to the often idiosyncratic and inconsistent views of Chinese students in the United States advocating reform in China and punishment for the Chinese authorities suppressing the demonstrators at Tiananmen. [14]

For more than a decade, the annual congressional consideration of the president's decision to renew most favored nation (MFN) trade status for China provided an opportunity for American human rights advocates to publicize their criticisms of China and to seek government as well as media and broader public support for their efforts. Human rights advocates were soon joined by other Americans with interests regarding economic and security relations involving China, and advocates for stronger US support for Taiwan, Tibet, and political rights in Hong Kong. As noted in chapter 5, the criticism of Chinese policies and practices in Congress was pervasive, though congressional commitment to a harder line against China often seemed thin. Partisan motives apart from concern with human rights and other differences with China frequently appeared to motivate critics of Chinese policies involved in the annual debates over whether to renew MFN trade treatment for China. When crises emerged in other areas affecting Sino-American interests, as they did during the war over Iraq's invasion of Kuwait in 1990 and the Taiwan Straits crisis of 1995–96, the congressional criticism of China's human rights policies and practices subsided as American officials pursued pragmatic interaction with the Chinese government. The Bill Clinton administration succeeded in ending the annual congressional deliberations over China by reaching agreement with China on entry into the WTO and getting Congress to pass related legislation granting China permanent normal trade relations with the United States. [15]

Developments in the twenty-first century have reinforced American tendencies to deal pragmatically with China and to play down differences. The terrorist attack on America in 2001 and the global economic crisis beginning in 2008–9 prompted US leaders to minimize differences over human rights and related values in pursuit of closer cooperation with China for the sake of other American interests. However, these issues continued to be raised by US leaders in discussions with China. President George W. Bush continued to voice concern with human rights issues, especially freedom of religion in China. He met several times with the Dalai Lama and also met with prominent political dissidents from China.[16]

President Barack Obama seemed to capture the recent balance in the US government's concerns with human rights issues when he spoke to the annual Sino-American leadership dialogue meeting in Washington in July 2009. He advised his Chinese colleagues that the American government did not seek to force China to conform to its view of human rights, but it would nonetheless continue to press China and others to conform to the values of human rights so important to the United States. He said:

> Support for human rights and human dignity is ingrained in America. Our nation is made up of immigrants from every part of the world. We have protected our unity and struggled to perfect our union by extending basic rights to all our people. And those rights include the freedom to speak your mind, to worship your God, and to choose your leaders. They are not things that we seek to impose—this is who we are. It guides our openness to one another and the world.[17]

Chinese leaders for their part highlighted the great progress made in advancing economic, social, and other considerations affecting the lives of the vast majority of Chinese people during the post-Mao period. Public opinion in China tended to be supportive of prevailing conditions in the country. Chinese officials also underlined China's increasing cooperation with foreign governments and international organizations to promote human rights abroad. They nonetheless drew a line against US and other foreign government and nongovernment efforts to interfere in Chinese internal affairs in ways that would undermine the sovereignty of China and the integrity of its Communist institutions. They also strongly opposed US and Western-backed efforts supporting popular empowerment against foreign authoritarian rulers in various so-called color revolutions (peaceful democratic movements involving mass demonstrations supported by Western governments and nongovernment groups that toppled post-Communist authoritarian administrations in such former Soviet states as Georgia, Ukraine, and Kyrgyzstan)[18] and the uprisings seen in the Middle East in the so-called Arab Spring. They resisted foreign efforts to spotlight Chinese deviations from international norms in international organizations or world media.[19]

At times, these diverging Sino-American approaches have come together in ways that complicate US-China relations. For example, an unanticipated uprising in Tibet in March 2008 saw a strenuous Chinese crackdown against dissent in Tibet. The developments received widespread negative media treatment in the United States and other Western countries. They coincided with an international Olympic Torch Relay that the Chinese government had organized leading up to the summer Olympic Games in China in 2008. The Olympic Torch Relay traveled through several Western countries, including the United States, and was greeted by hostile demonstrators supporting Tibetan rights and condemning Chinese policies. Some Western leaders vacillated on whether to participate in the opening ceremony of the Summer Olympics. Chinese official and public resentment against the Western demonstrations, supportive media coverage, and political leaders sympathetic to the Dalai Lama and Tibetan rights were strong. President Bush said firmly that he would attend the summer games in China, easing the tension in Sino-American relations over the episode, but the Tibet issue remained highly sensitive in Chinese interaction with some West European countries, and it then became a focal point of Chinese pressure on the incoming Obama administration. President Obama delayed a meeting with the Dalai Lama so as not to complicate his first visit to China in November 2009. He met with the Tibetan leader in February 2010, prompting much tougher Chinese criticism than seen in earlier US presidential meetings with the Dalai Lama. That Chinese pressure was viewed by Americans as one of several signs of growing Chinese assertiveness over differences with the United States.[20]

Broadly speaking, human rights remained a secondary concern in American policy toward China during the Obama administration. Incoming President Donald Trump promised a "pragmatic" approach to human rights issues in China and elsewhere, treating them with lower priority than economic and security interests of the United States. Despite such US government practice, the impact of policies and practices of China's more assertive and international active leader, Xi Jinping, strongly affected American concerns about human rights in China. His government tightened political controls over the media, academic institutions, and cultural activities; arrested dissidents and lawyers defending dissidents; and curbed NGOs supported by the United States and others in the West that were promoting change seen as challenging to CCP rule. The Xi government's push for the CCP's greater authoritarianism and firmer control of public discourse, social interchange, and key elements of the Chinese economy added to the perception widely held among specialists, media, various interest groups, and members of Congress that the decades of American and Western engagement in China were moving in the wrong direction and perhaps leading to failure. The above-noted anticipated result of closer engagement with China was a hoped-for, gradual political liberalization in China going along with China's greater involvement in world affairs. The actual result was increasingly seen as a much stronger Chinese government more capable of societal and economic management and control that effectively squelched signs of dissent or other liberalization.[21]

CONTEMPORARY HUMAN RIGHTS PRACTICES AND ISSUES

Early in the twenty-first century, the Chinese government and party leader Hu Jintao (2002–12) continued efforts to deal with public grievances and domestic and foreign calls for redress and reform while suppressing activists who attempted to organize mass protests or create organizations at odds with CCP rule. The results were some improvements in human rights along with continued serious abuses. On the one hand, China's developing legal system still featured corruption and political interference, but it also provided activists in China with tools with which to promote human rights. Although generally supportive of the status quo, the urban middle class showed increased willingness to engage in narrowly targeted protests against local government policies. Their activism added to more widespread social unrest among wage laborers and rural residents demonstrating against local government policies and practices and other conditions. Despite a massive effort by the Chinese authorities to control and censor information available to the public, the Internet and other communications technologies made it more difficult for the government to clamp down on information as fully as before. On the other hand, the human rights abuses by Chinese authorities included unlawful killings by security forces, torture, unlawful detention, the excessive use of state security laws to imprison political dissidents, coercive family planning policies and practices, state control of information, and religious and ethnic persecution. Tibetan, ethnic Uighur Muslims, and Falun Gong adherents were singled out for especially harsh treatment.[22]

The US government duly acknowledged Chinese advances and shortcomings, notably in a series of congressionally supported official reports including the State Department's annual report on human rights conditions in world countries. US government efforts to promote human rights in China included formal criticism of the Chinese government's policies and practices, official bilateral dialogues, public diplomacy, congressionally sponsored legislation, hearings, visits, and research. The US government also provided funding for rule of law, civil society development, participatory government, labor rights, preserving Tibetan culture, Internet access, and other related programs in China. The US government attention to human rights conditions in China was backed by more wide-ranging media coverage of human rights conditions in China and issues in US-China relations and by reports and other publicity from prominent nongovernment groups and individuals in the United States with a strong interest in promoting advancement of human rights conditions in China.[23]

American activism and pressure on China regarding human rights issues were tempered by an ongoing debate on whether human rights conditions in China were improving or not. On the negative side were US media, congressional, and other commentators who highlighted evidence of increasing Chinese legal restrictions on freedoms and cases of political and religious persecution. The annual State Department reports on human rights conditions in China were said by some to register no major or overall improvements. On the positive side were those who emphasized the expansion of economic and social freedoms in people's lives. [24]

Further complicating the debate were the efforts of the Chinese government to become more populist, accountable, and law-based, while rejecting Western democracy and more far-reaching political reforms. Party leader and President Hu Jintao and other senior officials showed sympathy with segments of the population who were left behind in the Chinese economic advance. The central leadership also acknowledged human rights as a concern of the state, continued to develop legal institutions, and implemented limited institutional restraints on the exercise of state power. These steps forward came amid continuing administrative practices that retained a large degree of arbitrary power for the ruling authorities. [25]

Indeed, the American debate about human rights conditions in China mirrored a debate among Chinese authorities on where to strike the balance between efforts to improve governance and reduce sources of social and political instability through anticorruption campaigns, and the implementation of political reforms and efforts to check mass pressures for greater change. Some Chinese leaders expressed fears that China's small but growing civil society, combined with foreign government and nongovernment assistance for advocacy groups in China, could bring about a "color revolution" in China. With this kind of fear in mind and with continuing determination to sustain and support CCP rule in China, the Chinese authorities enacted legislation aimed at preventing human rights abuses, but without protecting the activities of human rights activists who were subject to apparently arbitrary arrest and detention; it tolerated protests against official policies, but arrested protest leaders and organizers; public discourse on a wide variety of topics became routine, but politically sensitive issues remained off-limits. [26]

Getting the right balance of flexibility and coercion seemed especially important as increasing economic and social changes fostered tensions along with growing rights consciousness and social activism. Many efforts by citizens to express grievances and demand redress, having been met by government inaction or opposition, erupted into large-scale public protests. [27]

The mixed picture of positives and negatives in Chinese human rights policies and behavior was well illustrated in the annual State Department reports on conditions in China, which tended to focus on infractions and other negative developments, and assessments by Chinese and foreign specialists highlighting various positive Chinese reforms and advances. Thus, the State Department reports in this period noted episodes of unlawful or politically motivated killings, including people who died in detention because of torture. Torture seemed to be used commonly against Falun Gong adherents, Tibetans, Uighur Muslims, and other prisoners of conscience as well as criminal suspects. The Re-Education through Labor system, in which individuals were held in administrative detention for antisocial activity, without formal charges or trial, for a period up to four years, remained a central feature of social and political control in China. Unlawful detention and house arrest remained widespread, particularly against human rights activists, lawyers, and journalists sympathetic to their cause, and leaders of unofficial Christian churches. Thousands of persons were viewed by the State Department as political prisoners, serving jail time for "endangering state security" or the former political crime of "counterrevolution." China's "one-child policy" continued with fewer reports of occurrences that were more common in earlier decades[28] of coercive abortions, forced sterilization, and other unlawful government actions against individuals.

This list of infractions and violations of human rights from the perspective of the American government was balanced by positive developments assisting greater freedom and helping ensure human rights. NGOs were often encouraged by the authorities to remain active in order to improve governance and to allow people to give vent to their frustrations in ways that do not directly oppose one-party rule. Some representatives from these organizations and others outside the CCP-controlled system became more involved in advising with regard to government policies and behavior on a variety of topics. Media freedom was expanded in order to target corruption and other abuses of power. Freedom of worship within the range of government-approved religious organizations and churches remained strong; freedom of movement was enhanced by government policies that tried to accommodate the more than 10 percent of Chinese citizens who left their rural homesteads to pursue opportunities in the wealthier urban areas.[29]

The purpose and scope of NGOs grew substantially in this period. At this time early in the twenty-first century. there are more than three hundred thousand registered NGOs in China and more than one million in total, including more than two hundred international organizations. Environmental groups were at the forefront of NGO development in China. Other areas of NGO activity included poverty alleviation, rural development, public health, education, and legal aid. The Chinese government from time to time tightened restrictions on NGOs and voiced opposition to foreign support for groups pushing reforms not favored by the Chinese authorities, but the overall scope and activism of the NGOs continued to grow.[30]

Another area of positive development was the human rights legislation and reforms enacted by the Chinese government. In 2006 the government enacted prohibitions of specific acts of torture and requirements that interrogations of suspects of major crimes be recorded. Use of the death penalty, still egregiously high by international standards, declined markedly under instituted review by the Supreme People's Court. A new Labor Contract Law went into effect in 2008, prompting increases in dispute arbitration cases and lawsuits over wages and benefits. Farmers were provided with new measures in 2008 that allowed them more easily to lease, transfer, and sell rights to property allocated to them by the state. Government measures took effect in 2008 to require government institutions, especially local government administrations seen as more prone to corruption than other government bodies, to reveal financial accounts related to land seizures in rural areas. Responding to international criticism of organ transplants for profit from executed prisoners, the government enacted new regulations stipulating that the donation of organs for transplant must be free and voluntary.[31]

The advent of party and government leader Xi Jinping (2012–) has seen much greater emphasis on Communist Party control and the dangers posed by liberalizing forces inside China that are supported from abroad. There has been particularly strong concern over the activities of NGOs potentially challenging authoritarian rule. There has been a resurgence of official state-sponsored Chinese propaganda focused on the United States and other so-called hostile foreign forces as threats to China's stability and well-being. Domestically, the overall message fosters public suspicion of the United States and of individuals and NGOs in China with ties to the United States, Japan, or others associated with Western values. Meanwhile, China's impressive, well-financed and broad-ranging public diplomacy and propaganda efforts abroad feature media distortions, censorship, and defamation of democratic values. When combined with stepped-up Chinese pressure tactics and control efforts targeted against individuals and organizations abroad that are seen as adverse by the CCP regime, the result is a more serious challenge to American-supported values and norms.[32]

When Xi Jinping became general secretary of the CCP in 2012, he began carrying out a crackdown on dissent and activism that surprised many observers for its scope and severity; it included the detentions and arrests of hundreds of government critics, human rights lawyers, well-known bloggers, investigative journalists, outspoken academics, civil society leaders, and ethnic minorities. Indictments for state security crimes, which often are political in nature, rose in 2013 to 1,384 cases, the highest level since the Tibetan unrest of 2008. The government imposed growing restrictions on Chinese microblogging and mobile text services, which have become important sources of news for many Chinese people and platforms for public opinion. The Chinese government passed or considered new laws that

- strengthened the role of the state security apparatus in overseeing a wide range of social activities, including those of foreign NGOs
- placed additional restrictions on defense lawyers
- authorized greater governmental controls over the Internet[33]

Summarizing adverse conditions in 2016, the State Department disclosed in its annual human rights report that severe repression and coercion was targeted against organizations and individuals involved in civil and political rights advocacy; and such severe repression also was targeted against organizations and individuals involved with public interest and ethnic minority issues. Past hopes that free elections would spread from use in the very lowest levels of governance were thwarted. Citizens did not have the right to choose their government. Authorities prevented independent candidates from running in elections, even on such low levels as selecting delegates to local people's congresses. Citizens had limited forms of redress against official abuse. Other serious human rights abuses included arbitrary or unlawful deprivation of life; executions without due process; illegal detentions at unofficial holding facilities known as "black jails"; torture and coerced confessions of prisoners; and detention and harassment of journalists, lawyers, writers, bloggers, dissidents, petitioners, and others whose actions the authorities deemed unacceptable. There was also a lack of due process in judicial proceedings; political control of courts and judges; closed trials; the use of administrative detention; failure to protect refugees and asylum seekers; extrajudicial disappearances of citizens; restrictions on NGOs; and discrimination against women, minorities, and persons with disabilities. The government imposed a coercive birth-limitation policy that, despite lifting one-child-per-family restrictions, denied women the right to decide the number of their children and in some cases resulted in forced abortions (sometimes at advanced stages of pregnancy). On the work front, severe labor restrictions continued.[34]

Human Rights Issues

A wide range of human rights issues continue to prompt critical attention from American officials in the Congress and the executive branch of government as well as American media, human rights groups, and other groups and individuals with an interest. Some issues—like the status of student demonstrators and others arrested during the Tiananmen crackdown and those suffering as a result of widespread abuses in China's family planning regime—have subsided with the passage of time and changed circumstances. Others, like the human rights conditions in Tibet and among Uighur Muslims in China's restive Xinjiang region, have become more salient as a result of violence in both Tibet and Xinjiang in recent years. Still others, like the status and prospects of pro-democracy advocates in Hong Kong, have waned and then revived as a result of changing circumstances in Hong Kong. Meanwhile, China's increasingly strong and assertive efforts abroad to manipulate opinion and squelch dissent and opposition to the Communist government and its policies and practices have raised a new set of recently prominent human rights concerns.[35]

Persecution of Political Dissent

China's state security law is used liberally and often arbitrarily against political dissidents. In May 2013 the CCP issued a classified directive (Document No. 9) identifying seven "false ideological trends, positions, and activities," largely aimed at the media and liberal academics. According to the document, topics to be avoided in public discussion include universal values, constitutional democracy, freedom of the press, civil society, civil rights, an independent judiciary, and criticism of the CCP. Universities have been warned against using textbooks that spread "Western values" and making remarks that "defame the rule of the Communist Party."[36]

According to the Congressional Research Service and the Department of State, a concurrent crackdown included detentions and arrests of well-known bloggers, investigative journalists, outspoken academics, civil society leaders, human rights attorneys, and ethnic minorities. Many of them had no apparent political agenda or for years had avoided criminal charges. An estimated 160 to 200 activists were arrested or detained in 2013, and this trend accelerated in 2014. In July 2015 roughly 300 human rights lawyers and activists were arrested, detained, or put under surveillance. Many of the lawyers were released after receiving warnings to cease their activities, but several remained in detention or their whereabouts remained unknown. As of the end of 2016, 16 individuals detained as a result of the July 2015 roundup remained in pretrial detention at undisclosed locations without access to attorneys or to their family members.[37]

Other focal points of Chinese authorities cracking down on dissent involved a number of extraterritorial disappearances occurring during 2015–16. As disclosed in the State Department's human rights report, journalist Li Xin, who fled to India in 2015 after allegedly leaking documents detailing the CCP's propaganda policies, went missing on a train in Thailand in January and later reappeared in China in custody of security officials. He told his wife by telephone that he had returned voluntarily, but Thai immigration officials told the media they had no exit record for Li. Five men working in Hong Kong's publishing industry disappeared between October and December 2015. In addition to being Hong Kong residents, two had foreign citizenship, which was ignored by the Chinese government in its repression efforts. Gui Minhai was a Swedish citizen and was taken while he was in

Thailand; Lee Bo was a British citizen taken from Hong Kong. Media coverage of the cases noted that the men worked for a publishing house and bookstore in Hong Kong that was known for selling books critical of the CCP and its leaders. In a televised "confession" released by Chinese authorities, Gui Minhai said he had "voluntarily returned" to China to "bear the responsibility" for a traffic accident that supposedly occurred more than a decade before. Another bookseller, Hong Kong resident Lam Wing Kee, was detained at the border crossing into Shenzhen in October 2015 and released after five months. Upon his return to Hong Kong, Lam immediately recanted his televised confession, saying it was scripted and recorded under extreme pressure. He also said he was forced to sign away his legal rights when he was taken to Ningbo by men who claimed they were from a "central special unit." With the exception of Swedish citizen Gui Minhai, the other detained booksellers were released during the year but remained under surveillance, travel restrictions, and the threat of punishment after returning to Hong Kong. In early 2017 Gui's location—presumably under incommunicado detention in the mainland—remained unknown.[38]

Meanwhile the government still had not provided a comprehensive, credible accounting of all those killed, missing, or detained in connection with the violent suppression of the 1989 Tiananmen demonstrations. As reported by the Department of State, the Dui Hua Foundation said that Miao Deshun, the last known political prisoner dating from the Tiananmen era, was released during 2016. Many activists who were involved in the 1989 demonstrations and their family members continued to suffer official harassment. Chen Yunfei, arrested in 2015 for visiting the grave of a Tiananmen victim, was formally brought to trial in July 2016 on charges of "picking quarrels and provoking troubles." Chengdu authorities subsequently postponed his trial without explanation. In December a rescheduled hearing was also reportedly delayed after Chen dismissed his lawyers, citing their harassment at the hands of local security officials outside the courthouse. Others who attempted to commemorate the protests and associated deaths were themselves detained or otherwise targeted. In late May 2016, seven activists who appeared in a photograph marking the massacre's twenty-seventh anniversary were detained on suspicion of "picking quarrels and provoking troubles." They were released several weeks later. In June, Chengdu activists Fu Hailu, Zhang Junyong, Luo Yufu, and Chen Bing were detained for allegedly creating and marketing a liquor whose label commemorated the 1989 crackdown. They faced charges of "inciting subversion" and were held in the Chengdu Municipal Detention Center.[39]

Government officials continued to deny holding any political prisoners, asserting that persons were detained not for their political or religious views but because they violated the law. Authorities, however, continued to imprison citizens for reasons related to politics and religion. According to the

Department of State, tens of thousands of political prisoners remained incarcerated, most in prisons and some in administrative detention. The government did not grant international humanitarian organizations access to political prisoners.[40]

As reported by the Department of State, political prisoners were granted early release at lower rates than other prisoners. The Dui Hua Foundation estimated that more than one hundred prisoners were still serving sentences for counterrevolution and hooliganism, two crimes removed from the criminal code in 1997. Thousands of others were serving sentences for political and religious offenses, including "endangering state security" and "cult" offenses covered under Article 300 of the criminal code, crimes introduced in 1997. The government neither reviewed the cases of those charged before 1997 with counterrevolution and hooliganism nor released persons jailed for nonviolent offenses under repealed provisions.[41]

State Control of Information

The state authorities directly control the largest mass media outlets; they pressure other media regarding major or sensitive stories, and they impose severe measures against state critics. The CCP and government have continued to maintain ultimate authority over all published, online, or broadcast material. Officially, only state-run media outlets have government approval to cover CCP leaders or other topics deemed sensitive. While it did not dictate all content to be published or broadcast, the CCP and the government had unchecked authority to mandate if, when, and how particular issues were reported or to order that they not be reported at all.

As disclosed by the Department of State and other observers,[42] the government continued to strictly monitor the press and media, including film and television, via its broadcast and press regulatory body, the State Administration of Press, Publication, Radio, Film, and Television (SAPPRFT). The Cyberspace Administration of China (CAC) regulates online news media. As of 2017, all books and magazines continue to require state-issued publication numbers, which are expensive and often difficult to obtain. As in the past, nearly all print and broadcast media as well as book publishers are affiliated with the CCP or government. There are a small number of print publications with some private ownership interest but no privately owned television or radio stations. There are growing numbers of privately owned online media. The CCP has directed the domestic media to refrain from reporting on certain subjects, and traditional broadcast programming requires government approval. The SAPPRFT has announced that satellite television channels may broadcast no more than two imported television programs each year during prime-time hours and that imported programs must receive the approval of local regulators at least two months in advance.

In a well-publicized February 19, 2016, visit to the three main state and CCP news organizations—the Xinhua News Agency, CCTV, and the *People's Daily*—President Xi said, "Party and state-run media are the propaganda battlefield of the party and the government, [and] must bear the surname of the party. All of the party's news and public opinion work must embody the party's will, reflect the party's ideas, defend the authority of the Party Central Committee, [and] defend the unity of the party."[43]

China has the world's largest number of Internet users, estimated at more than 730 million people.[44] The Congressional Research Service said that the government of the People's Republic of China (PRC), with one of the most thorough and aggressive Internet censorship systems in the world, has attempted to control and monitor Internet use in China, with mixed results. Internet users have developed ways to circumvent censorship, and politically sensitive news and opinion often get widely disseminated, if only fleetingly, due to the sheer volume of online traffic. The government and Chinese netizens have engaged in a game of cat and mouse, with new communications technologies and services and novel censorship circumvention methods challenging the government's technological and human efforts to control the Web, followed by new government regulations and counter efforts, and then a repeat of the cycle. The state has the capability to block news of events and to partially shut down the Internet. In Xinjiang, the government blocked the Internet for ten months following the ethnic unrest of 2009, and it continues to do so in selected areas of the country from time to time. The monitoring and disruption of telephone and Internet communications reportedly were widespread in Xinjiang and Tibetan areas in 2013. Google services, including Gmail, were intermittently blocked in 2014.[45]

Censorship of microblog posts reportedly increased fivefold during the height of the Hong Kong democracy protests in September 2014. Continuously blocked websites, social networking sites, and file sharing sites include Radio Free Asia; Voice of America (Chinese language); international human rights websites, including those related to Tibet and Falun Gong; many Taiwanese news sites; Facebook; Twitter; and YouTube. Many English-language news sites, including the *Washington Post* and the *Wall Street Journal*, are generally accessible or occasionally or selectively censored. The *New York Times* and Bloomberg websites have been blocked since 2012 after they reported on the personal wealth of Chinese leaders. In 2014 access to the BBC was interrupted.[46]

As reported by the Congressional Research Service, commonly barred Internet searches and microblog postings include those with direct and indirect or disguised references to Tibetan policies; the Tiananmen suppression of 1989; Falun Gong; PRC leaders and dissidents who have been involved in recent scandals, events, or issues that authorities deem to be politically sensitive; discussions of democracy; sensitive foreign affairs issues; and sexual material. Other major areas that authorities target for occasional censorship include the following: controversial policies and government wrongdoing, public health and safety, foreign affairs, civil society, and media and censorship policies.[47]

Other developments highlighted by the Congressional Research Service include reported assessments that the majority of Internet users in China do not engage the medium for political purposes, or that they accept the government's justification that it regulates the Internet in order to control illegal, harmful, or dangerous online content, services, and activities. A reported two million censors, mostly young college graduates, are employed as "public opinion analysts" in the government and at major Internet service providers to scan messages already screened by computer and delete or block posts with sensitive or inappropriate political or social content. And the government reportedly also has employed tens of thousands of students and other Internet commentators, known as the "50 Cent Army," to post pro-government comments and express views critical of the United States and democracy on websites, bulletin boards, and chat rooms. Meanwhile, US communications and media companies are being excluded from China unless they comply with Chinese demands to put their servers inside the country, hand over proprietary codes, and comply with the censorship of content.[48]

Religious and Ethnic Issues

American media and other foreign sources have shown that the extent of religious freedom varies widely within China. Participation in officially sanctioned religious activity has increased in recent years. The PRC Constitution protects "normal" religious activities and those that do not "disrupt public order, impair the health of citizens or interfere with the educational system of the state." Chinese regulations enacted in 2005 protect the rights of registered religious groups to publish literature, collect donations, possess property, and train and approve clergy. In 2008 the State Administration for Religious Affairs (SARA) established a new unit to supervise folk religions as well as religions outside the five officially recognized major religions (Buddhism, Protestantism, Roman Catholicism, Daoism, and Islam), including the Eastern Orthodox Church and the Church of Jesus Christ of Latter-day Saints. The foreign media and other accounts asserted that these laws grant the government continued broad authority in determining what religious groups are lawful and to deny protections to others.[49]

As reported by US government agencies and various US and other foreign media, the religious and religious-ethnic groups that have clashed the most with the state in recent years have been unregistered Protestant and Catholic congregations, Tibetan Buddhists, and the Uighur Muslims in the Xinjiang Uighur Autonomous Region (XUAR). The International Religious

Freedom Act of 1998 (PL 105-292) established the United States Commission on International Religious Freedom to monitor religious freedom around the world and make policy recommendations to the president and Congress. Based largely on Commission reports, the State Department has annually identified China as a "country of particular concern" on account of "particularly severe violations of religious freedom." This designation has subjected China to US sanctions in accordance with provisions of PL 105-292, which have involved bans of US exports of crime control and detection instruments and equipment to China.[50]

Chinese Christians

American-based interest groups, American media, and US government reports disclose that Christians in China find increasing acceptance in Chinese society and, within limits, from the Chinese government. The Chinese leadership at times has acknowledged the positive roles that Christianity has played and can play in promoting social development and welfare. Yet it remains wary of the Christian church's power as a source of autonomous organization potentially challenging Communist rule.[51]

By some estimates of foreign specialists and reporters, the number of Christians in China ranges from about forty million to more than sixty million, with nearly two-thirds gathering in unofficial churches not approved by the Chinese authorities. A rise of religious memberships in China is attributed by foreign reports to the greater freedom and affluence among many Chinese and the need to cope with dramatic social and economic changes.[52]

Many unofficial Protestant churches, also known as "house churches" or "home gatherings" by the government, lack legal protection and remain vulnerable to the often unchecked authority of local officials. According to reports from American agencies, interest groups, media, and other foreign sources, in some regions and large cities, particularly in southern China, unregistered congregations meet with little or no state interference, while in other provinces and many rural areas, such independent gatherings experience harassment by local authorities, and their leaders have been beaten, detained, and imprisoned.[53]

Many Chinese Protestants reject the official church, known as the Three-Self Patriotic Movement, for political and theological reasons. The government claims it has encouraged unofficial Protestant churches to register with the state but that many of them have been discouraged from doing so by foreign Christian groups. Chinese pressure on such unofficial churches has included arresting leaders of house churches, harassing members of congregations, shutting down places of worship, and denying visas to foreign missionaries.[54]

China has engaged in dialogue with the Vatican, which broke ties with China in 1951. Both sides express an interest in improved relations. One of the key obstacles to normalization has been China's rejection of the Holy See's authority to appoint bishops. In April 2015 a Chinese bishop was ordained in Guangdong province with the tacit consent of the Vatican. Beijing and Pope Francis have expressed interest in improving relations. Obstacles remain, however, particularly regarding the appointment of bishops, the Vatican's diplomatic ties with Taiwan, and the Vatican's stances on religious freedom in China.[55]

Tibetans

Religious freedom and human rights issues in Tibet have a long history in Sino-American relations. Partly because of past clandestine US support for Tibetan insurgencies against Chinese rule following the escape to India from Chinese rule in Tibet by the Dalai Lama and many thousands of his followers in the late 1950s, the Chinese government remains wary of American intentions regarding Tibet. Even after the normalization of US diplomatic relations with China, US ambitions to challenge Chinese sovereignty over Tibet have been revealed from time to time as Congress has asserted its view of Tibet as a separate country, though the US administration consistently accepts Chinese sovereignty over Tibet. The intertwined issues of sovereignty, border security, and ethnic and religious freedom make the issue of Tibet difficult to manage in Sino-American relations. Added to the mix is the attraction of many Americans to the Dalai Lama, the leader of Tibetans abroad who also enjoys a strong but suppressed following among Tibetans in China.[56]

Coming against this background, a series of demonstrations on March 10, 2008, began in Lhasa and other Tibetan regions of China to mark the forty-ninth anniversary of an unsuccessful Tibetan uprising against Chinese rule in 1959. The demonstrations appeared to begin peacefully with small groups that were then contained by security forces. But the protests and the response of the PRC authorities escalated in the ensuing days, spreading from the Tibetan Autonomous Region into parts of Sichuan, Gansu, and Qinghai Provinces with Tibetan populations. By March 14, 2008, mobs of angry people were burning and looting establishments in downtown Lhasa. Authorities of the PRC responded by sealing off Tibet and bringing in large-scale security forces. The Chinese government defended its actions as appropriate and necessary to restore civil order and prevent further violence. Media, interest groups, and some officials in the West responded to the Chinese actions by calling for boycotts of the opening ceremonies of the Beijing Olympics and calling on China to hold talks with the Dalai Lama.[57]

The Chinese government and many Chinese people see China as having provided Tibet with extensive economic assistance and development using money from central government and provincial government coffers, and Chinese officials often seem perplexed at the simmering anger many Tibetans nevertheless retain against them. Despite economic development, Tibetans charge that the PRC interferes with Tibetan culture and religion. They cite as examples: Beijing's interference in 1995 in the choice of the Panchen Lama, Tibet's second-highest-ranking personage; enactment of a "reincarnation law" in 2007 requiring Buddhist monks who wish to reincarnate to obtain prior approval from Beijing; and China's policy of conducting "patriotic education" campaigns, as well as efforts to foster atheism, among the Tibetan religious community. The PRC defends the campaigns as tools that among other things help monks become loyal, law-abiding citizens of China.[58]

Increasingly expansive government controls on Tibetan religious life and practice have caused or contributed to discontent in Tibetan areas. The State Department has annually reported "serious human rights abuses" of Tibetans, including extrajudicial detentions and killings, arbitrary arrests, and severe mistreatment, torture, and deaths of Tibetan detainees and prisoners of conscience. In addition to chafing at religious controls, many Tibetans complain of the domination of the local economy by Han Chinese, particularly in urban areas; forced resettlement; cultural preservation that amounts to cultural regulation; and the adverse environmental effects of Beijing's development projects in the region. China's leaders remain resolute. In August and September 2015 they convened the Sixth Work Forum on Tibet and issued a white paper on Tibet, both of which touted PRC achievements in Tibet, reaffirmed PRC policies, and condemned the Dalai Lama's "separatist activities." As the CCP has sought to control the reincarnation process for Tibetan spiritual leaders, Beijing has asserted that the government has the prerogative to determine the reincarnation of the Dalai Lama. For his part, the 14th Dalai Lama has suggested that he may not be reincarnated at all.[59]

The Obama administration sought to show its support for religious freedom for Tibetans in China, notably through presidential meetings with the Dalai Lama. President Obama met with the Dalai Lama four times.[60]

Uighur Muslims

Violent clashes in July 2009 between Uighur and Han Chinese people in Urumchi, the capital city of the XUAR, left almost two hundred dead and hundreds arrested. American leaders, media, and NGOs supported Chinese government efforts to separate and arrest the fighters and end the violence, but they also were inclined to place blame on Chinese policies and practices seen to discriminate against and otherwise treat unfairly the Uighur Muslim people.[61]

As reported by the Congressional Research Service, in the past decade, Chinese authorities have carried out especially harsh religious and ethnic policies against Uighurs. Once the predominant ethnic group in the XUAR, Xinjiang's roughly ten million Uighurs now constitute less than half of the region's population of twenty-two million as many Han Chinese have migrated there, particularly to Urumqi, the capital. Uighurs have complained of restrictions on religious and cultural practices, the regulation and erosion of ethnic identity, economic discrimination, arbitrary harassment by PRC public security forces, and a lack of consultation on regional policies. Government restrictions affect the training and role of imams, the celebration of Ramadan, participation in the hajj, and use of the Uighur language. Uighur children are forbidden from entering mosques or studying the Koran while CCP members, civil servants, and teachers are not allowed to openly practice Islam and are discouraged from fasting during Ramadan. In December 2014 the Urumqi government banned the wearing of veils in public areas. The XUAR government's redevelopment of the ancient heart of Kashgar, a center of Islamic and Uighur history and culture, also has angered many Uighurs. [62]

PRC leaders often mix the religious and cultural practices of Uighurs in Xinjiang with criminal and subversive activities or the "three evils of religious extremism, splittism, and terrorism." The East Turkestan Islamic Movement (ETIM) and the Turkestan Islamic Party (TIP) are blamed by Beijing for violent attacks in various parts of China since the 1990s. ETIM and TIP are Uighur groups that advocate the creation of an independent Islamic state in Xinjiang, are believed to be based in Afghanistan and Pakistan, and have had some ties to Al Qaeda and the Taliban. PRC officials assert that Islamic fundamentalism, jihad, and terrorist techniques, much of them promoted over the Internet, have contributed to violence in Xinjiang, and have referred to Islamist-inspired attacks in Beijing and Kunming as well as Xinjiang as "the greatest threat since the founding of the PRC." They also claim that one hundred to three hundred Uighur Muslims have been identified among ISIS fighters. The United States designated the ETIM as a terrorist organization under Executive Order 13224 in 2002 (to block terrorist financing) and placed it on the Terrorist Exclusion List in 2004 (to prevent entry of terrorists). The ETIM also is on the United Nations' lists of terrorist organizations. [63]

The PRC government's three-pronged strategy in response to Uighur grievances and unrest involves (1) carrying out a "strike hard" campaign against "religious extremism," "separatism," and "terrorism"; (2) developing the XUAR economy; and (3) introducing policies to assimilate Uighurs into Han society. Foreign critics say the policies do not address long-standing Uighur religious, ethnic, and political grievances well, and Uighurs accused of criminal acts have been deprived of procedural protections that are provided under China's constitution and laws. Meanwhile, assimilation policies may contribute to the erosion of Uighur identity and breed further resentment.[64]

Falun Gong

Falun Gong is a movement that combines spiritual beliefs with an exercise and meditation regimen derived from traditional Chinese practices known as *qigong*. The movement remained out of the public spotlight while it gained millions of adherents across China in the 1990s. On April 25, 1999, thousands of adherents gathered in Beijing to protest the government's growing restrictions on their activities. The demonstration seemed to take the Chinese leadership by surprise. The ability of the movement to mobilize such an impressive show of support at the seat of Chinese administrative power was viewed as a threat—one that reflected infiltration of Falun Gong supporters throughout the police and security forces and other sensitive apparatus of the Chinese government.[65]

Party leader Jiang Zemin led a major crackdown against the movement that continued for years. The harsh measures against suspected adherents who refused to recant their beliefs and cooperate with the authorities led to widespread reports by the Department of State, US-based and other human rights groups, and foreign media of torture; estimates of adherents who have died in state custody range from several hundred to a few thousand. The Chinese government acknowledges that deaths while in custody have occurred but has denied that they were caused by mistreatment. As the Chinese suppression succeeded in wiping out the movement in China, its salience as a human rights issue in US-China relations declined.[66]

Hong Kong

The US government, especially the Congress, took a special interest in working to ensure that Hong Kong's transfer to Chinese sovereignty in 1997 under terms of a Sino-British agreement reached in 1984 did not impinge on Hong Kong's autonomy and on the nascent democracy movement in the territory. As time passed and Chinese rule caused few major controversies, American interest in Hong Kong as a human rights issue declined for several years.

A series of sit-in street protests, often called the Umbrella Movement, occurred in Hong Kong from September to December 2014. They registered widespread discontent with, among other things, the limited franchise of Hong Kong voters who were not able under provisions of the Chinese-passed Basic Law governing Hong Kong to directly elect the chief executive of Hong Kong. Beijing used an indirect election by a group of several hundred local notables to ensure that the chief executive was compatible with China's interests in Hong Kong.[67]

The Umbrella Movement captured the attention of US media, interest groups, and Congress, who showed their strong support for the movement's objective of direct election and more accountable government. These Americans primarily paid attention to Beijing's perceived encroachment on Hong Kong rights and interference in the territory's affairs in ways that violated the spirit of the "One Country, Two Systems" concept incorporated into the Sino-British Joint Declaration signed in 1984. According to a list provided by the Asia Society, Hong Kong grievances voiced by many, but often not a majority of, political economic and social leaders in Hong Kong included:

- Beijing's perceived manipulation of the nomination procedures for direct election of the chief executive of Hong Kong in 2017
- Beijing's banning in 2016 of elected members of the city's legislative council because of their association with Hong Kong independence
- Political and economic pressure on local student activists and their families who are associated with the Umbrella Movement protests demanding more local democracy
- Increased pressure and tightened censorship on the press and local media
- Increased scrutiny and pressure on both foreign and Hong Kong NGOs
- Instances of perceived encroachment on the autonomy of the local judiciary
- Instances of encroachment on local academic freedom
- The kidnappings and rendition to the mainland of non-Chinese-passport-holding Hong Kong booksellers by mainland security personnel (discussed above)[68]

US influence in Hong Kong–Beijing relations seemed small. The Obama government officials generally eschewed comment. The State Department's annual reports on human rights in Hong Kong registered a long list of American concerns. There were some congressional hearings and statements. Overall, the issue of Beijing's interference in Hong Kong reinforced negative trends in US-China relations.

China's International Challenges to Human Rights

With its expanding international profile and greater assertiveness under President Xi Jinping, Chinese government and Chinese Communist Party organs have been expanding the reach of their censorship and control activities beyond purely domestic affairs into the United States and other countries. Examples reported by the Asia Society and other observers include the abductions and detaining of foreign nationals and Hong Kong residents, which were discussed above. Chinese consular and embassy officials warn US and other foreign think tanks, churches, media outlets, NGOs, and universities against giving public platforms to people they deem politically unacceptable. Chinese officials also have pressured or boycotted international cultural events ranging from book fairs to beauty pageants in order to censor certain topics or expel certain participants for political reasons. Beijing agents target relatives of Chinese living abroad who express views that challenge party orthodoxy, not only by denying them visas to visit ailing and dying parents but also by threatening the human rights of family relatives within China. Meanwhile, as also noted above are China's massive public diplomacy/propaganda efforts that feature media distortions, censorship, and defamation of democratic values.[69]

US Government Policy Options

Contemporary US government policies and practices regarding human rights issues in relations with China reflect the generally secondary importance of these issues in recent Sino-American relations. The US government has a range of approaches endeavoring to promote democracy, individual rights, and the rule of law in China; their impact has not had a substantial effect on the continuation of one-party authoritarian rule in China. Despite recent negative trends in US-China relations, there remain optimists among American officials, specialists, journalists, and others with an interest in human rights in China. They tend to argue that US policies and practices of political and economic engagement with China that seek cooperation and avoid confrontation are helping foster trends in China that create conditions in which progress in democracy and other aspects of human rights has been and will continue to be made. Pessimists among these groups of Americans point out that US policies of engagement and avoidance of confrontation have apparently failed to produce political transformation of China's continued authoritarian political system and have not even worked effectively in setting in motion meaningful political change. The pessimists aver that efforts to promote democracy and better human rights conditions through quiet diplomacy and dialogues have been ineffectual; some argue for a much tougher US public stance regarding human rights issues with China.[70]

The George W. Bush administration from time to time, and congressional leaders more frequently, pressured China though public criticism of human rights conditions and calls on Chinese leaders to honor the rights guaranteed under its own constitution, bring its policies and practices into line with international standards, release prisoners of conscience, and undertake major political reforms. President Bush appealed personally to President Hu Jintao to allow more religious freedom; the president met in the White House with Chinese independent Christian leaders, the Dalai Lama, and prominent Chinese political dissidents. The Democratic-led 110th Congress (2007–8) sponsored around twenty resolutions aimed at promoting improved human rights conditions in China. The US government also provided funding for programs within China that helped strengthen the rule of law, civil society, government accountability, and labor rights. In addition, Washington supported US-based NGOs and Internet companies that monitored human rights conditions in China and helped enable Chinese Internet users to access Voice of America, Radio Free Asia, and other websites that are frequently blocked by the Chinese government.[71]

The Obama administration and the congressional leaders generally pursed the above courses of action. In public interactions with Chinese leaders, human rights issues received secondary priority. President Obama went to extraordinary efforts to avoid offending China by not meeting the Dalai Lama when he visited Washington in October 2009, a few weeks before the president's first visit to China. Obama did meet the Tibetan leader in Washington several weeks after he returned home from Beijing. Despite their actions in China in the 1990s showing strong opposition to Chinese human rights practices, both Secretary of State Hillary Clinton and House of Representatives Speaker Nancy Pelosi adopted a generally low profile on human rights issues during their official visits to China.[72]

The Chinese government has cooperated with the United States on some programs promoting the rule of law, civil society, village elections, and other programs dealing with aspects of human rights seen as beneficial for China's development; Chinese officials engage in human rights dialogues with the United States and other governments. The Chinese authorities remain sensitive to perceived US or other foreign interference in Chinese internal affairs affecting the continuation of authoritarian one-party rule in China. Beijing takes or threatens strong action against perceived infringements on sensitive issues. Chinese officials have been especially sensitive regarding Tibetan matters and issues involving Uighur dissent in Xinjiang in recent years. Chinese statements affirm China's commitment to a number of broad principles and practices governing international human rights. They sometimes offer negative commentaries regarding the human rights practices of the United States and other countries that tend to be critical of Chinese human rights policies and practices.[73]

Some activists argue that the United States should take principled stands against China's human rights abuses more openly, forcefully, and frequently. Many prominent Chinese dissidents have emphasized that international pressure and attention has protected them from harsher treatment by PRC authorities. Other experts believe that more overt efforts may undermine human rights objectives. Some observers contend that US open criticism of PRC human rights policies can strengthen hard-liners in the PRC leadership or create greater suspicion of foreign influences and ties.

Against that background, US experts and policy makers have disagreed over the best methods to apply toward promoting democracy and human rights in China. Congress and successive administrations often have employed a range of means simultaneously. Policy tools include open criticism of PRC human rights policies and practices, quiet diplomacy, hearings, foreign assistance programs, support for dissident and pro-democracy groups in China and the United States, sanctions, coordination of international pressure, bilateral dialogue, Internet freedom efforts, and public diplomacy. Some experts recommend a "whole-of-government" strategy whereby human rights policies are coordinated across US government departments, agencies, and delegations to China.[74]

Offering a comprehensive approach for American policy options in this issue area, the Asia Society Task Force on US-China Relations reported in 2017 an overall negative assessment of recent trends in US-China relations that gave special attention to human rights. Its recommendations were in line with the group's emphasis on US insistence on reciprocity with China in all areas of the relationship.

Following are its recommendations on human rights:[75]

- Seek Chinese agreement to allow US counterparts to China's Confucius Institutes, such as government-funded American Corners or privately funded Jefferson Institutes or Lincoln Centers, to operate in China.
- Increase support for US government–funded media and research outlets— such as the Voice of America, Radio Free Asia, and the National Endowment for Democracy—and support the development of technology that would enable more Chinese citizens to circumvent the Great Firewall blocking their access to the global Internet.
- Open high-level bilateral government discussions seeking similar access for US media outlets to operate, publish, and broadcast in Chinese markets that their Chinese counterparts enjoy in US markets.
- Seek a negotiated end to the harassment, delays, cancellations, and outright denials of visas for US journalists, academics, and NGO representatives who end up on political "blacklists."
- Urge university and NGO boards to review their programs and campuses in China to make sure they meet their own campuses' principles for academic freedom.
- Pay more attention to the UN's Human Rights Council in Geneva by fielding a larger and more active US delegation that should continue to urge China to end its practice of repatriating North Korean refugees in violation of international law.
- Change the ground rules of the bilateral human rights dialogues to increase the role of independent NGOs, and focus agendas of meetings more sharply to make them more substantive and productive.

- Make the so-called People-to-People track in the Strategic and Economic Dialogue more substantive.
- Work with civil society organizations, including universities, think tanks, and cultural-exchange organizations, to formulate a code of conduct for interacting with China, especially when Chinese authorities attempt to dictate what can be discussed or who can participate.
- Urge talks between Chinese leaders and the Dalai Lama concerning Tibetan religious and cultural freedoms while continuing to recognize Chinese sovereignty over Tibet, and urge President Trump to meet with the Dalai Lama in his capacity as a spiritual leader, just as other US presidents have done in the past.
- Collaborate with other like-minded democratic countries to coordinate common responses to human rights violations.

Chapter Twelve

Outlook

The twists and turns in US-China relations assessed in this book argue for caution in predicting the future direction of the relationship. Powerful elements of convergence and divergence have long characterized US-China relations. In the modern period, since the opening of official relations seen in President Richard Nixon's summit with Mao Zedong in 1972, the changing mix of areas of close cooperation with enduring differences has seen relations shift in positive or negative directions.

This volume has depicted tenets of realism in international relations (IR) theory as useful in understanding these shifts from negative to positive and vice versa, especially since the Cold War. The kinds of cost-benefit analysis seen in realism seem evident in decision making in Beijing and Washington during key episodes—notably, the breakthrough under Nixon and Mao in the 1970s, Deng Xiaoping's pullback from pressing the Ronald Reagan administration in the 1980s, the mutual accommodation in line with China's avowed "peaceful rise" during the George W. Bush administration, and the Chinese government's greater international assertiveness at US expense in the past decade.

Liberalism in IR theory has been employed to explain promoting cooperation through increased engagement—notably, economic interchange. Liberalism also has been used to explain the strong US disapproval of the Tiananmen crackdown of 1989 as Chinese leaders reversed nascent politically liberal trends in the period of reform. US disappointment also was registered to some degree recently in the face of the Xi Jinping government's tightening of control over Chinese civil society.

Constructivism in IR theory has been used to explain the positive significance of mutual learning by participants on both sides as they discerned and acted upon areas of common ground and mutual interest. At the same time, constructivism has also explained the distinct and often strongly divergent identities of China and the United States that seriously impede improving relations, especially in sensitive policy areas involving ideology, sovereignty, and security.

Looking ahead in 2017, the changeable mix of positive and negative elements in US-China relations now features two assertive and dynamic presidents who avow a close and cooperative relationship, at least for the present. As reviewed in chapter 7, the Donald Trump government's seemingly high expectations regarding China's role in halting North Korea's nuclear weapons amid warnings of confrontation and unspecified US military action against Pyongyang will be disappointed unless China reverses past policy calculations and is prepared to apply a lot more pressure and risk major tensions with its recalcitrant neighbor. Whether President Trump's positive rhetoric about the Chinese president is contingent on the US leader getting what he wants from China on North Korea remains to be seen. Meanwhile, as explained in chapter 7, the US administration's defense plans seem at odds with China's interests and its economic policy is conflicted on how to deal with various trade and investment issues.

In the pursuit of his top priority of Chinese rejuvenation in accord with what Beijing calls the "China Dream," Chinese President Xi Jinping has overseen substantial advances in Chinese control in the disputed South China Sea at America's expense. As explained in chapter 7, Xi also has challenged US economic leadership through massive Chinese economic initiatives highlighted by various silk road investment and infrastructure plans. By collaborating more closely with Russian President Vladimir Putin on a variety of issues challenging the United States, the Chinese president underscores rivalry with America. Under his rule, Chinese trade and investment practices disadvantaging American interests persist as does the massive Chinese military buildup focused on the American military presence in the Asia-Pacific region. The Chinese security forces confront and try to intimidate Taiwan and US ally Japan. The Chinese government's negative turn against US and other Western interests in China, the nongovernment organizations (NGOs) they support, and gross violations of US-backed human rights at home and abroad have negatively affected American attitudes toward China.

Such differences offset the many positive mutual benefits in the Sino-American relationship and have moved recent ties in a negative direction. As shown in chapter 6, in the first decade of the twenty-first century, such important differences were held in check by pragmatism of leaders on both sides who recognized the benefits of positive engagement, the perceived costs of friction given the increasingly interdependent US-China relationship, and preoccupations by leaders of both countries with other important problems. Unfortunately, the Xi Jinping government calculated that it could be more bold and assertive in pursuing various challenges to American interests without upsetting the overall US-China relationship in ways disadvantageous to China. As explained in chapter 7, in retrospect, that calculation seemed broadly correct as the Barack Obama government continued to give priority to maintaining stable and positive relations with China despite the challenges to American interests coming from the Xi government's often bold initiatives.

For the time being in 2017, the Xi government has not followed the path it used with President Obama and thus far has avoided challenges likely to prompt sharp reactions from the more unpredictable Trump government. In addition to concern about President Trump's possible responses to Chinese assertiveness, another reason that the current Chinese government may be following a less assertive posture is China's stated assessment that international trends are moving in its favor, notably in the all-important Asia-Pacific region,[1] especially as the Trump government's policies and practices in the region seem fragmented and less than effective.

TRUMP ADMINISTRATION POLICY IN THE ASIA-PACIFIC

The Trump government's preoccupation with North Korea and China reinforced a prevailing drift in American policy in Southeast Asia and much of the rest of the region. Trump and his officials have announced the end of the Obama government's "pivot to Asia" policy and repudiated its economic centerpiece, the Trans-Pacific Partnership (TPP).[2]

The Obama administration attached high priority to Southeast Asia, which has traditionally been second in American attention to Northeast Asia. In contrast, Southeast Asia was rarely mentioned in the long 2015–16 US presidential campaign. Trump's only references to the region were occasional criticisms of China's island-building in the South China Sea.[3]

As of mid-2017, President Trump's policy in Southeast Asia, South Asia, and Central Asia at best reflected belated and episodic attention based on a poorly staffed administration with no coherent strategic view. In contrast with a sharp focus on North Korea, China, and Northeast Asia, only very recently did administration officials begin to take steps to show interest in positive engagement with other parts of the Asia-Pacific.[4]

On security, Secretary of Defense James Mattis and Vice President Michael Pence were leading administration officials in persuading the president to play down his campaign rhetoric on Japan and South Korea—namely, that American alliance commitments to these allies were dependent on their payments to the United States. US military presence in these countries is viewed as a stabilizing influence by US partners in Southeast Asia and the Asia-Pacific.

There were some efforts to further assuage Southeast Asian partners. Vice President Pence visited Indonesia in April and told officials that President Trump would attend the upcoming US–ASEAN and East Asian summits in the Philippines, as well as the APEC summit in Vietnam scheduled for November 2017. The vice president's stop in Australia was broadly reassuring, but administration commentary devoted little attention to the troubled US alliances with the Philippines and Thailand.

At the end of April 2017, President Trump called leaders of Singapore, the Philippines, and Thailand. Inviting the latter two to visit the White House represented a break from the Obama government's arms-length treatment of both governments on human rights grounds. But the president then left town after the House of Representatives passed its controversial health care bill. He was at his estate in New Jersey and unavailable to meet with ASEAN foreign ministers visiting Washington that week.

On the South China Sea disputes, the Trump government followed a cautious approach. It waited until late May 2017 to allow a freedom-of-navigation exercise to take place by a US Navy ship targeted against land features claimed by the Chinese—a claim that had been deemed illegal by an international tribunal in 2016. In Indonesia, Pence repeated the administration's insistence on so-called fair trade with Indonesia, one of many Asian countries whose trade surplus with the United States placed them under review by the new administration.

Human rights issues in Southeast Asia—ranging from authoritarian strong-man rule in Cambodia and Communist dominance in Vietnam to the newly democratic Myanmar government's controversial crackdown on the oppressed Rohingya community—have received much less attention from the Trump government than from previous administrations. Recent presidential invitations to Philippine and Thai leaders underlined this new US pragmatism on human rights issues.

Southeast Asian and other Asia-Pacific officials were correct in complaining that they had few counterparts in the Trump government, particularly in the State and Defense departments, due to the administration's remarkable slowness in nominating appointees. Some governments, notably Vietnam, made the best of the situation, carrying out agreed-upon visits from senior leaders in spring 2017. More common among Southeast Asian and other Asia-Pacific states was a wait-and-see approach, as the Trump government slowly filled the ranks with appointees who could formulate US foreign and security policies relevant to the region.

As they waited, those seeking a coherent and well-integrated US strategy toward Southeast Asia and the Asia-Pacific seemed likely to be disappointed. Barring an unanticipated crisis, the preoccupation of the Trump administration with other priorities was likely to continue for the foreseeable future. Perhaps lower-ranking officials, once in office, would be able to craft a strategy worthy of the name. But they would have to convince their superiors of the importance of accepting and carrying out this strategy amid a din of other problems at home and abroad.

As noted in chapter 7, on key issues in Southeast Asia and the broader Asia-Pacific, there has appeared to be general agreement within the Trump government—shared by congressional leaders—on the need to strengthen the American security position in Southeast Asia along with the rest of the Asia-Pacific. President Trump's proposed increase in defense spending was presumably in support of congressional legislation of the period, such as the Asia-Pacific Stability Initiative and the Asian Reassurance Initiative Act. How far the initiatives will go in actually expanding US presence in the region will depend on administration and congressional willingness to modify or end the ongoing sequestration that has placed limits on defense and other discretionary government spending.

Though many Republicans are willing to consider deficit financing in order to increase defense spending, Republican "budget hawks," who reportedly include the current director of the Trump government's Office of Management and Budget along with many in Congress, oppose it. Increases in defense spending may therefore be contingent on cuts elsewhere.

Congressional Republicans include strong advocates of human rights, democracy, and American values in the conduct of US foreign policy. However, the early Trump government has largely followed a pattern of pragmatic treatment of these issues. Consistency in this stance will presumably be welcomed by more authoritarian Southeast Asian and Asian-Pacific leaders, as well as leaders in more pluralistic states like the Philippines, Myanmar, and Malaysia who were targeted for criticism by the Obama government and continue to be attacked by congressional and US nongovernment advocates.

Achieving a unified and sustained position on US economic and trade issues—with Southeast Asia, the broader Asia-Pacific, or elsewhere—promises to be more difficult than garnering consistency on security and foreign policy values. As explained in chapters 7 and 9, key appointees have records very much at odds with one another. Some strongly identified with the president's campaign rhetoric pledging to deal harshly with states that "treat the United States unfairly" and "take jobs" from American workers. Others stick to conservative Republican orthodoxy in supporting free trade. Reports of political alliances in the White House have been widespread, often with President Trump's adviser and son-in-law, Jared Kushner, and Economic Council Director Gary Cohn on one side and Commerce Secretary Wilbur Ross and US Trade Representative Robert Lighthizer on the other.

Policy is said to move back and forth between these two camps, though the circumstances behind this dynamic remain unclear. The president chose these officials and has a long record of welcoming sharply alternative views among his staff. Where Trump himself will come down in this debate and whether he will stick with a position are very unclear.

In sum, US policy is muddled and US attention is episodic and drifting.

THE IMPORTANCE OF POWER SHIFT IN ASIA

As noted in chapter 1 and explained in chapter 7, China's recent advances and the mediocre performance of the Trump administration in the Asia-Pacific have intensified debate in the United States and China over the implications of a possible power shift in Asia and what it means for future US-China relations.[5] Assertive Chinese actions challenging the United States in Asia and elsewhere have damaged US-China relations; they were widely seen as based on Chinese calculation of US decline following the global economic crisis of 2008–9. They have been influenced by US reluctance to bear more onerous international burdens seen under the rubric of the so-called Obama Doctrine and of the Trump administration's so-called America First foreign policy orientation. Meanwhile, there has been a widely held view in the US government, highlighted notably in an unclassified National Intelligence Estimate released in 2017, that one reason for increased challenges for the United States posed by Vladimir Putin and Xi Jinping was a perception of decline in the United States and Western-aligned powers.[6]

Against this background, a main determinant of greater tensions in US-China relations centers on China and whether it will continue assertive advances into disputed nearby territories and other challenges to US leadership in the Asia-Pacific and elsewhere. Such Chinese actions could be seen eventually as a direct Chinese test of US resolve as a regional security guarantor in the Asia-Pacific. The Chinese advances could make more likely a confrontation between a more assertive China and the United States. Thus the willingness and ability of China's leaders to curb recent assertiveness and deflect public and elite pressures for tougher foreign policy approaches represent an important indicator in the current period of whether US-China relations are likely to worsen.

For its part, the Trump government has appeared distracted from the Asia-Pacific except for the crisis with North Korea. The main danger the US government seemed to pose for the course of US-China relations centered on how it might react to challenges from China deemed provocative by the US government. As noted earlier, the Trump government has been more likely than the Obama government to take a wide range of actions, possibly including use of force, in response to China or other foreign governments seen provoking the United States.

From this perspective, the longer-term outlook for conflict or cooperation in Sino-American relations is influenced by the significance of China's rising influence and the perceived decline of the United States. China's ascendance as a world power represents the most important change in the still-developing international dynamics of the twenty-first century. A wide range of expert commentaries and assessments judges that China in recent decades has established a clear strategy of developing wealth and power in world affairs. They see China's recently assertive posture along its periphery as part of expanding Chinese economic, military, and political influence that entails a change in leadership in the Asia-Pacific region and a power shift in world affairs. The United States and its partners among developed countries are viewed in decline as China rises, and thus their choices are depicted in sometimes stark terms. They are advised by some to appease and accommodate China, and by others to resist.[7]

Whether we have reached such a tipping point in Asian and international politics has important implications for the course of Sino-American relations and particularly for American policy toward China. Discussed below are indicators that can be used by readers to assess just how powerfully China has advanced vis-à-vis the United States in the important Asia-Pacific region and elsewhere in world affairs, in order to judge whether we have reached a point where China is willing and able to confront the United States and others over contested territories along its rim and other sensitive issues in the period ahead.

There is a large literature assessing China's rising role in world affairs. Common in the literature is a tendency to employ a selected set of indicators focused on the growing size of China's economy; China's leading role as an international manufacturer and trader, consumer of raw materials, and holder of foreign exchange reserves; and China's widespread international impact backed by active diplomacy and steadily increasing military capabilities. These indicators support assessments of China's rapid growth globally. They contrast with indicators of slow growth or stagnation on the part of other world powers, notably Japan, Europe, and the United States. As a result, many specialists come to the conclusion that China has risen to the point where a power transition is underway in China's surroundings in Asia, with Beijing emerging as the region's new leader and with the United States, heretofore the leading power around Asia's rim, moving to a secondary position. Some specialists go further in judging that the power transition from the US leadership to that of China is more global in scope.[8]

Of course, there are specialists—including this writer--who employ other indicators and evidence to conclude that rising China probably has a long way to go to be in a position to challenge America's leading role in Asian and world affairs. Those indicators are discussed below. They depict China as growing in influence but still constrained and far from dominant in the Asia-Pacific, and for this and other reasons unwilling and unable to effectively confront the United States, even with America's recent problems and uncertain prospects.[9] Even if America remains ineffective and preoccupied, they see China as more likely to seek incremental gains at US expense that do not risk crisis and confrontation with the still substantial American power.

CHINESE LIMITATIONS AND CONSTRAINTS

Constraints on the Chinese challenges to American leadership involve domestic preoccupations, strong Chinese interdependence with the United States, and China's continued weak position relative to the United States in Asia and the world.[10]

Domestic Preoccupations

There is a general consensus among specialists in China and abroad about some of the key domestic concerns preoccupying the Xi Jinping leadership:[11]

- Weak leadership legitimacy highly dependent on how the leaders' performance is seen at any given time
- Pervasive corruption viewed as sapping public support and undermining administrative efficiency
- Widening income gaps posing challenges to the communist regime ostensibly dedicated to advancing the disadvantaged
- Incidents of social turmoil reportedly involving one hundred thousand to two hundred thousand mass events annually that are usually directed at state policies, with budget outlays for domestic security greater than China's impressive national defense budget[12]
- A highly resource-intensive economy (e.g., until recently, China used four times the amount of oil to advance its economic growth to a certain level than did the United States, even though the United States is inefficient and wasteful in how it uses oil),[13] with enormous and rapidly growing environmental damage being done in China as a result of such intensive resource use
- The need for major reform of an economic model in use in China for more than three decades that is widely seen to have reached a point of diminishing returns

That China's leadership remains uncertain and fractious in how to deal with these issues was underlined by the resort to state intervention (notably at odds with the announced economic reforms) to try to limit the damage from the 2015 stock market sell-off and the negative consequences for Chinese trade resulting from the upward valuation of the Chinese currency at that time. And reports of the results of the leaders' annual retreat at the seaside resort Beidaihe in August 2015 said that Xi's reform efforts were encountering extraordinarily "fierce resistance."[14] How much these domestic priorities preoccupy Chinese leaders and affect their policy toward America is not known, but on balance they seem to incline Chinese leaders to avoid big problems with the United States.

Strong Interdependence

The second set of constraints on tough Chinese measures against the United States involves strong and ever-growing interdependence in US-China relations. As discussed in chapter 6, beginning at the turn of the century, each government used engagement to build positive and cooperative ties and to build interdependence and webs of relationships that had the effect of constraining the other power from taking actions that opposed its interests. As noted in chapter 6, the policies of engagement pursued by the United States and China toward one another featured respective "Gulliver strategies" that were designed to tie down the aggressive, assertive, and other negative policy tendencies of the other power through webs of interdependence in bilateral and multilateral relationships.[15]

The power of interdependence to constrain assertive and disruptive actions has limits. Nevertheless, China's uncertain domestic situation seems unprepared to absorb the shock of an abrupt shutdown of normal economic interaction that might result from a confrontation with America. And both sides have become increasingly aware of how their respective interests are tied to the well-being and success of the other, thereby limiting the tendency of the past to apply pressure on one another.

China's Insecure Position and Recent Troubles in the Asia-Pacific

The third set of constraints on tough Chinese measures against the United States involves China's insecure position in the Asia-Pacific region. The Asian countries on China's periphery are historically where China has exerted greatest influence. They have long been the arena of the majority share of Chinese foreign policy effort. This area is where China interacts most with the United States, the world's remaining superpower. It features sovereignty issues (e.g., Taiwan) and security issues (e.g., US defense presence) that have been uppermost among Chinese foreign policy priorities. The Chinese military plays a major role in Asia, in contrast to other parts of the world where its role is minimal. Chinese involvement in other regions has focused in recent years on trade and related economic interests. Nevertheless, Asia is much more important for China's economic growth than other world regions.

Even after more than two decades of repeated efforts following the Cold War, China's rise in the region, despite its importance, remains encumbered and appears to make China unprepared to challenge US regional leadership.

The Xi Jinping government's assertive policies toward its neighbors arguably have made the situation worse. Without a secure foundation in nearby Asia, China will be inclined to avoid serious confrontation with the United States.[16]

China's Advances and Limitations in Asia

China's advances in Asia have depended heavily on the growth of Chinese trade with neighboring states, which made China the leading trading partner of most nearby Asian countries. Led by foreign-invested enterprises in China, which accounted for one-half of China's foreign trade, consumer and industrial goods were produced in China with materials and components imported from foreign enterprises, frequently in other parts of Asia. China was often the final point of assembly and the majority of the goods went to markets in developed countries, notably the European Union (EU) and the United States. Overall, the result was that China's importance as a recipient of Asian investment, a leading trading partner, and an engine of economic growth rose dramatically in Asia. China's attentive bilateral and multilateral diplomacy emphasized willingness to trade and provide financing, investment, and other support to countries, with "no strings attached."

Along land borders with Southeast Asian and Central Asian states, China built, often with the support of international financial institutions, networks of roads, railways, waterways, hydroelectric dams and electric power transmission grids, and pipelines that linked China ever more closely with these nations. A similar close integration developed between China and Taiwan, with the strength of the Taiwanese economy becoming increasingly determined by the island's interchange with mainland China. Another feature of China's outreach to Asia was emphasis on Chinese language, culture, and personal exchanges. This included support for Confucius Institutes and other organizations promoting student exchanges, the teaching of Chinese language and culture, and the facilitating of ever larger numbers of Chinese tourist groups traveling to neighboring countries.

China's limitations and shortcomings in relations with Asia are based on its past belligerence throughout the Cold War, a legacy of which most Chinese people are unaware, and Beijing's recent assertiveness. Popular ignorance of past Chinese aggression came because the Chinese government, employing its massive propaganda apparatus, successfully promoted to its own people an image of consistent, principled, and righteous Chinese behavior in foreign affairs. Conditioned by this thinking, Chinese elites and the general public have a poor appreciation of regional and US concerns about the rise of China. These Chinese citizens also remain heavily influenced by the Chinese media's emphasis on China's historic victimization at the hands of outside powers like the United States and Japan. As a result, the Chinese people are inclined to react very negatively to outside complaints and perceived infringements of Chinese interests and rights.

Against this background, Chinese media commentary applauded Xi Jinping's assertiveness and firmness in advancing Chinese interests at the expense of neighbors and in opposition to the United States. The commentary played well with audiences in China imbued with a strong sense of self-righteous nationalism. Xi's approach was depicted as consistent with China's aspiring for regional and international influence under the broad rubric of the "China Dream." Unfortunately, the reality was an overall worsening in Chinese relations with several key neighbors and concurrent instability in the most important arena in Chinese foreign relations.

The Xi government's policies drove relations with Japan to their lowest point since the Second World War. Japan's effective firmness backed with stronger support from an increasingly concerned United States saw Xi moderate his policies—predictably without acknowledging any failure of past policy—in seeking more normal interchange with Japan in 2015, but tensions continued to flare periodically. Xi's policies dealing with the conundrum in North Korea effectively drove relations with Pyongyang to their lowest point ever, underlining China's inability to secure its interests in this critically important area for China. And relations with South Korea declined sharply with the deployment of an advanced US antiballistic missile system in South Korea in 2017.

Most Southeast Asian nations remained reluctant to challenge China publicly over its recent advances in the South China Sea, but the Chinese expansion put the United States increasingly on alert as it prepared, with the assistance of Japan and Australia among others, for contingencies; the United States also garnered overt and tacit support of some key Southeast Asian governments. In South Asia, the Xi government's mix of economic and political overtures, along with demonstrations of military force in disputed border areas and in the Indian Ocean, deepened suspicions in India; the government in New Delhi actively advanced diplomatic, economic, and security ties with the United States, Japan, and Australia as part of national strengthening to protect its interests as China grew in power.

Additionally, comparatively tranquil situations in areas of acute Chinese concern in Taiwan and Hong Kong experienced adverse developments for Beijing. Elections in Taiwan in 2014 and 2016 were sharply at odds with Chinese interests. The new Taiwan President Tsai Ing-wen refused to endorse the so-called 1992 Consensus that was seen by Beijing as supporting its one-China principle; the outgoing Taiwan government had supported the 1992 Consensus but Tsai's government saw the concept as undermining Taiwan's sovereignty. Beijing used strong levers of control to compel compliance in Hong Kong, but it had less leverage on Taiwan's new president; in neither case was there a smooth path for advancing Chinese influence and control.

The Xi government had an easier time improving relations with various silk road and other initiatives in Central Asia and in improving relations with Russian President Vladimir Putin, with Russia now isolated from the West. But the bottom line remained a series of serious challenges in the most important arena of Chinese foreign relations that seemed almost certain to complicate any notion of China attaining regional dominance and leadership.

Strengths and Shortcomings in China's Economic Influence

The Xi Jinping government's foreign policy toward developing countries in Asia and elsewhere in the world involved a massive push for Chinese investment and financing abroad, advancing and modifying the strong "going out" policies of Chinese investment and financing in these areas seen in the previous decade. The previous effort focused on attaining access to petroleum and other raw materials needed for China's resource-hungry economy. Chinese economic reforms during the Xi administration have sought to reduce such intense resource use. The push for foreign investment and financing has aimed to enable construction abroad of Chinese-supplied infrastructure, provided by the enormous excess capacity of Chinese companies for such construction and supply, now that major infrastructure development inside China has been curtailed under recent economic reforms.

The image purveyed by Chinese officials and lauding Chinese commentary was one of enormous Chinese largess, unprecedented in the annals of world affairs. China was depicted using its more than $3 trillion in foreign exchange reserves in seeking mutually beneficial development throughout the world. The results were multibillion-dollar commitments to various Chinese silk road funds; new development banks led by China; and regional initiatives in Africa, Latin America, Europe, and the Middle East. China pledged infrastructure in unstable Pakistan valued at $46 billion, a responsible Chinese official said Beijing's overall plan for investment in Africa over the next decade amounted to $1 trillion, and Xi personally pledged investment in Latin America of $250 billion over the next decade. Foreign commentary often came to echo the Chinese commentaries in seeing Beijing as the dominant leader of international economic relations in Asia and much of the developing world.[17]

By contrast, a closer look at Chinese trade and economic influence shows gaps and less impact than might be expected. Indeed, the decline in Chinese foreign trade in 2015 and 2016, combined with unsteadiness in China's economic conditions and policy management, undercut China's international importance.[18] Trade with China accounts for more than 20 percent of the trade of some Asia-Pacific countries like South Korea and Australia, but the trade situation does not provide a basis for Chinese dominance in those countries. China's important, but lower, percentage of trade in developing countries in Asia, Africa, and Latin America usually makes China just one among several important foreign actors in these countries and far from dominant. China's role as an investor in all these regions is surprisingly small, especially in view of all the attention Chinese leaders have given for more than a decade to stronger Chinese investments abroad. After more than a decade of multibillion-dollar investment pledges, China accounted for about 10 percent of the foreign investment in Southeast Asia and about 5 percent in both Africa and Latin America.[19]

A major weakness of the Xi government's pledges of large sums of investment and loans is that China often implements only a fraction of its very ambitious pledges. Promises of large Chinese investments and loans to Pakistan and Indonesia in 2015 came with reports that China had actually implemented less than 10 percent of the multibillion-dollar pledges made to each country over the previous decade. The reasons for the poor follow-through are readily seen in Chinese wariness after many years of less than successful international economic involvement. A responsible Chinese official averred that 80 percent of proposed Chinese mining deals (an important feature of Chinese economic interaction in developing countries) have failed to be implemented; and others showed that Chinese satisfaction with the push for greater Chinese foreign investment abroad has been tempered by the fact that the Chinese enterprises more often than not were losing money in foreign-invested deals. There was no accounting in official Chinese media of the losses incurred by Chinese enterprises that became heavily involved in financing and investing in risky locales. Multibillion-dollar planned Asian projects in Myanmar, the Philippines, Sri Lanka, and Afghanistan were stopped or put on hold along with a variety of similar setbacks for Chinese involvement in other countries, including Mexico, Brazil, Greece, Nigeria, and throughout the turbulent Middle East and North African regions.[20]

Corrupt practices, nontransparent agreements with unaccountable foreign governments, unstable conditions in many developing countries, and China's changing needs for imported raw materials have all complicated the implementation of the support the Chinese have promised. Foreign labor unions and other politically active constituencies often resent China's tendency, on the one hand, to import Chinese labor crews to carry out Chinese-supported projects and, on the other hand, to be less attentive to international labor standards when employing local workers. The environmental impact of Chinese development projects prompted local civil-society groups to mobilize protests against Chinese practices. Those countries recently facing repayment of large Chinese loans contend with Chinese creditors assiduous in assuring that China will be paid back. If not paid back in money or commodities, China, as seen in Venezuela, Ecuador, Cambodia, Sri Lanka, and elsewhere, has been known to sometimes seek control of equity, including a ninety-nine-year lease of land in Sri Lanka. Critics have labeled such Chinese financing to poorer countries, which leads to strong Chinese control of those countries' economies, as the "China debt trap."[21] Finally, China's image as a significant donor of foreign assistance is undercut by the fact that China still receives annually several billions of (US) dollars worth of loans and foreign assistance from international financial institutions and national governments. The *Economist* reported in 2015 that in its calculation China remained a net recipient of foreign assistance until 2011.[22]

US Strengths and Shortcomings in the Asia-Pacific Region

Until the advent of the Trump administration, a comparison of Chinese policies and practices in the Asia-Pacific region with those of the United States appeared to underline how far China had to go, despite more than two decades of post–Cold War efforts to strengthen its position in Asia, if it intended to be successful in seriously confronting and challenging the United States. And without a secure periphery, and facing formidable US presence and influence, China almost certainly calculated that challenging the United States under such circumstances would pose grave dangers for the PRC regime.

But after several months of erratic behavior by the Trump government, there remains uncertainty as to whether the United States will persist in its past leadership role in competition with China in the Asia-Pacific region. Other possibilities range from retrenchment to conflict, with both at the extremes having potentially massive negative consequences for the existing Asian order. In particular, if retrenchment is pursued, then the existing constraints on China in Asia very likely will weaken substantially and China will have a freer hand in advancing toward regional dominance.

Nevertheless, it seems important to realize that any diminishment of US power and influence will take time. In a word, if rising China has some momentum, the United States benefits from massive inertia as the region's leading power. America has a unique and remarkably strong foundation of nongovernment connections with Asian countries, topped off with many millions of Asians now settled in the United States and participating constructively in interchange connecting the United States and Asia. The deeply rooted US military and intelligence interchange with almost all Asia-Pacific governments has made the head of the US Pacific Command by far the most active senior US government representative in the region; these relationships remain of mutual benefit and do not depend on sentiment. And despite withdrawing from the TPP, the US market remains open and still absorbs a massive amount of manufactured goods from regional exporters and their component suppliers in the regional production chains.[23]

Past US weaknesses in the Asia-Pacific included the often unilateral and arbitrary foreign policy decisions of the G. W. Bush administration, which were very unpopular with regional elites and public opinion. As the Obama administration refocused US attention positively on the Asia-Pacific region, regional concerns shifted to worry that US budget difficulties and political gridlock in Washington would undermine the ability of the United States to sustain support for regional responsibilities. Overall, the Obama government's "rebalance" policy and recent US practice meshed well with the interests of the majority of Asia-Pacific governments that seek legitimacy through development and nation building in an interdependent world economic order and an uncertain security environment caused notably by Chinese assertiveness. However, major questions remained on whether the rebalance was sufficient to deal with China's recent challenges and whether it would be continued by the new US administration.

The basic determinants of US strength and influence in the Asia-Pacific region involve five factors, starting with security. In most of Asia, governments are viable and make the decisions that determine direction in foreign affairs. Popular, elite, media, and other opinion may influence government officials in policy toward the United States and other countries, but in the end the officials make decisions on the basis of their own calculus. In general, the officials see their governments' legitimacy and success resting on nation building and economic development, which require a stable and secure international environment. Unfortunately, Asia is not particularly stable, and most regional governments are privately wary of, and tend not to trust, each other. As a result, they look to the United States to provide the security that they need to pursue goals of development and nation building in an appropriate environment. They recognize that the US security role is very expensive and involves great risk, including large-scale casualties if necessary, for the sake of preserving Asian security. They also recognize that neither rising China, nor any other Asian power or coalition of powers, is able or willing to undertake even a small part of these risks, costs, and responsibilities.

Second, the nation-building priority of most Asian governments depends greatly on export-oriented growth. As noted above, much of Chinese and Asian trade depends heavily on exports to developed countries, notably the United States. America has run a massive trade deficit with China, and a total annual trade deficit with Asia valued at more than US $400 billion. Asian government officials recognize that China, which consistently runs an overall trade surplus, and other trading partners in Asia are unwilling and unable to bear even a fraction of the cost of such large trade deficits, which, nonetheless, are very important for Asian governments.

Third, the George W. Bush administration was generally effective in interaction with Asia's powers. The Obama administration built on these strengths. The Obama government's broad rebalancing with regional governments and multilateral organizations had a scope ranging from India to the Pacific island states to Korea and Japan. Its emphasis on consultation and inclusion of international stakeholders before coming to policy decisions on issues of importance to Asia and the Pacific also was broadly welcomed and stood in contrast with the previously perceived unilateralism of the Bush administration. Meanwhile, the US Pacific Command and other US military commands and security and intelligence organizations have been at the edge of wide-ranging and growing US efforts to build and strengthen webs of military and related intelligence and security relationships throughout the region.

Fourth, the United States for decades, reaching back to past centuries, has engaged the Asia-Pacific region through business, religious, educational, media, and other interchange. Such active nongovernment interaction puts the United States in a unique position and reinforces overall American influence. Meanwhile, more than fifty years of generally color-blind US immigration policy, since the ending of discriminatory American restrictions on Asian immigration in 1965, has resulted in the influx of millions of Asia-Pacific migrants who call America home and who interact with their countries of origin in ways that underpin and reflect well on the US position in the region.

Fifth, part of the reason for the success of US efforts to build webs of security-related and other relationships with Asia-Pacific countries has to do with active contingency planning by many Asia-Pacific governments. As power relations change in the region, notably on account of China's rise, regional governments generally seek to work positively and pragmatically with rising China on the one hand, but they seek the reassurance of close security, intelligence, and other ties with the United States, on the other hand, in case rising China shifts from its current avowed benign approach to one of greater assertiveness or dominance.

Against the background of recent Chinese demands, coercion, and intimidation, the Asia-Pacific governments' interest in closer ties with the United States meshed well with the Obama administration's engagement with regional governments and multilateral organizations. The US concern to maintain stability while fostering economic growth overlapped constructively with the priorities of the majority of regional governments as they pursued their respective nation-building agendas.

Under President Trump, the positive role of the Pacific Command, legal immigration, and nongovernment American engagement in Asia has continued. The president's campaign rhetoric raised questions about support for alliances, but they have subsided with high-level US reassurance. America's role as economic partner was in doubt with the scrapping of the TPP, but the US market has remained open to regional imports.

President Trump ended the rebalance and TPP. Employing unpredictable unilateral actions, he cast doubt on past US commitment to positive regional relations. He also junked related policy transparency; carefully measured responses; and avoidance of dramatic action, linkage, or spillover among competing interests. Early in his presidency, his record in the region showed episodic engagement featuring intense pressure to prevent North Korea's nuclear weapons development and overall drift in dealing with most other issues. President Trump's strong defense posture and pragmatism on human rights issues were welcomed by many regional governments, but they failed to overshadow a muddled picture of a poorly staffed administration with conflicting impulses and many preoccupations leading to flawed engagement in the Asia-Pacific.

In sum, readers are advised to monitor this set of indicators for evidence of greater regional acceptance of China's rise as a benign and positive force in regional affairs. Such a change would presumably reduce regional interest in sustaining close ties with the United States as a potential counter to possible Chinese intimidation and coercion. Also, readers should monitor this set of indicators for signs that regional governments may come to judge the United States as unable or unwilling to strike a proper balance that allows regional governments to remain secure in the face of China's rise without causing friction between China and the United States that destabilizes the regional environment.

CONCLUSION

The discussion above leads to the following four conclusions of use to readers interested in tracking developments and assessing the importance of China's rise in Asian and world affairs and the future course of Sino-American relations:

1. China's recent relationships in Asia can be measured accurately.
2. Salient strengths and limitations of China's rising influence in Asia can be measured accurately.
3. Significant strengths and limitations of the United States in the Asia-Pacific region can be measured accurately.
4. The contingency planning of Asia-Pacific governments can be measured accurately.

Taken together these conclusions show continued Chinese advance in importance and influence. But the United States remains the region's leading power, and other governments are wary of implications of China's rise as they seek mutual benefit in greater economic and other interaction with China. Asia is the international area where China has always exerted greatest influence and where it devotes the lion's share of Chinese foreign policy attention, but that does not mean that China will come to dominate the region. Prevailing conditions, even including the mediocre record of the Trump administration as of mid-2017, make it hard to foresee how China could emerge in a dominant position in Asia for some time.

As a result, the reported danger of confrontation and/or conflict or the need for dramatic US accommodation or appeasement of China, which has been predicted to emerge in Sino-American relations amid projections of China rising to challenge the leading position of the United States in Asian and world affairs, appear to be reduced. Moreover, if China is not in a position to challenge the United States in nearby Asia, it will be less able to do so in other areas farther from China's scope of influence and farther from China's scope of concern. Indeed, it appears more likely that Chinese policy makers and strategists will continue incremental efforts and adjustments in order to overcome existing and future obstacles as they seek to improve Chinese influence, interests, and status. This difficult and protracted task adds to China's long array of domestic challenges and other preoccupations. It argues for continued reserve in broader Chinese foreign policies and prac-tices as Chinese leaders take account of the sustained but substantial limits of Chinese international power and influence.

Variables that could upset the above forecast include how well China's leaders manage such a moderate approach to world affairs. As noted here and in chapter 7, a major challenge comes from Chinese elite and public opinion that reflect unawareness of the negative legacies China has as a result of past behavior in nearby areas. And the acute sense of righteousness of these Chinese groups is accompanied by prickly patriotic inclinations that are quick to find fault with the United States and some of China's neighbors. Popular and elite frustrations can grow and spill over to impact Chinese leaders and the policies they follow toward China's neighbors and the United States.

Other variables that could change the forecast obviously include US poli-cy. Should the United States reverse policy and withdraw from security commitments to the Asia-Pacific or close American markets to regional ex-porters, the prevailing order in the Asia-Pacific would change significantly, with the future order possibly very much in doubt. The United States also could craft its reengagement in Asia as balancing against and attempting to exclude China, thereby forcing Asian governments to choose between Bei-jing and Washington.

Meanwhile, abrupt and provocative actions by the always unpredictable North Korean government, by claimants in territorial disputes along China's rim, and by the bold leaders in power in Washington and Beijing could escalate tensions. Under extreme circumstances, they could possibly lead to military conflict that if not well managed could see China and the United States in a disastrous war.

Notes

1. INTRODUCTION

1. Wang Jisi, "Trends in the Development of U.S.-China Relations and Deep-Seated Reasons," *Danddai Yatai* (Beijing), June 20, 2009, 4–20; Yan Xuetong, "The Instability of China-U.S. Relations," *Chinese Journal of International Politics* 3, no. 3 (2010): 1–30; Aaron Friedberg, *A Contest for Supremacy: China, America, and the Struggle for Mastery in Asia* (New York: W. W. Norton, 2011); Michael Swaine, *America's Challenge: Engaging a Rising China in the Twenty-First Century* (Washington, DC: Carnegie Endowment for International Peace, 2011); Jeffrey Bader, *Obama and China's Rise* (Washington, DC: Brookings Institution, 2012); David Shambaugh, ed., *Tangled Titans: The United States and China* (Lanham, MD: Rowman & Littlefield, 2012).

2. Bader, *Obama and China's Rise*; Kenneth Lieberthal, "The China-U.S. Relationship Goes Global," *Current History* 108, no. 719 (September 2009): 243–46; "China-U.S. Dialogue Successful—Vice Premier," *China Daily*, July 29, 2009, 1; Hillary Clinton and Timothy Geithner, "A New Strategic and Economic Dialogue with China," *Wall Street Journal*, July 27, 2009, https://www.wsj.com/articles/SB10001424052970204886304574308753825396372 (accessed September 7, 2009).

3. Prominent Americans identified with this view include Zbigniew Brzezinski and C. Fred Bergsten. For critical response, see Elizabeth Economy and Adam Segal, "The G-2 Mirage," *Foreign Affairs* 88, no. 3 (May–June 2009): 56–72.

4. Jeffrey Bader, "U.S.-China Challenges: Time for China to Step Up," Brookings, January 12, 2017, https://www.brookings.edu/research/u-s-china-challenges-time-for-china-to-step-up.

5. Robert Sutter and Satu Limaye, *America's 2016 Election Debate on Asia Policy & Asian Reactions* (Honolulu: East-West Center, 2016). That report used campaign statements and other materials made available in "2016 Presidential Candidates on Asia," Asia Matters for America, http://www.asiamattersforamerica.org/asia/2016-presidential-candidates-on-asia.

6. Bader, "U.S.-China Challenges"; Harry Harding, "Has U.S. China Policy Failed?" *Washington Quarterly* 38, no. 3 (2015): 95–122; Robert Blackwill and Ashley Tellis, *Council Special Report: Revising U.S. Grand Strategy toward China* (Washington, DC: Council on Foreign Relations, April 2015); Orville Schell and Susan Shirk, Chairs, *U.S. Policy toward China: Recommendations for a New Administration*, Task Force Report (New York: Asia Society, 2017).

7. Interviews with Chinese officials and specialists, Beijing 2016, reviewed in Sutter and Limaye, *America's 2016 Election Debate*, 21–28.

8. Bonnie Glaser and Alexandra Viers, "China Prepares for Rocky Relations in 2017," *Comparative Connections* 18, no. 3 (January 2017): 21–22.

9. Shi Jiangtao, "Tempest Trump: China and U.S. Urged to Make Plans for 'Major Storm' in Bilateral Relationship," *South China Morning Post*, January 30, 2017.

10. The above developments are reviewed in Bonnie Glaser and Alexandra Viers, "Trump and Xi Break the Ice at Mar-a-Lago," *Comparative Connections* 19, no. 1 (May 2017): 21–32.

11. Dave Majumbar, "New Report Details Why a War between China and America Would Be Catastrophic," *National Interest* (blog), August 1, 2016, http://nationalinterest.org/blog/the-buzz/new-report-details-why-war-between-china-america-would-be-17210.

12. On Chinese perspectives see Nina Hachigian, ed., *Debating China* (New York: Oxford University Press, 2014). See also contrasting US views of various differences in China-US relations in Michael Swaine, *Creating a Stable Asia: An Agenda for a U.S.-China Balance of Power* (Washington, DC: Carnegie Endowment for International Peace, 2016); Bader, "U.S.-China Challenges"; Harding, "Has U.S. China Policy Failed?"; Blackwill and Tellis, *Council Special Report*; Schell and Shirk, *U.S. Policy toward China*; Shambaugh, *Tangled Titans*; Friedberg, *A Contest for Supremacy*; and Swaine, *America's Challenge*. Earlier contrasting perspectives are seen in David M. Lampton, *The Three Faces of Chinese Power* (Berkeley: University of California Press, 2008); Bates Gill, *Rising Star: China's New Security Diplomacy* (Washington, DC: Brookings Institution, 2007); and Susan Shirk, *China: Fragile Superpower* (New York: Oxford, 2007).

13. Susan Lawrence and David MacDonald, *U.S.-China Relations: Policy Issues*, Report RL41108 (Washington, DC: Congressional Research Service of the Library of Congress, August 2, 2012); Schell and Shirk, *U.S. Policy toward China*.

2. PATTERNS OF US-CHINA RELATIONS PRIOR TO WORLD WAR II

1. John K. Fairbank, *Trade and Diplomacy on the China Coast: The Opening of the Treaty Ports, 1842–1854* (Cambridge, MA: Harvard University Press, 1953); Li Changjiu and Shi Lujia, *Zhongmei guanxi liangbainian* [Two hundred years of Sino-American relations] (Peking: Xinhua Publishing House, 1984).

2. Warren Cohen, *America's Response to China: A History of Sino-American Relations* (New York: Columbia University Press, 2010), 8–28; Michael Hunt, *The Making of a Special Relationship: The United States and China to 1914* (New York: Columbia University Press, 1983).

3. Daniel Bays, ed., *Christianity in China* (Stanford, CA: Stanford University Press, 1996).

4. Michael Hunt, *Frontier Defense and the Open Door: Manchuria in Chinese-American Relations, 1895–1911* (New Haven, CT: Yale University Press, 1973); Michael Schaller, *The United States and China: Into the Twenty-First Century* (New York: Oxford University Press, 2015), 26–48.

5. Akira Iriye, *After Imperialism: The Search for a New Order in the Far East, 1921–1931* (Cambridge, MA: Harvard University Press, 1965); Dorothy Borg, *The United States and the Far Eastern Crisis of 1933–1938* (Cambridge, MA: Harvard University Press, 1964).

6. John K. Fairbank, *The United States and China* (Cambridge, MA: Harvard University Press, 1983); Cohen, *America's Response to China*; Schaller, *The United States and China*; Gordon H. Chang, *Fateful Ties: A History of America's Preoccupation with China* (Cambridge, MA: Harvard University Press, 2015).

7. Ernest R. May and John K. Fairbank, eds., *America's China Trade in Historical Perspective: The Chinese and American Performance* (Cambridge, MA: Harvard University Press, 1986).

8. John Fairbank and Suzanne W. Barnett, eds., *Christianity in China* (Cambridge, MA: Harvard University Press, 1985).

9. Walter LaFeber, *The New Empire: An Interpretation of American Expansion, 1860–1898* (Ithaca, NY: Cornell University Press, 1963).

10. Cohen, *America's Response to China*, 29–88.

11. John Fairbank, Edwin Reischauer, and Albert Craig, *East Asia: Tradition and Transformation* (Boston: Houghton Mifflin, 1973), 593–95, 766.

12. Ronald Takaki, *Strangers from a Different Shore: A History of Asian America* (Boston: Little, Brown, 1998).

13. Hunt, *Making of a Special Relationship*; Li and Shi, *Zhongmei guanxi liangbainian* [Two hundred years of Sino-American relations].

14. Cohen, *America's Response to China*, 8–59.

15. Paul Cohen, *China and Christianity: The Missionary Movement and the Growth of Chinese Antiforeignism, 1860–1870* (Cambridge, MA: Harvard University Press, 1963).

16. Delber McKee, *Chinese Exclusion versus the Open Door Policy, 1900–1906* (Detroit, MI: Wayne State University Press, 1977).

17. Li Tien-yi, *Woodrow Wilson's China Policy, 1913–1917* (New York: Twayne, 1952).

18. Dorothy Borg, *American Policy and the Chinese Revolution, 1925–1928* (New York: Macmillan, 1947); Dorothy Borg, *The United States and the Far Eastern Crisis*; Akira Iriye and Warren I. Cohen, eds., *American, Chinese, and Japanese Perspectives on Wartime Asia, 1939–1949* (Wilmington, DE: Scholarly Resources, 1990).

19. Jonathan Goldstein, *Philadelphia and the China Trade* (University Park: Pennsylvania State University Press, 1978).

20. Cohen, *America's Response to China*, 4.

21. Peter Ward Fay, *Opium War, 1840–1842* (Chapel Hill: University of North Carolina Press, 1997).

22. Fairbank, *Trade and Diplomacy on the China Coast*.

23. Edward Gulick, *Peter Parker and the Opening of China* (Cambridge, MA: Harvard University Press, 1973).

24. Eugene Boardman, *Christian Influence upon the Ideology of the Taiping Rebellion 1850–1864* (Madison: University of Wisconsin Press, 1952).

25. David Anderson, *Imperialism and Idealism: American Diplomats in China, 1861–1898* (Bloomington: University of Indiana Press, 1985); Cohen, *America's Response to China*, 23–24.

26. Fairbank et al., *East Asia: Tradition and Transformation*, 558–96.

27. Immanuel C. Y. Hsu, *The Rise of Modern China* (New York: Oxford University Press, 2000), 297–99.

28. Schaller, *The United States and China*, 18–24.

29. Fairbank et al., *East Asia: Tradition . . .*, 570–75.

30. Anderson, *Imperialism and Idealism*, 154–70.

31. Tyler Dennett, *Americans in Eastern Asia: A Critical Study of the Policy of the United States with Reference to China, Japan, and Korea in the 19th Century* (New York: Macmillan, 1922), 485–504; Hunt, *Making of a Special Relationship*; Cohen, *America's Response to China*, 32–34.

32. Robert Sutter, *Historical Dictionary of United States–China Relations* (Lanham, MD: Scarecrow Press, 2006), 108.

33. Marilyn Young, *The Rhetoric of Empire: American China Policy, 1895–1901* (Cambridge, MA: Harvard University Press, 1968).

34. Cohen, *America's Response to China*, 29–88; Schaller, *The United States and China*, 26–48.

35. John Fairbank, Edwin Reischauer, and Albert Craig, *East Asia: The Modern Transformation* (Boston: Houghton Mifflin, 1965), 476–77.

36. Joseph Esherick, *The Origins of the Boxer Uprising* (Berkeley: University of California Press, 1987).

37. Cohen, *America's Response to China*, 42–55.

38. Hunt, *Frontier Defense and the Open Door*; Cohen, *America's Response to China*, 56–58.

39. Sutter, *Historical Dictionary*, 25–26.

40. Cohen, *America's Response to China*, 52–57, 65.

41. Sutter, *Historical Dictionary*, 25–26.

42. Edward Rhodes, *China's Republican Revolution: The Case of Kwangtung, 1895–1913* (Cambridge, MA: Harvard University Press, 1975), 176–81.

43. Hunt, *Frontier Defense and the Open Door.*

44. Sutter, *Historical Dictionary*, 192.

45. Cohen, *America's Response to China*, 68–70.

46. Hunt, *Frontier Defense and the Open Door.*

47. Li, *Woodrow Wilson's China Policy*; Fairbank et al., *East Asia: The Modern . . .* , 571, 645, 665.

48. Iriye, *After Imperialism*; Fairbank et al., *East Asia: The Modern . . .* , 674–76.

49. James Sheridan, *China in Disintegration: The Republican Era in Chinese History, 1912–1949* (New York: The Free Press, 1975).

50. Fairbank et al., *East Asia: The Modern . . .* , 685.

51. Benjamin Schwartz, *Chinese Communism and the Rise of Mao* (Cambridge, MA: Harvard University Press, 1958).

52. Cohen, *America's Response to China*, 107–9; Fairbank et al., *East Asia: The Modern . . .* , 688–91.

53. Schaller, *The United States and China*, 42–43.

54. Borg, *The United States and the Far Eastern Crisis*; Cohen, *America's Response to China*, 126–27.

55. Schaller, *The United States and China*, 51.

56. Sutter, *Historical Dictionary*, 78–79.

57. Fairbank et al., *East Asia: The Modern . . .* , 608–12.

58. Schaller, *The United States and China*, 54, 63.

59. Cohen, *America's Response to China*, 137–38.

60. Patricia Neils, *China Images in the Life and Times of Henry Luce* (Lanham, MD: Rowman & Littlefield, 1990); Graham Peck, *Two Kinds of Time* (Boston: Houghton Mifflin, 1967).

61. James C. Thomson Jr., *While China Faced West: American Reformers in Nationalist China, 1928–1937* (Cambridge, MA: Harvard University Press, 1968).

62. Fairbank et al., *East Asia: The Modern . . .* , 701–6.

3. RELATIONS DURING WORLD WAR II, CIVIL WAR, COLD WAR

1. Michael Schaller, *The U.S. Crusade in China, 1938–1945* (New York: Columbia University Press, 1979); Herbert Feis, *The China Tangle: The American Effort in China from Pearl Harbor to the Marshall Mission* (Princeton, NJ: Princeton University Press, 1953); Barbara Tuchman, *Stilwell and the American Experience in China, 1911–1945* (New York: Macmillan, 1971); Tsou Tang, *America's Failure in China, 1941–1950* (Chicago: University of Chicago Press, 1963); Jay Taylor, *The Generalissimo: Chiang Kai-shek and the Struggle for Modern China* (Cambridge, MA: Harvard University Press, 2009); Wang Taiping, ed., *Xin Zhongguo waijiao wushinian* [Fifty years of diplomacy of the new China] (Beijing: Beijing Chubanshe, 1999).

2. Feis, *The China Tangle.*

3. Russell Buhite, *Patrick J. Hurley and American Foreign Policy* (Ithaca, NY: Cornell University Press, 1973).

4. Dorothy Borg and Waldo Heinrichs, eds., *Uncertain Years: Chinese-American Relations, 1947–1950* (New York: Columbia University Press, 1980).

5. Taylor, *The Generalissimo*; Schaller, *The U.S. Crusade in China.*

6. Buhite, *Patrick J. Hurley and American Foreign Policy*; John Beal, *Marshall in China* (Garden City, NY: Doubleday, 1970).

7. Warren Cohen, "The Development of Chinese Communist Policy toward the United States, 1922–1938," *Orbis* 2 (1967): 219–37.

8. James Reardon-Anderson, *Yenan and the Great Powers: The Origins of Chinese Communist Foreign Policy, 1944–1946* (New York: Columbia University Press, 1980).

9. Odd Arne Westad, *Brothers in Arms: The Rise and Fall of the Sino-Soviet Alliance, 1945–1963* (Stanford, CA: Stanford University Press, 1998).

10. Borg and Heinrichs, *Uncertain Years*; Zi Zhongyun, *Meiguo duihua zhengce de yuanqi he fazhan, 1945–1950* [The origins and development of American policy toward China, 1945–1950] (Chongqing: Chongqing, 1987).

11. Tsou, *America's Failure in China*.

12. Charles Romanus and Riley Sunderland, *Time Runs Out on CBI* (Washington, DC: Department of the Army, 1959).

13. Charles Romanus and Riley Sunderland, *Stilwell's Command Problems* (Washington, DC: Department of the Army, 1956).

14. Tuchman, *Stilwell and the American Experience in China*.

15. Michael Schaller, *The United States and China: Into the Twenty-First Century* (New York: Oxford University Press, 2002), 59–61.

16. Ibid., 72; Warren Cohen, *America's Response to China: A History of Sino-American Relations* (New York: Columbia University Press, 2010), 138.

17. Tuchman, *Stilwell and the American Experience in China*.

18. Kenneth Shewmaker, *Americans and the Chinese Communists, 1927–1945: A Persuading Encounter* (Ithaca, NY: Cornell University Press, 1971).

19. Robert Sutter, *China Watch: Toward Sino-American Reconciliation* (Baltimore: Johns Hopkins University Press, 1978), 12–14.

20. Sutter, *China Watch*, 14–18.

21. Immanuel C. Y. Hsu, *The Rise of Modern China* (New York: Oxford University Press, 2000), 603–4.

22. Sutter, *China Watch*, 18–23.

23. Hsu, *The Rise of Modern China*, 604–5.

24. Buhite, *Patrick J. Hurley and American Foreign Policy*.

25. Schaller, *The United States and China*, 94–96.

26. Cohen, *America's Response to China*, 159–62.

27. Robert Sutter, *Historical Dictionary of United States–China Relations* (Lanham, MD: Scarecrow Press, 2006), 57–58.

28. Schaller, *The United States and China*, 99–102.

29. Cohen, *America's Response to China*, 192.

30. John Fairbank, Edwin Reischauer, and Albert Craig, *East Asia: The Modern Transformation* (Boston: Houghton Mifflin, 1965), 858–59.

31. Schaller, *The United States and China*, 115.

32. Nancy Bernkopf Tucker, *Strait Talk: United States-Taiwan Relations and the Crisis with China* (Cambridge, MA: Harvard University Press, 2009), 13.

33. Schaller, *The United States and China*, 116–17; Zi, *Meiguo duihua zhengce de yuanqi he fazhan* [The origins and development of American policy toward China].

34. Yu-ming Shaw, *An American Missionary in China: John Leighton Stuart and Chinese-American Relations* (Cambridge, MA: Harvard University Press, 1992).

35. Tucker, *Strait Talk*, 13; Sutter, *China Watch*, 31–34.

36. Chen Jian, *China's Road to the Korean War* (New York: Columbia University Press, 1994); Westad, *Brothers in Arms*; Zi Zhongyun and He Di, eds., *Meitai Guanxi Sishinian* [Forty years of US-Taiwan relations] (Beijing: People's Press, 1991).

37. Allen Whiting, *The Chinese Calculus of Deterrence: India and Indochina* (Ann Arbor: University of Michigan Press, 1975); Robert S. Ross and Jiang Changbin, eds., *Re-examining the Cold War: U.S.-China Diplomacy, 1954–1973* (Cambridge, MA: Harvard University Press, 2001).

38. Chen Jian, *Mao's China and the Cold War* (Chapel Hill: University of North Carolina Press, 2001); Thomas Christensen, *Useful Adversaries: Grand Strategy, Domestic Mobiliza-

288 *Notes*

tiontion, *and Sino-American Conflicts, 1949–1958* (Princeton, NJ: Princeton University Press, 1996).

39. Richard Wich, *Sino-Soviet Crisis Politics* (Cambridge, MA: Harvard University Press, 1980).

40. Ralph Clough, *Island China* (Cambridge, MA: Harvard University Press, 1978), 5–10.

41. Tucker, *Strait Talk*, 13–26.

42. Robert Blum, *Drawing the Line: The Origins of the American Containment Policy in East Asia* (New York: W. W. Norton, 1982); William Stueck, *The Korean War: An International History* (Princeton, NJ: Princeton University Press, 1997); Chen, *China's Road to the Korean War*.

43. Schaller, *The United States and China*, 152–62.

44. Bruce Cumings, *The Origins of the Korean War* (Princeton, NJ: Princeton University Press, 1990).

45. Cohen, *America's Response to China*, 186–91.

46. Schaller, *The United States and China*, 129–35.

47. Rosemary Foot, *A Substitute for Victory: The Politics of Peacemaking and the Korean Armistice Talks* (Ithaca, NY: Cornell University Press, 1990).

48. Barry Naughton, *The Chinese Economy: Transitions and Growth* (Cambridge, MA: MIT Press, 2007), 55–83.

49. Chen, *Mao's China and the Cold War*.

50. Christensen, *Useful Adversaries*.

51. Schaller, *The United States and China*, 144–46.

52. Ross Koen, *The China Lobby in American Politics* (New York: Harper and Row, 1974).

53. Tucker, *Strait Talk*, 13–15.

54. Clough, *Island China*, 10–14.

55. Sutter, *China Watch*, 34–46.

56. Zhang Baijia and Jia Qingguo, "Steering Wheel, Shock Absorber, and Diplomatic Probe in Confrontation: Sino-American Ambassadorial Talks Seen from the Chinese Perspective," in Ross and Jiang, eds., *Re-examining the Cold War*, 173–99; Sutter, *China Watch*, 34–46.

57. Sutter, *Historical Dictionary of United States–China Relations*, 4.

58. Steven Goldstein, "Dialogue of the Deaf? The Sino-American Ambassadorial-Level Talks, 1955–1970," in Ross and Jiang, eds., *Re-examining the Cold War*, 200–237.

59. Tucker, *Strait Talk*, 14–17.

60. Chen, *Mao's China and the Cold War*.

61. Schaller, *The United States and China*, 152–56.

62. Tucker, *Strait Talk*, 17–21.

63. Cohen, *America's Response to China*, 210–13; Goldstein, "Dialogue of the Deaf?" 229–37.

64. Tony Saich, *Governance and Politics of China* (New York: Palgrave Macmillan, 2004), 44–56.

65. Hsu, *The Rise of Modern China*, 689–702.

66. Roderick MacFarquhar and Michael Schoenhals, *Mao's Last Revolution* (Cambridge, MA: Harvard University Press, 2006).

67. Sutter, *China Watch*, 65–67.

68. Peter Van Ness, *Revolution and Chinese Foreign Policy* (Berkeley: University of California Press, 1970).

69. Jisen Ma, *The Cultural Revolution in the Foreign Ministry of China* (Hong Kong: Chinese University Press, 2004).

70. Schaller, *The United States and China*, 156–62.

71. Tucker, *Strait Talk*, 21–26.

4. RAPPROCHEMENT AND NORMALIZATION

1. A. Doak Barnett, *A New U.S. Policy toward China* (Washington, DC: Brookings Institution, 1971); Rosemary Foot, *The Practice of Power: U.S. Relations with China since 1949* (New York: Oxford University Press, 1997); Evelyn Goh, *Constructing the U.S. Rapprochement with China, 1961–1974* (New York: Cambridge University Press, 2005); Gong Li, *Kuayue: 1969–1979 nian Zhong-Mei guanxi de yanbian* [Across the chasm: The evolution of relations between China and the United States, 1969–1979] (Henan: Henan People's Press, 1992).

2. Chen Jian, *Mao's China and the Cold War* (Chapel Hill: University of North Carolina Press, 2001).

3. Foot, *The Practice of Power*; Goh, *Constructing the U.S. Rapprochement with China*.

4. Robert Ross, *Negotiating Cooperation: The United States and China, 1969–1989* (Stanford, CA: Stanford University Press, 1995); Robert Sutter, *China Watch: Toward Sino-American Reconciliation* (Baltimore: Johns Hopkins University Press, 1978), 83–102; Thomas Gottlieb, *Chinese Foreign Policy Factionalism and the Origins of the Strategic Triangle* (Santa Monica, CA: Rand, 1977); John Garver, *China's Decision for Rapprochement with the United States, 1968–1971* (Boulder, CO: Westview Press, 1982); Wang Zhongchun, "The Soviet Factor in Sino-American Normalization, 1969–1979," in *Normalization of U.S.-China Relations*, ed. William Kirby, Robert Ross, and Gong Li (Cambridge, MA: Harvard University Press, 2005).

5. James Mann, *About Face: A History of America's Curious Relationship with China, from Nixon to Clinton* (New York: Knopf, 1999).

6. Sutter, *China Watch*, 1–62.

7. The developments in the United States during 1968 noted here and below are covered in *American History Online—Facts on File* (http://www.fofweb.com) and *CQ Almanac 1968* (Washington, DC: Congressional Quarterly News Features [1968]).

8. Mann, *About Face*, 13–25.

9. Li Jie, "China's Domestic Politics and the Normalization of Sino-U.S. Relations, 1969–1979," in Kirby, Ross, and Li, eds., *Normalization of U.S.-China Relations*, 56–89; Philip Bridgham, "Mao's Cultural Revolution: The Struggle to Seize Power," *The China Quarterly* 41 (1970): 1–25.

10. Gottlieb, *Chinese Foreign Policy Factionalism*; Roderick MacFarquhar and Michael Schoenhals, *Mao's Last Revolution* (Cambridge, MA: Harvard University Press, 2006).

11. Harlan Jencks, *From Muskets to Missiles: Politics and Professionalism in the Chinese Army, 1945–1981* (Boulder, CO: Westview Press, 1982).

12. Thomas Robinson, "The Sino-Soviet Border Dispute: Background, Development and the March 1969 Clashes," *American Political Science Review* 66, no. 4 (December 1972): 1175–78; Alice Lyman Miller and Richard Wich, *Becoming Asia* (Stanford, CA: Stanford University Press, 2011), 116–36, 182–93.

13. John Garver, *Foreign Relations of the People's Republic of China* (Englewood Cliffs, NJ: Prentice Hall, 1993), 304–20.

14. Gottlieb, *Chinese Foreign Policy Factionalism*.

15. Sutter, *China Watch*, 72–75.

16. Ibid., 75–78.

17. Garver, *Foreign Relations of the People's Republic of China*, 306–10.

18. Sutter, *China Watch*, 78–102.

19. Michael Schaller, *The United States and China: Into the Twenty-First Century* (New York: Oxford University Press, 2002), 170.

20. Ross, *Negotiating Cooperation*, 28, 34–35.

21. Immanuel C. Y. Hsu, *The Rise of Modern China* (New York: Oxford University Press, 2000), 711–14, 822.

22. Sutter, *Historical Dictionary of United States–China Relations* (Lanham, MD: Scarecrow Press, 2006), 190–91.

23. Hsu, *The Rise of Modern China*, 710–14, 820–23.

24. Nancy Bernkopf Tucker, *Strait Talk: United States-Taiwan Relations and the Crisis with China* (Cambridge, MA: Harvard University Press, 2009), 35–40.

25. Ibid., 52, 68; Mann, *About Face*, 51–52.

26. An authoritative account of the U.S.-China opening is in Tucker, *Strait Talk*.

27. Ibid., 52.

28. House Committee on Foreign Affairs, *Executive-Legislative Consultations over China Policy, 1978–1979* (Washington, DC: US Government Printing Office, 1980).

29. Schaller, *The United States and China*, 178–84; Tucker, *Strait Talk*, 29–68; Ross, *Negotiating Cooperation*, 17–54.

30. Warren Cohen, *America's Response to China: A History of Sino-American Relations* (New York: Columbia University Press, 2010), 220.

31. Hsu, *The Rise of Modern China*, 763–73.

32. John K. Fairbank and Merle Goldman, *China: A New History* (Cambridge, MA: Harvard University Press, 1999), 404–5.

33. Hsu, *The Rise of Modern China*, 817–23.

34. Fairbank and Goldman, *China*, 406–10; Ezra Vogel, *Deng Xiaoping and the Transformation of China* (Cambridge, MA: Harvard University Press, 2011), 91–183.

35. Nayan Chanda, *Brother Enemy: The War after the War* (New York: Harcourt Brace Jovanovich, 1986).

36. Garver, *Foreign Relations of the People's Republic of China*, 166–77, 310–11.

37. Cohen, *America's Response to China*, 221–25.

38. Mann, *About Face*, 82–92.

39. Tucker, *Strait Talk*, 101–15.

40. Harry Harding, *A Fragile Relationship: The United States and China since 1972* (Washington, DC: Brookings Institution, 1992), 80–81.

41. Ross, *Negotiating Cooperation*, 125–26; Mann, *About Face*, 98–100.

42. House Committee on Foreign Affairs, *Executive-Legislative Consultations over China Policy*.

43. Harding, *A Fragile Relationship*, 86–87.

44. Schaller, *The United States and China*, 193–96.

45. Tucker, *Strait Talk*, 129–52.

46. Schaller, *The United States and China*, 177.

47. On the costs, see Tucker, *Strait Talk*, 52, 68, 153; Ross, *Negotiating Cooperation*, 163–245; Mann, *About Face*, 125–36; Schaller, *The United States and China*, 177; House Committee on Foreign Affairs, *Executive-Legislative Consultations over China Policy*.

48. See discussion of congressional debates on China policy in chapter 5, below.

49. Tucker, *Strait Talk*, 153–60.

50. Harding, *A Fragile Relationship*; Ross, *Negotiating Cooperation*; Mann, *About Face*. Major works covering later developments are Tucker, *Strait Talk*; David M. Lampton, *Same Bed, Different Dreams: Managing U.S.-China Relations, 1989–2000* (Berkeley: University of California Press, 2001); Robert Suettinger, *Beyond Tiananmen: The Politics of U.S.-China Relations, 1989–2000* (Washington, DC: Brookings Institution, 2003); Jean Garrison, *Making China Policy: From Nixon to G. W. Bush* (Boulder, CO: Lynne Rienner, 2005). Garrison's analysis (80–85) identifies two competing groups of US decision makers regarding China policy in the early 1980s as the "China-first" group and the "pan-Asian" group. The analysis in this book builds on the Garrison analysis.

51. Ross, *Negotiating Cooperation*, 170–245; Mann, *About Face*, 119–36; Garrison, *Making China Policy*, 79–106; Tucker, *Strait Talk*, 153–60.

52. Harding, *A Fragile Relationship*, 131–45. David Shambaugh, "Patterns of Interaction in Sino-American Relations," in *Chinese Foreign Policy: Theory and Practice*, ed. Thomas Robinson and David Shambaugh (New York: Oxford University Press, 1994), 203–5.

53. Garver, *Foreign Relations of the People's Republic of China*, 310–19.

54. Robert Sutter, *Chinese Foreign Relations: Developments after Mao* (New York: Praeger, 1986), 18–96.

55. Garver, *Foreign Relations of the People's Republic of China*, 98–103, 317–19.

56. Ross, *Negotiating Cooperation*, 164–74.

57. Sutter, *Chinese Foreign Relations*, 182.

58. Ibid., 178.

59. Garver, *Foreign Relations of the People's Republic of China*, 98–103; Ross, *Negotiating Cooperation*, 170–200.

60. Tucker, *Strait Talk*, 153–60; Mann, *About Face*, 128–33.

61. Sutter, *Chinese Foreign Relations*, 178.

62. Richard Nations, "A Tilt Towards Tokyo," *Far Eastern Economic Review*, April 21, 1983, 36; Ross, *Negotiating Cooperation*, 228–33.

63. Sutter, *Chinese Foreign Relations*, 178–79.

64. Ibid.

65. On Deng's role in these foreign policy issues and overall political standing, see Vogel, *Deng Xiaoping and the Transformation of China*.

66. Ross, *Negotiating Cooperation*, 233–45; Tucker, *Strait Talk*, 160–61.

67. Sutter, *Chinese Foreign Relations*, 180–81.

68. Ross, *Negotiating Cooperation*, 233–44; Sutter, *Chinese Foreign Relations*, 181–82.

69. Tucker, *Strait Talk*, 155–60.

70. Gerald Segal, *Sino-Soviet Relations after Mao*, Adelphi Papers, no. 202 (London: International Institute for Strategic Studies, 1985).

71. The review of Sino-Soviet relations in the remainder of this section is adapted from Sutter, *Chinese Foreign Relations*, 182–86. See also Segal, *Sino-Soviet Relations after Mao*.

5. TIANANMEN, TAIWAN, AND POST–COLD WAR REALITIES, 1989–2000

1. Tony Saich, *Governance and Politics of China* (New York: Palgrave Macmillan, 2004), 70–74; Ezra Vogel, *Deng Xiaoping and the Transformation of China* (Cambridge, MA: Harvard University Press, 2011)

2. Jean Garrison, *Making China Policy: From Nixon to G. W. Bush* (Boulder, CO: Lynne Rienner, 2005), 210–17; Steven Mufson, "Coverage of China in the American Press," in *China in the American Political Imagination*, ed. Carola McGiffert (Washington, DC: CSIS Press, 2003); David M. Lampton, *Same Bed, Different Dreams: Managing U.S.-China Relations, 1989–2000* (Berkeley: University of California Press, 2001), 276–78; Kenneth Lieberthal, "Why the US Malaise over China?" YaleGlobal Online, January 19, 2006, http://yaleglobal.yale.edu/content/why-us-malaise-over-china (accessed September 27, 2009); Kenneth Lieberthal and Wang Jisi, *Addressing U.S.-China Strategic Distrust* (Washington, DC: Brookings Institution, 2012).

3. Lampton, *Same Bed, Different Dreams*, 17–55.

4. Barry Naughton, *The Chinese Economy: Transitions and Growth* (Cambridge, MA: MIT Press, 2007), 98–100.

5. Carola McGiffert, ed., *Chinese Images of the United States* (Washington, DC: CSIS Press, 2006).

6. Kenneth Lieberthal, "China: How Domestic Forces Shape the PRC's Grand Strategy and International Impact," in *Strategic Asia 2007–2008*, ed. Ashley Tellis and Michael Wills (Seattle, WA: National Bureau of Asian Research, 2007), 63.

7. Garrison, *Making China Policy*, 182–83; Michael Swaine, *Reverse Course? The Fragile Turnabout in U.S.-China Relations*, Policy Brief 22 (Washington, DC: Carnegie Endowment, February 2003).

8. Warren Cohen, *America's Response to China: A History of Sino-American Relations* (New York: Columbia University Press, 2000), 229.

9. Michael Schaller, *The United States and China: Into the Twenty-First Century* (New York: Oxford University Press, 2015), 211–14.

10. John Garver, *Face Off: China, the United States, and Taiwan's Democratization* (Seattle: University of Washington Press, 1997).

11. Lampton, *Same Bed, Different Dreams*, 55–63.

12. Robert L. Suettinger, *Beyond Tiananmen: The Politics of U.S.-China Relations, 1989–2000* (Washington, DC: Brookings Institution, 2003), 358–409.

13. Robert Sutter, *U.S. Policy toward China: An Introduction to the Role of Interest Groups* (Lanham, MD: Rowman & Littlefield, 1998).

14. Harry Harding, *Public Engagement in American Foreign Policy* (New York: The American Assembly, Columbia University, February 23–25, 1995), 8–9.

15. Charlotte Preece and Robert Sutter, *Foreign Policy Debate in America*, CRS Report 91–833F (Washington, DC: Congressional Research Service of the Library of Congress, November 27, 1991).

16. Sutter, *U.S. Policy toward China*, 12.

17. "Ross Perot on the Issues," On the Issues, http://www.issues2000.org/Ross_Perot.htm (accessed September 21, 2009).

18. Sutter, *U.S. Policy toward China*, 13–14; Joseph Nye, *Bound to Lead* (Cambridge, MA: Harvard University Press, 1992).

19. Sutter, *U.S. Policy toward China*, 14–15; Lampton, *Same Bed, Different Dreams*, 17–63.

20. "John McCain on the Issues," On the Issues, http://www.issues2000.org/John_McCain.htm (accessed September 21, 2009).

21. Lampton, *Same Bed, Different Dreams*, 332–35, 338–39.

22. Kerry Dumbaugh, "Interest Groups: Growing Influence," in *Making China Policy: Lessons from the Bush and Clinton Administrations*, ed. Ramon Myers, Michel Oksenberg, and David Shambaugh (Lanham, MD: Rowman & Littlefield, 2001), 113–78.

23. Sutter, *U.S. Policy toward China*, 16.

24. Kent Wong, "The AFL-CIO and China," *U.S.-China Media Brief*, 2008, UCLA Asian American Studies Center, http://www.aasc.ucla.edu/uschina/ee_aflciochina.shtml (accessed September 21, 2009).

25. Dumbaugh, "Interest Groups," 150, 158–59, 161, 162, 170–71.

26. Sutter, *U.S. Policy toward China*, 16–17.

27. Nancy Bernkopf Tucker, *Strait Talk: United States-Taiwan Relations and the Crisis with China* (Cambridge, MA: Harvard University Press, 2009).

28. Suettinger, *Beyond Tiananmen*, 294, 330.

29. The four crises are identified and reviewed in Lampton, *Same Bed, Different Dreams*, 17–63. See also Suettinger, *Beyond Tiananmen*.

30. Schaller, *The United States and China*, 204–5.

31. Sutter, *U.S. Policy toward China*, 26–44.

32. James Mann, *About Face: A History of America's Curious Relationship with China, from Nixon to Clinton* (New York: Knopf, 1999), 274–78.

33. Cohen, *America's Response to China*, 229–31.

34. Schaller, *The United States and China*, 214–19.

35. Cohen, *America's Response to China*, 234–39.

36. For this and the next two paragraphs, see Robert Sutter, *Historical Dictionary of United States–China Relations* (Lanham, MD: Rowman & Littlefield, 2006), lxix–lxx.

37. Schaller, *The United States and China*, 219–27.

38. Cohen, *America's Response to China*, 235–36.

39. Tucker, *Strait Talk*, 217–18, 231–43.

40. Sutter, *Historical Dictionary of United States–China Relations*, lxxi.

41. Suettinger, *Beyond Tiananmen*, 369–77.

42. Tucker, *Strait Talk*, 239–44.

43. Lampton, *Same Bed, Different Dreams*, 95–97.

44. Garrison, *Making China Policy*, 148–52.

45. Ibid., 165–82; Robert Sutter, "The Democratic-Led 110th Congress: Implications for Asia," *Asia Policy* 3 (January 2007): 125–50.

46. The following analysis summarizes points made at greater length in Robert Sutter, "U.S. Domestic Debate over Policy toward Mainland China and Taiwan: Key Findings, Outlook, and

Lessons," *American Journal of Chinese Studies* 8, no. 2 (October 2001): 133–44; and Robert Sutter, "The Bush Administration and U.S. China Policy Debate," *Issues and Studies* 38, no. 2 (June 2002): 14–22.

47. Tucker, *Strait Talk*; Myers, Oksenberg, Shambaugh, eds., *Making China Policy*; Lampton, *Same Bed, Different Dreams*; Mann, *About Face*; Sutter, *U.S. Policy toward China*; Robert Sutter, *The China Quandary* (Boulder, CO: Westview Press, 1983).

48. Tucker, *Strait Talk*, 29–52.

49. Reviewed in ibid., 116–28; Sutter, *The China Quandary*, 5, 19, 85, and 146.

50. House Committee on Foreign Affairs, *Executive-Legislative Consultations over China Policy, 1978–1979* (Washington, DC: US Government Printing Office, 1980).

51. Ramon Myers, Michel Oksenberg, and David Shambaugh, eds., *Making China Policy: Lessons from the Bush and Clinton Administrations* (Lanham, MD: Rowman & Littlefield, 2001), 79–222.

52. Robert Sutter, "U.S. Domestic Debate over Policy toward Mainland China and Taiwan," in *Making China Policy: Lessons from the Bush and Clinton Administrations*, ed. Ramon Myers, Michel Oksenberg, and David Shambaugh (Lanham, MD: Rowman & Littlefield, 2001), 37.

53. Bill Gertz and Rowan Scarborough, "Inside the Ring," *Washington Times*, March 22, 2002 (Internet version); Murray Hiebert and Susan Lawrence, "Crossing Red Lines," *Far Eastern Economic Review*, April 4, 2002 (Internet version).

54. Sutter, "The Bush Administration and U.S. China Policy Debate," 16.

55. Lampton, *Same Bed, Different Dreams*; Chu Shulong, "Quanmian jianshe xiaokang shehui shiqi de zhongguo waijiao zhan-lue," *Shijie Jingji yu Zhengzhi* 8 (August 2003); Fu Hao and Li Tongcheng, eds., *Lusi shui shou? Zhongguo waijiaoguan zai Meiguo* [Who will win the game? Chinese diplomats in the United States] (Beijing: Hauqiao Chubanshe, 1998).

56. Song Qiang, Zhang Changchang, and Qiao Bian, *Zhongguo keyi shuo bu: Lengzhanhou shidai de zhengzhi yu qinggan jueze* [China can say no: The decision between politics and sentiment in the post–Cold War] (Beijing: Zhonghua Gongshang Lianhe Chubanshe, 1996).

57. Robert Sutter, *Chinese Policy Priorities and Their Implications for the United States* (Lanham, MD: Rowman & Littlefield, 2000), 40–41; Wang Jisi, *China's Changing Role in Asia* (Washington, DC: The Atlantic Council of the United States, January 2004), 1–5, 16–17; Qian Qichen, "Adjustment of the United States National Security Strategy and International Relations in the Early New Century," (Beijing) *Foreign Affairs Journal* 71 (March 2004): 1–7; Wang Jisi, "Xinxingshi de zhuyao tedian he Zhongguo waijiao," *Xiabdai Guoji Guanxi* (Beijing) 4 (April 2003): 1–3; Yuan Peng, "Bumpy Road Ahead for Sustainable Sino-U.S. Ties," *China Daily*, May 8, 2007, 11; Lieberthal, "Why the US Malaise over China?"; Fu Mengzi, "Sino-U.S. Relations," *Xiandai Guoji Guanxi* (Beijing) 17 (January 2007): 32–46.

58. Suettinger, *Beyond Tiananmen*, 340–51; Schaller, *The United States and China*, 223–24.

59. Sutter, *Chinese Policy Priorities*, 41–42.

60. "Experts Appraise Sino-U.S. Relations," *Jeifang Junbao* (June 1995), 5; Wang Jisi, "Deepening Mutual Understanding and Expanding Strategic Consensus," *Renmin Ribao* (June 16, 1998), 6; "Questions and Answers at Qian Qichen's Small-Scale Briefing," *Wen Wei Pao* (Hong Kong; November 4, 1997), A6; Sutter, *Chinese Policy Priorities*, 42.

61. Lampton, *Same Bed, Different Dreams*, 39–45; Sutter, *U.S. Policy toward China*, 47–65.

62. David M. Lampton, "America's China Policy in the Age of the Finance Minister: Clinton Ends Linkage," *China Quarterly* 139 (September 1994): 597–621.

63. Sutter, *Chinese Policy Priorities*, 43–44.

64. Lampton, *Same Bed, Different Dreams*, 45.

65. Sutter, *Chinese Policy Priorities*, 52; Garver, *Face Off*. See also Su Ge, *Meiguo: Dui hua Zhengce yu Taiwan wenti* [America: China policy and the Taiwan issue] (Beijing: Shijie Zhishi Chubanshe, 1998).

66. *U.S. News and World Report*, October 23, 1995, 72.

67. Suettinger, *Beyond Tiananmen*, 264–357.

68. Sutter, *Chinese Policy Priorities*, 57–58.

69. Susan Shirk, *China: Fragile Superpower* (New York: Oxford University Press, 2007), 220.

70. Robert Sutter, *China's Rise in Asia* (Lanham, MD: Rowman & Littlefield, 2005), 12–13.

6. PRAGMATISM AMID DIFFERENCES DURING THE GEORGE W. BUSH ADMINISTRATION

1. Murray Hiebert, *The Bush Presidency: Implications for Asia* (New York: Asia Society, 2001), 5–9.

2. Robert Sutter, "Grading Bush's China Policy: A−," *PacNet* 10 (March 8, 2002), https://www.csis.org/analysis/pacnet-10-grading-bushs-china-policy.

3. James Shinn, ed., *Weaving the Net: Conditional Engagement with China* (New York: Council on Foreign Relations, 1996).

4. Bonnie Glaser, "Bilateral Relations on Reasonably Sound Footing as 2000 and the Clinton Administration Come to a Close," *Comparative Connections* (January 2001), https://csis-prod.s3.amazonaws.com/s3fs-public/legacy_files/files/media/csis/pubs/0004qus_china.pdf.

5. Bonnie Glaser, "First Contact: Qian Qichen Engages in Wide-Ranging, Constructive Talks with President Bush and Senior U.S. Officials," *Comparative Connections* (April 2001), https://csis-prod.s3.amazonaws.com/s3fs-public/legacy_files/files/media/csis/pubs/0101qus_china.pdf.

6. John Keefe, *Anatomy of the EP-3 Incident* (Alexandria, VA: Center for Naval Analysis, 2002).

7. Nick Cummings-Bruce, "Powell Will Explain Bush's Asia Policy," *Wall Street Journal*, July 23, 2001, A11.

8. Michael Swaine and Zhang Tuosheng, eds., *Managing Sino-American Crises* (Washington, DC: Carnegie Endowment for International Peace, 2006).

9. "Concern over U.S. Plans for War on Terror Dominate Jiang Tour," Reuters, April 7, 2002, http://www.taiwansecurity.org (accessed April 9, 2002); Willy Wo-Lap Lam, "U.S., Taiwan Catch Jiang Off-Guard," CNN.com, March 19, 2002, http://edition.cnn.com/2002/WORLD/asiapcf/east/03/18/willy.column.

10. Bonnie Glaser, "Playing Up the Positive on the Eve of the Crawford Summit," *Comparative Connections* (October 2002), http://cc.csis.org/2002/10/playing-positive-eve-crawford-summit.

11. "U.S. Says China Regulations Should Free Up Soybean Exports," statement of the Office of the U.S. Trade Representative, October 18, 2002, http://ustr.gov; "Mainland Offers Taiwan Goodwill Gesture," *China Daily*, October 18, 2002, http://www.taiwansecurity.org (accessed October 20, 2002); "China Tightens Rules on Military Exports," Reuters, October 21, 2002, http://www.taiwansecurity.org (accessed October 23, 2002); "Ashcroft to Open China FBI Office," Reuters, October 22, 2002, http://www.taiwansecurity.org (accessed October 24, 2002); "U.S. and China Seal Billion Dollar Deals," *BBC*, October 22, 2002, http://www.taiwansecurity.org (accessed October 24, 2002); "U.S. and China Set New Rights Talks," *Washington Post*, October 24, 2002, http://www.taiwansecurity.org (accessed October 26, 2002).

12. Lu Zhenya, "Jiang Zemin, Bush Agree to Maintain High-Level Strategic Dialogue," *Zhongguo Xinwen She* (Beijing), October 26, 2002 (Internet version).

13. Shirley Kan, *U.S.-China Military Contacts: Issues for Congress*, CRS Report RL32496 (Washington, DC: Congressional Research Service of the Library of Congress, June 19, 2012), 2–4.

14. "Bush, Kerry Square Off in 1st Debate," *Japan Today*, October 1, 2004, http://www.japantoday.com/jp/news/313422/all (accessed March 21, 2008; site discontinued).

15. Robert Sutter, "The Taiwan Problem in the Second George W. Bush Administration—U.S. Officials' Views and Their Implications for U.S. Policy," *Journal of Contemporary China* 15, no. 48 (August 2006): 417–42.

16. Secretary of State Condoleezza Rice, remarks at Sophia University, Tokyo, Japan, March 19, 2005, http://www.state.gov/secretary/rm/2005/43655.htm (accessed March 21, 2008; site discontinued); Evan Medeiros, "Strategic Hedging and the Future of Asia-Pacific Stability," *Washington Quarterly* 29, no. 1 (2005–6): 15–28.

17. Rosemary Foot, "Chinese Strategies in a U.S.-Hegemonic Global Order: Accommodating and Hedging," *International Affairs* 82, no. 1 (2006): 77–94; Wang Jisi, "China's Search for Stability with America," *Foreign Affairs* 84, no. 5 (September–October 2005): 39–48; Yong Deng and Thomas Moore, "China Views Globalization: Toward a New Great-Power Politics," *Washington Quarterly* 27, no. 3 (Summer 2004): 117–36.

18. Off-the-record interviews with US officials reviewed in Robert Sutter, "Dealing with a Rising China: U.S. Strategy and Policy," in *Making New Partnership: A Rising China and Its Neighbors*, ed. Zhang Yunlin (Beijing: Social Sciences Academic Press, 2008), 370 -74.

19. Among published sources, see U.S.-China Economic and Security Review Commission, *2005 Report to Congress* (Washington, DC: US Government Printing Office, 2005), 143–90.

20. Remarks of Deputy Secretary of State Robert Zoellick, "Wither China? From Membership to Responsibility," National Committee for U.S.-China Relations, September 21, 2005, http://www.cfr.org/china/whither-china-membership-responsibility/p8916 (site discontinued).

21. Victor Cha, "Winning Asia: Washington's Untold Success Story," *Foreign Affairs* 86, no. 6 (November–December 2007): 98–133; Daniel Twining, "America's Grand Design in Asia," *Washington Quarterly* 30, no. 3 (2007): 79–94; Robert Sutter, *The United States in Asia* (Lanham, MD: Rowman & Littlefield, 2008), 270–76, 281–83.

22. Kerry Dumbaugh, *China-U.S. Relations: Current Issues and Implications for U.S. Policy*, CRS Report RL33877 (Washington, DC: Congressional Research Service of the Library of Congress, May 25, 2007).

23. David M. Lampton, *Same Bed, Different Dreams: Managing U.S.-China Relations, 1989–2000* (Berkeley: University of California Press, 2001).

24. Kerry Dumbaugh, *China-U.S. Relations*, IB 98018 (Washington, DC, Library of Congress, July 17, 2001).

25. Robert Sutter, *U.S. Policy toward China: An Introduction to the Role of Interest Groups* (Lanham, MD: Rowman & Littlefield, 1998), 94.

26. Bates Gill, *Meeting the Challenges and Opportunities of China's Rise* (Washington, DC: Center for Strategic and International Studies, October 2006), 6–12.

27. As cited in notes below, the following discussion relies on reports on China-U.S. relations done by the Congressional Research Service of the Library of Congress. Other sources include *Congressional Quarterly Weekly Report*, *CQ Weekly*, *Congressional Quarterly Almanac*, and *CQ Almanac*.

28. Tony Saich, *Governance and Politics of China* (New York: Palgrave Macmillan, 2004), 83.

29. Dumbaugh, *China-U.S. Relations*, IB 98018, 5.

30. Kerry Dumbaugh, *China and the 105th Congress: Policy Issues and Legislation, 1997–1998*, CRS Report RL30220 (Washington, DC: Congressional Research Service of the Library of Congress, June 8, 1999).

31. Larry Q. Nowels, *U.S. International Population Assistance: Issues for Congress*, CRS IB 96026 (Washington, DC: Congressional Research Service of the Library of Congress, June 15, 2001).

32. "Religion in China: When Opium Can Be Benign," *Economist*, February 1, 2007, http://www.economist.com/node/8625817 (accessed November 9, 2007).

33. Erica Werner, "U.S. Lawmakers Criticize Yahoo Officials," *Washington Post*, November 6, 2007, A1.

34. Richard Weitz, "Persistent Barriers to Sino-American Military Dialogue," Jamestown Foundation China Brief, September 6, 2006, https://jamestown.org/program/persistent-barriers-to-sino-american-military-dialogue (accessed July 29, 2017).

35. Kerry Dumbaugh, *China-U.S. Relations in the 109th Congress*, CRS Report RL32804 (Washington, DC: Congressional Research Service of the Library of Congress, December 31, 2006), 20.

36. Shirley Kan, et al., *China: Suspected Acquisition of U.S. Nuclear Weapons Data*, CRS Report RL30143 (Washington, DC: Congressional Research Service of the Library of Congress, 1999).

37. Amy Argetsinger, "Spy Case Dismissed for Misconduct," *Washington Post*, January 7, 2005, A-4; Steve Lohr, "State Department Yields on PC's from China," *New York Times*, May 23, 2006, http://www.nytimes.com/2006/05/23/washington/23lenovo.html (accessed November 9, 2007).

38. Wayne Morrison, *China-U.S. Trade Issues*, CRS Report RL33536 (Washington, DC: Congressional Research Service of the Library of Congress, April 23, 2007).

39. Dumbaugh, *China-U.S. Relations in the 109th Congress*, 19.

40. Morrison, *China-U.S. Trade Issues*.

41. Ibid.

42. Dumbaugh, *China-U.S. Relations in the 109th Congress*, 4.

43. Ibid., 27.

44. Bonnie Glaser, "Mid-Air Collision Cripples Sino-U.S. Relations," *Comparative Connections* (April–June 2001), https://csis-prod.s3.amazonaws.com/s3fs-public/legacy_files/files/media/csis/pubs/0102qus_china.pdf.

45. Dumbaugh, *China-U.S. Relations in the 109th Congress*, 8.

46. Dumbaugh, *China-U.S. Relations*, IB 98018, 10–11.

47. Peter Grier, "Why Bush Risks China's Ire to Honor Dalai Lama," *Christian Science Monitor*, October 17, 2007, 1.

48. Thomas Friedman, "China: Scapegoat or Sputnik," *New York Times*, November 10, 2006, http://select.nytimes.com/2006/11/10/opinion/10friedman.html (accessed November 13, 2006).

49. The analysis in and sources for this section are reviewed in Robert Sutter, "The Democratic-Led 110th Congress: Implications for Asia," *Asia Policy* 3 (January 2007): 125–50; and Robert Sutter, "The Democratic Victory in Congress: Implications for Asia," *Brookings Northeast Asian Commentary* no. 4, December 2006.

50. "New Study Reveals Most Americans Remain Committed to Steady Internationalism Despite Frustration over Iraq War," Chicago Council on Global Affairs Media Advisory, October 11, 2006.

51. Robin Toner, "After Many Years, Now It's His Turn at the Helm," *New York Times*, January 8, 2007, A1. Carl Hulse, "Leadership Tries to Restrain Fiefs in New Congress," *New York Times*, January 7, 2007, http://www.nytimes.com/2007/01/07/us/politics/07chairmen.html (accessed September 27, 2009).

52. For sources and examples, see Robert Sutter, *Chinese Foreign Relations: Power and Policy since the Cold War*, 3rd ed. (Lanham, MD: Rowman & Littlefield, 2012), 1–2.

53. David Shambaugh, "China's 17th Party Congress: Maintaining Delicate Balances," *Brookings Northeast Asia Commentary*, November 1, 2007, https://www.brookings.edu/opinions/chinas-17th-party-congress-maintaining-delicate-balances (accessed November 11, 2007).

54. Denny Roy, *China's Foreign Relations* (Lanham, MD: Rowman & Littlefield, 1998).

55. Robert Sutter, *Chinese Policy Priorities and Their Implications for the United States* (Lanham, MD: Rowman & Littlefield, 2000), 18. See review of this period in Barry Naughton, *The Chinese Economy: Transitions and Growth* (Cambridge, MA: MIT Press, 2007), and Saich, *Governance and Politics of China*.

56. Kerry Dumbaugh, *China's 17th Party Congress, October 15–21, 2007*, Congressional Research Service Memorandum, October 23, 2007.

57. Maureen Fan, "China's Party Leadership Declares New Priority: 'Harmonious Society,'" *Washington Post*, October 12, 2006, A18.

58. These developments and determinants are reviewed in Sutter, *Chinese Foreign Relations*, 2–3.

59. This dualism and respective Gulliver strategies are discussed in Robert Sutter, "China and U.S. Security and Economic Interests: Opportunities and Challenges," in *US-China-EU Relations: Managing the New World Order*, ed. Robert Ross and Oystein Tunsjo (London: Routledge, 2010).

60. See reviews of Chinese leaders' priorities following the major party and government meetings in the Jamestown Foundation's weekly publication *China Brief*, http://www. jamestown.org/index.php, and the quarterly publication *China Leadership Monitor*, http://www.hoover.org (Publications tab).

61. Testimony on US-China relations before the House Foreign Affairs Committee of Deputy Secretary of State John Negroponte, May 1, 2007, https://2001-2009.state.gov/s/d/2007/84118.htm (accessed May 5, 2007); Cha, "Winning Asia," 98–113.

62. See contrasting views of China's approach to the United States at this time and of various differences in China-US relations in Bates Gill, *Rising Star: China's New Security Diplomacy* (Washington, DC: Brookings Institution, 2007); Susan Shirk, *China: Fragile Superpower* (New York: Oxford University Press, 2007); David M. Lampton, *The Three Faces of Chinese Power: Might, Money, and Minds* (Berkeley: University of California Press, 2008); Michael Swaine, *America's Challenge: Engaging a Rising China in the Twenty-First Century* (Washington, DC: Carnegie Endowment, 2011); Aaron Friedberg, *A Contest for Supremacy: China, America, and the Struggle for Mastery in Asia* (New York: W. W. Norton, 2011); and Jeffrey Bader, *Obama and China's Rise* (Washington, DC: Brookings Institution, 2012).

63. Kerry Dumbaugh, *China-U.S. Relations: Current Issues and Implications for U.S. Policy*, CRS Report RL33877 (Washington, DC: The Congressional Research Service of the Library of Congress, February 10, 2009); Susan Lawrence and David MacDonald, *U.S.-China Relations: Policy Issues*, CRS Report RL41108 (Washington, DC: Congressional Research Service of the Library of Congress, August 2, 2012).

64. Gill, *Rising Star*; Avery Goldstein, *Rising to the Challenge: China's Grand Strategy and International Security* (Stanford, CA: Stanford University Press, 2005); Evan Medeiros and R. Taylor Fravel, "China's New Diplomacy," *Foreign Affairs* 82, no. 6 (November–December 2003): 22–35; People's Republic of China State Council Information Office, "China's Peaceful Development Road," *People's Daily Online*, December 22, 2005 (accessed July 7, 2006); Sutter, *Chinese Foreign Relations*, 3–13; Shirk, *China*; Aaron Friedberg, "The Future of U.S.-China Relations: Is Conflict Inevitable?" *International Security* 30, no. 2 (2005): 7–45.

7. BARACK OBAMA, DONALD TRUMP, AND XI JINPING

1. See contrasting views of China's approach to the United States and of various differences in China-US relations in Michael Swaine, *America's Challenge: Engaging a Rising China in the Twenty-First Century* (Washington, DC: Carnegie Endowment, 2011); Aaron Friedberg, *A Contest for Supremacy: China, America, and the Struggle for Mastery in Asia* (New York: W. W. Norton, 2011); and Jeffrey Bader, *Obama and China's Rise* (Washington, DC: Brookings Institution, 2012).

2. See assessments of prominent Chinese specialists in Nina Hachigian, ed., *Debating China: The U.S.-China Relationship in Ten Conversations* (New York: Oxford University Press, 2014); and Wu Xinbo, "Chinese Visions of the Future of U.S.-China Relations," in *Tangled Titans: The United States and China*, ed. David Shambaugh (Lanham, MD: Rowman & Littlefield, 2013), 371–88.

3. Christopher Johnson, "Thoughts from the Chairman: Xi Jinping Unveils his Foreign Policy Vision," Center for Strategic and International Studies, December 8, 2014, https://www.csis.org/analysis/thoughts-chairman-xi-jinping-unveils-his-foreign-policy-vision; Yun Sun, "China's Peaceful Rise: Peace Through Strength?" *PACNET 25* (Honolulu, HI: CSIS Pacific Forum, March 31, 2014); Yong Deng, "China: The Post-Responsible Power," *Washington Quarterly* 37, no. 4 (Winter 2015): 117–32.

4. Robert Sutter and Satu Limaye, *America's 2016 Election Debate on Asia Policy and Asian Reactions* (Honolulu, HI: East-West Center, 2016).

5. Kerry Dumbaugh, *China-U.S. Relations: Current Issues and Implications for U.S. Policy*, CRS Report RL33877 (Washington, DC: Congressional Research Service of the Library of

Congress, February 10, 2009); Susan Lawrence and David MacDonald, *U.S.-China Relations: Policy Issues*, CRS Report RL41108 (Washington, DC: Congressional Research Service of the Library of Congress, August 2, 2012); Dave Majumdar, "America Reveals 'Great Power' Plans against Russia and China," *National Interest* (blog), February 3, 2016, http://nationalinterest. org/blog/the-buzz/america-reveals-great-power-plan-against-russia-china-15103.

6. G. John Ikenberry, "The Rise of China, the United States and the Future of the Liberal International Order," in Shambaugh, ed., *Tangled Titans*, 53–74; Ashley Tellis and Robert Blackwill, "Revising U.S. Grand Strategy toward China," Council on Foreign Relations, April 2015, https://www.cfr.org/report/revising-us-grand-strategy-toward-china; Lyle Goldstein, "Is It Time to Meet China Halfway?" National Interest, May 12, 2015, http://nationalinterest.org/ feature/it-time-meet-china-halfway-12863.

7. On the contrasting views, see Aaron Friedberg, *Beyond Air-Sea Battle: The Debate over US Military Strategy in Asia* (London: IISS/Routledge, 2014); Ashley Tellis and Robert Blackwill, "Revising U.S. Grand Strategy toward China," Council on Foreign Relations, April 2015; Thomas Christensen, *The China Challenge: Shaping the Choices of a Rising Power* (New York: W. W. Norton, 2016); Lyle Goldstein, *Meeting China Halfway* (Washington, DC: Georgetown University Press, 2015); Michael Swaine, *Creating a Stable Asia: An Agenda for a U.S.-China Balance of Power* (Washington, DC: Carnegie Endowment, 2016).

8. Robert Sutter, "Obama's Cautious and Calibrated Approach to an Assertive China," YaleGlobal, April 19, 2016, http://yaleglobal.yale.edu/content/obamas-cautious-and-calibrated-approach-assertive-china.

9. Sutter and Limaye, *America's 2016 Election Debate*, 19–20.

10. Ibid., 21.

11. Bonnie Glaser and Alexandra Viers, "China Prepares for Rocky Relations in 2017," *Comparative Connections* 18, no. 3 (January 2017): 21–22; Bonnie Glaser and Alexandra Viers, "Trump and Xi Break the Ice at Mar-a-Lago," *Comparative Connections* 19, no. 1 (May 2017): 21–32.

12. Martin Indyk, Kenneth Lieberthal, and Michael O'Hanlon, *Bending History: Barack Obama's Foreign Policy* (Washington, DC: Brookings, 2012), 24–69.

13. Bonnie Glaser and Brittany Billingsley, "Friction and Cooperation Co-exist Uneasily," *Comparative Connections* 13, no. 2 (September 2011): 27–40; Minxin Pei, "China's Bumpy Ride Ahead," Diplomat, February 16, 2011, http://thediplomat.com/2011/02/chinas-bumpy-ride-ahead; Robert Sutter, *Positive Equilibrium in US-China Relations: Durable or Not?* (Baltimore: University of Maryland School of Law, 2010).

14. Elisabeth Bumiller, "US Will Counter Chinese Arms Buildup," *New York Times*, January 8, 2011, http://www.nytimes.com/2011/01/09/world/asia/09military.html; David Sanger, "Superpower and Upstart: Sometimes It Ends Well," *New York Times*, January 22, 2011, http:// www.nytimes.com/2011/01/23/weekinreview/23sanger.html.

15. Bader, *Obama and China's Rise*, 69–129; "Interview [of Hillary Clinton] with Greg Sheridan of the *Australian*," US Department of State, November 8, 2010, https://2009-2017. state.gov/secretary/20092013clinton/rm/2010/11/150671.htm.

16. Bonnie Glaser and Brittany Billingsley, "Strains Increase and Leadership Transitions," *Comparative Connections* 14, no. 3 (January 2012): 29–40; Mark Manyin et al., *Pivot to the Pacific? The Obama Administration's "Rebalancing" toward Asia*, CRS Report 42448 (Washington, DC: Congressional Research Service of the Library of Congress, March 28, 2012).

17. Kurt Campbell, *The Pivot* (New York: Twelve-Hachette Book Group, 2016); Robert Sutter, *The United States and Asia: Regional Dynamics and Twenty-First Century Relations* (Lanham, MD: Rowman & Littlefield, 2015).

18. Yong Deng, "China: The Post-Responsible Power," *Washington Quarterly* 37, no. 4 (Winter 2015): 117–32; Denny Roy, *Return of the Dragon: Rising China and Regional Security* (New York: Columbia University Press, 2013); Yun Sun, "China's New Calculations in the South China Sea," *Asia-Pacific Bulletin* 267, June 10, 2014.

19. Assessments of US-China relations in this period include Bader, *Obama and China's Rise*; Indyk, Lieberthal, and O'Hanlon, *Bending History*, 24–69; Aaron Friedberg, *A Contest for Supremacy*; Kenneth Lieberthal and Wang Jisi, *Addressing U.S.-China Strategic Distrust* (Washington, DC: Brookings Institution, 2012); Andrew Nathan and Andrew Scobell, *China's*

Search for Security (New York: Columbia University Press, 2012); Roy, *Return of the Dragon*; Hachigian, ed., *Debating China*; Goldstein, *Meeting China Halfway*; Christensen, *The China Challenge*; Shambaugh, ed., *Tangled Titans*; Tellis and Blackwill, "Revising U.S. Grand Strategy toward China"; Campbell, *The Pivot*; Sutter, *The United States and Asia*.

20. Shannon Tiezzi, "American Government Torn on How to Handle China," Diplomat, August 4, 2015, http://thediplomat.com/2015/08/americas-government-is-torn-on-how-to-handle-china; Robert Sutter, "Americans Speak to U.S.-China Policy: Let's Be Frank," National Bureau of Asian Research, September 18. 2015, http://xivisit.nbr.org/2015/09/18/americans-speak-to-u-s-china-policy-robert-sutter (site discontinued).

21. Orville Schell and Susan Shirk, Chairs, *US Policy toward China: Recommendations for a New Administration*, Task Force Report (New York: Asia Society, 2017); Sutter, *The United States and Asia*, 307–14; and Robert Sutter, *Chinese Foreign Relations: Power and Policy since the Cold War*, 4th ed. (Lanham, MD: Rowman & Littlefield, 2016), 133–49.

22. Robert Sutter, "Foreword: Russia-China Relations," in *Russia-China Relations: Assessing Common Ground and Strategic Fault Lines* (Seattle, WA: National Bureau of Asian Research, 2017), http://nbr.org/publications/element.aspx?id=950.

23. Johnson, "Thoughts from the Chairman"; Yun Sun, "China's Peaceful Rise"; Yong Deng, "China: The Post-Responsible Power."

24. Author consultations with US administration officials, Washington, DC, August 2016.

25. Sutter and Limaye, *America's 2016 Election Debate*, 20.

26. Sutter, "Obama's Cautious and Calibrated Approach to an Assertive China"; Jeffrey Bader, "A Framework for U.S. Policy toward China," Asia Working Group Paper 3, March 2016, Brookings, https://www.brookings.edu/wp-content/uploads/2016/07/us-china-policy-framework-bader-1.pdf; Deputy Secretary Blinken Testimony on US-China Relations: Strategic Challenges and Opportunities, Senate Foreign Relations Committee, April 27, 2016.

27. David M. Lampton, "A Tipping Point in U.S.-China Relations Is upon Us," *US-China Perception Monitor*, May 11, 2015; Harry Harding, "Has U.S. China Policy Failed?" *Washington Quarterly* 38, no. 3 (2015): 95–122.

28. Sutter, "'Obama's Cautious and Calibrated Approach to an Assertive China."

29. "China's ZTE to Pay Massive U.S. Fine over Iran, North Korea Sanctions Busting," Euronews, March 7, 2017, http://www.euronews.com/2017/03/07/china-s-zte-to-pay-massive-us-fine-over-iran-north-korea-sanctions-busting.

30. The coverage of the US election in this article builds on the findings of Sutter and Limaye, *America's 2016 Election*. That report used campaign statements and other materials made available in "2016 Presidential Candidates on Asia," Asia Matters for America, http://www.asiamattersforamerica.org/asia/2016-presidential-candidates-on-asia; other news and commentary; interviews and discussions with senior Republican and Democratic Asian specialists conducted in Washington, DC, during June 2016; and with Asian specialists, commentators, and officials in Beijing, Seoul, Taipei, Tokyo, and Washington during July 2016. The principal findings and implications of the report were discussed with and validated by those interviewed, most of whom requested anonymity.

31. Harding, "Has U.S. China Policy Failed?"

32. Jeffrey M. Jones, "Americans See China's Economic Power as Diminished Threat," Gallup, February 26, 2015, http://www.gallup.com/poll/181733/americans-china-economic-power-diminished-threat.aspx; Lydia Saad, "Americans See China as Top Economy Now, but U.S. in Future," Gallup, February 22, 2016, http://www.gallup.com/poll/189347/americans-china-top-economy-future.aspx.

33. Hillary Clinton, "Issues: National Security: With Policies That Keep Us Strong and Safe, America Can Lead the World in the 21st Century," *Hillary for America*; Hillary Clinton, "Remarks to AFL-CIO [AFL-CIO Convention, Philadelphia, PA]," April 6, 2016.

34. Bernie Sanders, interview by Ezra Klein, *Vox*, July 28, 2015, http://www.vox.com/2015/7/28/9014491/bernie-sanders-vox-conversation.

35. "Cruz on the Issues: China," Council on Foreign Relations, http://www.cfr.org/campaign2016/ted-cruz/on-china.

36. "A Conversation With John Kasich," Council on Foreign Relations, December 9, 2015, http://www.cfr.org/united-states/conversation-john-kasich/p37304; John Kasich, in "Transcript

of Republican Debate in Miami, Full Text," CNN, March 10, 2016, http://www.cnn.com/2016/03/10/politics/republican-debate-transcript-full-text/index.html.

37. Marco Rubio, "How My Presidency Would Deal with China," *Wall Street Journal*, August 27, 2015, http://www.wsj.com/articles/how-my-presidency-would-deal-with-china-1440717685.

38. Maggie Haberman, "Donald Trump Says He Favors Big Tariffs on Chinese Exports," *New York Times*, January 7, 2016, http://www.nytimes.com/politics/first-draft/2016/01/07/donald-trump-says-he-favors-big-tariffs-on-chinese-exports; Donald Trump, "'America First' Foreign Policy Speech," Washington, DC, April 27, 2016.

39. Sutter and Limaye, *America's 2016 Election Debate*, 21.

40. Jane Parlez, "China Sees New Ambiguity in Donald Trump's Taiwan Call," *New York Times*, December 3, 2016, https://www.nytimes.com/2016/12/03/world/asia/taiwan-call-gives-china-a-clue-on-what-to-expect-from-donald-trump.html.

41. Barak Ravid, "Trump's Israel Pick at Senate Confirmation hearing," HAARETZ, February 16, 2017, http://www.haaretz.com/us-news/LIVE-1.772078/Friedman-confirmation-two-state.

42. "Trump's Unpredictability on Foreign Policy Keeps the World Guessing," *Financial Times*, January 19, 2017, https://www.ft.com/content/31b5d958-ddc1-11e6-9d7c-be108f1c1dce.

43. Samuel Osbourne, "Japanese Prime Minister Shinzo Abe Says Donald Trump Encouraged Him to Improve Relations with Vladimir Putin," *Independent*, February 14, 2017, http://www.independent.co.uk/news/world/americas/us-politics/japan-prime-misiter-shinzo-abe-donald-trum-p-improve-russia-relations-valdimir-putin-us-president-a7579166.html.

44. Jeremy Page and Teping Chen, "Syria Attack Throws U.S.-China Summit Off-Balance," *Wall Street Journal*, April 7, 2017, https://www.wsj.com/articles/syria-attack-throws-u-s-china-talks-off-balance-1491555629.

45. Bonnie Glaser and Alexandra Veers, "Trump and Xi Break the Ice at Mar-a-Lago," 21–32.

46. David Brown and Kevin Scott, "China-Taiwan Relations," *Comparative Connections* 19, no. 1 (May 2017): 62–63.

47. Shi Jiangtao, "US Doubts over One-China Linchpin to Stalk Key Sino-US Security Talks," *South China Morning Post*, June 16, 2017, 1; Mark Landler, "Trump Takes More Aggressive Stance with U.S. Friend and Foes in Asia," *New York Times*, June 30, 2017, https://www.nytimes.com/2017/06/30/world/asia/trump-south-korea-china.html.

48. Emily Rauhala, "As Trump Pushes for Bigger U.S. Defense Budget, China Slows Growth Rate of Its Military Spending," *Washington Post*, March 4, 2017, https://www.washingtonpost.com/world/as-trump-pushes-for-bigger-us-defense-budget-china-slows-growth-rate-of-its-military-spending/2017/03/04/ace6105c-0094-11e7-a51a-e16b4bcc6644_story.html?utm_term=.489451bdd660.

49. Mark Lander and Michael Shear, "Trump Administration to Take a Harder Tack on Trade with China," *New York Times*, April 6, 2017, https://www.nytimes.com/2017/04/06/us/politics/trump-xi-jinping-china-summit-mar-a-lago.html.

50. Tracy Wilkinsen, "Human Rights Fade from U.S. Foreign Policy Agenda under Trump," *Los Angeles Times*, April 5, 2017, http://www.latimes.com/nation/la-fg-trump-human-rights-20170405-story.html.

8. SECURITY ISSUES IN CONTEMPORARY US-CHINA RELATIONS

1. In addition to sources noted in chapter 4, see Wang Zhongchun, "The Soviet Factor in Sino-American Normalization, 1969–1979," in *Normalization of U.S.-China Relations*, ed. William Kirby, Robert Ross, and Gong Li (Cambridge, MA: Harvard University Press, 2005).

2. John Garver, *Foreign Relations of the People's Republic of China* (Englewood Cliffs, NJ: Prentice Hall, 1993), 166–77, 310–11.

3. James Mann, *About Face: A History of America's Curious Relationship with China, from Nixon to Clinton* (New York: Knopf, 1999), 33–35.

4. Garver, *Foreign Relations of the People's Republic of China*, 166–73; Harry Harding, *A Fragile Relationship: The United States and China since 1972* (Washington, DC: Brookings Institution, 1992), 119–22, 332–33.

5. House Committee on Foreign Affairs, Subcommittee on Asian and Pacific Affairs, *Playing the China Card: Implications for United States-Soviet Union-Chinese Relations* (Washington, DC: US Government Printing Office, 1979).

6. Robert Sutter, *The China Quandary: Domestic Determinants of U.S. China Policy, 1972–1982* (Boulder, CO: Westview Press, 1983), 99–100, 111–26.

7. Mann, *About Face*, 98–100, 109–14; Yitzhak Shichor, "The Great Wall of Steel: Military and Strategy in Xinjiang," in *Xinjiang: China's Muslim Borderland*, ed. S. Frederick Starr (Armonk, NY: M. E. Sharpe, 2004), 148–50.

8. Harding, *A Fragile Relationship*, 224–34.

9. David M. Lampton, *Same Bed, Different Dreams: Managing U.S.-China Relations, 1989–2000* (Berkeley: University of California Press, 2001), 39–63; Jean Garrison, *Making China Policy: From Nixon to G. W. Bush* (Boulder, CO: Lynne Rienner, 2005), 165–72.

10. Shirley Kan, *U.S.-China Military Contacts: Issue for Congress*, CRS Report RL32496 (Washington, DC: Congressional Research Service of the Library of Congress, April 15, 2009), 6–11.

11. Lampton, *Same Bed, Different Dreams*, 71–110.

12. The Chinese reactions and motivations concerning these developments are reviewed in Lampton, *Same Bed, Different Dreams*, and Robert Suettinger, *Beyond Tiananmen: The Politics of U.S.-China Relations, 1989–2000* (Washington, DC: Brookings Institution, 2003).

13. Evan Medeiros, *China's International Behavior: Activism, Opportunism, and Diversification* (Santa Monica, CA: Rand Corporation, 2009), 48–53; Bonnie Glaser and Brittany Billingsley, "Creating a New Type of Great Power Relations," *Comparative Connections* 14, no. 2 (September 2012): 25–32; and author's consultations with Chinese specialists, Beijing, March 25, 2015.

14. Bonnie Glaser and Evan Medeiros, "The Ecology of Foreign Policy Decision-Making in China: The Ascension and Demise of the Theory of Peaceful Rise," *China Quarterly* 190 (June 2007): 291–310.

15. Robert Sutter, *China's Rise in Asia* (Lanham, MD: Rowman & Littlefield, 2005), 265–76.

16. Avery Goldstein, *Rising to the Challenge: China's Grand Strategy and International Security* (Stanford, CA: Stanford University Press, 2005).

17. Robert Sutter, *Chinese Foreign Relations: Power and Policy since the Cold War* (Lanham, MD: Rowman & Littlefield, 2008), 177.

18. Ibid., 178.

19. David M. Lampton, *The Three Faces of Chinese Power: Might, Money, and Minds* (Berkeley: University of California Press, 2008), 27.

20. People's Republic of China State Council Information Office, "China's Peaceful Development Road," *People's Daily Online*, December 22, 2005, http://english.peopledaily.com.cn/200512/22/eng20051222_230059.html (accessed July 7, 2006); "Full text of Chinese President Hu Jintao's Speech at Opening Session of Boao Forum," *China Daily*, April 15, 2011, http://www.chinadaily.com.cn/china/2011-04/15/content_12335312.htm (accessed August 11, 2017); People's Republic of China State Council Information Office, "China's National Defense in 2004" (Beijing, December 27, 2004); People's Republic of China State Council Information Office, "China's National Defense in 2006" (Beijing, December 29, 2006). People's Republic of China State Council Information Office, "China's National Defense in 2008" (Beijing, January 2009); People's Republic of China State Council Information Office, "China's National Defense in 2010" (Beijing, March 2011).

21. Briefings, Academy of Military Science, Beijing, June 2008 and June 2011; briefings by senior representatives of the Academy at a public meeting at Georgetown University, Washington, DC, on October 2, 2008.

22. Paul Godwin, "China as a Major Asian Power: The Implications of Its Military Modernization (A View from the United States)," in *China, the United States, and Southeast Asia: Contending Perspectives on Politics, Security, and Economics*, ed. Evelyn Goh and Sheldon Simon (New York: Routledge, 2008), 145–66; Ashley J. Tellis and Travis Tanner, eds., *Strategic Asia 2012–2013: China's Military Challenge* (Seattle, WA: National Bureau of Asian Research, 2012); Chu Shulong and Lin Xinzhu, "It Is Not the Objective of Chinese Military Power to Catch Up and Overtake the United States," *Beijing Huanqiu Shibao*, June 26, 2008, 11; Christopher Twomey, "The Military-Security Relationship," in *Tangled Titans: The United States and China*, ed. David Shambaugh (Lanham, MD: Rowman & Littlefield, 2012), 235–62.

23. United States Department of Defense, *Annual Report on the Military Power of the People's Republic of China, 2009* (Washington, DC: US Department of Defense, March 2009); United States Department of Defense, *Annual Report to Congress: Military and Security Developments Involving the People's Republic of China 2012*, https://www.defense.gov/Portals/1/Documents/pubs/2012_CMPR_Final.pdf (accessed January 25, 2013).

24. People's Republic of China State Council Information Office, "China's National Defense in 2004," 2–4.

25. Andrew Scobell and Larry M. Wortzel, eds., *Shaping China's Security Environment: The Role of the PLA* (Carlisle, PA: Strategic Studies Institute, US Army War College, 2006), 2; Andrew Nathan and Andrew Scobell, *China's Search for Security* (New York: Columbia University Press, 2012).

26. Briefings, Beijing, June 2008; Georgetown University, Washington, DC, October 2, 2008.

27. Hu Xiao, "Japan and U.S. Told, Hands Off Taiwan," *China Daily*, March 7, 2005, 1; for background see Michael Yahuda, *Sino-Japanese Relations after the Cold War* (New York: Routledge, 2014).

28. "China-Southeast Asia Relations," *Comparative Connections* 9, no. 3 (October 2007): 75.

29. On the military aspects of the Obama government's reengagement policies, see Mark Manyin et al., *Pivot to the Pacific? The Obama Administration's "Rebalancing" toward Asia*, CRS Report 42448 (Washington, DC: Congressional Research Service of the Library of Congress, March 28, 2012) and Kurt Campbell, *The Pivot* (New York: Twelve-Hachette Book Group, 2016).

30. United States Department of Defense, *Annual Report to Congress . . . 2012*; Nathan and Scobell, *China's Search for Security*; Tellis and Tanner, eds., *Strategic Asia 2012–2013*; Ian Rinehart, *The Chinese Military: Overview and Issues for Congress*, CRS Report 44196 (Washington, DC: Congressional Research Service of the Library of Congress, March 24, 2016).

31. Robert S. Ross, "The Geography of Peace: East Asia in the Twenty-First Century," *International Security* 23, no. 4 (Spring 1999): 81–118.

32. Aaron Friedberg, *A Contest for Supremacy: China, America, and the Struggle for Mastery in Asia* (New York: W. W. Norton, 2011).

33. Kan, *U.S.-China- Military Contacts*.

34. Evan Medeiros, *Reluctant Restraint: The Evolution of China's Nonproliferation Policies and Practices, 1980–2004* (Stanford, CA: Stanford University Press, 2007).

35. Bonnie S. Glaser, "China's Policy in the Wake of the Second DPRK Nuclear Test," Asia Foundation, https://asiafoundation.org/resources/pdfs/GlaserChinaSecurity2.pdf (accessed July 19, 2017); Jeffrey Bader, *Obama and China's Rise* (Washington, DC: Brookings Institution, 2012) 26–39, 83–93.

36. Evan Medeiros, *China's International Behavior*, 96–101; Bader, *Obama and China's Rise*, 140–50; "China to Become Second-Largest Contributor to UN Peacekeeping Budget," *China Watch*, June 6, 2016, http://www.telegraph.co.uk/sponsored/china-watch/politics/12210677/china-contributions-un-peacekeeping-budget.html.

37. Godwin, "China as a Major Asian Power," 145–66; Tellis and Tanner, *Strategic Asia 2012–2013*; United States Department of Defense, *Annual Report to Congress . . . 2012*; Rinehart, *The Chinese Military.*

38. Michael Swaine, "China's Regional Military Posture," in *Power Shift: China and Asia's New Dynamics*, ed. David Shambaugh (Berkeley: University of California Press, 2005), 266; Lampton, *The Three Faces of Chinese Power*, 40–42; Tellis and Tanner, *Strategic Asia 2012–2013*; Michael Swaine, *Creating a Stable Asia: An Agenda for a U.S.-China Balance of Power* (Washington, DC: Carnegie Endowment for International Peace, 2016); Aaron Friedberg, *Beyond Air-Sea Battle: The Debate over US Military Strategy in Asia* (London: IISS/ Routledge, 2014).

39. Bates Gill, *Rising Star: China's New Security Diplomacy* (Washington, DC: Brookings Institution, 2007); David Shambaugh, *China Goes Global* (New York: Oxford University Press, 2013), 269–306; Ankit Panda, "China Creates New 'Asia for Asians' Security Forum," Diplomat, September 15, 2014, http://thediplomat.com/2014/09/china-creates-new-asia-for-asians-security-forum.

40. The discussion in the following several paragraphs is adapted from Swaine, "China's Regional Military Posture," 268–72. See also Michael Swaine, *America's Challenge: Engaging a Rising China in the Twenty-First Century* (Washington, DC: Carnegie Endowment for International Peace, 2011), 147–82; Tellis and Tanner, *Strategic Asia 2012–2013*, 3–196; Friedberg, *Beyond Air-Sea Battle*; Swaine, *Creating a Stable Asia: An Agenda for a U.S.-China Balance of Power* (Washington, DC: Carnegie Endowment for International Peace, 2016).

41. Garver, *Foreign Relations of the People's Republic of China*, 249–64.

42. Suettinger, *Beyond Tiananmen*, 200–263; Twomey, "The Military-Security Relationship"; Susan Lawrence and David MacDonald, *U.S.-China Relations: Policy Issues*, CRS Report RL41108 (Washington, DC: Congressional Research Service of the Library of Congress Report, August 2, 2012), 8–24; Robert Ross, "The Problem with the Pivot," *Foreign Affairs* (November–December 2012).

43. Reviewed in Friedberg, *Beyond Air-Sea Battle.*

44. See Swaine, *Creating a Stable Asia.*

45. Ralph Cossa and Brad Glosserman, "The Pivot Is Dead; Long Live the Pivot," *Comparative Connections* 19, no. 1 (May 2017): 2–3.

46. Bonnie Glaser and Alexandra Viers, "Trump and Xi Break the Ice at Mar-a-Lago," *Comparative Connections* 19, no. 1 (May 2017): 26–30.

47. Jane Parlez, Yufan Huang, and Paul Mozur, "How North Korea Managed to Defy Years of Sanctions," *New York Times*, May 12, 2017, A1.

9. ECONOMIC AND ENVIRONMENTAL ISSUES IN CONTEMPORARY US-CHINA RELATIONS

1. Arthur Kroeber, *China's Economy* (New York: Oxford University Press, 2016); Barry Naughton, *The Chinese Economy: Transitions and Growth* (Cambridge, MA: MIT Press, 2007); David M. Lampton, *The Three Faces of Chinese Power: Might, Money, and Minds* (Berkeley: University of California Press, 2008), 78–116; David Shambaugh, *China Goes Global* (New York: Oxford University Press, 2013), 156–206; C. Fred Bergsten, Charles Freeman, Nicholas Lardy, and Derek Mitchell, *China's Rise: Challenges and Opportunities* (Washington, DC: Peterson Institute for International Economics, 2008), 105–37; Nicholas Lardy, *Sustaining China's Economic Growth after the Global Financial Crisis* (Washington, DC: Peterson Institute for International Economics, 2012); Wayne Morrison, *China's Economic Conditions*, CRS Report RL33534 (Washington, DC: Congressional Research Service of the Library of Congress, December 4, 2012); Wang Jisi, "Trends on the Development of U.S.-China Relations and Deep-Seated Reasons," lecture delivered at the Chinese Academy of Social Science, Asia Pacific Institute, *Dangdai Yatai* (Beijing), June 20, 2009, 4–20.

2. Bergsten et al., *China's Rise*, 9–32; C. Fred Bergsten, Bates Gill, Nicholas Lardy, and Derek Mitchell, *China: A Balance Sheet* (New York: Public Affairs, 2006), 73–117; Wayne Morrison, *China-U.S. Trade Issues*, CRS Report RL33536 (Washington, DC: Congressional Research Service of the Library of Congress, May 21, 2012); Jeffrey Bader, *Obama and China's Rise* (Washington, DC: Brookings Institution, 2012), 111–27.

3. Kenneth Lieberthal, "How Domestic Forces Shape the PRC's Grand Strategy and International Impact," in *Strategic Asia 2007–2008*, ed. Ashley Tellis and Michael Wills (Seattle: National Bureau of Asian Research, 2007), 29–68; Lampton, *The Three Faces of Chinese Power*, 207–51; Lardy, *Sustaining China's Economic Growth*; Kroeber, *China's Economy*, 233–62.

4. Robert Suettinger, *Beyond Tiananmen: The Politics of U.S.-China Relations, 1989–2000* (Washington, DC: Brookings Institution, 2003), 358–409.

5. Bader, *Obama and China's Rise*, 111–27; Yuan Peng, "China, U.S. Should Find Common Ground in Strategic Dialogue," *China Daily*, July 27, 2009, 4; Kenneth Lieberthal and Wang Jisi, *Addressing U.S.-China Strategic Distrust* (Washington, DC: Brookings Institution, 2012); Nina Hachigian, ed., *Debating China: The U.S.-China Relationship in Ten Conversations* (New York: Oxford University Press, 2014), 21–42.

6. Robert Sutter and Satu Limaye, *America's 2016 Election Debate on Asia Policy and Asian Reactions* (Honolulu, HI: East-West Center, 2016), 18–22; Orville Schell and Susan Shirk, Chairs, *US Policy toward China: Recommendations for a New Administration*, Task Force Report (New York: Asia Society, 2017), 60–64.

7. Schell and Shirk, *US Policy toward China*, 60.

8. Wayne Morrison, *China-U.S. Trade Issues*, CRS Report RL33536 (Washington, DC: Congressional Research Service of the Library of Congress, December 29, 2016), 26–34.

9. David Dollar, *Trade Is Front and Center as Trump and Xi Meet* (Washington, DC: Brookings Institution, April 3, 2017); Bonnie Glaser and Alexandra Viers, "Trump and Xi Break the Ice at Mar-a-Lago," *Comparative Connections* 19, no. 1 (May 2017): 21–32; Wayne Morrison, *China-U.S. Trade Issues*, CRS Report RL33536 (Washington, DC: Congressional Research Service of the Library of Congress, April 24, 2017).

10. Wayne Morrison, *China's Economic Rise*, CRS Report RL33534 (Washington, DC: Congressional Research Service of the Library of Congress, October 9. 2014), summary page; Yu Yongding, "An Opportunity for China," *Japan Times*, April 12, 2015, http://www.japantimes.co.jp/opinion/2015/04/12/commentary/world-commentary/opportunity-china/#.VXLETdJViko (site discontinued).

11. "Catching the Eagle," *Economist* (blog), August 22, 2014, http://www.economist.com/blogs/graphicdetail/2014/08/chinese-and-american-gdp-forecasts.

12. U.S. China Business Council, *China Economic Reform Scorecard*, February 2015, https://www.uschina.org/reports/china-economic-reform-scorecard-february-2015 (the reviews are published four times a year); Dan Blumenthal and Derek Scissors, "China's Great Stagnation," *National Interest*, October 16, 2017, http://nationalinterest.org/feature/chinas-great-stagnation-18073.

13. "China's Outward Investment Tops $161 Billion in 2016," Reuters, December 26, 2016, http://www.reuters.com/article/us-china-economy-investment-idUSKBN14F07R.

14. Wayne Morrison, *China's Economic Conditions*, CRS Report 33534 (Washington, DC: Library of Congress, Congressional Research Service, June 26, 2012), 10–25.

15. Lampton, *The Three Faces of Chinese Power*, 88–101.

16. Robert Sutter, *Chinese Foreign Relations: Power and Policy since the Cold War*, 4th ed. (Rowman & Littlefield, 2016), 64–65; Xu Hongcai, "Changing Trade Structure," *China Daily*, January 28, 2013, 8; Liu Yantang, "Political Bureau Study Session: Seizing Initiative in International Competition," *Liaowang* (Beijing) (June 6, 2005): 12–15; "China's Reforms: The Second Long March," *Economist*, December 11, 2008, http://www.economist.com/node/12758848. Trade figures taken from the United Nations Comtrade database, http://comtrade.un.org/db.

17. Morrison, *China-U.S. Trade Issues* (April 24, 2017), 10; Xu Hongcai, "Changing Trade Structure"; Diao Ying, "Firms Urged to Diversify Export Markets," *China Daily*, December 24, 2008, 1.

18. Wayne Morrison, *China-U.S. Trade Issues*, Issue Brief IB 91121 (Washington, DC: Congressional Research Service of the Library of Congress, May 15, 2006), 1; Xu Hongcai, "Changing Trade Structure"; "China's Exports to US," Geopolitical Futures, December 9, 2016, https://geopoliticalfutures.com/chinas-exports-to-the-us.

19. "Foreign Firms Dominate China's Exports," *China Business*, June 30, 2006, http://www.taiwansecurity.org (accessed July 3, 2006); "Investment Overseas and Imports a Priority," *China Daily*, December 8, 2006, 1; Morrison, *China's Economic Conditions* (December 4, 2012), 10–11; Wayne Morrison, *China's Economic Rise*, CRS Report 33534 (Washington, DC: Congressional Research Service of the Library of Congress, October 21, 2015), 13.

20. Australian Parliamentary Library Research Service, *Directions in China's Foreign Relations: Implications for East Asia and Australia* (Canberra: Parliamentary Library Research Brief 9: 2005–2006, December 5, 2005), 6–10.

21. Trade figures used in this section are from the United Nations Comtrade database, http://comtrade.un.org/db.

22. Thomas Lum, *Comparing Global Influence: China's and the U.S. Diplomacy, Foreign Aid, Trade, and Investment in the Developing World*, CRS Report RL34620 (Washington, DC: Congressional Research Service of the Library of Congress, August 15, 2008), 46–47; "China Eclipses U.S. as Biggest Trading Nation Measured in Goods," *Bloomberg News*, February 10, 2013, http://www.bloombergnews.com (accessed February 11, 2013).

23. "China's Reforms"; Li Jiabao, "Export Woes Highlight Need for Change in Trade Structure," *China Daily*, February 5, 2012, 13.

24. Lum, *Comparing Global Influence*, 46–47. Trade figures used in this section are from United Nations Comtrade database, http://comtrade.un.org/db.

25. Morrison, *China's Economic Conditions* (December 4, 2012), 12; "China's FDI Inflow Rises 4.1% in 2016," *China Daily*, January 14, 2017, http://www.chinadaily.com.cn/business/2017-01/14/content_27953171.htm.

26. Randall Morck, Bernard Yeung, and Minyuan Zhao, "Perspectives on China's Outward Foreign Direct Investment" (working paper, International Monetary Fund, Washington, DC, August 2007).

27. Lum, *Comparing Global Influence*, 59.

28. Morrison, *China's Economic Rise*, 17; "China's Outward Investments Top $161 Billion in 2016."

29. Fu Jing, "Be Bold in Expanding Overseas, Firms Told," *China Daily*, December 23, 2008, 1; Yi Gang, "How to Implement the 'Going Out' Strategy," *Caixin*, January 18, 2013, http://www.chinafile.com/reporting-opinion/caixin-media/how-implement-going-out-strategy (original accessed January 18, 2013).

30. Carol Lancaster, *The Chinese Aid System* (Washington, DC: Center for Global Development, June 2007); Bao Chang and Ding Qingfen, "No Hidden Strings Tied to Aid," *China Daily*, April 27, 2011, 3.

31. Lum, *Comparing Global Influence*, 33–34.

32. Ibid.; Robert Sutter, *Chinese Foreign Relations: Power and Policy since the Cold War*, 4th ed. (Lanham, MD: Rowman & Littlefield, 2016), 74.

33. Robert Sutter, *Chinese Foreign Relations: Power and Policy since the Cold War*, 3rd ed. (Lanham, MD: Rowman & Littlefield, 2012), 83–84, 94, 291, 311.

34. "China's Financial Diplomacy: Rich but Rash," *Economist*, January 31, 2015, http://www.economist.com/news/finance-and-economics/21641259-challenge-world-bank-and-imf-china-will-have-imitate-them-rich.

35. Wayne Morrison, *China's Economic Conditions*, CRS Report RL33534 (Washington, DC: Congressional Research Service of the Library of Congress, March 5, 2009), 17–19.

36. Robert G. Sutter and Chin-Hao Huang, "China-Southeast Asia: Economic Concerns Begin to Hit Home," *Comparative Connections* 10, no. 4 (January 2009), http://cc.csis.org/2009/01/economic-concerns-begin-hit-home.

37. Wang Xu, "Currency Crosses Borders," *China Daily*, December 25, 2008, 1; "China Rolls Out Aid Package for ASEAN," Xinhua, April 12, 2009, http://ww.xinhuanet.com (accessed April 15, 2009; site discontinued).

38. Susan Lawrence and David MacDonald, *U.S.-China Relations: Policy Issues*, CRS Report RL41108 (Washington, DC: Congressional Research Service of the Library of Congress, August 2, 2012), 24–25.

39. Morrison, *China-U.S. Trade Issues* (December 29, 2016), 30–34.

40. Morrison, *China-U.S. Trade Issues* (May 21, 2012), 2; Howard Schneider, "U.S. Trade Deficit Drops for 2012," *Washington Post*, February 8, 2013, https://www.washingtonpost.com/business/economy/us-trade-deficit-drops-for-2012/2013/02/08/36dd01f0-7235-11e2-8b8d-e0b59a1b8e2a_story.html?utm_term=.e35e7f89dabe (accessed February 12, 2013); Morrison, *China-U.S. Trade Issues* (April 24, 2017), 10.

41. Morrison, *China-U.S. Trade Issues* (April 24, 2017), 9–10.

42. "China Criticizes US Trade Protectionism Measures," Xinhua, April 17, 2012, http://www.globaltimes.cn/content/705258.shtml (accessed February 9, 2013).

43. Morrison, *China-U.S. Trade Issues* (December 29, 2016), 3–8, 11–14.

44. Morrison, *China-U.S. Trade Issues* (December 29, 2016), 3; Office of the United States Trade Representative, "The People's Republic of China," https://ustr.gov/countries-regions/china-mongolia-taiwan/peoples-republic-china (accessed July 20, 2017).

45. Discussed in Morrison, *China-U.S. Trade Issues* (April 24, 2017), 27–31.

46. See review of complaints in Schell and Shirk, *US Policy toward China*, 60–64.

47. Morrison, *China-U.S. Trade Issues* (December 29, 2016), 27–29.

48. Schell and Shirk, *US Policy toward China*, 61.

49. This paragraph is taken from Morrison, *China-U.S. Trade Issues* (December 29, 2016), 40–41.

50. Morrison, *China-U.S. Trade Issues* (April 24, 2017), 35.

51. Robert Sutter, *Chinese Policy Priorities and Their Implications for the United States* (Lanham, MD: Rowman & Littlefield, 2000), 11, 46, 53.

52. Robert Sutter, *Chinese Foreign Relations: Power and Policy since the Cold War* (Lanham, MD: Rowman & Littlefield, 2008), 99.

53. Morrison, *China-U.S. Trade Issues* (May 16, 2006), 13–14; Morrison, *China-U.S. Trade Issues* (June 3, 2009), 20; Morrison, *China-U.S. Trade Issues* (May 21, 2012), 29–30; Morrison, *China-U.S. Trade Issues* (April 24, 2017), 37–46.

54. U.S. Special Trade Representative, "Priority Watch List," annual report, April 25, 2008, http://www.ustr.gov/sites/default/files/asset_upload_file558_14870.pdf (accessed November 3, 2009).

55. *Hearing on China: Intellectual Property Infringement, Indigenous Innovation Policies, and Framework for Measuring Effects on the U.S. Economy* (testimony of Jeremie Waterman, senior director, Greater China, US Chamber of Commerce, before the US International Trade Commission, June 15, 2010).

56. Morrison, *China-U.S. Trade Issues* (April 24, 2017), 42–46.

57. Sutter, *Chinese Foreign Relations* (2008), 97.

58. Deepak Bhattasali, Shantong Li, and Will Martin, eds., *China and the WTO* (Washington, DC: World Bank, 2004).

59. David Barboza, "Trade Surplus Tripled in '05, China Says," *New York Times*, January 12, 2006, http://www.nytimes.com/2006/01/12/business/worldbusiness/trade-surplus-tripled-in-05-china-says.html (accessed January 12, 2006); Morrison, *China-U.S. Trade Issues* (May 21, 2012), 35–39.

60. Sutter, *Chinese Foreign Relations* (2008), 76.

61. Cited in Morrison, *China-U.S. Trade Issues* (December 29, 2016), 46.

62. Morrison, *China-U.S. Trade Issues* (April 24, 2017), 48.

63. Lawrence and MacDonald, *U.S.-China Relations*, 30–31.

64. William Pentland, "China Pulls Back Indigenous Innovation Policies," *Forbes*, July 3, 2001, https://www.forbes.com/sites/williampentland/2011/07/03/china-pulls-back-indigenous-innovation-policies/#d61709d425c6 (accessed February 15, 2013).

65. Morrison, *China-U.S. Trade Issues* (May 21, 2012), 26–28.

66. Morrison, *China-U.S. Trade Issues* (December 29, 2016), 50–52; Donald Keyser, "President Obama's Re-election: Outlook for U.S.-China Relations in the Second Term," *China*

Policy Institute: Analysis (blog), November 12, 2012, http://blogs.nottingham.ac.uk/chinapolicyinstitute/2012/11/07.

67. Wayne Morrison, *China's Currency: A Summary of the Economic Issues*, CRS Report RS21625 (Washington, DC: Congressional Research Service of the Library of Congress, May 8, 2008); Morrison, *China-U.S. Trade Issues* (May 21, 2012), 40.

68. Rebecca Nelson, "Treasury's Recent Report on Foreign Exchange Rate Policies," CRS Insight IN10601, cited in Morrison, *China-U.S. Trade Issues* (December 29, 2016), 50.

69. Morrison, *China-U.S. Trade Issues* (December 29, 2016), 51.

70. Ibid.

71. "President Trump's WSJ Interview: Highlights," *Wall Street Journal*, April 12, 2017, http://www.wsj.com/podcasts/president-trump-wsj-interview-highlights/632F7842-135C-407A-AB30-6F6D7409F38B.html.

72. Morrison, *China-U.S. Trade Issues* (April 24, 2017), 19.

73. Morrison, *China-U.S. Trade Issues* (May 21, 2012), 15; Morrison, *China-U.S. Trade Issues* (December 29, 2016), 18; Department of the Treasury, *U.S. Portfolio Holdings of Foreign Securities as of December 31, 2015*, October 2016, http://ticdata.treasury.gov/Publish/shca2015_report.pdf.

74. Morrison, *China-U.S. Trade Issues* (June 3, 2009), 9; Morrison, *China-U.S. Trade Issues* (May 21, 2012), 17–20: Morrison, *China-U.S. Trade Issues* (December 29, 2016), 20.

75. Lawrence and MacDonald, *U.S.-China Relations*, 30.

76. Morrison, *China-U.S. Trade Issues* (November 29, 2012), 17.

77. Morrison, *China-U.S. Trade Issues* (May 21, 2012), 20–23.

78. Schell and Shirk, *US Policy toward China*, 60–61.

79. Claire Read, "U.S.-China Economic Relations: The Propeller Needs Oil" (Washington, DC: CSIS, August 27, 2015).

80. Hachigian, ed., *Debating China*, 28–42, 137–43.

81. Morrison, *China-U.S. Trade Issues* (December 29, 2016), 54.

82. Schell and Shirk, *US Policy toward China*, 62–64.

83. "George W. Bush on Environment," Issues 2000, http://www.issues2000.org/George_W__Bush_Environment.htm (accessed November 3, 2009).

84. Robert Sutter, *Chinese Foreign Relations: Power and Policy since the Cold War*, 2nd ed. (Lanham, MD: Rowman & Littlefield, 2010), 97–99.

85. Kenneth Lieberthal and David Sandalow, *Overcoming Obstacles to U.S.-China Cooperation on Climate Change*, John L. Thornton China Center Monograph Series Number 1 (Washington, DC: Brookings Institution, January 2009).

86. Kerry Dumbaugh, *China-U.S. Relations: Current Issues and Implications for U.S. Policy*, CRS Report R40457 (Washington, DC: Congressional Research Service of the Library of Congress, March 17, 2009), 18–19.

87. Elizabeth Economy and Adam Segal, "The G-2 Mirage," *Foreign Affairs* 88, no. 3 (May–June 2009): 14–23; Lawrence and MacDonald, *U.S.-China Relations*, 32–34.

88. Ibid.

89. Joanna I. Lewis, "China's Strategic Priorities in International Climate Change Negotiations," *Washington Quarterly* 31, no. 1 (Winter 2007–2008): 155–74; Joanna Lewis, "The State of U.S.-China Relations on Climate Change," *Woodrow Wilson International Center for Scholars China Environmental Series* 11 (2010/2011): 7–47.

90. Sutter, *Chinese Foreign Relations* (2012), 97–99.

91. Sutter, *Chinese Policy Priorities*, 188.

92. Elizabeth Economy, "China's Environmental Challenge," *Current History* (September 2005): 278–79; Sutter, *Chinese Policy Priorities*, 189.

93. Sutter, *Chinese Foreign Relations* (2012), 98.

94. Te Kan, "Past Successes and New Goal," *China Daily*, December 26, 2005–January 1, 2006, Supplement, 9.

95. Sutter, *Chinese Foreign Relations* (2012), 98.

96. Lawrence and MacDonald, *U.S.-China Relations*, 34.

97. The White House, Office of the Press Secretary, "FACT SHEET: U.S.-China Cooperation on Climate Change," September 3, 2016, https://obamawhitehouse.archives.gov/the-press-office/2016/09/03/fact-sheet-us-china-cooperation-climate-change-0.

98. Schell and Shirk, *US Policy toward China*, 37–38.

10. TAIWAN AND EAST ASIAN MARITIME DISPUTES IN CONTEMPORARY US-CHINA RELATIONS

1. David Brown, "Taiwan Sets a New Direction," *Comparative Connections* 18, no. 1 (May 2016), 67–78.

2. Steven Goldstein, *China and Taiwan* (Cambridge: Polity Press, 2015), 99–118.

3. Richard Bush and Michael O'Hanlon, *A War Like No Other* (New York: John Wiley and Sons, 2007); Office of the Secretary of Defense, *Annual Report to Congress: Military and Security Developments Involving the People's Republic of China 2012* (Washington, DC: Department of Defense, May 2012); Nancy Bernkopf Tucker, *Strait Talk: United States-Taiwan Relations and the Crisis with China* (Cambridge, MA: Harvard University Press, 2009); Richard Bush, *Uncharted Strait* (Washington, DC: Brookings Institution, 2013); Su Ge, *Meiguo: Dui hua Zhengce yu Taiwan wenti* [America: China policy and the Taiwan issue] (Beijing: Shijie Zhishi Chubanshe, 1998); Zi Zhongyun and He Di, eds., *Meitai Guanxi Sishinian* [Forty years of US-Taiwan relations] (Beijing: People's Press, 1991).

4. Shirley Kan, *U.S.-Taiwan Relationship: Overview of Policy Issues*, CRS Report R41592 (Washington, DC, Congressional Research Service of the Library of Congress, December 11, 2014).

5. Alan Romberg, "Tsai Ing-wen Takes Office: A New Era in Cross-Strait Relations," *China Leadership Monitor* no. 50 (Summer 2016), http://www.hoover.org/research/tsai-ing-wen-takes-office-new-era-cross-strait-relations.

6. Richard Bush, *Untying the Knot* (Washington, DC: Brookings Institution, 2005), 22–57; Denny Roy, *Taiwan: A Political History* (Ithaca, NY: Cornell University Press, 2003), 146–50, 195–202, 212–22, 235–40; T. Y. Wang, "Taiwan's Foreign Relations under Lee Teng-hui's Rule, 1988–2000," in *Sayonara to the Lee Teng-hui Era*, ed. Wei-chin Lee and T. Y. Wang (Lanham, MD: University Press of America, 2003), 250–60; Dennis Van Vranken Hickey, *Foreign Policy Making in Taiwan* (New York: Routledge, 2007). An earlier version of this assessment appeared in Robert Sutter, "Taiwan's Future: Narrowing Strait," *NBR Analysis* 96, (Seattle, WA: National Bureau of Asian Research, May 2011).

7. Bush, *Untying the Knot*, 57–71; Steven Goldstein and Julian Chang, eds., *Presidential Politics in Taiwan: The Administration of Chen Shui-bian* (Norwalk, CT: EastBridge, 2008).

8. Steven Goldstein, "Postscript: Chen Shui-bian and the Political Transition in Taiwan," in Goldstein and Chang, *Presidential Politics*, 296–98.

9. Ibid., 299–304.

10. David Brown, "Taiwan Voters Set a New Course," *Comparative Connections* 10, no. 1 (April 2008): 75.

11. Dennis V. Hickey, "Beijing's Evolving Policy toward Taipei: Engagement or Entrapment," *Issues and Studies* 45, no. 1 (March 2009): 31–70; Alan Romberg, "Cross Strait Relations: 'Ascend the Heights and Take a Long-Term Perspective,'" *China Leadership Monitor* no. 27 (Winter 2009), http://www.hoover.org/research/cross-strait-relations-ascend-heights-and-take-long-term-perspective; author's interviews and consultations with international affairs officials, including repeated meetings with senior officers, Taipei, May–December 2008, April 2009.

12. David Brown, "Economic Cooperation Framework Agreement Signed," *Comparative Connections* 12, no. 2 (July 2010): 77–79.

13. David Brown, "Looking Ahead to 2012," *Comparative Connections* 12, no. 4 (January 2011).

14. Donald Zagoria, "Trip to Seoul, Taipei, Beijing, Shanghai, and Tokyo—May 8–25, 2010," National Committee on American Foreign Policy (NCAFP), 2010, 2–6.

15. Author's interviews and consultations with international affairs officials, including repeated meetings with senior officers, Taipei, May–December 2008 and April 2009.

16. Shirley Kan, *Taiwan: Major U.S. Arms Sales since 1990*, CRS Report RL30957 (Washington, DC: Congressional Research Service of the Library of Congress, November 29, 2012); Kathrin Hille and Demetri Sevastopulo, "U.S. and China Set to Resume Military Talks," *Financial Times*, June 21, 2009.

17. Author's interviews and consultations, Taiwan, December 2008 and April 2009; Jeffery Bader, *Obama and China's Rise* (Washington, DC: Brookings Institution, 2012), 18–19; David Shear, "Cross-Strait Relations in a New Era of Negotiation" (remarks at the Carnegie Endowment for International Peace, Washington, DC, July 7, 2010), http://carnegieeurope.eu/2010/07/07/cross-strait-relations-in-new-era-of-negotiation-event-2955.

18. Bonnie Glaser, "The Honeymoon Ends," *Comparative Connections* 12, no. 1 (April 2010): 23–27. Kan, *Taiwan: Major U.S. Arms Sales*.

19. Robert Sutter, *Chinese Foreign Relations: Power and Policy since the Cold War*, 4th ed. (Lanham, MD: Rowman & Littlefield, 2016), 170.

20. Robert Sutter, "Taiwan's Elections, China's Response and America's Policy," Diplomat, February 1, 2016, http://thediplomat.com/2016/02/taiwans-elections-chinas-response-and-americas-policy.

21. David Brown, "Adjusting to New Realities," *Comparative Connections* 18, no. 3 (January 2017): 51–57.

22. David Brown and Kevin Scott, "Adrift without Dialogue," *Comparative Connections* 19, no. 1 (May 2017): 61–66.

23. Robert Sutter, "The Taiwan Elections: Don't Expect a US Policy Change," *Interpreter*, January 20, 2016, http://www.lowyinterpreter.org/post/2016/01/20/The-Taiwan-elections-Dont-expect-a-US-policy-change.aspx.

24. These differing approaches are reviewed in Sutter, "Taiwan's Elections, China's Response and America's Policy." Evidence of one or more of the three viewpoints are seen in Richard C. Bush III, "Cross-Strait relations: Not a one-way street," *Brookings Institution* (blog), April 22, 2016, https://www.brookings.edu/blog/order-from-chaos/2016/04/22/cross-strait-relations-not-a-one-way-street; Mark Stokes and Sabrina Tsai, "The United States and Future Policy Options in the Taiwan Strait," Project 2049, February 1, 2016, http://www.project2049.net/documents/Future_US%20Policy%20Options%20in%20the%20Taiwan%20Strait_Project%202049.pdf; T. X. Hammes, "Strategy for an Unthinkable Conflict," Diplomat, July 27, 2012, http://thediplomat.com/2012/07/military-strategy-for-an-unthinkable-conflict; John Bolton, "China-Taiwan Tensions are Rising," John Bolton PAC, April 25, 2016, http://www.boltonpac.com/2016/04/bolton-china-taiwan-tensions-rising-obama-responds-critical; William Lowther, "US Presidential Candidate Pledges to Defend Taiwan," *Taipei Times*, January 9, 2016, http://www.taipeitimes.com/News/taiwan/archives/2016/01/09/2003636798.

25. William Lowther, "US Presidential Candidate Pledges to Defend Taiwan," *Taipei Times*, January 9, 2016, http://www.taipeitimes.com/News/taiwan/archives/2016/01/09/2003636798.

26. Ted Cruz, "Sen. Cruz: Taiwan Is Exemplar of Liberty and Best Hope for Peace in East Asia," Senate Office of Ted Cruz, January 16, 2016, https://www.cruz.senate.gov/?p=press_release&id=2576.

27. William Lowther, "Tsai Has 'Very Successful' US Meetings," *Taipei Times*, June 4, 2015, http://www.taipeitimes.com/News/front/archives/2015/06/04/2003619870.

28. Peter Navarro, "America Can't Dump Taiwan," National Interest, July 19, 2016, http://nationalinterest.org/feature/america-cant-dump-taiwan-17040 (accessed July 29, 2016).

29. William Lowther, "Clinton Would Not Change US' Taiwan Policy: Aide," *Taipei Times*, July 27, 2016, 3.

30. Robert Sutter and Satu Limaye, *America's 2016 Election Debate on Asia Policy and Asian Reactions* (Honolulu: East-West Center, 2016), 25–26.

31. Sutter and Limaye, *America's 2016 Election Debate*, 26.

32. Brown and Scott, "Adrift without Dialogue"; Bonnie Glaser and Alexandra Viers, "Trump and Xi Break the Ice at Mar-a-Lago," *Comparative Connections* 19, no. 1 (May 2017): 21–32.

33. Robert Sutter, "Trump and China," *EastAsia Forum Quarterly* 9, no. 2 (April–June 2017): 21–24.

34. Bader, *Obama and China's Rise,* 69–92.

35. Ronald O'Rourke, *Maritime Territorial and Exclusive Economic Zone (EEZ) Disputes Involving China: Issues for Congress*, CRS Report 42784 (Washington, DC: Congressional Research Service of the Library of Congress, December 10, 2012).

36. There appeared to be serious disagreement within the Obama government: Military leaders like Defense Secretary Ashton Carter and Pacific Commander Admiral Harry Harris adopted much tougher public postures than the Obama White House staff regarding Chinese provocations in the East China Sea and the South China Sea. There were repeated media reports that Harris was muzzled by the president's aides. David Larter, "4-Star Admiral Wants to Confront China; White House Says 'Not So Fast,'" *Navy Times*, April 6, 2016 (republished September 26, 2016), https://www.navytimes.com/articles/4-star-admiral-wants-to-confront-china-the-white-house-says-not-so-fast.

37. Don Keyser, "President Obama's Re-election: Outlook for U.S China Relations in the Second Term," *China Policy Institute* (blog), November 7, 2012, http://blogs.nottingham.ac.uk/chinapolicyinstitute/2012/11/07.

38. Robert Ross, "The Problem with the Pivot," *Foreign Affairs* (November–December 2012); Shawn Brimley and Ely Ratner, "Smart Shift," *Foreign Affairs* (January–February 2013): 177–81. The full scope of the rebalance policy is addressed in Kurt Campbell, *The Pivot* (New York: Twelve-Hachette Book Group, 2016); see also Mark Manyin et al., *Pivot to the Pacific? The Obama Administration's "Rebalancing" toward Asia*, CRS Report 42448 (Washington, DC: Congressional Research Service of the Library of Congress, March 28, 2012); and Robert Sutter, *The United States and Asia: Regional Dynamics and Twenty-First Century Relations* (Lanham, MD: Rowman & Littlefield, 2015).

39. The following discussion comes from Robert Sutter and Chin-Hao Huang, "China Muscles Opponents on South China Sea," *Comparative Connections* 14, no. 2 (September 2012): 61–69; Robert Sutter and Chin-Hao Huang, "China Gains and Advances in South China Sea," *Comparative Connections* 14, no. 3 (January 2013): 69–76; and James Przystup, "China-Japan Relations," *Comparative Connections* 14, no. 3 (January 2013): 109–24.

40. Przystup, "China-Japan Relations."

41. Su Xiaohui, "Obama Will Be 'Smarter' in Rebalancing towards Asia and Engaging China," *China-US Focus*, November 8, 2012.

42. Bonnie Glaser, *Beijing as an Emerging Power in the South China Sea* (Washington, DC: CSIS, 2012).

43. Mark Valencia, "Asian Threats, Provocations Giving Rise to Whiffs of War," *Japan Times*, June 9, 2014, http://www.japantimes.co.jp/opinion/2014/06/09/commentary/world-commentary/asian-threats-provocations-giving-rise-whiffs-war/#.U6VP6JRdXxA.

44. White House Office of the Press Secretary, *Fact Sheet: U.S.-Japan Global and Regional Cooperation*, April 25, 2014; Matt Spetalnick and Nathan Layne, "Obama Accuses China of Flexing Muscles in Disputes with Neighbors," Reuters, April 28, 2015, http://www.reuters.com/article/2015/04/29/us-usa-japan-idUSKBN0NJ09520150429.

45. Emma Chanlette-Avery, coord., *Japan-US Relations*, CRS Report RL33436 (Washington, DC: Congressional Research Service of the Library of Congress, April 23, 2015), 2.

46. Sutter and Huang, "China Muscles Opponents on South China Sea": and Sutter and Huang, "China Gains and Advances in South China Sea."

47. The 2014 events are explained in greater detail in Robert Sutter and Chin-Hao Huang, "China Advances, More Opposition in South China Sea," *Comparative Connections* 16, no. 2 (September 2014), http://cc.csis.org/2014/09/china-advances-opposition-south-china-sea.

48. Michael Green and Ernest Bower, *Carter Defends South China Sea and Shangri-La* (Washington, DC: Center for Strategic and International Studies, May 29, 2015); "Facing U.S.-Led Resistance in the South China Sea," *Comparative Connections* 17, no. 2 (September 2015): 65–73.

49. The above developments are reviewed in Dean Cheng, "South China Sea after the Tribunal Ruling—Where Do We Go from Here?" *National Interest* (blog), July 16, 2016, http://nationalinterest.org/blog/the-buzz/south-china-sea-after-the-tribunal-ruling-where-do-we-go-17011; "Countering Adverse Tribunal Ruling," *Comparative Connections* 18, no. 2 (September 2016): 59–67; "Beijing Presses Its Advantages," *Comparative Connections* 18, no. 3 (January 2017): 43–48.

50. "Countering Adverse Tribunal Ruling," 59–67; "Beijing Presses Its Advantages," 43–48.

51. "China Consolidates Control and Advances Influence," *Comparative Connections* 19, no. 1 (May 2017): 51–58; Steven Stashwick, "US Freedom of Navigation Challenges in South China Sea on Hold," Diplomat, May 8, 2017, http://thediplomat.com/2017/05/us-freedom-of-navigation-challenges-in-south-china-sea-on-hold.

11. ISSUES OF HUMAN RIGHTS IN CONTEMPORARY US-CHINA RELATIONS

1. For historical treatment of these differences, see John K. Fairbank, *The United States and China* (Cambridge, MA: Harvard University Press, 1983).

2. See the discussion of human rights issues in Harry Harding, *A Fragile Relationship: The United States and China since 1972* (Washington, DC: Brookings Institution, 1992); James Mann, *About Face: A History of America's Curious Relationship with China, from Nixon to Clinton* (New York: Knopf, 1999); David M. Lampton, *Same Bed, Different Dreams: Managing U.S.-China Relations, 1989–2000* (Berkeley: University of California Press, 2001); and Ming Wan, *Human Rights in Chinese Foreign Relations: Defining and Defending National Interests* (Philadelphia: University of Pennsylvania Press, 2001). See also People's Republic of China State Council Information Office, *National Human Rights Action Plan of China (2009–2010)*, April 13, 2009, http://www.china.org.cn/archive/2009-04/13/content_17595407.htm (accessed November 8, 2009).

3. "Don't Call It the New Chinese Global Order (Yet)," *Foreign Policy*, March 7, 2017, http://foreignpolicy.com/2017/03/07/dont-call-it-the-chinese-global-order-yet-xi-jinping-donald-trump-values.

4. Yu Keping, "Ideological Change and Incremental Democracy in Reform-Era China," in *China's Changing Political Landscape: Prospects for Democracy*, ed. Cheng Li (Washington, DC: Brookings Institution, 2008), 44–60.

5. Jacques deLisle, "Legalization without Democratization in China under Hu Jintao," in Cheng Li, ed., *China's Changing Political Landscape*, 185–211.

6. Gong Li, "The Difficult Path to Diplomatic Relations: China's U.S. Policy, 1972–1978," in *Normalization of U.S.-China Relations: An International History*, ed. William Kirby, Robert Ross, and Gong Li (Cambridge, MA: Harvard University Press, 2005).

7. Harding, *A Fragile Relationship*, 198–99; Warren Cohen, *America's Response to China: A History of Sino-American Relations* (New York: Columbia University Press, 2000), 213.

8. Cohen, *America's Response to China*, 212–13.

9. Harding, *A Fragile Relationship*, 198–206; Mann, *About Face*, 100–109.

10. Michael Schaller, *The United States and China into the Twenty-First Century* (New York: Oxford University Press, 2002), 197.

11. John K. Fairbank and Merle Goldman, *China: A New History* (Cambridge, MA: Harvard University Press, 1999), 419–26.

12. Lampton, *Same Bed, Different Dreams*, 130–53.

13. Song Qiang, Zhang Changchang, and Qiao Bian, *Zhongguo keyi shuo bu: Lengzhanhou shidai de zhengzhi yu qinggan jueze* [China can say no: The decision between politics and sentiment in the post–Cold War] (Beijing: Zhonghua Gongshang Lianhe Chubanshe, 1996).

14. Mann, *About Face*, 200–201.

15. Lampton, *Same Bed, Different Dreams*, 15–63.

16. Sheryl Gay Stolberg, "Bush Meets 5 Dissidents from China before Games," *New York Times*, July 30, 2008, http://www.nytimes.com/2008/07/30/sports/olympics/30prexy.html? mcubz=1 (accessed November 7, 2009).

17. "Remarks by the President at the U.S./China Strategic and Economic Dialogue," The White House, Office of the Press Secretary, July 27, 2009, https://obamawhitehouse.archives. gov/the-press-office/remarks-president-uschina-strategic-and-economic-dialogue (original accessed November 7, 2009).

18. Gideon Rachman, "China's Strange Fear of Colour Revolution," *Financial Times*, February 9, 2015, https://www.ft.com/content/9b5a2ed2-af96-11e4-b42e-00144feab7de.

19. C. Fred Bergsten, Bates Gill, Nicholas Lardy, and Derek Mitchell, *China: The Balance Sheet* (New York: Public Affairs, 2006), 62–72; "China Hits Back on U.S. Human Rights," CNN, May 25, 2012, http://www.cnn.com/2012/05/25/world/asia/china-us-human-rights/ index.html.

20. Kerry Dumbaugh, *Tibet: Problems, Prospects, and U.S. Policy*, CRS Report RL34445 (Washington, DC: Congressional Research Service of the Library of Congress, July 30, 2008); Jeffrey Bader, *Obama and China's Rise* (Washington, DC: Brookings Institution, 2012), 48–52, 72–75.

21. Orville Schell and Susan Shirk, Chairs, *U.S. Policy toward China: Recommendations for a New Administration*, Task Force Report (New York: Asia Society, 2017), 53.

22. Bergsten et al., *China*, 62–72; Cheng Li, "Will China's 'Lost Generation' Find a Path to Democracy?" in *China's Changing Political Landscape*, 98–120; Joseph Fewsmith, "Staying in Power: What Does the Chinese Communist Party Have to Do?" in Cheng Li, ed., *China's Changing Political Landscape*, 212–28; US Department of State, Bureau of Democracy, Human Rights and Labor, *Country Reports on Human Rights Practices for 2011: China* (includes Tibet, Hong Kong, and Macau), https://www.state.gov/j/drl/rls/hrrpt/2011/eap/186268.htm; US Department of State, Bureau of Democracy, Human Rights and Labor, *Country Reports on Human Rights Practices for 2016: China* (includes Tibet, Hong Kong, and Macau), https:// www.state.gov/documents/organization/265540.pdf.

23. US Department of State, *Country Reports on Human Rights Practices for 2011*; Congressional-Executive Commission on China, *Annual Report 2012*, October 10, 2012, https:// www.cecc.gov/publications/annual-reports/2012-annual-report; US Commission on International Religious Freedom, *Annual Report of the U.S. Commission on International Human Rights*, March 2012, http://www.uscirf.gov/sites/default/files/resources/ Annual%20Report%20of%20USCIRF%202012(2).pdf; Amnesty International, *Annual Report 2012—China, 2012*, https://www.amnestyusa.org/files/air12-report-english.pdf (accessed March 5, 2013); Human Rights Watch, *World Report 2013-China*, https://www.hrw.org/world-report/2013/country-chapters/china-and-tibet (accessed March 5, 2013).

24. Thomas Lum and Hannah Fischer, *Human Rights in China: Trends and Policy Implications*, CRS Report RL34729 (Washington, DC: Congressional Research Service of the Library of Congress, July 17, 2009), 1; Susan Lawrence and David MacDonald, *U.S.-China Relations: Policy Issues*, CRS Report R41108 (Washington, DC: Congressional Research Service of the Library of Congress, August 2, 2012), 35–42.

25. Andrew Nathan, "China at the Tipping Point?" *Journal of Democracy* 24, no. 1 (January 2013): 20–25; People's Republic of China State Council Information Office, *National Human Rights Action Plan of China (2012–2015)*, June 14, 2012, http://news.xinhuanet.com/english/ china/2016-06/14/c_135435326.htm (accessed March 5, 2013).

26. Bergsten, *China*, 62–64; Lawrence and MacDonald, *U.S.-China Relations*, 35–42; Lum and Fischer, *Human Rights in China*, 2. As seen from source notes below, reports from the Department of State and the Congressional Research Service of the Library of Congress provide comprehensive and balanced coverage of human rights issues in China of use to researchers and specialists.

27. "Recent High-Profile Mass Protests in China," BBC News, July 3, 2012, http://www. bbc.co.uk/news/world-asia-china-18684903 (accessed March 5, 2013).

28. Thomas Lum and Hannah Fischer, *Human Rights in China: Trends and Policy Implications*, CRS Report RL34729 (Washington, DC: Congressional Research Service of the Library

of Congress, October 31, 2008), 3–4; US Department of State, *Country Reports on Human Rights Practices for 2011.*

29. Yu Keping, *Democracy Is a Good Thing* (Washington, DC: Brookings Institution, 2008); C. Fred Bergsten, Charles Freeman, Nicholas Lardy, and Derek Mitchell, *China's Rise: Challenges and Opportunities* (Washington, DC: Peterson Institute for International Economics, 2008), 38; Nathan et al., "China at the Tipping Point?"

30. Paul Mooney, "How to Deal with NGOs—Part 1, China," YaleGlobal Online, August 1, 2006, http://yaleglobal.yale.edu/content/how-deal-ngos-part-i-china; Raymond Li, "Li Keqiang Wants Tax Breaks for NGOs Specializing in AIDS/HIV Work," *South China Morning Post*, November 29, 2012, http://www.scmp.com/news/china/article/1093457/li-keqiang-wants-tax-breaks-ngos-specialising-aidshiv-work (accessed March 5, 2013).

31. Lum and Fischer, *Human Rights in China* (2008), 5–7.

32. Schell and Shirk, *U.S. Policy toward China*, 53–55; US Department of State, *Country Reports on Human Rights Practices for 2016* (see "Executive Summary").

33. Thomas Lum, *Human Rights in China and U.S. Policy*, CRS Report R43964 (Washington, DC: Congressional Research Service of the Library of Congress, September 17, 2015); see "summary" pages.

34. US Department of State, *Country Reports on Human Rights Practices for 2016* (see "Executive Summary").

35. Kerry Dumbaugh, *China-U.S. Relations: Current Issues and Implications for U.S. Policy*, CRS Report R40457 (Washington, DC: Congressional Research Service of the Library of Congress, March 17, 2009); Bonnie Glaser, "U.S.-China Relations," *Comparative Connections* 11, no. 3 (October 2009): 36–37; Lawrence and MacDonald, *U.S.-China Relations*, 39–42. Lum, *Human Rights in China and U.S. Policy*, 21–28; US Department of State, *Country Reports on Human Rights Practices for 2016*, 97–98; Schell and Shirk, *U.S. Policy toward China*, 54.

36. Lum, *Human Rights in China and U.S. Policy*, 6; Linda Yeung, "Campus Crackdown on 'Western Values,'" University World News, February 6, 2015, http://www.universityworldnews.com/article.php?story=2015020710141145.

37. Lum, *Human Rights in China and U.S. Policy*, 6; US Department of State, *Country Reports on Human Rights Practices for 2016*, 1.

38. US Department of State, *Country Reports on Human Rights Practices for 2016*, 5–6; "Swedish Rights Groups Honours Detained Bookseller Gui Minhui," AFP via HKFP, April 22, 2017, https://www.hongkongfp.com/2017/04/22/swedish-rights-group-honours-detained-bookseller-gui-minhai.

39. US Department of State, *Country Reports on Human Rights Practices for 2016*, 6.

40. Ibid., 18–19.

41. Ibid., 19.

42. Ibid., 24–25; Lum, *Human Rights in China and U.S. Policy*, 11–14.

43. "Xi Completes Media Tour, Stresses Party Leadership," Xinhua, February 20, 2016, http://news.xinhuanet.com/english/2016-02/20/c_135114528.htm.

44. Steven Millward, "China Now Has 731 Million Internet Users," *TECHINASIA*, January 22, 2017, https://www.techinasia.com/china-731-million-internet-users-end-2016.

45. Lum, *Human Rights in China and U.S. Policy*, 11–12.

46. Ibid., 11–13; US Department of State, *Country Reports on Human Rights Practices for 2016*, 28–34.

47. Lum, *Human Rights in China and U.S. Policy*, 12.

48. Ibid., 12–13.

49. Lum and Fischer, *Human Rights in China* (2008), 14.

50. United States Commission on International Religious Freedom, "Frequently Asked Questions," http://www.uscirf.gov (accessed March 5, 2013).

51. Lum and Fischer, *Human Rights in China* (2009), 13.

52. "Poll Shows 300M in China 'Religious,'" *South China Morning Post*, February 7, 2007, http://www.scmp.com; "Survey Finds 300M China Believers," BBC News, February 7, 2007, http://news.bbc.co.uk/2/hi/asia-pacific/6337627.stm; Ian Johnson, "In China, Unregistered Churches Are Driving a Religious Revolution," *Atlantic*, April 23, 2017, https://www.

theatlantic.com/international/archive/2017/04/china-unregistered-churches-driving-religious-revolution/521544.

53. US Department of State, *Country Reports on Human Rights Practices for 2011*; Lawrence and MacDonald, *U.S.-China Relations*, 36.

54. Maureen Fan, "Beijing Curbs Rights It Says Citizens Have to Worship," *Washington Post*, August 1, 2008, http://www.washingtonpost.com.

55. Lum, *Human Rights in China and U.S. Policy*, 21.

56. Melvyn Goldstein, Tashi Tsering, and William Siebenschuh, *The Struggle for Modern Tibet* (Armonk, NY: M. E. Sharpe, 2000); Warren Smith, *China's Tibet: Autonomy or Assimilation* (Lanham, MD: Rowman & Littlefield, 2009); Dumbaugh, *Tibet*.

57. Warren Smith, *Tibet's Last Stand? The Tibetan Uprising of 2008 and China's Response* (Lanham, MD: Rowman & Littlefield, 2009).

58. Dumbaugh, *Tibet*, 6–9.

59. US Department of State, *Country Reports on Human Rights Practices for 2014 (Tibet)*, June 25, 2015, https://www.state.gov/documents/organization/236644.pdf; "China Issues White Paper on Tibet," Xinhua, September 6, 2015; US Department of State, *Country Reports on Human Rights Practices for 2016*, 76–96.

60. "Obama Meets Dalai Lama in Spite of China's Protest," Reuters, June 15, 2016, http://www.reuters.com/article/us-usa-obama-dalilama-idUSKCN0Z1221.

61. Hugo Restall, "The Urumqi Effect," *Wall Street Journal*, July 10, 2008, https://www.wsj.com/articles/SB124716357455819069; Nicholas Bequelin, "Behind the Violence in Xinjiang," *New York Times*, July 10, 2008, http://www.nytimes.com/2009/07/10/opinion/10iht-edbequelin.html?mcubz=1.

62. Lum, *Human Rights in China and U.S. Policy*, 25.

63. Ibid., 26.

64. US Department of State, *Country Reports on Human Rights Practices for 2016*, 62–65.

65. Maria Hsia Chang, *Falun Gong: The End of Days* (New Haven, CT: Yale University Press, 2004).

66. Thomas Lum, *China and Falun Gong*, CRS Report 33437 (Washington, DC: Congressional Research Service of the Library of Congress, May 25, 2006).

67. Richard Bush, *Examining the Impact of the Umbrella Movement* (Washington, DC: Brookings Institution, December 3, 2014).

68. Schell and Shirk, *U.S. Policy toward China*, 50–52.

69. Ibid., 54–55.

70. James Mann, *The China Fantasy* (New York: Viking, 2007); David M. Lampton, "*The China Fantasy*, Fantasy," *China Quarterly* 191 (September 2007): 745–54; Nathan, "China at the Tipping Point?"

71. Lum and Fischer, *Human Rights in China* (2008), 27–28.

72. John Pomfret, "Obama Postpones Dalai Lama Meeting," *Washington Post*, October 5, 2009, http://www.washingtonpost.com; Ariana Eunjung Cha and Glenn Kessler, "Pelosi, Like Clinton, Plays Down Human Rights before China Trip," *Washington Post*, May 24, 2009, http://www.washingtonpost.com.

73. People's Republic of China State Council Information Office, *National Human Rights Action Plan of China (2009–2010)*; "China Hits Back on U.S. Human Rights," CNN, May 25, 2012, http://www.cnn.com/2012/05/25/world/asia/china-us-human-rights/index.html.

74. Lum, *Human Rights in China and U.S. Policy*, 36–38.

75. Schell and Shirk, *U.S. Policy toward China*, 56–57.

12. OUTLOOK

1. Timothy Heath, "China Intensifies Effort to Establish Leading Role in Asia, Dislodge U.S.," *China Brief* 17, 2 (February 6, 2017), https://jamestown.org/program/china-intensifies-effort-establish-leading-role-asia-dislodge-u-s.

2. Among other sources assessing the Trump administration's policies in the Asia-Pacific, see Sheldon Simon, "Mixed Messages," *Comparative Connections* 19, no. 1 (May 2017): 41–50; Prashanth Parameswaran, "What Mattis' Shangri-La Dialogue speech Revealed about Trump's Asia Defense Policy," Diplomat, June 6, 2017, http://thediplomat.com/tag/trump-asia-policy; Benjamin Lee, "Trump's First 100 Days in Asia," Diplomat, April 28, 2017, http://thediplomat.com/2017/04/trumps-first-100-days-in-asia; Robert Sutter, "Trump and China: Implications for Southeast Asia," *East Asia Forum Quarterly* 9, no. 2 (April–June 2017): 21–24.

3. Robert Sutter and Satu Limaye, *Washington Asia Policy Debates: Impact of 2015–2016 Presidential Campaign and Asian Reactions* (Washington, DC: East-West Center, 2016), 22–24.

4. See Simon, "Mixed Messages"; Bonnie Glaser and Alexandra Veers, "Trump and Xi Break the Ice at Mar-a-Lago," *Comparative Connections* 19, no. 1 (May 2017): 21–32; Parameswaran, "What Mattis' Shangri-La Dialogue speech revealed about Trump's Asia Defense Policy"; Lee, "Trump's First 100 Days in Asia." The following details are taken from Sutter, "Trump and China."

5. See among others, Jeffrey Bader, *U.S.-China Challenges: Time for China to Step Up* (Washington, DC: Brookings Institution, 2017); Michael Swaine, *Creating a Stable Asia: An Agenda for a U.S.-China Balance of Power* (Washington, DC: Carnegie Endowment for International Peace, 2016); Harry Harding, "Has U.S. China Policy Failed?" *Washington Quarterly* 38, no. 3 (2015): 95–122; Robert Blackwill and Ashley Tellis, *Council Special Report: Revising U.S. Grand Strategy toward China* (Washington, DC: Council on Foreign Relations, April 2015); Orville Schell and Susan Shirk, Chairs, *US Policy toward China: Recommendations for a New Administration*, Task Force Report (New York: Asia Society, 2017); Bonnie Glaser and Alexandra Viers, "China Prepares for Rocky Relations in 2017," *Comparative Connections* 18, no. 3 (January 2017): 21–22; Shi Jiangtao, "Tempest Trump: China and U.S. Urged to Make Plans for 'Major Storm' in Bilateral Relationship," *South China Morning Post*, January 30, 2017, http://www.scmp.com/news/china/diplomacy-defence/article/2065707/tempest-trump-china-and-us-urged-make-plans-major-storm.

6. US National Intelligence Council, *Global Trends: Paradox of Progress*, Report NIC 2017-001 (Washington, DC, January 2017), x, 31, 33.

7. Aaron Friedberg, *A Contest for Supremacy: China, America, and the Struggle for Mastery in Asia* (New York: W. W. Norton, 2011); Hugh White, *The China Choice* (Collingwood, Australia: Black Inc., 2012).

8. Arvind Subramanian, "The Inevitable Superpower: Why China's Rise Is a Sure Thing," *Foreign Affairs* 90, no 5 (September–October 2011): 66–78; Stefan Halper, *The Beijing Consensus: How China's Authoritarian Model Will Dominate the 21st Century* (New York: Basic Books, 2010); Martin Jacques, *When China Rules the World: The Rise of the Middle Kingdom and the End of the Western World* (New York: Penguin, 2009).

9. Stephen Brooks and William Wolfforth, "The Once and Future Superpower: Why China Won't Overtake the United States," *Foreign Affairs* (May–June 2016), https://www.foreignaffairs.com/articles/united-states/2016-04-13/once-and-future-superpower; Paul Dibb and John Lee, "Why China Will Not Become the Dominant Power in Asia," *Security Challenges* 10, no. 3 (2014): 1–21; Robert Sutter, *Chinese Foreign Relations: Power and Policy since the Cold War*, 4th ed. (Lanham, MD: Rowman & Littlefield, 2016), 327–33.

10. The following is based on Sutter, *Chinese Foreign Relations*, 327–33, and Robert Sutter, "China's Rise: Evolution and Implications," in *The Far East and Australasia, 2017* (London: Routledge, forthcoming). See also Robert Sutter, *Foreign Relations of the PRC* (Lanham, MD: Rowman & Littlefield, 2013), 215–17; Robert Sutter, *The United States and Asia* (Lanham, MD: Rowman & Littlefield, 2015), 112–32.

11. David M. Lampton, *Following the Leader: Ruling China from Deng Xiaoping to Xi Jinping* (Berkeley: University of California Press, 2015); David Shambaugh, ed., *The China Reader* (New York: Oxford University Press, 2016); Andrew Nathan and Andrew Scobell, *China's Search for Security* (New York: Columbia University Press, 2012); Thomas Christensen, *The China Challenge: Shaping the Choices of a Rising Power* (New York: W. W. Norton, 2016).

12. Ben Blanchard and John Ruwitch, "China Hikes Defense Budget, to Spend More in Internal Security," Reuters, March 5, 2013, http://www.reuters.com/article/2013/03/05/us-china-parliament-defence-idUSBRE92403620130305.

13. Feng Zhaokui, "China Still a Developing Nation," *China Daily*, May 6, 2010, 12.

14. Keira Lu Huang, "Xi Jinping's Reforms Encounter 'Unimaginably Fierce Resistance,'" *South China Morning Post*, August 21, 2015, http://www.scmp.com/news/china/policies-politics/article/1851314/xi-jinpings-reforms-encountering-fierce-resistance.

15. Robert Sutter, "China and U.S. Security and Economic Interests: Opportunities and Challenges," in *U.S.-China-EU Relations: Managing the New World Order*, ed. Robert Ross and Oystein Tunsjo (London: Routledge, 2010); James Shinn, ed., *Weaving the Net: Conditional Engagement with China* (New York: Council on Foreign Relations, 1996).

16. This section summarizes findings in Sutter, *Chinese Foreign Relations*, 327–33; Sutter, "China's Rise: Evolution and Implications"; Sutter, *Foreign Relations of the PRC*, 1–26 and 311–27; and Sutter, *The United States and Asia,* 109–34.

17. Sutter, *Chinese Foreign Relations*, 65–73.

18. Ibid., 63–65.

19. Ibid., 68–69.

20. Ibid., 67–71.

21. Veasna Var and Sovinda Po, "Cambodia, Sri Lanka and the China Debt Trap," *East-AsiaForum*, March 18, 2017, http://www.eastasiaforum.org/2017/03/18/cambodia-sri-lanka-and-the-china-debt-trap.

22. "China's Financial Diplomacy: Rich but Rash," *Economist*, January 31, 2015, http ://www.economist.com/news/finance-and-economics/21641259-challenge-world-bank-and-imf-china-will-have-imitate-them-rich.

23. This section follows the review in Sutter, *United States and Asia*, 120–23.

Selected Bibliography

Accinelli, Robert. *Crisis and Commitment: United States Policy toward Taiwan, 1950–1955.* Chapel Hill: University of North Carolina Press, 1996.
Bachrack, Stanley D. *The Committee of One Million: "China Lobby" Politics, 1953–1971.* New York: Columbia University Press, 1976.
Bader, Jeffrey. *Obama and China's Rise.* Washington, DC: Brookings Institution, 2012.
Barnett, A. Doak. *China and the Major Powers in East Asia.* Washington, DC: Brookings Institution, 1977.
———. *U.S.-China Relations: Time for a New Beginning—Again.* Washington, DC: Johns Hopkins University, School for Advanced International Studies, 1994.
Bays, Daniel H., ed. *Christianity in China.* Stanford, CA: Stanford University Press, 1996.
Beal, John R. *Marshall in China.* Garden City, NY: Doubleday, 1970.
Bernstein, Richard, and Ross H. Munro. *Coming Conflict with China.* New York: Knopf, 1998.
Borg, Dorothy. *American Policy and the Chinese Revolution, 1925–1928.* New York: Macmillan, 1947.
———. *The United States and the Far Eastern Crisis of 1933–1938.* Cambridge, MA: Harvard University Press, 1964.
Borg, Dorothy, and Waldo Heinrichs, eds. *Uncertain Years: Chinese-American Relations, 1947–1950.* New York: Columbia University Press, 1980.
Buhite, Russell D. *Patrick J. Hurley and American Foreign Policy.* Ithaca, NY: Cornell University Press, 1973.
Bush, Richard. *At Cross Purposes: U.S.-Taiwan Relations since 1942.* Armonk, NY: M. E. Sharpe, 2004.
———. *Untying the Knot.* Washington, DC: Brookings Institution, 2005.
———. *Uncharted Strait.* Washington, DC: Brookings Institution, 2013.
———. *Hong Kong in the Shadow of China.* Washington, DC: Brookings Institution, 2016.
Chang, Gordon. *Friends and Enemies: The United States, China, and the Soviet Union, 1948–1972.* Stanford, CA: Stanford University Press, 1990.
———. *Fateful Ties: A History of America's Preoccupation with China.* Cambridge, MA: Harvard University Press, 2015.
Chen Jian. *Mao's China and the Cold War.* Chapel Hill: University of North Carolina Press, 2001.
Christensen, Thomas. *Useful Adversaries: Grand Strategy, Domestic Mobilization, and Sino-American Conflicts, 1949–1958.* Princeton, NJ: Princeton University Press, 1996.
———. *The China Challenge: Shaping the Choices of a Rising Power.* New York: W. W. Norton, 2016.

Cohen, Warren I. *America's Response to China: A History of Sino-American Relations*. New York: Columbia University Press, 2010.

Dennett, Tyler. *Americans in Eastern Asia: A Critical Study of the Policy of the United States with Reference to China, Japan, and Korea in the 19th Century*. New York: Macmillan, 1922.

Dong Mei, ed. *Zhong-Mei guanxi ziliao xuanbian* [Selected materials on Sino-American relations]. Beijing: Shishi Chubanshe, 1982.

Dulles, Foster Rhea. *American Policy toward Communist China, 1949–1969*. New York: Thomas Y. Crowell, 1972.

Fairbank, John K. *The United States and China*. Cambridge, MA: Harvard University Press, 1983.

Fairbank, John K., and Suzanne W. Barnett, eds. *Christianity in China*. Cambridge, MA: Harvard University Press, 1985.

Foot, Rosemary. *The Practice of Power: U.S. Relations with China since 1949*. New York: Oxford University Press, 1997.

Friedberg, Aaron. *A Contest for Supremacy: China, America, and the Struggle for Mastery in Asia*. New York: W. W. Norton, 2011.

———. *Beyond Air-Sea Battle: The Debate over US Military Strategy in Asia*. London: IISS/ Routledge, 2014.

Fu Hao, and Li Tongcheng, eds. *Lusi shui shou? Zhongguo waijiaoguan zai Meiguo* [Who will win the game? Chinese diplomats in the United States]. Beijing: Hauqiao Chubanshe, 1998.

Garrison, Jean. *Making China Policy: From Nixon to G. W. Bush*. Boulder, CO: Lynne Rienner, 2005.

Garver, John W. *China's Decision for Rapprochement with the United States, 1968–1971*. Boulder, CO: Westview Press, 1982.

———. *Face Off: China, the United States, and Taiwan's Democratization*. Seattle: University of Washington Press, 1997.

———. *The Sino-American Alliance: Nationalist China and American Cold War Strategy in Asia*. Armonk, NY: M. E. Sharpe, 1997.

Goh, Evelyn. *Constructing the U.S. Rapprochement with China, 1961–1974*. New York: Cambridge University Press, 2005.

Goldstein, Lyle. *Meeting China Halfway*. Washington, DC: Georgetown University Press, 2015.

Goldstein, Steven. *China and Taiwan*. Cambridge: Polity Press, 2015.

Gong Li. *Kuayue: 1969–1979 nian Zhong Mei guanxi de yanbian* [Across the chasm: The evolution of China-US relations, 1969–1979]. Henan: Henan People's Press, 1992.

Gong Li, William Kirby, and Robert Ross, eds. *Zong jiedong zouxiang jianjiao: Zhong Mei guanxi zhengchanghua jincheng zai tantuo* [From thaw to normalization: A reexamination of the normalization of US-China relations]. Beijing: Zhongyang Wenxian Chubanshe, 2004.

Griswold, A. Whitney. *The Far Eastern Policy of the United States*. New York: Harcourt Brace, 1938.

Hachigian, Nina, ed. *Debating China: The U.S.-China Relationship in Ten Conversations*. New York: Oxford University Press, 2014.

Han Nianlong, and Xue Mouhong, eds. *Dangdai Zhongguo waijiao* [Contemporary Chinese diplomacy]. Beijing: Zhongguo Shehui Kexue Chubanshe, 1990.

Harding, Harry. *A Fragile Relationship: The United States and China since 1972*. Washington, DC: Brookings Institution, 1992.

Harding, Harry, and Yuan Ming, eds. *Sino-American Relations, 1945–1955*. Wilmington, DE: Scholarly Resources, 1989.

Herzstein, Robert Erwin. *Henry R. Luce, Time, and the American Crusade in Asia*. New York: Cambridge University Press, 2005.

House Committee on Foreign Affairs. *Executive-Legislative Consultations over China Policy, 1978–1979*. Washington, DC: US Government Printing Office, 1980.

Hu Sheng, ed. *Zhongguo gongchandang de qishi nian* [Seventy years of the Chinese Communist Party]. Beijing: Zhonggong Dangshi Chubanshe, 1991.

Hunt, Michael H. *The Making of a Special Relationship: The United States and China to 1914.* New York: Columbia University Press, 1983.

Iriye, Akira. *Across the Pacific: An Inner History of American–East Asian Relations.* New York: Harcourt, Brace and World, 1967.

Iriye, Akira, and Warren I. Cohen, eds. *American, Chinese, and Japanese Perspectives on Wartime Asia, 1939–1949.* Wilmington, DE: Scholarly Resources, 1990.

Isaacs, Harold R. *Scratches on Our Minds: American Images of China and India.* New York: John Day, 1958.

Jacoby, Neil H. *U.S. Aid to Taiwan.* New York: Praeger, 1966.

Jespersen, T. Christopher. *American Images of China, 1931–1949.* Stanford, CA: Stanford University Press, 1996.

Jia Qingguo. *Wei Shixian de Hejie: Zhongmei Guanxi de Gehe yu Weiji* [The unmaterialized rapprochement: Estrangement and crisis in Sino-American talks in retrospect]. Beijing: Shijie Zhishi Chubanshe, 1985.

Jiang Changbin, and Robert S. Ross, eds. *1955–1971 Nian de Zhong Mei Guanxi—Huanhe Zhigian: Lengzhan Chongtu yu Keshi de Cai Tantao* [US-China relations 1955–1971—before détente: An examination of Cold War conflict and restraint]. Beijing: Shijie Zhishi Chubanshe, 1998.

———. *Cong Duizhi zouxiang Huanhe: Lengzhan Shiqi Zhong Mei Guanxi zai Tantao* [From confrontation toward détente: A reexamination of US-China relations during the Cold War]. Beijing: Shijie Zhishi Chubanshe, 2000.

Jing Li. *China's America: The Chinese View of the United States, 1900–2000.* New York: State University of New York Press, 2011.

Kirby, William, Robert Ross, and Gong Li, eds. *Normalization of U.S.-China Relations.* Cambridge, MA: Harvard University Press, 2005.

Koen, Ross Y. *The China Lobby in American Politics.* New York: Harper and Row, 1974.

Lampton, David M. *Same Bed, Different Dreams: Managing U.S.-China Relations, 1989–2000.* Berkeley: University of California Press, 2001.

Lardy, Nicholas. *Sustaining China's Economic Growth after the Global Financial Crisis.* Washington, DC: Peterson Institute for International Economics, 2012.

Latourette, Kenneth S. *The History of Early Relations between the United States and China, 1784–1844.* New Haven, CT: Yale University Press, 1917.

Li Changjiu, and Shi Lujia. *Zhongmei guanxi liangbainian* [Two hundred years of Sino-American relations]. Peking: Xinhua Publishing House, 1984.

Lieberthal, Kenneth, and Wang Jisi. *Addressing U.S.-China Strategic Distrust.* Washington, DC: Brookings Institution, 2012.

Lin Qing. *Zhou Enlai zaixiang shengya* [The career of Prime Minister Zhou Enlai]. Hong Kong: Changcheng Wenhua Chubanshe, 1991.

Liu Xiaoyuan. *A Partnership for Disorder: China, the United States, and Their Policies for the Postwar Disposition of the Japanese Empire.* New York: Cambridge University Press, 1996.

MacMillian, Margaret. *Nixon in China.* Toronto: Viking Canada, 2006.

Mann, James. *About Face: A History of America's Curious Relationship with China, from Nixon to Clinton.* New York: Knopf, 1999.

———. *The China Fantasy.* New York: Viking 2007.

May, Ernest R. *The Truman Administration and China, 1945–1949.* New York: Lippincott, 1975.

May, Ernest R., and John K. Fairbank, eds. *America's China Trade in Historical Perspective: The Chinese and American Performance.* Cambridge, MA: Harvard University Press, 1986.

Miller, Stuart Creighton. *The Unwelcome Immigrant: The American Image of the Chinese, 1785–1882.* Berkeley: University of California Press, 1969.

Myers, Ramon, ed. *A Unique Relationship: The United States and the Republic of China under the Taiwan Relations Act.* Stanford, CA: Hoover Institution, 1989.

Myers, Ramon, Michel Oksenberg, and David Shambaugh, eds. *Making China Policy.* Lanham, MD: Rowman & Littlefield, 2001.

Nathan, Andrew, and Andrew Scobell. *China's Search for Security.* New York: Columbia University Press, 2012.

Neils, Patricia. *United States Attitudes toward China: The Impact of American Missionaries.* Armonk, NY: M. E. Sharpe, 1990.

Peck, Graham. *Two Kinds of Time.* Boston: Houghton Mifflin, 1967.

Pei Jianzhang. *Yanjiu Zhou Enlai: Waijiao sixiang yu shijian* [Researching Zhou Enlai: Diplomatic thought and practice]. Beijing: Shijie Zhishi Chubanshe, 1989.

———. *Zhonghua renmin gongheguo waijiao shi, 1949–1956* [A diplomatic history of the People's Republic of China, 1949–1956]. Beijing: Shijie Zhishi, 1994.

Qian Qichen. *Ten Episodes in China's Diplomacy.* New York: HarperCollins, 2005.

Pillsbury, Michael. *The Hundred-Year Marathon.* New York: St. Martin's Press, 2015.

Romberg, Alan. *Rein In at the Brink of the Precipice.* Washington, DC: Henry Stimson Center, 2003.

Ross, Robert S. *Negotiating Cooperation: The United States and China, 1969–1989.* Stanford, CA: Stanford University Press, 1995.

Ross, Robert S., and Jiang Changbin, eds. *Re-examining the Cold War: U.S.-China Diplomacy, 1954–1973.* Cambridge, MA: Harvard University Press, 2001.

Roy, Denny. *Return of the Dragon: Rising China and Regional Security.* New York: Columbia University Press, 2013.

Schaller, Michael. *The U.S. Crusade in China, 1938–1945.* New York: Columbia University Press. 1979.

———. *The United States and China: Into the Twenty-First Century.* New York: Oxford University Press, 2015.

Shambaugh, David. *Beautiful Imperialist: China Perceives America, 1972–1980.* Princeton, NJ: Princeton University Press, 1991.

———, ed. *Tangled Titans: The United States and China.* Lanham, MD: Rowman & Littlefield, 2012.

Shaw, Yu-ming. *An American Missionary in China: John Leighton Stuart and Chinese-American Relations.* Cambridge, MA: Harvard University Press, 1992.

Shewmaker, Kenneth E. *Americans and the Chinese Communists, 1927–1945: A Persuading Encounter.* Ithaca, NY: Cornell University Press, 1971.

Shinn, James, ed. *Weaving the Net: Conditional Engagement with China.* New York: Council on Foreign Relations, 1996.

Snow, Edgar. *Red Star over China.* New York: Random House, 1938.

Solomon, Richard H. *The China Factor: Sino-American Relations and the Global Scene.* Englewood Cliffs, NJ: Prentice Hall, 1982.

Song Qiang, Zhang Changchang, and Qiao Bian. *Zhongguo keyi shuo bu: Lengzhanhou shidai de zhengzhi yu qinggan jueze* [China can say no: The decision between politics and sentiment in the post–Cold War]. Beijing: Zhonghua Gongshang Lianhe Chubanshe, 1996.

Su Ge. *Meiguo: Dui hua Zhengce yu Taiwan wenti* [America: China policy and the Taiwan issue]. Beijing: Shijie Zhishi Chubanshe, 1998.

Suettinger, Robert L. *Beyond Tiananmen: The Politics of U.S.-China Relations, 1989–2000.* Washington, DC: Brookings Institution, 2003.

Sutter, Robert G. *U.S. Policy toward China: An Introduction to the Role of Interest Groups.* Lanham, MD: Rowman & Littlefield, 1998.

Swaine, Michael. *America's Challenge: Engaging a Rising China in the Twenty-First Century.* Washington, DC: Carnegie Endowment for International Peace, 2011.

———. *Creating a Stable Asia: An Agenda for a U.S.-China Balance of Power.* Washington, DC: Carnegie Endowment for International Peace, 2016.

Swaine, Michael, and Zhang Tuosheng, eds. *Managing Sino-American Crises.* Washington, DC: Carnegie Endowment for International Peace, 2006.

Tang Tsou. *America's Failure in China, 1941–1950.* Chicago: University of Chicago Press, 1963.

Tao Wenzhao. *Zhong Mei guanxi shi* [The history of Sino-US relations]. Shanghai: Renmin Chubanshe, 2004.

Taylor, Jay. *The Generalissimo: Chiang Kai-shek and the Struggle for Modern China.* Cambridge, MA: Harvard University Press, 2009.

Thomson, James C., Jr. *While China Faced West: American Reformers in Nationalist China, 1928–1937.* Cambridge, MA: Harvard University Press, 1968.

Tian Zengpei, ed. *Gaige kaifang yilai de Zhongguo waijiao* [Chinese diplomacy since reform and opening]. Beijing: Shijie Zhishi Chubanshe, 1993.

Tuchman, Barbara. *Stilwell and the American Experience in China, 1911–1945.* New York: Macmillan, 1971.

Tucker, Nancy Bernkopf. *China Confidential: American Diplomats and Sino-American Relations, 1945–1996.* New York: Columbia University Press, 2001.

———. *Strait Talk: United States-Taiwan Relations and the Crisis with China.* Cambridge, MA: Harvard University Press, 2009.

Varg, Paul A. *Missionaries, Chinese and Diplomats: The American Protestant Missionary Movement in China, 1890–1952.* Princeton, NJ: Princeton University Press, 1958.

———. *The Making of a Myth: The United States and China, 1897 1912.* East Lansing: Michigan State University Press, 1968.

Wachman, Alan M. *Taiwan: National Identity and Democratization.* Armonk, NY: M. E. Sharpe, 1994.

———. *Why Taiwan?* Stanford, CA: Stanford University Press, 2007.

Wang Bingnan. *Zhongmei huitan jiunian huigu* [Nine years of Sino-American ambassadorial talks]. Beijing: Shijie Zhishi, 1985.

Wang Dong. *The United States and China: A History from the Eighteenth Century to the Present.* Lanham, MD: Rowman & Littlefield, 2013.

Wang Taiping, ed. *Xin Zhongguo waijiao wushinian* [Fifty years of diplomacy of the new China]. Beijing: Beijing Chubanshe, 1999.

White, Hugh. *The China Choice.* Collingwood, Australia: Black Inc., 2012.

Xia Yafeng. *Negotiating with the Enemy: U.S.-China Talks during the Cold War, 1949–1972.* Bloomington: Indiana University Press, 2006.

Xie Xide, and Ni Shixiong. *Quzhe de licheng: Zhong Mei jianji ershi nian* [From normalization to renormalization: Twenty years of Sino-US relations]. Shanghai: Fudan Daxue Chubanshe, 1999.

Xue Mouhong, and Pei Jianhang, eds. *Danggai Zhongguo waijiao* [The diplomacy of contemporary China]. Beijing: Zhongguo Shehui Kexue Chubanshe, 1987.

Yan Xuetong. *Zhongguo guojia liyi fenxi* [The analysis of China's national interest]. Tianjin: Tianjin Renmin Chubanshe, 1996.

———. "The Instability of China-U.S. Relations." *Chinese Journal of International Politics* 3, no. 3 (2010): 1–30.

Yan Xuetong, Wang Zaibang, Li Zhongcheng, and Hou Roushi. *Zhongguo jueqi: Guoji huanjing pinggu* [International environment for China's rise]. Tianjin: Renmin Chubanshe, 1998.

Young, Kenneth T. *Negotiating with the Chinese Communists: The United States Experience, 1953–1967.* New York: McGraw-Hill, 1968.

Young, Marilyn B. *The Rhetoric of Empire: American China Policy, 1895–1901.* Cambridge, MA: Harvard University Press, 1968.

Zhang Shu Guang. *Deterrence and Strategic Culture: Chinese-American Conflicts, 1949–1959.* Ithaca, NY: Cornell University Press, 1992.

Zhang Yunling, ed. *Hezou haishi duikang: Lengzhanhou de Zhongguo, Meiguo he Riben* [Cooperation or confrontation: China, the United States, and Japan after the Cold War]. Beijing: Zhongguo Shehui Kexue Chubanshe, 1997.

Zi Zhongyun. *Meiguo duihua zhengce de yuanqi he fazhan, 1945–1950* [The origins and development of American policy toward China, 1945–1950]. Chongqing: Chongqing, 1987.

Zi Zhongyun, and He Di, eds. *Meitai Guanxi Sishinian* [Forty years of US-Taiwan relations]. Beijing: People's Press, 1991.

Zou Jing-wen. *Li Denghui Zhizheng Gaobai Shilu* [Record of revelations on Lee Teng-hui's administration]. Taipei: INK, 2001.

Index

About the Author

Robert G. Sutter has been professor of practice of international affairs at the Elliott School of International Affairs (ESIA) at George Washington University since 2011. He also directs the ESIA Bachelor of Arts in International Affairs program, involving more than one thousand students.

A PhD graduate in history and East Asian languages from Harvard University, Sutter taught full-time at Georgetown University (2001–11) and part-time during the previous thirty years at Georgetown, George Washington, and Johns Hopkins Universities and the University of Virginia. He has published twenty-one books, more than two hundred articles, and several hundred government reports dealing with the United States, China, and contemporary Asian and Pacific affairs. His most recent, newly published book is *The United States and Asia: Regional Dynamics and Twenty-First Century Relations* (Rowman & Littlefield, 2015). The fourth edition of his book *Chinese Foreign Relations: Power and Policy Since the Cold War* (Rowman & Littlefield) was published in 2016.

Sutter's government career (1968–2001) involved work on Asian and Pacific affairs and US foreign policy. He was for many years the senior specialist and director of the Foreign Affairs and National Defense Division of the Congressional Research Service. He was also the national intelligence officer for East Asia and the Pacific at the US government's National Intelligence Council, the China Division director at the Department of State's Bureau of Intelligence and Research, and a professional staff member of the Senate Foreign Relations Committee.